WALKING *to* JERUSALEM

WALKING *to* JERUSALEM

ENDURANCE AND HOPE ON A PILGRIMAGE
FROM LONDON TO THE HOLY LAND

JUSTIN BUTCHER

PEGASUS BOOKS
NEW YORK LONDON

WALKING TO JERUSALEM

Pegasus Books, Ltd.
148 West 37th Street, 13th Floor
New York, NY 10018

First Pegasus Books hardcover edition September 2019

ISBN: 978-1-64313-211-2

10 9 8 7 6 5 4 3 2 1

For Nancy

who has walked with me
up hill and down dale
through wind and rain
through thick and thin

Contents

	Foreword	xiii
1.	First Steps	1
2.	Preamble	17
3.	Esprit de Corps	37
4.	Au Chemin de la Guerre	55
5.	Champagne Trail	73
6.	À Piedmont à Pied	91
7.	*Aut viam inveniam aut faciam*	105
8.	Balkanisation	127
9.	Refugee Road	151
10.	Walking Turkey	175
11.	Crossing Jordan	199
12.	Jerusalem Syndrome	225
	Epilogue	283
	Acknowledgements	286
	Notes	289
	Index	293

Hope imagines the future and then acts as if that future is irresistible.

(Walter Wink)

There is no hope without risk.

(Zoughbi Al-Zoughbi)

The real changes happen by what I would call the conversion of the feet.

(Fr Michael Czerny SJ,
Migrants and Refugees Section, Vatican City)

Hope is by its nature something projected into the dark.

(Rowan Williams)

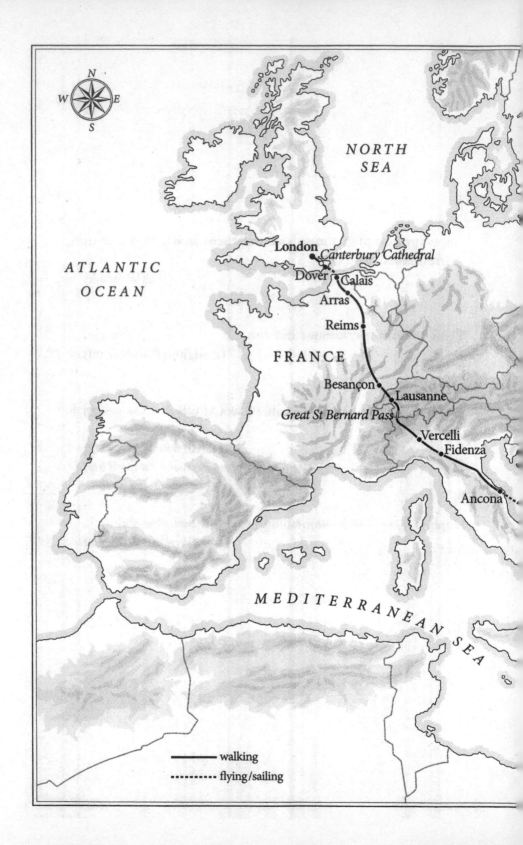

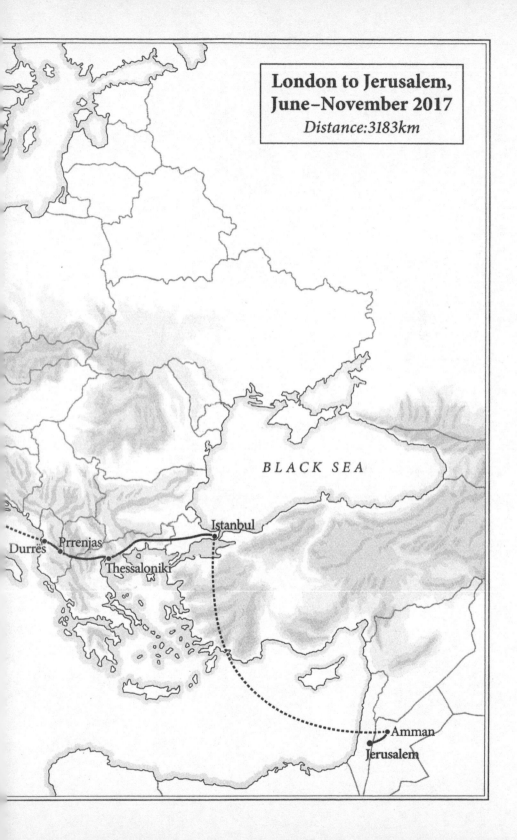

London to Jerusalem,
June–November 2017
Distance: 3183km

BLACK SEA

Durrës
Prrenjas
Thessaloniki
Istanbul
Amman
Jerusalem

Foreword

FOR THIRTY YEARS Amos Trust has chosen to walk a path of faithful and active solidarity with the Palestinian people. It's built strong partnerships with the dwindling Christian community in the West Bank and Gaza Strip; it's taken 'pilgrims' to see the reality of the Occupation up close; it's rebuilt Palestinian homes demolished by Israel's discriminatory planning regulations; and it's encouraged and funded creative and non-violent resistance to an oppression the world is fully aware of but refuses to take meaningful action against. The mantra Amos has adopted to express what the future of Israel/ Palestine should look like cuts through all the possible constitutional arrangements to focus on one non-negotiable point: *Equal rights for all who call the Holy Land home.* It always surprises me just how controversial this statement turns out to be.

The centenary of the Balfour Declaration presented a particular challenge for Amos. It was an anniversary likely to be little remembered by the general public in the UK but hugely significant to Palestinians who date their suffering from this act of British imperial hubris. As an organisation that took seriously its commitment to find creative ways to express justice for the forgotten, it needed an act that was bold and distinctive and would be welcomed by Palestinians even if it was ignored back home. A conference or a demonstration or a petition would hardly fit the bill. Something else was required. Justin Butcher, a longtime friend of Amos, had the answer. That thirty-year walk of active solidarity should have a literal expression in this anniversary year. An actual walk. A real pilgrimage. A collective penance. A 'Just Walk to Jerusalem' to deliver a simple, clear message that said 'we're sorry this has happened to you, it was wrong'.

The idea was beautiful and crazy. The logistics alone would be an organisational nightmare. The risk assessment would run for pages. It would be a five-month, 3,300-kilometre trek across eleven countries with mountains, rivers and seas to navigate. And then there was no guarantee that the walkers would even be allowed to cross the border into the occupied West Bank, let alone reach Jerusalem. Every step would be a leap of faith. It was typical of Amos Trust's culture of moral audacity to say 'let's do it!'.

Justin's account of *Walking to Jerusalem* is a wonderful, unique mix of travelogue, activist's diary, history lesson, spiritual reflection and, occasionally, first aid for healing wounded feet. It works on all these fronts, reflecting the daily experience of the walkers themselves – especially the nine aged from 18 to 67 who undertook the entire journey.

Perhaps an unanticipated consequence of walking to Jerusalem was the encounter it created with a thousand years of European history in all its power, glory and acts of injustice. The medieval cathedrals with their stories of heroic crusades to the Holy Land; the rusting weaponry of the Great War still being ploughed up by French farmers each year; the Jewish experience of Europe, good, bad and deadly; and now, Syrian refugees, the latest arrivals struggling for acceptance.

It's never easy to know if anything we do in the name of equality and human rights will make a difference. Will the powers that be see the light? Will lives be made better? Will our message be remembered by tomorrow morning? It's the perennial dilemma faced by activists for the common good all over the world. The odds are stacked against us. If they weren't, we wouldn't need activists in the first place.

In the context of Israel/Palestine, the standard dilemmas are multiplied. There are good reasons for this. The Palestinian people have had, to quote their most articulate advocate Edward Said, 'the extraordinarily bad luck' to have as their adversary the Jewish people, 'the most morally complex of all opponents' with 'a long history of victimization and terror behind them'. In other words, the Palestinians have paid a very high price for the rest of the world's anti-Semitism. The activist's call for Palestinian rights becomes interpreted (sometimes spun) as an attack on Jewish safety in a world that's proved itself catastrophically unreliable in assuring that safety.

This undoubtedly complicates matters. But it doesn't change the 'facts on the ground' for the Palestinian people. Their dispossession and ongoing oppression is also real. The challenge is to remain mindful of past iniquities without it blinding us to present injustices.

While the walkers were making their way across the continent, I was back home criss-crossing the UK wrestling with what Edward Said meant by 'the most morally complex of all opponents'. In numerous church halls and Quaker meeting houses I gave my talk on Jewish opposition to Balfour, in 1917 and since then. Sadly I never spoke at a synagogue, although that's where I most wanted to tell my story. I tried to make the point that the Balfour Declaration had profound, but vastly contrasting, consequences for Jews and Palestinians. As we got closer to the anniversary, I watched as Jewish religious and community leaders, and Israel's Ambassador to the UK, Mark Regev, attempted to turn Balfour from a piece of *realpolitik* into 'holy scripture'. They were turning criticism of Balfour into a curious mix of blasphemy and anti-Semitism. I knew there was nothing blasphemous or anti-Semitic about the Just Walk to Jerusalem. The sanctification of Balfour could only create another roadblock on the path to justice and peace.

We have to thank the Prime Minister, Theresa May, for turbo-charging the final days of the pilgrimage. Helpfully, she repeated her wish to 'celebrate' the Balfour anniversary with 'pride' during a Prime Minister's Question time in the House of Commons a week before the Balfour anniversary. It was a comment that revealed much about the Prime Minister's willingness to dismiss the lived experience of millions of Palestinians. Mrs May's acknowledgement that there was still 'work to be done' to achieve peace was either a wonderful example of British understatement or, more likely, a failure to recognise the fundamental injustice crammed into those sixty-seven words of diplomatic duplicity. The Prime Minister's remarks weren't headline news in the UK but the Palestinian media were all over it. And here were a bunch of Brits, some of whom had walked a couple of thousand miles, determined to make the apology that their government refused to countenance. The Just Walk to Jerusalem was succeeding in one of its key aims – to disrupt the official UK narrative and show the Palestinian people that they were not forgotten.

The day of the Balfour anniversary itself was an intense, emotional and at times surreal experience for me and for many of the walkers, especially those who'd undertaken the full journey from London to Jerusalem.

I never imagined that I'd have the opportunity to hand my sixty-seven-word re-write of the Balfour Declaration, composed a year earlier, directly to Her Majesty's representative in Jerusalem; or that a couple of hours later I'd be in the centre of Ramallah, probably the only British Jew there, protesting alongside thousands of Palestinians; or that the walkers would all be having lunch as the guests of President Abbas in the Palestinian Authority compound; or that evening I'd be hearing Revd Naim Ateek, the 'father of Palestinian liberation theology', preaching in St George's Cathedral back in East Jerusalem.

But the most telling moment of that day, which seemed to sum up exactly why we were there, was the near failure of the Bethlehem Choir to reach the Cathedral service. With the privilege of free movement, our walkers had travelled a continent to reach Jerusalem. But a Palestinian Christian choir from Bethlehem, a short car drive away, nearly didn't make it because they couldn't get through an Israeli security checkpoint. The six members of the choir arrived, apologetic and out of breath, and slipped their way to the front of the Cathedral to sing Arab melodies to us. Another example of beautiful Palestinian resistance.

The question as to whether the Just Walk to Jerusalem made a difference is, at this moment in time, impossible to answer. Future historians may have the perspective needed. We do not. But it may also be entirely the wrong question.

As Alexandra, one of the volunteer drivers, said to Justin in Turkey, ' ... ordinary people like us don't particularly want to put themselves through potentially life-changing risks by getting involved in activism. It's because governments and international bodies fail to sort out these terrible situations of injustice. Ordinary people have to get involved.' I would argue, in the case of Alexandra and all the 'Just Walkers', that their passion and conviction makes them not quite so 'ordinary'.

As the second century of Balfour began, with no sign of a just peace in sight, I published a new blog post from Jerusalem that ended with this thought: 'When hope is so difficult to find there is only one thing left. We can choose where to walk and who to walk alongside.' Amos Trust has chosen to walk alongside the Palestinian people. And there are times when that must be enough.

Robert Cohen
Amos Trust, trustee
November 2018

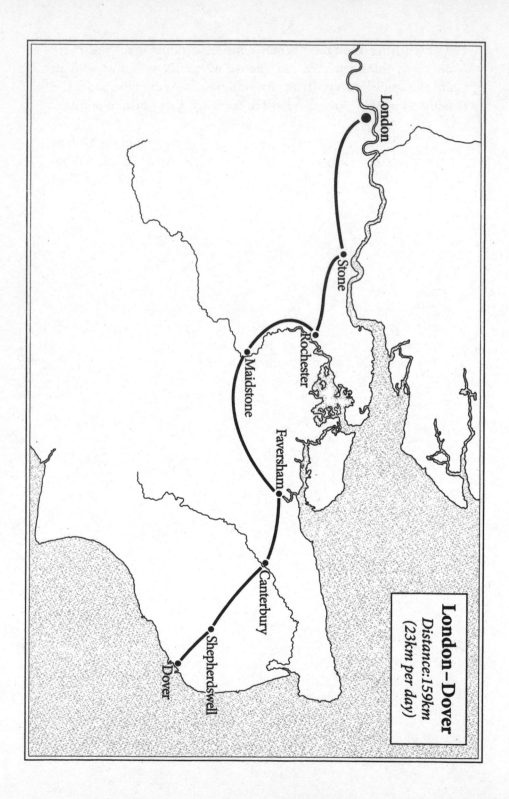

London

Stone

Rochester

Maidstone

Faversham

Canterbury

Shepherdswell

Dover

London–Dover
Distance:159km
(23km per day)

I

First Steps

I'M STANDING IN Trafalgar Square on a bright Saturday morning in June. All around is the hubbub and bustle of tourists and shoppers milling and browsing, selfie sticks bristling and shopping bags swinging. There's a fizz and crackle on the breeze that ricochets from face to face, in the ebb and flow of chit-chat and the melee of lipstick smiles, sunglasses, nail varnish, suntanned shoulders, Union Jack baseball caps, straw summer hats, ice cream and Coca-Cola, open-top tour buses, ticket stalls and ticket touts and all the riot and swirl of the global village out on the town. Over there on the fourth plinth is David Shrigley's 'Really Good', grotesque black thumbs-up stabbing at the sky, and, high above it all, Nelson on his column dwindles with Olympian disdain to a dizzying pinhead amid a haze of vapour trails. Youngsters from the four corners of the earth drape themselves over the giant recumbent lions, or bathe their faces in the sparkling fountains.

Two days ago was the general election, a glorious kamikaze debacle in which Theresa May's ruling Tory party, wrongly sniffing an easy kill, went to the polls only to have their majority wiped out by a resurgent Labour, led by career backbencher Jeremy Corbyn. The biter bit, the bloodhound poleaxed by a knockout punch from the hare. Nobody's quite clear who's in charge now. Will May be able to form a minority government? She's rumoured to be planning a pact with the extreme Ulster Protestant Democratic Unionist Party founded by the late Ian Paisley, who's no doubt chortling in his grave. What about Corbyn? Will he attempt a coalition with the Lib Dems and SNP? Who knows? Not the media and not the crowd, but a pro-Corbyn demonstration is

I

brewing in Parliament Square this morning, and the buzz in the air is palpable . . .

Just one week ago, a white van was mounting the pavement of London Bridge and mowing down pedestrians, then knife-wielding Islamist fanatics ran amok through Borough Market, with bewildered crowds fleeing in terror and, amid the frenzy, many acts of heroic courage. Eleven dead, scores wounded, and a city traumatised for the second time in two months, but still defiant. Paris, London, Manchester, then London again.

And here in front of me, gathered on the steps of St Martin-in-the-Fields, is a crowd of forty-odd adventurers, all ages from eighteen to eighty, from every walk of life and many nations – Americans, Australians, Brits and Irish, Kiwis and even Maltese, artists, architects, priests, farmers, doctors, musicians, youth workers, students – all here with one goal: to walk to Jerusalem. Time to fire the starting pistol. I feel hopelessly unready. They all look like pretty serious grown-ups (well, most of them), not actor-scallywag-writer-activists like me. What have they let themselves in for?

'Good morning, everybody, and welcome!' I yell. 'Welcome to the Just Walk to Jerusalem! Thank you all for being here today, to set off together on this big, crazy adventure!' Given the heightened security in London at the moment, I half expect to be shut down and moved on before we've even started. 'I'm Justin Butcher, the originator of the Walk, so it's all my fault, and I'm thrilled to be here today with Amos Trust, and such an amazing troupe of intrepid walkers, come together from all over the world. Hats off to you all, and thank you!'

One older gentleman is cupping his ear and squinting. I need to inspire them, and they can't even hear what I'm saying. The background din of taxis, buskers, bustling crowds and diesel-bus engines wheezing and groaning doesn't help.

'Three years ago, I made a promise,' I say, raising my voice a few decibels. 'Almost exactly three years ago, in June 2014, I was in a village in Palestine called Al-Khader, near Bethlehem, visiting a family whose house had been demolished two days earlier by the Israeli army. They were welcoming us, pulling chairs out of the rubble to seat us in the shade of their fig tree.' The poignancy of the story seizes me afresh. 'The farmer, Ali Salim, said, "Please, we

2

request the nations of the world to do something, to stop this humiliation and cruelty against us."' I sense the attention of the group, their interest pricked, some of them filming me on their phones. "'Our hearts are broken for you," we said. "We know that your voice is silenced. But we promise to use our voices to tell your story." And that's why we're here today . . .'

Almost all of us are wearing pale green T-shirts emblazoned with the slogan, 'Just Walk to Jerusalem – Change the Record'. Amos Trust, the small human rights charity who are my partner in this venture, have conceived this strapline, and on the T-shirt design, above and below the Amos flame logo, WiFi-symbol wedges suggest an old seven-inch vinyl, the cracked record we want to change, but also an outburst of energy, a new rumour spreading.

'That's why we're here today: to use our voices – and our feet, our legs, our knees, hips and blisters – to change the record of a hundred years of injustice for the Palestinian people. Today marks the fiftieth anniversary of Israel's military occupation of East Jerusalem, the West Bank, Gaza and the Golan Heights. Next month marks the tenth year of Israel's land, sea and air blockade of the Gaza Strip, devastated in three major wars, fast becoming one of the worst humanitarian crisis zones on the planet, where 80 per cent of Palestinians are dependent on food aid and 30 per cent of children have acute anaemia. At the end of our Walk, *insha'Allah*, we will arrive in Jerusalem on the second of November, the centenary of the Balfour Declaration.'

Will we? I wonder. *Will any of us actually make it that far? And if we do, will we get in? And will anyone notice? Will anyone care?*

'The Hungarian–Jewish author Arthur Koestler, writing from the new State of Israel in 1949, described the Balfour Declaration as "one of the most improbable political documents of all time, in which one nation solemnly promised a second the country of a third". For the Palestinian people, the Balfour Declaration precipitated a century of dispossession, conflict and suffering. We walk today in penance for Britain's historic responsibility for this injustice. We walk in solidarity with the Palestinian people, whose right of return is denied. And we walk in hope, calling for full equal rights for all peoples in the Holy Land, who call it their home. Let's walk!'

There are barriers up along the west side of Whitehall. The police would clearly prefer us to stick to the pavement. As we wave everyone across to head down to the Cenotaph, I find myself musing on the bizarre history that led from Britain's deadlock in the trenches of the Western Front to our conquest of Palestine, the British Mandate and the creation of Israel, the Palestinian *Nakba* and exile, all the way back to us here today.

His Majesty's government view with favour . . .

The first time I ever heard of Balfour was six years ago, sitting at my kitchen table with my friend Ahmed Masoud and his mother Fatima, from Gaza. The Rafah crossing from Gaza into Egypt was open for the first time in four years, and Fatima had managed somehow to get a visa to travel to the UK, to visit her son in London, meet his wife Heather for the first time and make the acquaintance of her two-year-old grandson Zino. What made our dinner that evening all the more remarkable was the fact that the previous year, Ahmed and I had written a play about Fatima for BBC Radio, without me ever having met her.

His Majesty's government view with favour the establishment in Palestine of a national home for the Jewish people and will use their best endeavours to facilitate the achievement of this object . . .

Originally, Ahmed's family were olive farmers from the village of Deir Sneid, now part of Israeli territory, close to the border with Gaza. Then came the *Nakba* (Arabic for 'catastrophe') of May 1948, when the British Mandate withdrew from Palestine and 700,000 Palestinians fled or were driven from their homes into exile.

. . . it being clearly understood that nothing shall be done which may prejudice the civil and religious rights of existing non-Jewish communities in Palestine . . .

Ahmed's family fled to Gaza, where they have lived ever since, in Jabaliya Refugee Camp. Most Palestinian families still hold the keys of the houses they left behind in 1948, heirlooms of a bitter heritage. These keys to houses, which for the most part no longer exist, are cherished fiercely as family totems symbolising the Palestinians' right of return, denied for seventy years.

. . . or the rights and political status enjoyed by Jews in any other country.

The Israeli 'Law of Return' entitles anyone, anywhere in the world, who can adduce one Jewish grandparent, to an Israeli passport, along with their spouse, on the basis of the Jewish claim to the land from biblical times. Meanwhile, the universal right of return of refugees, enshrined in the 1948 UN Declaration of Human Rights, has yet to be extended to exiled Palestinians, who lost their homes and land rather more recently.

Ahmed's mother was diagnosed with cancer in 2009, just after Israel's 'Cast Lead' onslaught on Gaza, and had to undergo major surgery, complicated by the fact that medical supplies essential for her subsequent care, such as chemotherapy drugs and colostomy bags, were embargoed by the Israeli blockade. Ahmed hadn't seen his family in Gaza for seven years, and was desperate to visit his mother, but all the borders were shut. Married to Heather, he had British residency, but his only passport was the Palestinian *hawiya*, an ID card which the Israeli government issues compulsorily to all Palestinians in the Occupied Territories. Added to this, they'd just discovered that Heather was pregnant with their first child. Ahmed's dilemma, his daring journey into Gaza, joyous reunion with his family and eventual escape formed the basis of the play *Escape From Gaza*, which we wrote together for BBC radio, broadcast in 2011. Rather wonderfully, BBC Arabic service broadcast the play into Gaza so that Ahmed's family were able to hear it. And here now, against all the odds, was Fatima herself, larger than life, at my kitchen table, just a few months later.

She was a vibrant dinner companion, and I could see where Ahmed got his creative spark and energy. At one point, astonished at her *joie de vivre*, I asked her, 'How do you cope, day to day, with the anger you must feel? At everything the Israelis have done to you, your family, your people?'

As Ahmed translated, she grinned, eyeing me rather puckishly. 'The anger goes further back,' she said, pointing, 'all the way back to you, your country, and your Balfour Declaration, when you promised our land to someone else, nearly a hundred years ago.'

'Ah.' I turned to Ahmed. 'Do a lot of Palestinians still think about that, remember that?'

'Every Palestinian,' he said. 'If you go to Gaza one day, you'll find, walking along the streets, as a Brit, all the kids will shout, "Balfour! Balfour!" It's where it all started. It's forgotten history for you, but for us it's still going on, we're still living with the consequences.'

And here I am in 2017, ambling down Whitehall to the building where those fateful sixty-seven words were penned a century ago. At the entrance to Horse Guards Parade, we're stopped by a royal cavalcade emerging on to Whitehall, coaches and mounted soldiers in burnished cuirasses, glittering sabres drawn and helmet plumes fluttering. And here in the foremost coach, a few inches from my face through the glass, is a living relic of the age of Balfour, H. R. H. Prince Philip himself, celebrating his ninety-sixth birthday today, off to the park for a 21-gun salute.

We cross over Whitehall, making our way down the east side to the Cenotaph and then back over to the original front door of the Foreign Office. Who will be its next incumbent? If the Tories can form a government – still a moot question – and if he keeps his old job – mooter still given his role in the Brexit fiasco – it will be Boris Johnson. Who not long ago described the Balfour Declaration as 'bizarre', 'tragicomically incoherent', an 'exquisite piece of Foreign Office fudgerama',which makes it all sound a good deal more cosy than the cold-blooded reality that the records show. While Jews enjoyed both 'rights' and 'political status' in Balfour's wording, the Palestinians were neither named nor accorded political rights. Their identity as the indigenous people, constituting 90 per cent of the population and owning 98 per cent of the land, was obfuscated by the deliberately misleading nomenclature: 'non-Jews' in this land in which Britain had chosen to build a Jewish 'national home'.

In Palestine we do not even propose to go through the form of consulting the wishes of the present inhabitants of the country . . . [we] are committed to Zionism. And Zionism, be it right or wrong, good or bad, is rooted in age-long traditions, in present needs, in future hopes, of far profounder import than the desires and prejudices of the 700,000 Arabs who now inhabit that ancient land. (Balfour's memorandum to Lord Curzon, August 1919)[1]

And, as the 'first military governor of Jerusalem since Pontius Pilate' (in his own words), Sir Ronald Storrs, wrote with Machiavellian cynicism, Zionism 'blessed him that gave as well as him that took, by forming for England "a little loyal Jewish Ulster" in a sea of potentially hostile Arabism'.

A little loyal Jewish Ulster. It's worth pondering that pungent phrase. The 'Plantation of Ulster' which followed its conquest in the 1590s was a calculated exercise in social engineering, the organised colonisation of nine counties by Protestant settlers from England and Scotland, overseen by James I and his ministers as a strategy for anglicising, 'civilising' and controlling the province. So began a 400-year ethnic and sectarian conflict which continues to this day, in no way eased by Brexit and the prospect of a new EU border in Ireland, not to mention Theresa May's Faustian pact with the DUP. At the time of the Balfour Declaration, resentment at centuries of British rule had exploded recently with the Easter Rising of 1916, and would erupt again within fourteen months into the Irish War of Independence (1919–22). So the invocation of 'Ulster' as a template for Zionist colonisation of Palestine under the British Mandate was less than felicitous.

As British rule in Ireland went up in flames, and centuries of settler-colonisation unravelled in a messy partition that would spark an ongoing guerrilla war in Northern Ireland lasting the whole of the twentieth century, far away in Palestine *at precisely the same moment* we were setting out to do it all over again. Following the outbreak of the Jaffa Riots in 1921, Colonial Secretary Winston Churchill proposed the recruitment of a 'picked force of white gendarmerie' who had served the Crown in the Irish War – the infamous Black and Tans. As ruthless enforcers of state coercion, infamous for their attacks on civilians and civilian property, the Black and Tans were second to none. House demolition was one of their specialities. Now they were reunited under their old boss, Britain's first High Commissioner for Palestine, Sir Herbert Samuel, who as Home Secretary in 1916 had overseen the internment of nearly 2,000 people allegedly involved in the Easter Rising. Britain's brutal *modus operandi* in Ireland was all set to play out again in Palestine, only this time the settlers weren't Scots Presbyterians.

7

Back in present-day Whitehall, I marshal the group for photographs in front of the handsome Victorian oak doors, framed with Portland stone friezes, which form the official front entrance to the Foreign and Commonwealth Office (FCO). I've never been inside (it's only open to the public one weekend of the year), but the FCO is fabled to be one of the most spectacular buildings in London, a Gilbert Scott treasure trove in which one magnificent atrium gives on to another, the Grand Staircase with its fabulous domed ceiling, the lustrous golden Locarno Suite and the marble-floored, glass-roofed magnificence of the Durbar Court, in the former India Office. These sober wooden doors give no hint of the splendours within. The entrance used nowadays is round the corner in King Charles Street, so we'll probably get away with our momentary annexation of the front steps.

One of the walkers, Peter, suggests I reprise my speech while he films it, so I belt out the salient points once more. 'Here we are, on the steps of the Foreign Office, where the Balfour Declaration was penned nearly one hundred years ago . . .' The weather, the gods and the police all seem to be smiling on us and I get through it uninterrupted, rounded off with a polite smattering of applause, and on we stride to Parliament Square.

On the corner between Portcullis House and Big Ben, Momentum activists are stacking placards emblazoned with rumbustious slogans: 'May out! Corbyn in!', 'DEFY TORY RULE – Strike, march, occupy!' (*Socialist Worker*), 'VICTORY FOR CORBYN' (arguably somewhat stretching the point), 'Out May. Be gone!' (hand-painted on a cardboard box), 'Migrants and refugees welcome here,' and a flock of anti-DUP placards: 'Don't be DUP-ed into hate!', 'DUP = ANTI-GAY, ANTI-GREEN, ANTI-WOMEN' and, cocking a snook at the DUP's religiously conservative stance, 'Pray DUP away'. More than half a million have signed an online petition calling on the Conservatives not to do this deal, and urging Theresa May to resign.

Roadside barriers on Westminster Bridge are a sad reminder of the attack on 22 March, when Khalid Masood drove into pedestrians along the south side of the bridge, injuring more than fifty people and killing four. After crashing the car into the perimeter fence of Parliament, he ran through the Carriage Gates into New Palace Yard and fatally stabbed PC Keith Palmer, before being shot dead himself by an armed officer.

Today the bridge is a surging swarm of happy tourists snapping each other against a Big Ben backdrop, admiring riverside sights and bringing foot traffic to a standstill. It's like trying to cross the Ponte Vecchio. We reconvene in dribs and drabs on the South Bank in front of County Hall, where 'Ken Livingstone' once ruled the GLC, and press on eastwards. Until a week ago, we had a beautiful riverside site next to the Oxo Tower booked for our 'Change the Record' event, the official launch for Just Walk to Jerusalem. Then, after last weekend's attacks, some residents of the flats in the Oxo Tower expressed misgivings about our event to the charitable body which manages the riverside spaces, and we were asked to move to somewhere less conspicuous.

'Green Space' is a scrubby patch of wasteland to the east of the Waterloo roundabout, pretty much enclosed by high walls and fences on all sides. What could be more fitting? In true make-do-and-mend spirit, Amos Trust and our event company have made it very festive, with an outdoor stage and banners flying the 'Change the Record' logo in the colours of the Palestinian flag. And yes, there are some decent-sized patches of grass here and there, so this invisible fenced-off brownfield enclave may – just about – be said to be 'green'. Baba Ganoush's sizzling falafels ('the best in town'), Palestinian dancers and a friendly crowd of supporters greet the walkers as we check our names on the stewards' list and join the throng. Throng perhaps is an exaggeration. Where is everyone? This is the fiftieth anniversary of the Occupation, after all, and, as far as I know, there are no other major Palestine events taking place today. All the key players are here with us – the Palestine Solidarity Campaign (PSC), the Palestinian Mission to the UK, Artists for Palestine UK, Jews for Justice for Palestinians, Friends of Al-Aqsa, Zaytoun CIC, and so on. A bit thin on the ground, but stout-hearted nonetheless, we mingle and meet and munch falafels as the afternoon programme unfolds.

Encouragingly, there's a good clutch of young Arabic Brits, no doubt drawn by the band 47Soul, rising stars of the Arabic music scene, who have top billing today. My family are all here, to my great encouragement, and many friends – Ahmed and Heather and their little beauties Zino and Serene; and here's Garth Hewitt, singer, priest and activist, founder of Amos Trust and pioneer for Palestinian

9

rights throughout the world church network, with his wife and
fellow-campaigner Gill. It was Garth's tireless work in championing
Palestinian rights that first brought many important Palestinian and
Israeli voices to the attention of Christian communities in the UK.
Through the crowd I spot Leanne Mohamad, the fifteen-year-old
British-Palestinian schoolgirl who won the Jack Petchey Speak Out
Challenge last year with her 'Birds not Bombs' speech on Gaza and
weathered a subsequent storm of online abuse. And here's Jim
Stewart, our indefatigable routemeister, who's given months of his
time to planning our routes and accommodation all across Europe
and Turkey – a gigantic labour of love.

'Jim, we really can't thank you enough,' I say, shaking his hand.

'Well, you guys are doing it,' he grins. 'I never had to leave my
desk! I wish I was coming with you. You're going to some amazing
places.'

Off to one side I spot Glyn Secker and Naomi Wimborne-Idrissi,
signatories of Jews for Justice for Palestinians and Labour Party
activists, unfurling a banner for the new solidarity group 'Free
Speech on Israel'. The banner shows the Israeli Separation Wall
with the caption, 'It's not anti-Semitic to oppose Zionism'. This is
a response to Theresa May's announcement last year at a Conservative
Friends of Israel meeting that the UK would be adopting formally
the definition of anti-Semitism agreed in 2016 by the International
Holocaust Remembrance Alliance. The illustrative examples accompanying this definition have been disputed as arguably conflating
criticism of the State of Israel with anti-Semitism. In a speech which
Israeli historian Avi Shlaim has dubbed 'Theresa in Wonderland',
she described Israel as 'a state which guarantees the rights of people
of all religions, races and sexualities'. Glyn and Naomi are dauntless
campaigners who refuse to be silenced by frequent accusations that
they are 'self-hating Jews'.

In 2010, Glyn skippered the yacht *Irene*, sailing from Cyprus to
Gaza with a cargo of children's therapeutic toys, schoolbooks, musical
instruments and medical supplies, in an attempt to break the sea
blockade. The passengers included Reuven Moskovitz, a Holocaust
survivor, and Lillian Rosengarten, a refugee from Nazi Germany.
One Israeli crew member, Rami Elhanan, lost his daughter to a
suicide bombing in 1997. I remember hearing Glyn speak at the

2011 Greenbelt Festival about his voyage: how they set sail from Cyprus with such hope, flying flags from the rigging representing the nationalities of the passengers and crew and the many peace organisations and charities supporting them. 'It looked so pretty, with all our flags flying,' he said, 'and the sun glittering on the sea at Famagusta.' But as they sailed towards Gaza, Israeli naval vessels swooped to surround the yacht. Glyn and his crew appealed to the Israeli marines, calling out through a megaphone, 'We are a Jewish humanitarian mission to Gaza, carrying schoolbooks, toys and medical supplies. All of us on board are Jews, from many nations, including an eighty-year-old Holocaust survivor and the children of Holocaust survivors. We are in international waters: you have no right to stop us.' He described how they sat down on the deck, linking arms in a circle and singing, 'We shall overcome,' as the Israeli marines boarded the *Irene*. Shockingly, they tasered one Israeli crew member in the heart, convulsing him in agony, but he survived. He and his brother were taken on to the Israeli gunboat while the others were towed to Ashdod in Israel and detained until deportation, and the yacht was impounded. In a touching coda, Glyn described how he and his partner, in solidarity, had chosen to give their children Arabic names when they were born. This last detail brought the audience to their feet, cheering him to the echo.

'Well, we did it!' I turn to see Chris Rose loping through the crowd, all six foot six of him, and stooping earthwards to exchange a manly hug. Director of Amos Trust, cycling nut, writer and Anglican priest (though you wouldn't know it most of the time), Chris is my chief partner-in-crime for this whole crazy venture. 'We made it to the launch!' he exclaims, through a mouthful of falafel, 'And lunch! Only another 2,000 miles to go . . .' Despite best-laid plans, two last work engagements in York and Prague over the next few days must be fulfilled before I'm at liberty, so Chris will lead the first group of walkers through Kent and I will join them in Dover on Friday.

Things are hotting up on stage now. After a virtuosic oud set by Kareem Samara, founder of Artists for Palestine UK, there's a gloriously daft display of percussive pyrotechnics by beatbox sensation Hobbit (aka Jack Hobbs, with whom I travelled to Palestine in 2014), using nothing but his voice and a microphone to create an entire polyphony of rhythms, melodies and bass lines. Next up is a typically pugnacious speech of encouragement from Manuel Hassassian, the Palestinian Delegate (whom we're not supposed to call ambassador because Palestine isn't recognised as a state by the UK), and then Ahmed takes the stage, with Katie Hagley from Amos Trust. A writer and academic, Ahmed has recently become an Amos trustee. His wife Heather is a co-founder of Zaytoun, an award-winning Fairtrade company which imports Palestinian olive oil and other produce to the UK. My wife Nancy has worked for them since 2012. Ahmed salutes the walkers and explains that, as a Palestinian from Gaza, he can't travel to Jerusalem. Last summer, he says, he was invited to the annual Palestinian Festival of Literature, Palfest, in Ramallah, to read from his newly published novel, *Vanished*. As Palestinians are not permitted to travel through Israel, he flew to Amman in Jordan and caught the bus to the King Hussein/Allenby Bridge crossing, where the Israelis refused him entry. 'The Israeli border officer yelled at me, "You are a Gaza citizen!" "What does that even mean?" I said. "I'm a British citizen – I have a UK passport." "Go back to Gaza!" he shouted. But I can't. I truly and honestly can't.'

I remember Ahmed describing at the time how the border guards took him to a side room and displayed all his details on a screen – pictures of his family in Gaza and London, even pictures of his son Zino.

'I was really freaked out,' he said. 'A soldier comes in with a big gun and they start showing you all the information they have on you, and you think, "What's going to happen to me?" I said, "I want to call my British Embassy." They just laughed and said, in a thick Arabic accent, "*Enta Falasteeni, khabebi!* (You are Palestinian, darling!) Call God if you want. No one's going to help you."

'My mother in Gaza was angry with me the next morning. "Go back to London!" she shouted over the phone. "Your life is there now, with your wife and children. You're stupid to put yourself in danger like this. Forget all about it, forget about Gaza too – and forget about us." But how could I?'

Now Ahmed's introducing another new Amos trustee, the writer and campaigner Robert Cohen.

'Our call is clear and simple,' Robert says. 'Equal rights for all who call the Holy Land home. It's astonishing how controversial that call is. This year I became the first Jew to be a trustee on the board of Amos Trust, an organisation that's spent thirty years bringing justice and hope to the forgotten all over the world. I'm glad to have found a spiritual home in an incredible organisation that draws its courage and inspiration from a Hebrew prophet. Three thousand years ago it was the prophet Amos who cut through all the hypocrisy and denial of his own community with a passionate, raging and poetic call for justice. He recognised that the Jewish leadership of his day had got it wrong, they were leading their people down a moral cul-de-sac and heading for disaster.

'And he called them out on it. His call was also clear and simple: Justice and Righteousness.

'Amos and his fellow Hebrew prophets certainly have a lot to answer for. They created a tradition. A tradition of principled countercultural, non-compliance. Radical dissent from oppressive power. A tradition that I and a great many other Jews think of as our primary Jewish inheritance. The values that remain true when so much else has become corrupted.

'All of you are here because you want to be part of a bold and creative response to some rather dismal anniversaries this year, and I've been speaking around the country about Jewish opposition to Balfour both in 1917 and today. I call the talk I've been giving "The Wrong Kind of Jews", which usually raises a few eyebrows of concern. But don't worry, there's nothing anti-Semitic about what I have to say.

'The man who would become the leader of the Zionist movement, Chaim Weizmann, first met Arthur Balfour at a hotel in Manchester in 1907. They spent about an hour together discussing Weizmann's ideas, and at the end of their meeting, Balfour said, "It's strange, Mr Weizmann. Most of the Jews I meet are not like you."

'To which Weizmann replied, "Mr Balfour, you meet the wrong kind of Jews."

'So there were the "wrong kind of Jews" then, and, one hundred years after Balfour, and fifty years after the start of the Occupation, there is good reason to be the "wrong kind of Jew" today.

'It's not widely understood, but there are many Jews in Britain deeply troubled by the actions of the State of Israel.

'There are many Jews in Britain who see fifty years of Occupation of the West Bank as morally indefensible.

'There are many Jews who see the siege of Gaza and the wars against its people as crimes.

'There are many Jews who believe Jerusalem must be a shared city.

'There are plenty of Jews, like me, who don't wish to build their Jewish identity around Zionism.

'Jews may be monotheistic in our theology but we are certainly not monolithic in our political outlook. Certainly not when it comes to Israel and the Palestinian people.

'Let me make special mention of a group here today: Free Speech on Israel is a Jewish-led initiative working hard to create space for an open and honest discussion about Israel that has no time for anti-Semitism or racism of any kind. Free Speech on Israel is punching above its weight and making common cause with others, including Christians and Muslims, who stand in solidarity with the Palestinian people. Thank you for being here.'

He waves to where Glyn and Naomi are flourishing their banner, amid warm applause.

'I'd also like to pass on greetings and solidarity from Jews for Justice for Palestinians, an organisation that for many years has provided a vital alternative UK Jewish perspective on Israel. Together with you, we awkward, rebellious, dissident "Wrong Kind of Jews" want to stand with the prophet Amos in that incredible river of justice than runs through all of human history. Like you, we are wading into that stream of righteousness.

'Let me tell you about one of my great heroes, Rabbi Abraham Joshua Heschel, whose family were murdered in the Holocaust, and who marched alongside Martin Luther King Jr at Selma for Black Civil Rights in the mid-1960s. At the end, physically and emotionally exhausted, he said it felt as if his legs had been praying. I think that's how it's going to be for our Amos pilgrims to Jerusalem too as they call for equal rights for all.

'So we wish you strong feet, strong legs and muscles full of prayer. Together, we're changing the record!'

Throughout all that follows – stirring speeches, a knockout comedy slot from Mark Thomas and a fabulously hip set from

47Soul, including the irresistibly danceable reggae anthem, 'Every land is a holy land' – Robert's words keep pulsing in my mind: 'strong feet, strong legs and muscles full of prayer . . .'

The last word – for now – is reserved for Garth Hewitt who, as a canon of St George's Cathedral in Jerusalem, will be there to welcome us, *insha'Allah*, at the end of our Walk.

'Congratulations to those who will walk!' he calls out across the crowd. 'Today we'll send off the first pilgrims; more will join at different stages. There are ninety people altogether walking sections ranging from odd days to several weeks. Ten will do the entire walk. So it's walking time! After a moment of quiet, the walkers will set off from Southwark Cathedral, the starting point for pilgrimages to Canterbury and Jerusalem since mediaeval times.'

Garth reads for the first time the words of the newly written liturgy which will become our daily observance on the Walk:

We walk this day with those whose freedom is denied.
We walk with those who have fled war, torture and despair.
We walk in penance for broken promises and political fixes.
We walk the long road with all those who strive for peace, justice
    and reconciliation.
We walk with those who long to return to home.
We walk in hope that one day all people in the Holy Land will live
    in peace,
as neighbours with full equal rights.

'So go in peace, walk for peace, live for peace and let all of us pray for peace – and have an amazing time. Free, free Palestine!'

And we're off.

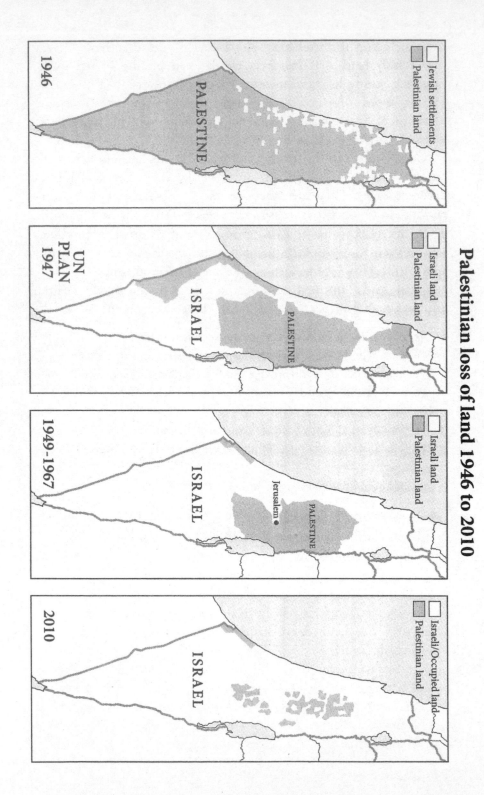

Palestinian loss of land 1946 to 2010

1946

Jewish settlements
Palestinian land

PALESTINE

UN PLAN 1947

Israeli land
Palestinian land

ISRAEL

PALESTINE

1949-1967

Israeli land
Palestinian land

ISRAEL

Jerusalem •

PALESTINE

2010

Israeli/Occupied land
Palestinian land

ISRAEL

2

Preamble

20 June 2014, The House at Al-Khader

WE'RE DRIVING OUT to a village near Bethlehem, in the Occupied West Bank, a group of British artists performing in the Bet Lahem Live Festival. We're going to visit a Palestinian family whose house was demolished two days ago in the mayhem of collective punishment following the disappearance of three teenage Israeli settlers from the Hebron area last week. Five Palestinian children have been shot dead, dozens wounded and hundreds arrested, refugee camps invaded and tear-gassed, the UNRWA offices of the camps ransacked, and many homes demolished – all supposedly part of a 'police action' to find the missing teenagers. Meanwhile, Palestinian prisoners due for release as part of the failed peace talks are on hunger strike, and the leader of the Palestinian Authority, President Mahmoud Abbas, has invited Hamas in from the cold to form an alliance with Fatch.

We've arrived at the remote hilltop farm, close to the village of Al-Khader – the 'Green Man', the Arabic name for St George who, according to legend, was imprisoned here before his martyrdom. It's a desperate sight: two ugly heaps of wreckage, twisted iron rods poking out of shattered plaster, smashed lintels, splintered timber, all strewn with odd bits of furniture, kitchen utensils, floor tiles, children's toys – and, lined up around the ruins of their home, a large Palestinian family: a father, four adult sons and many children, teenagers down to toddlers. They're pulling chairs out of the rubble to seat us in the shade of a large fig tree.

The father of the family, Ali Salim Mousa, and his eldest son embrace us as we approach, kissing us on both cheeks. The farmer is a wiry, slight man in his sixties with a leathery face and grizzled beard. They insist that we sit. One of the sons produces bottles of water and plastic cups, handing them round. When everyone is seated, Ali Salim stands in front of us, next to another older man, his cousin Ismail, and welcomes us 'in my land'.

Our guide, Marwan, translates: 'All my respect to everyone from Europe. We are a Palestinian nation under Israeli occupation. We received from this Occupation every kind of suffering in our life. Every home in Palestine, you will find suffering – someone martyred, someone arrested, someone exiled. The nations of Europe are like gentle people; you do not have this suffering. We receive all this pain and suffering because we do one big mistake: we stay in our land.' Ali Salim touches his chest with bunched fingers and flings them out to us. 'It's my honour to have you here and I say, thank God we still have kind people, nice people like you in the world.

'We have history here – from a long time we are living here. If you ask me what is my name, I have at least ten names – Ali Hassan Salim Mohammed Mousa . . .' he reels off a string of names. 'We have been here so long, but the settlers come here and take our land, under the eyes of their civil administration. For nearly fifty years we have had our land stolen, building military camps, building the Wall. I have a large family, with two wives and four sons. Then they came to demolish my house. I built again. After three years, they come again and demolish, and we build again. After three years they come and demolish again. Three times!'

Marwan puts his arm around Ali's cousin Ismail. 'He has no tears,' he says. 'They're stuck in his eyes.'

Ali continues, 'We asked the commander, "What wrong have we done?" They said, "This is against the security of Israel." You can tell how much they hate us. They said, "You have ten minutes." They threw away my cousin's fridge, threw it in the rubble so he couldn't use it again. They don't recognise us as human beings. We are like slaves who have to do service for Israel. They say, God gave the life to all people, but they don't look on us like that. They want us to give up, to lose hope. But this is my land and we stay here forever. I need to build my cemetery here. Even when I die, I will not move from here.'

The land slopes steeply down from the homestead across a dried-up stream-bed to where the Wall cuts across the farmland of

Al-Khader, annexing it to the settlement on the nearby hilltop. Ali points towards the settlement. 'The leader of this group of settlers is from Russia,' he says. 'He has a large pack of dangerous dogs. We don't let the children go near them. We don't ride donkeys any more, because they train their dogs to attack them. If an elderly person is riding their donkey down in the village and the settlers come with their dogs, they'll fall off and injure themselves.' He gestures to his grandchildren – three little girls and two boys. 'What kind of mistake have these children made against Israel? Going to school in the morning and coming home to find their house destroyed? These settlers have children. But they have no feeling, no sensitivity to us, to our children. My grandchildren ask us, "Why have they done this? Destroyed our house?"

'I tell my children, "This is the Zionist movement, from one hundred years ago." I'm not talking about Jewish people!' He shakes his finger emphatically. 'I'm talking about Zionists and the Occupation.' He throws out his arms, encompassing our group. 'We request all the nations of the world to put some kind of pressure on Israel's government to stop this cruelty, this humiliation against us.'

His eldest son, Ahmed, holding his own two-year-old lad, says, 'What I'm pleased – my children didn't see the bulldozers. I have six children; my father has eight. We have twenty children in this house. I teach my children to grow up in the world and have respect for everybody, but *they* are teaching my children to hate. What will my son learn from this? Please, please share our story with the world. We're not just talking about demolished houses – all the people in jail . . .'

His uncle Ismail says, 'My son is in jail for eighteen months for working without a permit in Israel. A 2,000-shekel fine and one and a half years in jail – because he followed the work. Really, by God, we need peace.'

Ali Salim explodes suddenly, slapping his hand against his palm. 'I couldn't even say, "Ay!"' he exclaims. 'They put their feet on my neck, and I couldn't even say, "Ow!" If he needs water, I'll give him water from my house. But to come and . . . look, I'll show you the well I built. They destroyed it.' He leads us over to the edge of the slope and points down to a deep gash in the ground, where the wellhead has been bulldozed and choked with boulders. He's almost spitting with anguish. 'Are you here with any kind of international law? They demolish, they put the boot on our heads and say, "*Shekit, shekit, shekit*, shut up, you can't say anything." Could anyone live under this Occupation? They could not. We sleep like sardines, ten in the tent, suffocating.

'They demolish my house four times, but even if they drive over us with tanks, we will not move. We will not be moved.'

Now another son, Khaled, has produced a pot of coffee and is filling plastic cups for us all. It's rich, dark Arabic coffee, sweetened with cardamom.

Our group leader, Nive Hall, is thanking Ali Salim. 'Our hearts are broken for you,' he says, as Marwan translates. 'We have heard you. We know that your voice is silenced, and we promise to use our voices to tell your story.'

'Everything I tell you is the truth,' says Ali Salim. Once again, he spreads his arms to include all of us. 'God bless you, give you a nice and relaxed life. We will pray for you. All my respect. Thank you for coming to hear my story.'

In March 2012, I visited Israel/Palestine for the first time, as part of a delegation sponsored by Amos Trust and the Greenbelt Festival. This trip, it seemed, would represent a great spiritual and cultural moment for me. From this small, bitterly contested patch of land in the Middle East, a cosmic narrative radiates across human history. Like Christians down the ages and across the world, I'd spent half a lifetime reading, studying and singing this narrative – and now I was poised to set foot on the hallowed stage myself. Jerusalem, Jericho, Nazareth, Galilee – every name is a referential trigger for a thousand hymns, paintings and poems; every brick is laden with legends. Like the most innocent of religious pilgrims, I experienced a kind of 'Indiana Jones'-style mystical thrill as our plane began its descent to Tel Aviv. *This is the place. I'm here at last. The land of the Bible stories, the land of Christ Himself.* Would I find Him here? On the Palm Sunday path down the Mount of Olives, in the Garden of Gethsemane or the Church of the Holy Sepulchre, or the grotto shrine of the Nativity Church amid the snow-clad, starlit hills of the 'little town' of Bethlehem?

Well, no, of course. What we found in most of the holy sites was a kind of biblical theme park, staffed by heavily bearded, stressed-out Greek Orthodox monks policing thronging queues of tourists, pushing and shoving, each eagerly awaiting their holy moment, their special encounter with the Divine in the magical location where X marks the spot. Quick prayer, quick photograph, buy a candle, on to the next miracle.

What we did encounter, on arriving at last in Bethlehem, was the Wall. The eight-metre high concrete, barbed-wire, watchtower and search-camera monolith, symbol and fact of occupation and oppression, monument to despair. And my immediate, almost flippant reaction was to turn to my companions and say, 'We should build the Wall in London. Then people would see what it's like.'

The idea grew on me. How could one go about it? What would we need to pull it off? In the wake of the 'Occupy' movement, the word from inside the Westminster village was that online petitions are all very well, but if you really want to make people sit up and take notice, you've got to get people out on the streets. So what would we need to bring the Bethlehem Wall to the notice of the public in the UK?

Well, it would have to be in central London – and at Christmas, because that's the only time anyone ever thinks of Bethlehem. It would have to be on private property – we'd surely never get permission from Westminster Council. Ideally, it would need the collaboration of a supportive faith community with a vision for creative, radical projects. All the arrows were pointing towards St James's Piccadilly and their talented and inspiring rector, Lucy Winkett. It so happened that she was chair of trustees for Amos Trust, she'd visited Israel/Palestine many times, and we'd collaborated successfully on a large, ambitious project ten years before at St Paul's Cathedral. So we met, and I asked her if I could build an eight-metre high concrete Wall across her church courtyard for the whole of Christmas 2013. I expected her to laugh. I didn't expect her to say yes.

Eight metres high and twenty-four metres across, with twenty tons of water ballast to weigh it down. How much would it cost? Don't know. Did we have the money? Never mind. Think big and aim high.

With the vision still firmly under wraps, an astonishing artistic programme was building around the putative Wall. Working in the theatre world, I'm used to most people saying no, most of the time. But to my imaginary, secret and unfunded Wall at St James's Piccadilly, the most amazing people kept saying yes. The legendary violinist Nigel Kennedy, comedians Jeremy Hardy and Mark Steel, performance poet Rafeef Ziadah, superstar chefs Yotam Ottolenghi and Sami Tamimi, singers from the Tallis Scholars, film-makers Leila and Larissa Sansour: everybody loved the idea, its audacity and simplicity. It was unnerving. What if we couldn't get the funding? What if the Council closed us down?

It was Lucy's inspiration that the Wall in Piccadilly should be not only a provocative piece of public art, but also a festival of 'Beautiful Resistance' – a term coined by Dr Abdelfattah Abusrour, director of Alrowwad Cultural & Arts Society in Aida Refugee Camp, Bethlehem. In this bleak, impoverished setting, right in the shadow of the Wall, among a cramped population living as refugees since 1948, Alrowwad teaches theatre, dance, music and photography to Palestinian teenagers as an expression of hope, to counter the daily humiliation and despair of the Occupation. 'I don't want to die for my country,' Abdelfattah told us. 'I want to live for my country. As Palestinian refugees, we don't have the luxury of despair. Instead, we choose beautiful resistance.'

Despite the magnitude of injustice heaped upon them, most Palestinians I've met prefer to celebrate life, love, laughter and hospitality. So, back in London, we decided to build a Christmas festival around our replica Wall – not just in solidarity with, but in *celebration* of Bethlehem today, because the reality of the Wall isn't the only thing that people in the West can't see and don't understand.

Everywhere we went in Palestine, certainly we saw the oppression and suffering, but, springing up all around the checkpoints, concrete barriers and razor wire fences, we also encountered communities of hope. People in the West can't see, because they're always looking at governments and official processes – just as most religious pilgrims, seeking an encounter with God in the Holy Land, look in the wrong places. 'By all means, visit the holy sites, the dead stones,' said Nidal Abu Zuluf of the East Jerusalem YMCA, 'but we'd prefer it if you come and visit us, the living stones, under Occupation, behind the Wall.'

'We are going through the Stations of the Cross, the Via Dolorosa, on a daily basis,' said Dr Zoughbi Al-Zoughbi, the charismatic director of Wi'am Conflict Transformation Centre in Bethlehem. 'Every day we could be angry – legitimately! – but as the Israelis are destroying our lives, we are transforming them, turning the garbage of our anger and hate into the flower and tree of compassion.'

With the watchtowers and skunk water cannon of the Wall overlooking their playground, Wi'am works with Palestinian children to heal the trauma of the Occupation through art therapy and sports, runs women's gender empowerment programmes and provides a safe space to local communities for conflict resolution. It is an astonishing community of hope.

No more do people see the remarkable example of Daoud Nassar, founder of the Tent of Nations, a sustainable eco-farm outside Bethlehem, besieged on a hilltop between louring settlements, which draws visitors and volunteers from all over the world, and brings Palestinian schoolchildren for summer breaks in green fields, *because their land is their future*, says Daoud. He has decided to use the near-impossible conditions imposed by the Occupation as a spring-board for eco-innovation. 'We have no running water, so we've had to become very efficient in our use of rainwater, recycling our "grey" water to irrigate the crops. If we were to build any new structures, the Israelis would demolish them, so instead we have tunnelled out caves in the hillside and are planning to build wind-mills on wheels. If it moves, it's not a structure!'

Unusually, Daoud's family has paperwork dating back to the Ottoman era demonstrating their ownership of the land, so they have proved extremely difficult to dislodge. They have been fighting a record-breaking twenty-five-year legal action against the Israeli government to retain their land. Nevertheless, the occupying forces make regular and destructive incursions. The last time I visited Daoud, in 2014, the IDF had just bulldozed his entire fruit crop, claiming it was grown on land that didn't belong to him. Daoud said, 'You have to feel sorry for the people who did this. These acts they commit – they will follow them for the rest of their lives.' *We refuse to be your enemy*, proclaims the stone gatepost at the entrance to his farm.

Nor do people in the West hear nearly enough about the work of Jeff Halper, founder of the Israeli Committee Against House Demolitions. A Jewish Israeli activist for Palestinian rights, Jeff campaigns tirelessly on the issue that he considers to epitomise the cruelty and injustice of the Occupation: house demolitions. He and other Israeli activists place themselves regularly in front of IDF bulldozers, and they organise house rebuilding projects with volunteers from the West. Short, stout and voluble, with a Father Christmas beard and a broad New York drawl, Jeff is an infectiously engaging embodiment of 'Beautiful Resistance.' He's been arrested more times than he can remember, written several books, gives speaking tours all over the world and has picked up a Nobel Peace Prize nomination along the way.

Together with his Palestinian friend Salim Shawamreh, whose house had just been demolished for the fifth time, Jeff sat and ate with us in a chilly tent on the hillside of Anata, in East Jerusalem. Salim's family made us welcome in their tent, and in breaking bread together we celebrated another community of hope.

And how I wish that more people around the world could hear the heart-stirring words of Sami Awad, founder of the Holy Land Trust in Bethlehem, whom I sometimes describe as a kind of Palestinian Gandhi. The following diary piece attempts to convey a sense of the impression he made on me at our first meeting.

March 2012

We're sitting in a quiet, secluded meeting room in the old city of Bethlehem with one of the most extraordinary men I've ever met. The 'meditation room' is a cool, shaded enclave away from the fierce heat of the mid-morning sun, with low divans set round three walls and a pleasant stream of natural light from low windows either side of the door. Furnished in traditional Bedouin style, with oriental rugs on the floor and embroidered cushions scattered across the divans, the room has a low vaulted ceiling, almost like a tent. We're in the offices of the Holy Land Trust, a Palestinian organisation working for peace and equality through non-violence, and our host is its director, Sami Awad. He's a warm, charismatic guy, middling height and sturdy, whose easy-going sense of humour belies his remarkable *gravitas* and insight. His dark brown eyes, droll and ironic one moment, can glow like coals the next with a depth of soul suddenly revealed. He speaks with a gentle accent somewhere between educated north American and classic Arabic-English.

'What do we seek for this land that many people here call holy, but don't treat as such?' he asks. 'Well, there were two reasons for starting Holy Land Trust. The first was political. I returned from the USA in 1998, during the Oslo Peace Process, which represented a great hope for Palestinians but in reality was a huge disappointment. New structures of control were imposed on us, despite the creation of the Palestinian Authority and some measure of autonomy. New checkpoints sprang up, new restrictions of movement between Palestinian communities were forced on us. New structures of economic occupation and control arose, restricting the movement of farm produce, for example, from Gaza to the West Bank. Our markets were flooded with Israeli products. We saw also a massive increase of settlement-building in Palestinian territory, putting new "facts on the ground" and making future compromise inevitable. I concluded that we had to bring forms of non-violent action into the political arena. Palestinian politicians ignored the voice of the people, without which peace is impossible.

'The second reason was religious. This land is holy to the three Abrahamic faiths, but belongs in the end to no one but God. As the people of this land, we should be its trustees, to care for the land and proclaim the beautiful messages of God's love, peace and justice to the world, and welcome people of all faiths from everywhere. So, as the millennium approached, in celebration of this call, we organised the re-enactment of the journey of the Magi from Iran, through Syria and Jordan and into the Holy Land to Bethlehem – a truly amazing experience.

'Then, in 2000, the Second Intifada began. Here at Holy Land Trust, we asked, "What can we do to contribute to peace?" We believe non-violence is the only workable solution, so we have developed a whole programme of training courses, seminars, protests and activities. There is not yet a well-developed non-violent movement in Palestine, but soon I believe this will be widespread. We can help to spearhead and disseminate this movement.

'Also, we want to look to the future: what comes after the

Occupation ends? Gender equality, human rights and religious freedom are not guaranteed just because the Occupation ends. Decolonisation around the world often leads either to civil war or dictatorship. Holy Land Trust asks, "What can we do *now* to prepare the ground for a democracy?"

'So, alongside our programmes in non-violent and creative forms of resistance, we focus on activities and courses which support community building and democratic training.

'Of course, we also reflect continually on the question, what causes Israeli society to treat us this way? Does it come out of nothing? Is it genetic? The primary answer is the trauma and fear of the Israeli race, because of the Holocaust. And the world has ignored or perpetuated the trauma by feeding the addiction, piling political legitimacy and support on Israel, instead of being strong and saying, "No, if you do wrong, we will stop you."

'Israel looks for the possibility of threat anywhere. Israel will attack Iran, exploiting this perception of the possibility of threat. Israeli leaders exploit this threat, this trauma in the Israeli psyche, all the time.

'What would Jesus do in this situation? Non-violence, yes, as a social and political choice. But also "loving the enemy", as evidenced in the Gospels, for example John chapter 4: "He *had* to go through Samaria" – i.e., He wanted to engage with the enemy, to heal the wounds of the enemy, to show compassion for the woman of Samaria.

'Palestinians have to try to do this, and not act as the victim. The biggest problem is victimisation – in both communities; victimhood and depression are the modern ailments of stress. Holy Land Trust is also engaging with the Christian community worldwide – particularly in the West. There is a big challenge with American evangelical Zionist Christians, who are probably in reality the most threatening entity for Israelis and Jews out there. We are seeing cracks in the wall even with the most extreme groups. I tell them, "Have a heart for both Palestinians and Israelis." I attended a conference in the USA, in Virginia Beach, at Regents University, Pat Robertson's stamping ground. I spoke to 800 Christian leaders, real extremists, total Zionists. It was a big breakthrough in our relationships.

'Then in 2010 we held the conference "Christ at the Checkpoint", and invited evangelical leaders, Christian Zionists and Messianic Jews, to come and debate and study in Bethlehem. Tony Campolo came, and many others like him. There was lots of pushback, but the conference leaders lovingly responded with great confidence. Here were 600 delegates, 400 of them internationals. The Kairos Palestine document was showcased prominently at this conference, a declaration of the united churches of the Holy Land, modelled on the Kairos document that emerged from South Africa in the apartheid era, calling on Christians worldwide to stand in solidarity with black South Africans, naming apartheid as a sin against God and humanity. The Kairos Palestine document is the same, calling on churches across the world to stand in solidarity with us, to condemn the Occupation and join with us in our struggle.

'What else do we do? Well, we run a course called "Transformation" training, involving one-to-one coaching and leadership development, seeking creative ways to make the impossible possible. We run something called "Distinction" training, looking at the limitations of decision-making based exclusively on the past.

'Consider the checkpoint experience: an Israeli soldier does the one-finger beckoning move. What do we do? Well, our Pavlovian response is to slump, walk grudgingly over to the soldier, take out our ID card before we've even been asked, assuming we're going to be humiliated. Well, maybe not. Actually, we don't know what he wants. Maybe he just wants a light for his cigarette! So, we train Palestinians to make *self*-empowering choices: straighten up, walk smartly, look him in the eye, and say, "Yes? What can I do for you?"

'Ninety-eight per cent of Palestinians engaging in non-violent resistance are Muslim. Palestinian Christians, being a minority, can be very strident and competitive, always wanting to prove themselves, including in the armed resistance. So Holy Land Trust has some Muslim board members. After all, Jesus is the "Prince of Peace" in Islam as well as Christianity. Muslim Palestinians don't like evangelical Christians from the West telling them to convert, but they do revere Jesus as prophet!

'Our latest initiative? Well, you guys are all artists from the UK Greenbelt Festival, and I'm planning to get a Greenbelt-style festival going here in Bethlehem – Bet Lahem Live!'

Inspired by these encounters, on a wing and a prayer, and the generous collaboration of countless supporters, the Wall in London at Christmas 2013 and its accompanying festival, Bethlehem Unwrapped, was a creative and political success, even a landmark, with thousands of visitors, a sold-out programme of events and global media coverage.

When I returned to Bethlehem the following June, the 'facts on the ground' had gone from bad to worse. Against all the odds, Sami had succeeded in mounting the first Bet Lahem Live festival the previous summer, with support from Amos Trust and Greenbelt Festival. Now I had come with a group of UK artists to attend the 2014 Bet Lahem Live. The daily insecurity of the Occupation, with periods of relative calm constantly erupting into new crises, of course makes it extremely difficult to plan anything in Palestine, and just such a crisis had blown up the week before the festival: three Israeli teenagers had set out to hitchhike from one of the most extreme religious settlements, Gush Etzion, just south of Jerusalem and Bethlehem, in the West Bank, to their homes in central Israel, and had disappeared. Officially, Jewish Israelis are forbidden from entering the West Bank (despite the presence there of 700,000 Israeli settlers), and large red signs at points of road access to Palestinian areas warn that entry to the Occupied Territories is 'illegal and dangerous to your life'. Hitchhiking on Palestinian or joint access roads is forbidden to Israeli military personnel, but for mitzvah-observant adolescents it is a 'rite of passage, a way of life, a declaration of independence and of ownership of the land', according to *Haaretz* newspaper.

The disappearance of the teenagers led immediately to a massive outburst of collective punishment by Israeli forces up and down the Palestinian Territories. The demolition of the house at Al-Khader was only one among many. In Bethlehem, Sami found himself under considerable pressure to cancel the festival. In a piece entitled 'Will Sami Awad do the right thing?', *The Times of Israel* asked, 'Will he proceed with a festival that provides cover for anti-Israel activism? Or will he do the right thing and cancel the festival, slated to begin on Thursday, to avoid exacerbating the tension caused by the kidnapping of three Israeli teenagers last week?' The piece also questions the propriety of allowing a celebration to proceed 'while three Jewish teenagers . . . are being held hostage by Hamas a few miles away in Hebron'.

'Well, if we waited for things to be "normal", we'd never hold a festival at all,' said Sami. 'We're living under a military occupation! But many Palestinian voices have been raised in criticism as well: some people are saying, "Why are you having a festival when all these appalling things are being done to us?" So we've been out to many communities to try to get a sense of what people are feeling – should we go ahead, or cancel? And the majority opinion is that we should proceed. This is the whole point – to hold a festival as an act of cultural, non-violent resistance to the Occupation. Yes, things are appalling at the moment, but things are never right under an unjust occupation, and if we're intimidated into cancelling because of what's going on, the Occupation will have won. We need to hold firm and go ahead.'

Three days later, I sat with Sami once again in the meditation room at Holy Land Trust, as he spoke to the UK artists attending the festival.

19 June 2014

'Before 1948, my family lived in a prosperous suburb of Jerusalem,' Sami tells us, 'and we had very friendly relationships with all our neighbours, Jewish and Palestinian. One of the neighbouring families was Orthodox Jewish, and on the *shabat* (Jewish Sabbath), when they're not supposed to do any work of any kind, my grandparents used to go into their house to turn the lights on and off for them. That was the level of trust which existed between neighbours.

'Then, in 1948, came the war, what we call the *Nakba*, when Palestine was ethnically cleansed by the Zionist brigades. My grandfather was determined that his family would not be involved in any kind of violence. He was climbing on to the roof with a white flag, to hang it up to show that this was a house of peace, when he was shot dead by a sniper. The next day, the Zionist brigades came to the house and told my grandmother, "You all have to leave, immediately, otherwise you'll be killed," and so my family became refugees, fleeing into what is now called the West Bank, to stay with different relatives – some in Bethlehem, some elsewhere.

There wasn't enough room for all the kids to live with relatives, so my father and his siblings went into orphanages. So I grew up against a background of tragedy, dispossession and exile. I grew up with a lot of rage inside me.

'The inspiration for my family's work in peace and reconciliation came from my grandmother. Before she died, she spoke about my grandfather, and about the man who had killed him. "I don't even want to know his name," she said. "Never find out his name, even if you have the chance." When we asked her why, she said, "Because if he'd known my husband, he would never have shot him."'

Sami pauses as we absorb this story. Then, slowly, quietly, as if weighing the cost of his words, he continues. 'It's been said – and I believe this – that the greatest attainment of justice is to achieve reconciliation with those who have wronged you. This was my grandmother's vision. My uncle, Dr Mubarak Awad, established the Palestinian Centre for the Study of Non-Violence (PCSN) in East Jerusalem in 1983. He spent three years lecturing in East Jerusalem, the West Bank and the Gaza Strip on the philosophy and techniques of non-violent resistance, and the PCSN mounted all kinds of actions – protests, civil disobedience, planting olive trees on land under threat of confiscation, tax strikes, boycott campaigns, encouraging people to eat and drink only Palestinian products, and so on – until the Israeli government kicked him out of the country. He now lives and teaches in Washington DC.

'The First Intifada began in December 1987 as a non-violent movement of resistance to Israel's occupation, directly influenced by my uncle's ideas, and he was one of the prime movers, publishing a twelve-page blueprint for peaceful resistance in the Palestinian Territories. Mubarak in turn was influenced by the ideas of Mahatma Gandhi and Martin Luther King Jr, as well as the distinguished American academic Professor Gene Sharp, who founded the Albert Einstein Institution. Sharp's trilogy on *The Politics of Non-Violence* is the classic text on civil disobedience, and he's probably the world's leading academic on the theory and practice of non-violent resistance. My uncle has translated the writings of Gandhi and King into Arabic, and he's often referred to in the Middle East as the Arab Gandhi, because he drew directly on Gandhi's strategies of resistance in the non-violent overthrow of the British Raj.

'There is a big gap, a huge impoverishment in the culture of leadership in both communities: Israelis and Palestinians both play the victim game, and so our culture of leadership is all about mastering the art of victimhood. So at Holy Land Trust we've developed a course in "non-linear thinking" for leadership, which invites participants to ask, "What is the future I want to achieve, and how do I live and act today to bring that future into reality?" Or, as the late great Walter Wink wrote, "Hope imagines the future and then acts as if that future is irresistible."

'Every so often, the IDF commander in Bethlehem calls me in to see him. For a "chat", for "coffee". And I ask him about his family, his wife and kids. And he often says, "You know, Sami, I really respect your work." My work? Organising non-violent resistance? Against your Occupation? "Yes," he says, "I respect your work." "So, what then?" I say. "What are we doing here?" And he says, "Well, we're on different sides in this story, aren't we?" And I know for a fact that when he sends in his soldiers to break up a demonstration, he singles me out for punishment. "Get Sami," he tells them, "give him a good beating, chuck him in the van." Because he really respects my work.

'As Palestinian Christians, we reflect on Christ's injunction to love our enemies. Well, to love my enemy, I must try to understand him. This is why I went to visit Auschwitz. What I saw there helped me to understand the inherited trauma of the Israeli psyche. I saw groups of Israeli kids going round the museum exhibits, the huts and gas chambers, being instructed by their teachers and rabbis. "This is not just your past," they were telling the kids. "This is your present, and your future too."

'So we consider that the collective psyche of Israel is traumatised. They build walls, barbed-wire fences, checkpoints, watchtowers – they've surrounded this land with a cage of steel and concrete. Just as a woman who's been raped repeatedly will view the approach of any man as a threat, so Israel looks on any and every other state, people, tribe or entity as an enemy or future enemy who must be met and defeated pre-emptively with violence. Out of guilt for the Holocaust, the world has given "bad love" to Israel: yes, yes, carry on, do whatever you want, and we will always support you. If the world really loves Israel, they need to stop feeding their addiction.

As Palestinian Christians, we reflect on the meaning of our suffering. And we consider that perhaps the meaning of so much undeserved suffering . . . perhaps, somehow, our calling is to play a role in healing the traumatised psyche of the Israeli people.'

Seeking an encounter with the Divine in the Holy Land, I had a palpable sense that I had found God not in the shrines and monuments of the pilgrimage trail, but in people like Sami, Jeff, Daoud, Zoughbi and the others. 'Jesus was born, lived and died in a land under military occupation,' Sami reminded us. 'And he rose from the dead and proclaimed the new kingdom in a land under occupation. We Palestinians can't afford to wait for someone else to come and give us our freedom. We must claim and embrace our freedom *now*, in the mind, heart and actions, in preparation for the day when freedom becomes a political reality.'

'We promise to use our voices to tell your story.'

After the grief and horror of Israel's onslaught on Gaza in 2014, I found myself reflecting again on the promise we made to Ali Salim in the ruins of his house in Al-Khader. I was determined to use every creative resource at my disposal to try to find new ways to uphold the Palestinian story and celebrate the courage and humanity of their culture under siege and occupation. I wasn't short of opportunities: in September of that year, I was asked to produce the UK launch of *Open Bethlehem*, a remarkable documentary feature by the acclaimed Palestinian film-maker Leila Sansour, depicting the impact of the Occupation and the Wall on her home town of Bethlehem, to a packed audience of luminaries at the Royal Geographical Society, hosted by Melvyn Bragg. Leila's film, which has since had major releases in the UK and USA, was hailed in *The Guardian* as 'the kind of art that peace processes are built on'. Then, in 2015, Ahmed Masoud invited me to collaborate on a new play, a dark tragicomedy called *The Shroud Maker*, based on a real-life character he had encountered in Gaza City who made a living sewing shrouds for the dead. Our premiere performance at Amnesty International, on Armistice Day 2015, raised funds for the Al-Ahli Hospital in Gaza City. Then, in the summer of 2016, I worked with Amos Trust to bring fourteen teenage Palestinian dancers and singers from Alrowwad Youth Theatre to the UK for a three-week tour including performances at St Paul's Cathedral, the Scottish Parliament and the Pleasance at the Edinburgh Fringe. The young performers' joyful talent and effervescent spirit won the hearts of audiences up and down the UK, as well as prime-time television coverage and full-page spreads in the national press.

And all this time, the 'perfect storm' of upcoming Palestinian anniversaries was brewing. A big, crazy stunt, it seemed to me, was required. Something bigger and crazier than the Wall.

Soon after he came from Gaza to the UK to study, Ahmed told me, he made a train journey from London to Edinburgh. 'It was the most wonderful journey I'd ever made,' he said. 'Hundreds of miles through beautiful green countryside, and no one to stop you. I couldn't believe it – no borders, no fences, walls, checkpoints, nothing – just rolling on and on, free. I was sitting with my face glued to the window, just drinking it in, so much land and sky.' Maybe this is what gave me the idea of the Walk. The complete opposite of the Wall in Piccadilly – instead of a barbed-wire and concrete barrier, a massive celebration of freedom of movement – a gigantic walk. To where? To Palestine, of course, where exiled Palestinians aren't allowed to return. To Jerusalem.

'Jerusalem is at the heart of the Palestinian cause,' said Mustafa Barghouti, leader of the Palestine National Initiative, when I met him in Ramallah in March 2012. A medical doctor, member of the Palestinian parliament and founder of the Palestinian Medical Relief Society, which provides health care in the West Bank and Gaza Strip, he spoke about the importance of freedom of movement to Palestinians, and specifically about their yearning for Al-Quds, their holy city, Jerusalem. In an interview given around this time, he said, 'East Jerusalem should be the capital of the Palestinian State. If Jerusalem is lost, the whole concept and idea of Palestinian state-hood is lost, and the possibility of peace is lost. And Jerusalem is an important place for all of humanity, a holy place for Muslims, Christians and the Jewish people. It should be the place where peace begins.'

Europeans have been travelling to the Holy Land for nearly 2,000 years, as pilgrims, penitents, scholars, crusaders, conquerors and colonialists. Reflecting on this history, and Britain's complicity in the ongoing conflict in the Middle East, I conceived the idea of a pilgrimage, a 'Just Walk' to Jerusalem. I shared the idea with Chris Rose, who loved it. He put it to the Amos staff and trustees, who also loved it, albeit with a gulp or two of apprehension. When we tried it out on Sami, he *really* loved it, saying it was the perfect follow-up to their re-enactment of the Journey of the Magi. Then, when Chris and Nive shared the idea with the other Amos partners and friends in the West Bank, Alrowwad, Wi'am and the others, they were taken aback by the enthusiasm all round. Everyone wanted a piece of it.

I went to my friend Pen Hadow, the Polar explorer, who remains the only person in the world to have trekked solo to the North Pole, to ask him if we were mad. 'No, of course not,' he said. 'I mean, yes – but no. Of course you can do it.' Would we need to train for months in preparation? 'No. Just get on with it and build up your stamina as you go.' Pen introduced me to Harry Bucknall, who walked and wrote about the Via Francigena ('the way through France'), the ancient path from Canterbury to Rome, in his book *Like a Tramp, like a Pilgrim*. Harry in turn introduced me to Ian Brodrick and the Confraternity of Pilgrims to Jerusalem, and over the course of two years' planning with Amos Trust, the Walk to Jerusalem became a reality.

There is a brutal expression, 'Facts on the ground', which has become part of the lexicon of Israel's fifty-year occupation. The maxim 'possession is nine tenths of the law' pretty much sums it up – building settlements, grabbing land, bulldozing houses, erecting walls – putting 'facts on the ground' which will set the goalposts of any future territorial negotiations.

But is not hope a fact as well? The great American historian, playwright and activist Howard Zinn wrote in his 1994 autobiography:

> To be hopeful in bad times is not just foolishly romantic . . . If we see only the worst, it destroys our capacity to do something. If we remember those times and places – and there are so many – where people have behaved magnificently, this gives us the energy to act, and at least the possibility of sending this spinning top of a world in a different direction. And if we do act, in however small a way, we don't have to wait for some grand utopian future. The

future is an infinite succession of presents, and to live now as we think human beings should live, in defiance of all that is bad around us, is itself a marvelous victory.[1]

An infinite succession of presents – or, as walkers say, putting one foot in front of the other. Following pilgrimage routes and Roman roads across Europe; in the year of Brexit, traversing the continent from west to east on foot; walking the refugee road from the Syrian conflict, and enacting symbolically the Palestinians' right of return.

Changing the record. Putting some new 'facts on the ground'.

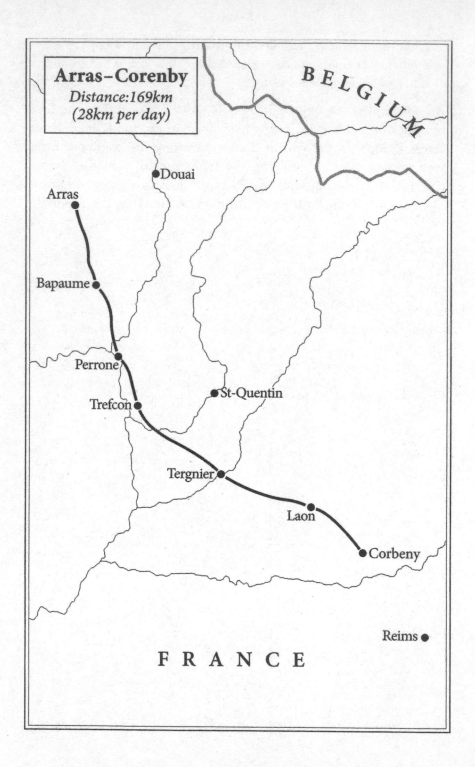

Arras–Corenby
Distance:169km
(28km per day)

BELGIUM

Douai

Arras

Bapaume

Perrone

Trefcon

St-Quentin

Tergnier

Laon

Corbeny

Reims

FRANCE

3

Esprit de Corps

Another world is not only possible; she is on her way.
On a quiet day, I can hear her breathing.

*You have been shown what is good, to act justly, to love mercy and
to walk humbly.*

We walk this day with those whose freedom is denied.
We walk with those who have fled war, torture and despair.
We walk in penance for broken promises and political fixes.
**We walk the long road with all those who strive for peace,
justice and reconciliation.**
We walk with those who long to return to home.
We walk in hope that one day all people in the Holy Land
Will live in peace, as neighbours with full equal rights.

Walk softly upon the earth. May its beauty surround you;
May its wisdom delight you, its music invite you.
*May you love and be loved; may you know peace and practise
compassion.*

Rejoice in the earth and in all of creation. Rejoice in life.

Ambulando Solvitur. **It will be solved by walking.**

(*Just Walk to Jerusalem* liturgy)

★ ★ ★

Friday 16 June 2017

DOVER IS THE unhappiest place to live in England, according to the 2017 iLiveHereUK poll, in which one contributor, borrowing a leaf from the Donald Trump lexicon of diplomacy, described the town as the 'herpes-infested sh*t-hole of the British Isles', but the town always awakens pleasant memories for me. My grandmother lived two miles north along the White Cliffs in the idyllic Wodehousian enclave of St Margaret's Bay, where Noel Coward wrote *Blithe Spirit* and *Brief Encounter* in his seaside cottage (sold subsequently to Ian Fleming), Henry Royce (of Rolls-Royce fame) developed the first British aeroplane engine in a clifftop retreat, and Peter Ustinov lived in the old coastguard lookout hut.

My brother Matthew and I spent half our childhood scrambling up and down this coastland, fishing and rock-pooling, building dams and setting snares, exploring every glade and spinney of the South Foreland Valley from the lighthouse to the low-tide sands. The cliffs and valley are riddled with old army bunkers and gun emplacements, which became for us the setting for innumerable secret missions, last stands and death-defying frontal assaults. St Margaret's took such a pounding from the German guns in the war, and the daily dogfights overhead were so intense, as Spitfires and Hurricanes battled desperately against swarms of Luftwaffe bombers, that the tranquil bay and surrounding chalk bluffs became known as Hellfire Corner.

Our trips to Dover were for tackle and bait in the fishing shop, twenty lugworm writhing in newspaper, or white ragworm brandishing pincers from their jaws. Leathery-faced sea dogs sold us hooks and spinners, hollow cheeks sucking at their pipes as they counted out change with mythically wrinkled hands. Fishing from Dover pier with my dad and brother in all weathers, freezing yellow with crab and lugworm guts and salt wind spraying our faces, coating our cheeks with rime. Tramping up and down the barnacled planks to keep warm, chasing gulls away from the bait bucket in squawking indignation, and sipping tea from flasks billowing steam in the sea breeze. Watching the heave and swell of the green sea through the cracks in the planks, vertiginous on solid ground as beneath your feet a yawning world of water surged and dropped away. 'Watch your rod!' my dad would bark as, marvellously, the tip juddered with a bite. Fumbling excitement, numbed fingers grappling the reel, yanking the rod back for the strike, then slipping the catch and reeling feverishly, desperate not to snarl the tackle, leaning out over the pier rails . . . and the thrill of that silver flash as the fish broke clear of the foam.

And if it was raining too hard to fish, there was always Dover Castle, flinty and massive on its green headland, battlements bristling with cannon snouts, a fabulous warren of dungeons and armouries and all the martial cornucopia of a thousand years of war. There's an ironic backstory to the doughty splendour of this fortress, on which Henry II lavished more money than any other castle in England.

On the fifth day of Christmas 1170, Archbishop Thomas Becket was murdered in Canterbury Cathedral by four knights who had ridden hotfoot from the king's court after his infamous outburst, 'Will no one rid me of this turbulent priest?' Championing the privilege of the Church against secular power, Becket had stood up to the king and lost his life. His murder shocked the crowned heads and courts of Europe, and turned Henry overnight into a pariah, despite his protestations of innocence. Then, as tales of miracles taking place at the site of Becket's martyrdom began to proliferate within just a few weeks, pilgrims began to arrive from all over Europe to visit his tomb. The trickle of pilgrims soon became a flood and, when the Pope declared Becket a saint and martyr in February 1173, Henry's reputation was in tatters. Simultaneous invasions of his realm the following year from Scotland, France and Flanders, coupled with a rebellion led by his wife Eleanor of Aquitaine and his elder sons, threatened to engulf Henry. Then, on 12 July 1174, he performed an elaborate show of public penance for Becket's murder, walking barefoot in sackcloth to the cathedral and allowing himself to be flogged naked, while kneeling at Becket's tomb, by every monk in the cloister, after which he spent the night alone in the martyr's crypt.

As Henry attended a farewell mass the next morning, the king of Scotland was captured at Alnwick. Later that same day the young king's invading fleet was defeated and dispersed. With God's favour restored and the saint's blessing secured, as it seemed, Henry's kingdom and rule were rescued. He became the leading devotee of the burgeoning cult of St Thomas, visiting his shrine every time he returned to England from Normandy, and Dover Castle became his 'show home' for entertaining the great and the good from across Europe and beyond. Welcoming royal pilgrims to Canterbury in the opulence of his mighty clifftop fortress, Henry made simultaneous demonstrations of pious reverence for the martyred saint and the reach of his formidable power, which had extinguished Becket's life. As part of his rehabilitation in the eyes of the Church, Henry 'took the cross' in 1172, vowing to go on crusade to defend the beleaguered Crusader Kingdom of Jerusalem, surrounded from east and north by the Seljuk Turks and Nur ad-Din of Damascus and from the south by the forces of Saladin, Sultan of Egypt. After Jerusalem fell to Saladin in 1187, Henry and his eldest son Richard, now known as the 'Lionheart', announced their intention to join the Third Crusade.

Nestling beneath the White Cliffs and the castle, the ferry port is as shabby and dreary as ever, but for me the spell of nostalgia is strong. This tangled conflux of traffic lanes, customs booths, barriers and fences has always been for me a two-way portal to enchantment. Departing on family holidays to France, we'd always stop off at my grandmother's old storm bungalow on Goodwin Road looking across the valley to the cliffs, to deposit our border terrier, Harry, for a two-week sojourn chasing rabbits with his country cousin Benjy, Grandma's Jack Russell. And when we returned, we always had the thrill of reunion to inspire us, as well as revisiting the cherished haunts of the South Foreland Valley. It was, as they say, the best of both worlds.

The walkers are Arthur from Blythburgh and Brussels; his sister Vanessa from Norwich; veteran peace-walkers Cressey and Jude from Perth in Western Australia; David, from the Gold Coast, Queensland; Denise from Washington DC and London; Ian and Mary from Lewes, Sussex; Chris Rose's eighteen-year-old son Jack, almost as tall as his father; Lynn from Southport, who has what my kids would describe as a 'bangin' tan'; Naomi and Robin from Cambridge, youth worker and software developer respectively; and Tim from Hertford, Buddhist and town planner. Robin and Tim are our walk leaders/navigators. Piloting our support bus is Ivor the driver, a droll Brummy beekeeper and retired Methodist minister. David, exotically, is Maltese *and* Australian, and on the bus from the foot passenger terminal to the ship, he's trying to fathom the logistics of getting the right exit stamps in his two passports, so he doesn't run into trouble with his three-month UK visa. Apparently, the UK passport, rated number two in the world on Arton Capital's 'Power Rank' index, is set to plummet in clout post-Brexit to number twenty-six, slightly below Mexico. Ah well, at least it'll be blue.

As the ferry pulls away with funnel blasts, churning sea and a convoy of gulls, from the deck I point out the South Foreland lighthouse, landmark of the sceptred isle, and tell Jude and Denise how my brother and I used to go to sleep each night in my grandmother's conservatory, watching the lighthouse beams rake across the night sky and listening to the sound of the sea swell sucking at the shingle down in the bay. Peering across the valley and over the dark sea on a clear night, you could see the lights of France twinkling, and across the black expanse of the Channel, here and there the lights of ships glimmered, sparking dreams of pirates, smugglers and spies. Every minute or so the lightship would flash its beacon flare, warning vessels away from the peril of Goodwin Sands, where 2,000 ships had foundered. Mr Blanche, the last lighthouse keeper before its decommission, used to do odd jobs for Grandma, and Mrs Blanche was her cleaner, an archetypal apple-cheeked housekeeper from one of Mr Mulliner's tales, bellowing rustic good cheer in a broad Kent accent, with forearms like a wrestler and a perpetual fag on her lip.

Jude is a doctor, in her mid-sixties, recently retired. 'Wanted a change,' she says. 'I spent two years nursing my husband Graham, until he died.'

'I'm sorry,' I say.

'It's OK,' she smiles, 'it was a good death, and it wasn't unexpected. I feel really happy that he made a good end, and I was with him all the way.' After he died she did the European Peace Walk, and most recently she's been in Serbia, working with refugees from Iraq, Afghanistan and north Africa. 'They offer you *their* food,' she says. 'They're sitting on the pavement with a morsel of food, and you ask them if they're OK, and they invite you to share their food! And the way we treat them in Australia, Europe, the UK . . . if only we could stop the arms trade, maybe this war in the Middle East would end.' Jude and I will become great buddies, over countless miles of walking and talking.

As we approach the French coast, a long, low, sandy strand surmounted by green hills, the ugly, bristling dock buildings of Calais hove into view and, beyond, the space rocket spikes of the Eglise Notre Dame (where Charles de Gaulle was married), the famous lighthouse and the Mairie de Calais. Walking out of the ferry terminal through barbed-wire walkways and fences is an immediate reminder of the refugee crisis and the former camps nearby, Sangatte and the Jungle. From Dover onwards, we're on the refugee road.

Away from the grimy ferry port, the old town is quaintly pretty. Jude tells me about her sons, stepsons and grandchildren as we walk through beautiful rose gardens and *parcs municipaux* to the Place du Soldat Inconnu, where Rodin's *Burghers of Calais* keep vigil, their poignant dignity offsetting the gaudy·extravagance of the Mairie. After the battle of Crécy in 1346, Edward III of England besieged and eventually captured Calais, but the town's citizens withstood the siege for so long that the enraged king at first ordered the entire population to be slaughtered *en masse*. Relenting somewhat, he agreed to spare the townspeople on condition that six of their principal citizens came to him, bareheaded and barefoot, with ropes around their necks, and gave themselves up to death. In flowing sinews of bronze, Rodin's masterpiece captures the moment when the heroic burghers walk out to die for their people, humbled and defenceless before the ruthless king. The first cast of the sculpture is here in Calais, set as Rodin wished at ground level, so that contemporary townsfolk would 'almost bump into' the figures and feel solidarity with them, but there are twelve other original casts around the world, including one in Parliament Square in London. Celebrating the sculpture as Britain's 'best work of public art', Jonathan Jones in *The Guardian* praised it as 'a poem to surrender. The emaciated bodies, tattered robes and, above all, the wonderfully delicate and melancholy gestures and poses of the figures express a strange and captivating mood of self-negation . . .

disconcertingly modern art. Rodin's masterpiece is sculpture as history painting, and it serves in London as a monument to humble, everyday heroes. It is true and it is beautiful. If only more public art rose to its level.'[1]

There's a sort of happy ending to the story: although the king had ordered their execution, his queen, Philippa of Hainault, was so moved by their courage she begged him to spare their lives. At her appeal, he pardoned them, but drove out most of the town's French inhabitants, and settled Calais with English subjects. As we drape our company of walkers over and around the sculpture for photographs, there's much speculation about the likely response of today's politicians to the ultimatum faced by the burghers. Somehow, no one can quite picture Boris Johnson barefoot in bronze with a noose around his neck.

Through more rose gardens and parks and past a faded Palladian opera house dominated by a statue of Jacquard (1752–1843), inventor of the first programmable loom, we follow the canal out of central Calais and plunge into a strange maze of roundabouts and motorway verges, hopping fences and improvising, all the time trying to head south-west to find our Ibis budget hotel somewhere close to the Eurotunnel and station. The reason we're having to scramble like this, Naomi points out, is that there are no walking routes to the Eurotunnel. Of course not: the authorities don't want to make it easy for anyone to approach on foot.

Once we're established at the Ibis budget, on a traffic island in a godforsaken retail park somewhere south-west of Calais, I venture out with a couple of the walkers to explore the local hostelries – a burger joint, a pizza joint and possibly a pasta joint, by the looks of it. As we trek across roundabouts and car parks, one of my companions mentions she comes from a large family.

'What fun,' I say, as she tells me about all her brothers and sisters.

'What fun,' she says drily. 'I hate my siblings.'

'Oh dear.'

'What about you? Brothers? Sisters?'

Deep breath. Here we go.

'Well, I have a brother. But he's no longer with us.'

'Oh?' she says. 'What happened to him?'

'Well, my father and brother were drowned off the north coast of Cornwall in an accident back in 1988. The three of us were fishing together. I was the survivor.'

No comment.

Behind us, Jack is somewhat flummoxed, poor chap. 'Oh. Oh dear. Very sorry to hear that, Justin. That's terrible.'

I bat him on the shoulder. 'It's OK, Jack. It's one of those things, you know. Happens in life.'

'Oh. Well . . . I'm glad you survived.'

Bless him, this gawky, gentle lad, finding exactly the right words. I thump him on the shoulder again. 'Bless you, Jack.'

We scope out the options for dinner. 'Eating in a chain hotel restaurant is utterly soulless,' pronounces my laconic companion. I concur. The best bet seems to be a *Pataterie* perched on a patch of scrub between a roundabout and a multiplex, with a two-course menu + drink for €14.50. The romance of pilgrimage.

Accommodation is basic: a cramped room with a double bed and a single bunk – for three of us. 'Well, this'll be cosy,' I say. One of my roommates offers to sleep on the floor. Hard, bare, cold formica. Then I remember that I have a sleeping bag and blow-up mattress. 'No, let me,' I say. 'I'm the youngster.'

After writing up notes till 1 a.m., I creep into the tiny budget room, insert myself into the cubicle shower–loo and clean teeth as quietly as possible, and then struggle, jammed in the narrow space between the loo and the iron bed frame, into pjs and sleeping bag liner (basically an envelope made of a sheet) and lie down on the very narrow inflatable mattress sandwiched on the very narrow strip of floor between the double bed and the wall. I'm almost under the bed. Any sudden movement and I will crack my skull on the metal undercarriage. I tuck my arm between pillow and floor, lay my head down and try to relax.

And then the torment begins.

From the bunk overhead, one of my roommates inhales with an astonishing, protracted snort like a lorry with a punctured exhaust, or maybe the receding gasp of a slow tide over shingle, and then exhales with a stertorous rasp like a draining cistern. *Please, God.* My other companion rumbles and wheezes in answer, and then comes the next shattering snore from A, astoundingly loud, the death rattle of a wounded warthog. B groans and sighs in the lull, a kind of antiphon of guttural snorts, and A's next snore rends the night with belief-beggaring volume. Chunks of plaster are falling off the walls. This is like a scene from Laurel and Hardy or the Marx Brothers. It's like sleeping in a barn with livestock. I start mentally composing vengeful prose, then try frantically to surrender my mind to some deeper level of Zen consciousness where A's snores will not reach me. To no avail. Every so often, it seems as if he's given up the ghost, or settled, or cleared his airways or something, and we have a moment or two of calm. But then B, lonely without his pacemaker, grunts and snuffles plaintively, and A's nose and throat judder into life once more like a corpse sitting up at a wake. I could cheerfully strangle him.

Somehow I drift into a hypnotic state of endurance.

5am. This ghastly little room is turning into a kind of aural torture chamber. B's in the shower now, about six inches from my head, through the wall, and he appears to be flexing and straightening out his creaking limbs in an orgy of sound and fury. Great sighs and groans cascade behind the shower stream. 'Ah! Oh! God!' he yells at one point. Is the man completely oblivious? I bury my head and vainly seek unconsciousness. The agony and ecstasy continue.

5.30am. I am definitely going mad. B now appears to be unpacking every item of his luggage, wrapped in tarpaulin by the sound of it, which rattles and clatters with every movement. Fossicking, rustling, emptying bags, unravelling whatever the hell it is that he's got seventeen of wrapped in the noisiest substance known to the human ear, doing God knows what with it, and then repacking, stowing, sorting and heaving. *What the hell is he doing at 5.30 in the morning?* As A emerges from the shower, B whispers considerately, *sotto voce*, that I'm asleep and they mustn't wake me. I want to murder him.

'Oh, hang on,' he says brightly, 'maybe we're still on UK time.' I roll over and pick up my phone. It's 6.15 a.m. 'Yes, you're not wrong,' says B, noticing me, 'it is that time.' He laughs – *laughs* – 'Hoo-hoo, I can't believe we've done this! Ah, well, breakfast's not until 7.30.' I groan and turn back over. When they finally leave me alone, at 7.30, B looks down at me from the doorway. 'Look at him,' he says fondly, 'he could sleep on a clothesline.'

My soul is heavy with dark thoughts.

Forty-five minutes' undisturbed rest until B returns to tell me it's 8.15 a.m., and I drag myself awake.

Saturday 17 June

Morning liturgy in the Ibis car park.

To escape the nest of converging roads and railways that lead to the Eurotunnel, we have to scramble through a hinterland of motorway verges, kerbs, fences and patches of wasteland like somewhere in the Occupied West Bank. Every major road, bridge and railway line is hedged with overhanging barbed-wire fences to prevent migrants leaping on to lorries or trains. As Rodin commemorates, Calais has seen famous sieges in the past millennium, but now, with the tunnel, it has become the siege-frontier of Fortress UK.

At last we escape and join a canal path south towards Coulogne, into the pleasant pastures and neat little villages of the Pas-de-Calais. Close by, Henry VIII jousted with Philip of France at the Field of the Cloth of Gold, 497 years ago to the day, as Halle's *Chronicle* records:

> On Saturday both kings entered the field and King Henry's armour-skirt and horse-trapper were decorated with 2,000 ounces of gold and 1,100 huge pearls, the price of which was incalculable, the Earl of Devonshire also appeared that day wearing cloth of gold, tissue-cloth and cloth of silver, all elaborately embroidered, with his retinue wearing the same uniform.
>
> When the French king and the Earl of Devonshire charged at each other, so fierce was their encounter that both their lances broke. In all they ran off eight times, during which the French king broke three lances while the earl broke two lances and the French king's nose.

A far cry from today's Brexit negotiations.

This stretch of land, adjoining the Normandy beaches and the Cap Blanc-Nez, from which Bleriot flew the first flight across the

Channel on 25 July 1909, is still popular for flying. Some kind of powered parachute or parahawk glides back and forth across the fields to our right as we follow the canal southwards. Overhead, a pair of buzzards wheel and soar, calling to each other. Strange to see shaggy, horned Highland cattle grazing the marshlands to the east; apparently it's their favourite terrain. The canal is pretty rank – not a lot of commerce these days, other than the odd child trying his luck angling amid festoons of duckweed. We pass a four-way lock, once an embodiment of civic pride, now concreted shut from east to west – against migrants, perhaps? – and without lock gates from north to south. Next to a 'lifting bridge' at the village of Marais-de-Guines, a late nineteenth-century plaque commemorates the town burghers responsible for this proud achievement of local engineering.

The village of Guines, liberated in January 1558 from the English by Francois, Duc de Guise, as its monument reads, has a famous moated castle and reservoir, marking an aquatic border, the meeting point of fresh and salt water. I remember a later Duc de Guise was principal villain in de Rostand's *Cyrano de Bergerac*. The military action in which Guines was liberated, part of the wider Siege of Calais of 1558, brought England's control of the 'Pale of Calais' to an end. There was shock and disbelief in England at the loss of her last continental territory, and a few months later, on her death bed, Queen ('Bloody') Mary was reputed to have said, 'When I am dead and cut open, they will find Philip and Calais inscribed on my heart.' Poor Mary. The continental princes, seeing her childless, were already eyeing up her kingdom – and her husband Philip of Spain was already eyeing up her sister Elizabeth.

We walk through the pretty town square, with its obligatory WWI memorial and Mairie, to a campsite adjoining the very pretty mini-chateau, in early eighteenth-century Palladian style, with a moat full of huge carp and an old farm courtyard around an impressive seventeenth-century dovecot. The courtyard restaurant is the *Auberge du Colombier* – the 'Dovecot Inn'. I find a garden in the chateau grounds and sit scribbling, blistered bare feet on the grass, cold beer to hand, as the doves and wood pigeons coo in the sunny late afternoon.

Today's *New York Times* carries a front-page piece about Palestine after fifty years of Occupation. Marine Le Pen is losing in further French parliamentary elections last Sunday and this coming Sunday, after her initial trouncing by Macron. Londoners are demonstrating in protest at purported government negligence regarding fire regulations in Grenfell Tower, following the tragic fire three days ago in which at least sixty people so far are known to have died, with a similar number badly injured and many more made homeless – poor, mainly ethnic minority council residents in the Royal Borough of Kensington and Chelsea, one of the wealthiest local authorities in the UK. The city of Marawi in the Philippines is under siege after ISIS-inspired militants seized areas of the city and went from house to house, killing non-Muslims.

In this little chateau garden, all is peaceful, an enclave of birdsong and sunshine. Ivor the driver joins me for a beer by the carp moat, and we chat about beekeeping, his career as a Methodist minister, his Palestine activism with McCabe Pilgrimages and his six years at theological college in north Derbyshire and Birmingham. 'Two Ulstermen tried to kill me once in Derbyshire – extreme Protestants – but the college offered me opportunities I couldn't get anywhere else, 'cause I had no formal education.' He tells me about his beekeeping charity in The Gambia, and about his grandson who had leukaemia as a kid, and when his son-in-law left, Ivor and his wife supported their daughter bringing up their grandchildren. Now he's driving with the Just Walk, aged seventy-seven.

Back at the campsite, Vanessa's prepared an artisan smorgasbord of pâté, cheese, salads and ham, set out in the forest clearing. We fall to with a will. The walkers' feet are an extraordinary collage of blisters and Gaffa Tape. It's faintly repulsive but somehow a great leveller. The received wisdom seems to be that Gaffa Tape is the best, if the skin isn't broken, as a preventative. If the skin's broken, the prescribed remedy is something called Compeed – a kind of magical plaster which bonds itself into your flesh and somehow replaces the torn skin. David is fabulously Bohemian – dark-skinned, long dark hair, pheasant feather in his cap – and gold toenail varnish, as I discover at this evening's picnic. What's that all about? Is it some other anti-blister remedy I don't know about, or just private peccadillo?²

Sunday 18 June – Feast of Corpus Christi, L'Abbaye de Notre Dame, Wisques

Tranquil, beautiful evening after a long – long – hot day of walking 35 km southeast from Guines. I'm sitting out on the terrace of the pilgrim guest house of the Abbaye de Notre Dame, Wisques, looking out over the valley. Pigeons are cooing, song thrushes twittering, sun and mist-haze in the pastures below. A paraglider is droning away up in the sky somewhere to the east.

When we arrived, footsore, hot and limb-weary after a day of striding through the wheat, barley and potato fields of the Pas-de-Calais, Sister Lucy welcomed us with much admiration in the kitchen. An elderly, bright-eyed nun of the enclosed Benedictine order of the Sisters of St Cécile of Solesmes, she exclaimed, 'J'aime beaucoup les pèlerins! Et vous marchez jusqu'à Gerusalemme, n'est-ce pas?'

'Oui, c'est ca.'

'Et pourquoi?'

Arthur invites me to explain, in my best O-level French.

'Alors, ma soeur,' I say, falteringly, 'nous marchons . . . pour la paix.'

'Pour la paix, ah oui.'

'Et pour les Palestiniens, pour les droits des Palestiniens, pour l'égalité . . . pour tous ceux qui habitent la terre sainte.'

'Oui, je comprends,' she nods. 'Alors, vous êtes très bienvenu ici. Vous êtes Catholique?'

'Non, je suis Anglican,' I say, 'et dans mon église à Londres, je suis le directeur de la musique.'

'Ah, oui! Et comment appelez-vous?'

'Je m'appelle Joo-stan.'

'Ah – Joo-stan! C'est mon saint préféré!' she exclaims. 'Peut-être vous connaissez l'histoire de Joo-stan? Il était Juif, et il a été converti au Christianisme, puis martyrisé.'

'Ah, Joo-stan Martyr.'

'Précisément. Et la fête de Joo-stan est le premier juin.'

Hobbling around in sweaty clothes and martyred feet. Blissful shower and first cold beer – some kind of super high-strength Bavarian blonde beer was all Ivor could find in the local shops.

Arthur's socks and pants are stewing in our basin – 'hissing hot!' as Falstaff laments in *Merry Wives*.

As the 8.6 per cent Bavarian beer starts to kick in, other moments from the day float to the surface: seeing the first poppies in the verges of the cornfields; meeting 'rival pilgrims' walking the Camino de Santiago, in the ruins of the thirteenth-century chapel of Guémy on the Saint Louis Mount, where several pilgrimage routes intersect ('Come on, let's beat them up,' I said to Jack); lunch in the pretty little town of Tournehem-sur-la-Hem (the Hem is the river running through this region), allegedly founded by an illegitimate son of Richard the Lionheart, Philip 'le Batard', where the café proprietress let us eat our picnic at her outdoor tables.

Mary told me many tales of family and childhood today as we walked. Her mother worked in the British Embassy in Madrid in the 1940s. On one occasion, when the embassy staff were told not to look out the front window into the courtyard (but she did), she saw Mussolini arriving in a car, to negotiate with the Brits about who knows what. Her father, who worked subsequently for the Bank of England throughout his career, was in Spain during the 1940s, supporting Franco to keep Spain out of the war, then in Latin America from the 1950s to 1960s. Mary's research into the bank's archives turned up his reports from Cuba: 'Met a young army officer the other day, someone-or-other Castro, don't think he'll amount to much . . .'

She has a wonderful, sunburnt, smiling, wrinkled face, spectacular blisters on her feet and amazing stamina. There's a dreamy, childlike quality to Mary – a high, sing-song voice and a perpetual smile and yet not in any way fake. She's very real, but from a rather enchanted planet, methinks.

A magical tableau hoves into view, a moment Jude described, watching her grandchildren's delight playing in the sea in Perth as the sun went down: sharks, stingrays and jellyfish notwithstanding, they persuaded her to let them stay in the water till dusk. 'Oh, Grandma, it's so beautiful!' they squealed, thrilled and a little scared all at once.

★ ★ ★

The refectory has the cloistered feel of an old public school dining hall, with oak panelling, handsome stained-glass mullioned windows overlooking the grounds, Romanesque arches and vaulting overhead. Acolyte nuns sing grace for us, and soup is served. *Beautiful soup, so rich and green, waiting in a hot tureen* . . . I would say it's probably nettle soup. Vanessa later describes it as algae floating in seawater. Tastes fine to me. Generously, the nuns have provided us with wine. The white is sweet, warm and disgusting; the red passable. I sit with two young French women, Anna-Louise and Matin. Matin is a trainee lawyer who's come here for some seclusion to prepare for her notary exams. Anna-Louise, I guess, is an acolyte of some sort.

'Do you think the Palestinians and the Israelis can live together?' asks Matin. 'I've heard of Christians and Jews – yes. Christians and Muslims – yes. But Muslims and Jews? No. My friend in Jerusalem says the Jews can't go to visit in the Muslim areas.'

'Well, before, under the Ottomans,' I say, 'the three peoples did live together: Christians, Muslims and Jews. My Palestinian friends say their problem is not with Jews, but with the Israeli government, and the army.'

Compline in the abbey church of an enclosed order of nuns is a first for me. We're admitted to the neo-Gothic chapel through a small postern door leading directly into the east end, where we sit and stand around the sanctuary and high altar, looking west through a screen of cage bars to the nave, where the nuns sit and stand and sing the office. In an ethereal plainchant reminiscent of the soaring incantations of Hildegard von Bingen, they sing three psalms, the office hymn *Te lucis ante terminum* and an 'Angel liturgy', sung from Pentecost to Advent, with bells, which I've never encountered before. Psalm 90 is salutary with regard to land disputes:

Lord, you have been our dwelling-place
throughout all generations.
Before the mountains were born
or you brought forth the whole world,
from everlasting to everlasting you are God.

Psalm 133 is no less apposite and wonderfully oriental:

> How good and pleasant it is
> when God's people live together in unity!
> It is like precious oil poured on the head,
> running down on the beard,
> running down on Aaron's beard,
> down on the collar of his robe.
> It is as if the dew of Hermon
> were falling on Mount Zion.
> For there the Lord bestows his blessing,
> even life forevermore.

Peering through the cage bars in the candlelit gloom suffused with wafting incense, I feel a bit like an intruder witnessing some esoteric rite, an interloper eavesdropping on the arcane mysteries of the *Bona Dea*. Several of my companions are completely nonplussed. They do their best to stand, sit, kneel and cross themselves at the right moments, coughing and spluttering from the clouds of incense. Down in the nave, there's much bowing and scraping to a huge leather-bound ceremonial Bible, but no reading. The sheer *otherness* of the nuns' life, and the oddity of our almost-encounter, reminds me of Seamus Heaney's poem 'Lightenings viii' about the monks of Clonmacnoise who, gathered for prayer in the oratory, see a mystical ship appear above them in the air. Realising it has run aground in their reality, they must release it to sail on its way.

Exiting via the postern door, we 'climb back out of the marvellous' and wander through the abbey gardens to watch the sunset over the valley. 'I think God's out here,' says Cressey, gesturing to the sky and fields, 'not in there.'

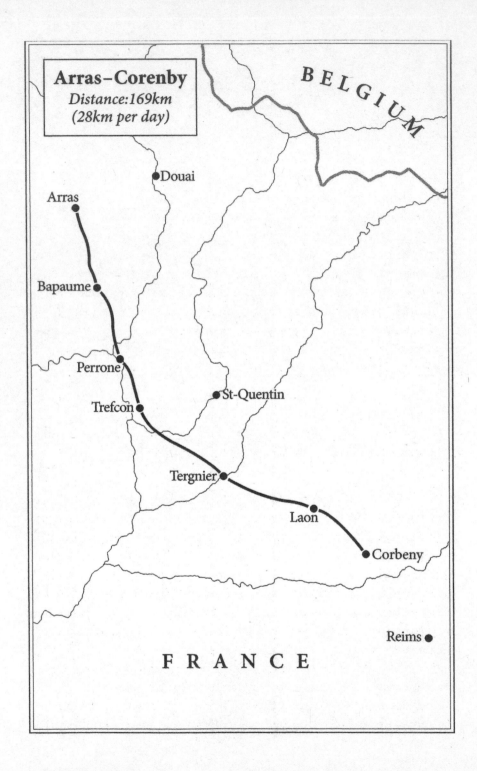

Arras–Corenby
Distance:169km
(28km per day)

BELGIUM

Douai

Arras

Bapaume

Perrone

St-Quentin

Trefcon

Tergnier

Laon

Corbeny

Reims

FRANCE

4

Au Chemin de la Guerre

AFTER A 6 a.m. breakfast and liturgy on the abbey lawn, we're following the Via Francigena through idyllic woodland to the south of Wisques. This is a blissful walk with magical early morning light in the treetops, angel-rays of sun sluicing and slanting down into clearings through translucent greenery, a sun-pierced canopy alive with birdsong. For this morning's reflection, I read R. S. Thomas's poem 'The Kingdom', which contains the lines,

> It's a long way off, but to get
> There takes no time and admission
> Is free, if you purge yourself
> Of desire, and present yourself with
> Your need only and the simple offering
> Of your faith, green as a leaf.

We've gathered round Arthur to admire a slowworm slithering over and over his hands, a sinuous figure-of-eight in gunmetal grey, when my phone pings with a text from Nancy, my wife: 'Attack at Finsbury Park Mosque last night van drove onto pavement by mosque we are all fine.'

I'm rather stunned. It's right around the corner from us. I cycle past there most days and my kids have friends who attend this mosque. Apparently, it's 'revenge' for the Borough Market attack. Later this morning, Nancy texts me again: 'Passing through FP just now and overcome suddenly and surprisingly by what was going on after last night. Ambushed by feelings and weeping with a young Muslim woman. We are a diverse but in parts divided society and that's not just about race and religion it's about dysfunctional recent evolution of many things . . . we don't know how to live together. We need to find and work in true common ground, while acknowledging different people, and stop ghettoisation.'

The glorious, sun-haunted forest setting prompts David to tell me about the tree-planting project which he and his wife Heidi have set up in Madagascar. David designs shops, cafes and restaurants for a living, but they've developed a sideline writing and publishing inspiring gift books, a commercial operation which they call 'The Next Big Think', from which the profits go to support the tree-planting project.

'We went on holiday to Madagascar and flying over the country and seeing the terrible devastation caused by logging – great stretches of bare earth, massive scars in the forests, like wounds, we looked at each other and said, "We have to do something about this." These forests are the last natural environment on earth for so many species of lemur. I mean, if you look at that little belt of woodland over there and just imagine – that could be the last refuge of one particular species. But you can understand why the local people take part in logging – they need an income. So we try to provide an alternative income – planting, tending and guarding trees. They have tree guards now, keeping watch all night on patches of newly planted forest. And we try to run it like a sustainable business – through the book sales – not like a charity.'

They've now planted more than 115,000 new trees in Madagascar.

'I needed to get away from Australia physically,' David says, 'in order to just stop working! I've made a good living designing shops and restaurants, but to be honest I'm fed up just spending all my time working. We don't have kids, and that's fine – that's a decision we took – but I need to stop and take stock. My wife has given me this gift – to go away for five months on this Walk – as a chance to take time out, seek a new direction. Maybe we'll go to Africa together to volunteer for a charity. Maybe Madagascar.'

He tells me about his time hitchhiking around Papua New Guinea. 'I wanted to see if I could survive on the absolute minimum, so I wore a pair of shorts and flip-flops and carried a rice bag. That was it! People had warned me about how dangerous it was going to be, but you know, travelling alone in Papua, everyone I met just wanted to look after me! I had the best time. I ran into a bunch of guys climbing Mount Wilhelm and they said, "Come along and join us," so I did. It was beautiful.' He shows me a gruesome gallery of pictures on his phone, leeches on his ankles, his calves running with blood, perforated with bites. 'Well, some people panic about leeches, but I just figured, let 'em feed as much as they want; I've got plenty of blood, and when they've had enough, they'll drop off. And they did!'

'And your feet didn't drop off as well?'

'Well, no, I think they're still there. Last time I looked. But I did get malaria.'

'From the leeches?'

'No, from the mozzies. They're nasty in Papua. Should've worn a shirt. Still, no worries.'

David has a little reflexive chuckle, a cheery little suffix tagged on to everything he says, which makes me chuckle in turn. I tell him he reminds me of one of the crazier Desert Fathers – a kind of Aussie tree-hugging version of St Simeon Stylites, who was equally generous to parasites.

Later that day, as the forest track emerges into a hummocky up-and-down path between fields and hedgerows, always heading south, south-east, Tim tells me about his childhood in Botswana, where his parents worked as missionaries, and sings the Botswanan national anthem in a very pleasing tenor voice. Vanessa and I discuss the thrills of extreme exertion in the open air, and I describe an epiphanic moment on the England coast-to-coast bike ride a few years ago when, after a gruelling five-mile climb from Penrith, we emerged on to the high breast of the north Pennines. A spell of unearthly stillness seemed to hang over the rugged heathland, with not a breath of wind, just the piercing call of the curlews piping across the moors. A euphoric sense of enlightenment and wellbeing suffused mind, body and soul. *This is what it's all about. This is why we're here. To live in the open air, to work our bodies, muscles, blood, bones and sinews, embrace the natural world, relish the ecstasy of feeling alive.*

'Well,' says Vanessa, 'that was dopamine.'

Alain, the host of our pilgrim gîte, tells us that one of the Popes of Avignon came from Thérouanne, during the period 1309–76 when seven successive popes resided in Avignon rather than Rome, and the subsequent Dual Papacy (1378–1417), when a series of 'antipopes' ruled the French Catholic church from Avignon, after a schism between the French cardinals and the newly elected Pope Urban VI in Rome. Later, he tells us, in 1553, Thérouanne was captured by the Holy Roman Emperor Charles V, razed to the ground, and the land ploughed up and salted in revenge for the defeat of his forces by the French at the Siege of Metz. *Carthago delenda est.*

Dr Jude has bought a big bag of salt, not for scorching the earth of enemy cities, but for foot-baths, to draw the moisture out of our blisters. As I sit writing these notes in the garden by moonlight, I have my bulbous feet in a bowl of tepid salt water. 'You'll feel the benefit in the morning,' Jude assures me. 'The Germans swear by it.' Well, they should know. Apparently, the gîte has a vibrating foot-massage machine for sore-footed *pèlerins*, but I'll start with the German remedy and see what the morning brings.

When I phone my wife, she tells me she's standing outside the Finsbury Park Mosque with our kids and some of our friends in a huge crowd, taking part in a silent, candlelit vigil in solidarity with our local Muslim community.

Wednesday 21 June

Two days later, we're walking through barley fields from the tiny hamlet of Amettes, where we stayed last night in an ancient half-timbered wattle-and-daub farmhouse, the remains of a fourteenth century stronghold built around a courtyard hung with antique farm implements, dotted with stone tubs overflowing with herbs and geraniums, sleepy sheepdogs basking in the sun and poultry clucking in coops beneath thatched eaves. Monsieur et Madame gave us a lavish welcome and a four-course *paysan* banquet around a farmhouse table groaning with local goodies – sausage pâté, salmon pâté-bread-bake, stuffed veal and vegetables, toothsome slabs of fresh bread and a pleasant, sweetish rosé, a home-grown Cabernet d'Anjou, and chocolate mousse. Every square inch of wall was crowded with antique crockery, devotional kitsch and photographs of the Pope blessing their statue of St Benoît-Joseph Labre, which apparently they carried in pilgrimage to Rome a few years ago. St Benoît was born here in Amettes in 1748, a mendicant Franciscan and Holy Fool revered as the 'Beggar of Perpetual Adoration'. Monsieur le fermier showed me a little shrine to St Benoît in the outer wall of the farmhouse courtyard, the remains of a mediaeval chapel adjoining the fortress.

Sun bathing the meadow mists conjures a magical golden haze, and skylarks overhead shower us with silver slivers of birdsong as we tramp alongside whispering waves of corn, barley, wheat and maize. Claw-prints in the puddle-mud speak of bird baths at dawn. Dawn was the name of my wife's mother, known to all and sundry as 'Marmar', a somewhat enchanted being from a batty, mystical planet which only occasionally crossed spheres with our own. The music accompanying her final send-off to the faerie-realm, five years ago, was Vaughan Williams' *Lark Ascending*. Lark song in the early morning pricks memories of Dawn and makes me smile.

Walking through the next village, Floringhem, I dive under a closing door-shutter into a *bar-tabac*, just as the madame is shutting up shop after her morning stint, select at random a pouch of poison weed which I hope most closely resembles my preferred brand, fork out some euros and duck back beneath the slats, calling, 'Merci, madame!' Catching up with Jude and Mary, I report that my poison-stock is replenished and all is well. 'Now I can not-smoke all day. As long as I have some in my backpack.'

Jude is amused. 'As long as you're in control, you can refrain,' she says.

'Something like that. Can't defend it. Totally ashamed. Don't like to smoke in front of my kids. It's the dark side.'

'Like me with Mars bars,' says Mary, 'and spiral bound notebooks.'

'Notebooks?'

'Yes.'

'That's a strange addiction.'

'After our first child was born. Bit of depression. Used to have a thing about Mars bars. And writing down my thoughts in note-books.'

Mary then tells me a shocking story of a young woman, Oxford-educated, in their church, who had severe postnatal depression. One day, she went along to the mums-and-toddlers Bible study group and left her kids, then went out and drove to Beachy Head. And jumped off.

Dear God. We walk. Eventually I say, 'But what a conundrum for the kids, later on – that they have to try to understand why their mum couldn't stay with them.'

'Yes,' she says, 'their grandmother came to look after them. They've grown up very well. One of them's at Oxford now.'

Later, walking through steep forest paths down to the chateau village of Ranchicourt with Robin and Mary, she tells me about a young man whom Ian 'led to the Lord', as she puts it, who was drowned swimming at sea, and then about a young woman whom she'd led to the Lord, who was an au pair for a four-year-old boy. They were walking on the seafront and the boy was swept away by a huge wave. The young au pair went in after him. The boy was saved, but she lost her life. Prompted by these strange echoes, I tell Mary and Robin about my bereavement.

Passing through the village of Division, Lynn and I notice plaques at the end of each street with quotations from French authors, in alphabetical order: Aragon, Baudelaire, Camus, Diderot, and so on. We play an A to Z game of French writers with Arthur and Naomi. *Flaubert, Gide, Hugo, Ionesco (does he count?), Jullien, K . . . K . . . can anyone think of a K?*

From Floringhem to Division to Houdain to Ranchicourt, strange conical hills dot the horizon, spoil tips from coal-mining days, Tim tells us. *(Madame de Lafayette, Leroux who wrote Le Fantôme de l'Opéra, Marivaux, Maupassant, Prosper Mérimée of 'Carmen' fame, Molière, there's loads of Ms . . .)* Mary tells me of her flair for Latin at school, curtailed by her mother sending her to nursing college at the age of eighteen. I debate faith schools with retired head teacher Denise – do they segregate further an already atomised society? Shouldn't we shove all our kids together and let them get on with it? I describe the pleasingly non-PC rudeness and ribaldry at my son Jacob's school, between him and his Muslim friends: 'Walahi, Allah-hu-akbar, you loser, thanks for 9/11, etc.' *(Charles Nodier, from Besançon, vampire stories and gothic tales, Gerard de Nerval, who wrote plays with Dumas, O . . . O . . . who begins with O?)*

Arthur asks me and I tell the saga of my arrest by CIA agents in Bucharest during a Bush presidential visit to Romania celebrating accession to NATO membership, and how my harassment by these goons spawned my anti-war satire *The Madness of George Dubya* in 2003. Naomi describes the feeling of powerlessness, shared by many young people, after the anti-war movement 'failed', as she puts it. Did it fail? Obviously, on one level, but wasn't it a milestone, a mass mobilisation of popular dissent like never seen before? Can we trace the flow of that same energy through the 'Occupy' movement, the Arab Spring, even to the swell tide of Corbyn's success? *(Pascal, Proust, Quinault, confederate of Corneille and Molière, Racine, Rostand, Sartre, Tardieu, what about U?)* Jude and I explore the village and chateau of Ranchicourt, bending down to smell the flocks of wild alyssum by the roadside, breathing honey-perfumed fragrance. *(V is for Voltaire, obviously, W . . . W . . . they don't use W; X . . . oh blimey, what about Saint Ex-upery? Who? Antoine de Saint-Exupéry, the guy who wrote 'The Little Prince'? Y's no better, Yves Saint Laurent. No, how about Yasmina Reza, the playwright. Never mind. Z's easy — Emile Zola, 'J'Accuse!' and the Dreyfus Affair, the Dreyfus Affair and the birth of the Zionist movement, all roads lead to Jerusalem . . .)*

And so we drag weary, blistered feet from the blistering heat of French high summer, 34°C in mid-afternoon, into the blessed cool of the glass-and-chrome spaceship-like Hotel International in the middle of an out-of-town retail estate somewhere near Olhain. In the blissfully air-conditioned foyer, I get acquainted with Lora on reception. I explain to her that we're walking to Jerusalem. For peace, for equal rights. Her eyes moisten.

'Why?' she says, 'For ze Palestinians?'

'Yes,' I explain. 'This year it's ten years, fifty years, one hundred years . . .'

She knows; she understands.

'So we're doing this for the Palestinians, to call for equal rights, for justice.'

She's streaming with tears, wiping her eyes. Yikes. 'I'm sorry,' she says. 'It's very . . . kind zat you do zis. Zat you sink about people so far away, zat you want to do zis for zem. It makes me cry.'

'I'm sorry,' I say, 'I didn't mean to make you cry.'

'It's OK. And do you sink they can live togezer, Jews and Palestinians?'

'Yes,' I say, 'because many of our Palestinian friends say that their parents and their grandparents lived happily with Jewish neighbours. It's not Jews; it's the government, the Occupation.'

I wonder why she's so moved. Maybe she has Palestinian antecedents. Or maybe the arrival of a travel-stained, footsore bunch of ragamuffins hoofing it to the fabled holy city of ancient times for the rights of a forgotten people is just so incongruous in this ultra-modern retail estate setting that it simply touches her, fast track, deep down. A dose of what Seamus Heaney called 'the redress of poetry'. Who knows?

Astonishing stories pop out of Ivor over dinner – starting up a bee-farming charity in The Gambia, running biennial trips to Palestine with McCabe Pilgrimages, staging a play at theological college, *Christ Recrucified* by Nikos Kazantzakis (of *Zorba the Greek* fame), being put in a 'Victorian mental asylum' after a nervous breakdown – all in the most inconsequential fashion, peppered with a comic Virgilian leitmotif of beekeeping metaphors. I'm forming the opinion that Ivor is, quietly, one of the most remarkable people I've ever met. From our first beer together in the gardens of the chateau at Guines, I suspected that beneath the veneer of a short, round Brummy with a white beard and a perpetually worried look on his face, beat the heart of a lion, and I was right.

'I was conceived out of wedlock, you see, in a really impoverished slum area of south Staffordshire. No education, no money.' He chuckles. 'When I got my place at theological college, in Derbyshire, they sent you a list of all the stuff you had to bring – so many pairs of socks, shirts, underwear and so forth – I'd never worn underpants! My mother said, "What d'you need all that for? Load of rubbish!" But I said, "I can't go to theological college without underpants, Mum," so that was the beginning of my elevation in the world.'

Earlier in the week, Ivor and I were buying bread and pastries for the walkers' lunch, when he muttered something about raising the funds for a bakery in The Gambia, and another in Al-Eizariya.

'Bethany?' I said. 'Al-Eizariya in Palestine, Jerusalem?'

'Yeah, they're very good bakers there. We wanted to do something to stimulate the local economy, you know. Very nice bakery. Lovely baklava. Wonderful honey in Palestine.' (One of the properties of

Palestinian honey, according to my extensive research, is to increase the sperm count in male rats.)

'I was stuck in Jericho with a bunch of McCabe pilgrims in 2010, when the Icelandic ash-cloud stopped all the flights, so one day I took them to visit the Monastery of St George in the Jordan Valley, an ancient sixth-century monastery hanging off the cliffs like a beehive in the Wadi Qelt. There were just three old monks in this huge old place, who couldn't stand each other. "We've got something to show you," they said. "Come and see." So they took us through a great honeycomb of caves to this kind of chapel, and there was a chap lying in a glass case, dead, in a monk's habit, with patent leather shoes, and his face was perfectly preserved. "It's our brother," they said, "he's been raised incorruptible." He'd been dead and buried for ten years, and they'd dug him up to move his tomb or something, and found him perfectly mummified. They were all convinced it was a miracle! Probably something to do with the chemicals in the rocks, and the extreme dryness.'

'Just three monks there?' I ask.

'Yeah, just three. Knocking around this vast labyrinth. Funny, isn't it? Mind you, I don't worry about church membership declining these days because, after all, at a certain point, Jesus' followers all abandoned him.'

Thursday 22 June, Olhain – Arras

Arras, Azincourt, Bapaume, Cambrai, Vimy . . . it's a haunting feeling to walk past these names on signs as we trek on down through the Pas-de-Calais into Picardy and the battlegrounds of the Somme, striding along chalky tracks through vast green and golden fields of wheat, corn, maize, oil seed rape and barley, the bread basket of the Hauts-de-France. I remember something Ivor said yesterday: 'I look at all these thousands of acres of arable land, and it's all so rich and abundant, and then the poppies in the verges remind you it's all been nourished and fertilised by the blood of millions of young men. The bread basket of Normandy, they call it, grown out of a bloodbath.'

One of those who heeded the summons was my great-uncle, Clarence Edward Butcher, my grandfather's younger brother, known as Clare, who lied about his age to join the London Regiment, aged sixteen. A photograph in my mother's dining room cabinet shows an elfin-faced Second Lieutenant Clare Butcher in July 1916, in a subaltern's uniform that looks like fancy dress on one so young. Because of the date handwritten on the photograph, I'd always assumed he was killed in the five-month apocalypse of the Somme, along with a million other young men. My grandfather, whom I knew sixty years later as 'Pop', was also in uniform, a captain in the Royal Naval Air Service. I remember him as a dreamy old gentleman in an overcoat, with a long thin face, sunken cheeks and far-away watery eyes, a wonderful painter with a great fondness for Milky Way chocolate bars, with whom I toddled around Hampstead Garden Suburb every Saturday morning while my father did his grocery shopping. But my father's younger sister Alison told me once how furious Pop had been when the recruiting office accepted Clare into the London Regiment, manifestly underage, and doubly furious when he was killed.

Unpacking our bags at the Arras Hotel bed and breakfast, another out-of-town retail park gem off a dual carriageway beyond the ring road, I discover that a camping water container has exploded in the van and drenched my suitcase. I have to cut the zip open with my penknife. All my bloody books are soaked and expanded to twice their size. With the walkers ensconced, I hang up my books and clothes to dry and head out to reccy the prospects for dinner. The best restaurant in the vicinity, the receptionist tells me, is the *Tomate Cerise*. After traipsing across half a mile of car park and traffic island wasteland, I come to something that looks like a drive-through McDonald's with a large red plastic tomato on the roof, then step through the doors into another world. An extraordinary replica *belle époque* interior of fountains, chandeliers, *chaises-longues* and potted palms, like a romantic Parisian bistro-cum-boudoir of the 1920s. Off a roundabout, off a motorway.

That night, I have a strange dream. I'm sitting cross-legged on the floor, cradling my father in my lap. In life, he was a rugged outdoors man, a farmer, fisherman and gardener, but also a lover of literature, music and theatre and, like his father, a gifted draughtsman. A great conversationalist with a broad knowledge of politics and history, he could also be a hilarious mimic and clown when the mood seized him, and he loved children's games, making toys, writing and illustrating stories with us and teaching us carpentry and bricklaying. Quick to laughter, sometimes irascible, but incapable of bearing a grudge, he could seem impatient, not one to suffer fools, but he was immensely kind and sensitive, with a generous reservoir of compassion and a fierce sense of fairness, and he had the 'common touch', able to get alongside pretty much anyone. He was also a man of deep faith. In my dream I am cradling him, utterly weary and surrendered, as if finally he has laid down the effort and vigour of so much striving, so much giving, so much living. And in our strange dream-*Pietà* tableau, he weeps, opening a lifetime's well of grief, as if releasing the anguish of generations of tragedy and sorrow in our family – the loss of his Uncle Clare, so desperately young, in the Great War; the deaths of his baby brother David and of his brother John's wife, killed in the Blitz; the murder of his niece Kasia; his own death in the sea at Zennor with my brother Matthew; then Kasia's daughter Polly, and his nephew Marek . . . a hundred years of grief for so many cheerful, bright lives extinguished by untimely death. His weeping flows into me and fills me. I soothe and comfort him and kiss his brow, and somehow sense that, for him, the burden is set down. As I cradle his weeping body, I feel that I am the inheritor of all this grief, that it is my task to hold it on behalf of them all.

When I wake, prompted by a sudden hunch, I look up the Commonwealth War Graves Commission database, and search for my great-uncle.

Butcher, Clarence Edward. Second Lieutenant, 4th Battalion, London Regiment (Royal Fusiliers). Date of death: Thursday, May 3rd 1917. Aged 19. Son of Edward John and Emily Butcher, of 'Lynton', Well End, Barnet, Herts. Commemorated at Arras Memorial, Pas de Calais, France. Number of casualties: 34,835. Cemetery/memorial reference: Bay 9.

Here? I was absolutely convinced he'd died at the Somme in 1916. Either way, my grandfather was adamant that Clare was seventeen, not nineteen, when he died, but the official records were obliged to perpetuate the lie. I email my Italian cousin David, the oracle on all Butcher family lore. When I was in Brescia for his wedding last year he showed me the Memorial Scroll sent to our great-grandparents after Clare's death, printed on parchment in calligraphic script beneath the royal crest, with his rank, name and regiment handwritten in red.

David replies with links to the CWGC listing and a digitalised *War History Of The 4th Battalion The London Regiment (Royal Fusiliers) 1914–1919* by Captain F. Clive Grimwade:

> Hi Justin, I'm glad to hear you can visit Clarence's memorial in Arras. It's exactly 100 years since he died! I understand the body was never recovered, so his name is on a memorial wall rather than a gravestone. Give our love to Nancy and the kids. It's a shame we live so far apart. God bless – David.

Scrolling through the *War History*, I find the account of the Arras Offensive in which Clare was killed:

> The night of the 2nd May was fine and cold, though the early hours were misty, and at 3.40am on the 3rd when our bombardment increased to hurricane intensity it was still almost dark. At this hour the Battalion stood to, and the vivid flashes of the guns and the streams of S.O.S. signals from the enemy lines showed that inferno had broken loose, and the attack had begun. The British barrage was good, but the enemy was evidently expecting the attack as his counter-barrage was quick and his machine-gun fire devastating in volume and accuracy.
>
> The 3rd May was a day of great disappointment all along the line, and comparatively little success was achieved. The 169th Brigade were held up by a German strong post in Cavalry Farm and, after occupying a precarious position between it and the river for some hours, were forced back by a heavy counter-attack to their original line. The 167th Brigade was also unable to progress.
>
> It seems clear that zero hour was too early. In the darkness it was impossible for the troops to see visual signals of command, and the delay caused by having to pass messages down the line owing to the din of the bombardment resulted in the attacking waves moving off zig-zag in shape with officers at the advanced points. In such a

formation they became an easy target for the enemy machine-guns. Some greater success might, moreover, have been achieved had the creeping barrage moved forward more quickly, which would have been quite possible in view of the comparatively unbroken state of the ground . . .[1]

It seems clear that zero hour was too early. They couldn't see what they were doing. I imagine my great-uncle squinting down the line in the darkness, a seventeen-year-old boy trying to marshal his platoon with the horrific din of bombardment erupting all around them, then catching a yelled message through the uproar, blowing his whistle and scrambling up out of the trench and into the hell-storm.

The Arras memorial is overwhelming. It stands on the western side of the old city, badly bombed and lovingly reconstructed after WWII, an elegant *ville historique* of Flemish-Baroque townhouses, cafes, fountains, tramways and neo-Gothic spires arrayed around and about two central eighteenth-century piazzas, the old Vauban Citadel and the river. And just to the west, along boulevards lined with immaculate *jardins publiques*, geraniums, pansies and busy Lizzies radiating through manicured lawns in geometric stripes of colour, the memorial rises serene and sad, its outer perimeter sweeping in a graceful curvature of blonde stone and red brick, a neo-Palladian temple to the dead built, of course, by Lutyens. It reminds me vividly of my Oxford college and my old school, and oak-panelled corridors bearing gold-lettered names of Old Boys' varsity scholarships, rowing trophies and cricket caps – and, of course, the honour roll of the glorious dead. Through the sandy beige pillars of its imposing gateway, from a distance I glimpse a heart-piercing vista that seems to rush away into an unknown recess, a vast field of white headstones summoning you to leave behind the noise of traffic, canned music and buzzing phones to enter the eternal present of the dead, forever young.

Looking up at the pillars and their portal to the world beyond, I find myself remembering lines from a poem which my lifelong friend Ben Hopkins wrote for me after my father and brother died. An avowed atheist, Ben has always enjoyed lampooning my beliefs, and we've argued the toss on matters of faith for nearly forty years, but in this poem, he wrote:

They were strong men, strong in body and spirit,
And now their strong arms are pulling them to another world,
And the sea which hurts them is only the tears they shed
for those they leave behind.
I do not believe, but I feel this,
because outside the sun is shining
And there is no darkness on land or sea.

I understand the body was never recovered. What does that mean? Presumably that Clare was blown literally to pieces, that nothing recognisable remained. Jung once wrote that the opposite of remembering is dismembering. Perhaps in reassembling the dismembered shreds of Clare's memory I am putting myself back together as well, stitching the boy in the old photograph in my mother's dining room into my grandfather's recollections and my aunt's and father's anecdotes, interweaving the words on the Memorial Scroll in David's flat in Brescia with the images conjured from the *War History*, and grafting this patchwork of threads and fibres into this moment in this place. To complete the collage I will go through those pillars to find his name, engraved on the white memorial wall, along with the 34,784 other names of British, New Zealand and South African soldiers who died here at Arras, reported 'missing in action', between 9 April and 16 May 1917.

I remember, back in 1988, the coroner's officer down in Cornwall telling me how unlikely it was, with each passing day, that my father's and brother's bodies would ever be recovered. Strong currents sweep the waters off West Penwith swiftly out into the Atlantic, he said, but he had a suggestion, one which astonished me.

'When we're searching for bodies lost at sea,' he said, 'I'm prepared to explore every possible avenue.'

Silence.

'What do you mean?' I asked, mystified.

'Well, I mean *every* possible avenue. I've sometimes consulted a medium in Penzance, in previous searches.'

'Oh, really?' I said, faintly.

'Yes, there was a young woman lost at sea a few years ago, and on the medium's advice I instructed my divers to search offshore in a certain area for a box-like structure, which they discovered – the remains of a wreck, and the body was found.'

It's difficult to explain how visceral is the need to recover the bodies of loved ones lost in tragic accidents or violence, the primal need to put an end to uncertainty and fulfil the painful but essential rituals of burial, mourning, honouring, saying goodbye. Walking through the Somme battlefields, we were told that an astounding 80 per cent of German war dead on the Western Front have no known grave. It's difficult to explain how extremely important it became to me and my mother, over a period of just a few days, that my father's and brother's bodies should be found. We were praying earnestly and repeatedly for this. But not this way. With the slightly dazed feeling of being in a dream, or maybe in a film, I thanked the coroner's officer and said we'd prefer to rely on prayer. And to our unspeakable relief, their bodies were found, several days apart, by fishing vessels.

And there they are buried, beneath rough-hewn headstones of Cornish granite in the graveyard of the tiny Norman church of St Senara, with its mermaid legend carved on the famous mediaeval bench, in the ancient tin-mining village of Zennor, against a hillside of gorse and rough pasture dotted with tumbled cromlechs, looking out across Zennor Head to the sea. And there I make my pilgrimage, every two or three years, to prune the hectic profusion of wild roses, honeysuckle and camellia which I planted nearly thirty years ago, and clean the lichen from the slate lettering on their headstones, sit in the cool of the church and watch the dipping sun shine like fire through the west windows, and drink a pint of Cornish ale in the Tinner's Arms, and walk the coastal path down to the bay of Wicca Pool, where they died.

A few years later, in a strange echo, our aged family dog Harry, arthritic and almost blind, staggered by accident one winter evening into my mother's garden pond, and couldn't get out. My mother found him later that night, drowned and frozen stiff. He had been bought for my brother's seventh birthday, when I was five, and was nearly eighteen when he died, so this felt, somehow, like the final knell of childhood, the severing of the last living link with those years of boyhood companionship – me, Matthew and Harry out together roaming the woods and clifftop paths. And of course the wretched task of burying him fell to me. I found it desperately upsetting, hacking a grave out of the frozen soil at the foot of the towering twisted willow my father had planted fifteen years before, and laying his poor rigid body in the earth, fur frozen in spikes, dead eyes opaque like milk, pink tongue stuck out stiff in *rigor mortis*. He was my childhood consolation when no one else understood or seemed to care, my sparring partner of countless play-fights, the incorrigible rabbit-chaser and absconding rascal of a thousand truancies, the lethal stinkbum of long car journeys and the mediator of familial strife, by all and to all unconditionally loved and loving. He was *Harry*. I was almost hyperventilating with the upset and effort as I shovelled the earth over his poor stiff limbs and covered up his frozen face. It was an awful task. And yet . . . and yet . . . I'm glad I did it. That *I* did it and not someone else. That he's buried in my mother's garden, at the foot of my father's willow tree, and not just left at a vet's surgery to be disposed of somewhere. His body became part of the soil to nourish the willow and red acer and sweet chestnut · trees, as it should. And I'm certain that choosing the place, digging the hole, handling his lifeless body and burying him myself, upsetting as it was, was a powerful ritual through which my grief could flow.

All of which is simply to say, I cannot imagine the pain, the suspended anguish and protracted torment, of those who cannot bury their loved ones.

The Battle of Arras secured the longest advance thus far in trench warfare, but the end result was a costly stalemate, with 160,000 British casualties and possibly an equal number on the German side. The British general commanding the attack was Edmund Allenby, nicknamed the 'Bloody Bull', a man of 'ferocious temper that his subordinates felt was often based only on slight provocation', according to the *International Encyclopedia of Military History*.[2] His rages, wrote one of his loyal staff officers in 1916, appeared to 'confirm the legend that "the Bull" was merely a bad-tempered, obstinate hot-head, a "thud-and-blunder" general'. Apparently he was also a devoted husband and father, constantly anxious about his son Michael, a lieutenant in the Royal Horse Artillery. He would check the daily casualty returns every night before going to bed, asking, 'Have you any news of my little boy today?'

The horrific casualties at Arras and the ultimate failure to achieve a breakthrough on the Western Front, combined with a campaign against him by his own officers and irreconcilable differences in outlook with Field-Marshal Douglas Haig, resulted in Allenby's replacement at the head of the British Third Army and his recall to London. His next appointment was to take command of British forces in the Middle East, as head of the Egyptian Expeditionary Force. One month after his arrival in Cairo, he received a telegram from his wife, informing him that their son had been wounded and later died, aged nineteen, on the Belgian Front. Of Allenby's grief, Wavell later wrote, 'He went on with his work and asked no sympathy. Only those close to him knew how heavy the blow had been, how nearly it had broken him, and what courage it had taken to withstand it.' With the War on the Western Front in stalemate once more, the British government was turning its attention elsewhere in hopes of a breakthrough. Courting the Zionist leadership in Britain on the one hand, and Sharif Hussein of Mecca on the other, while secretly negotiating the carve-up of Ottoman territories with France, Lloyd George and Balfour and others in the cabinet had decided the time was ripe for an attempt on Jerusalem. Allenby's next assignment would be the conquest of Palestine.

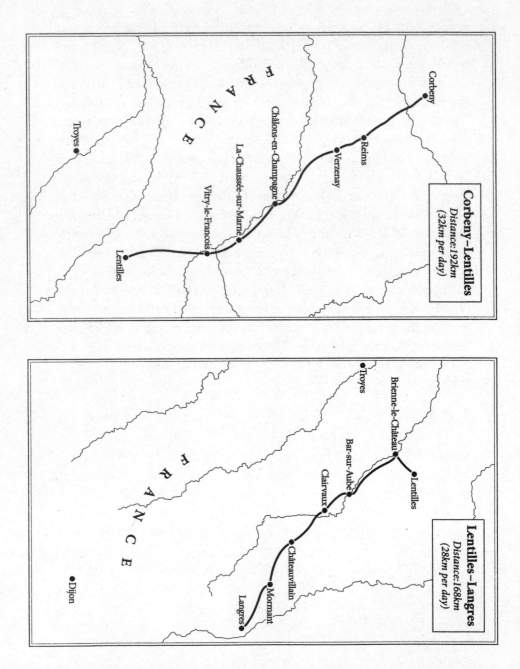

Corbeny–Lentilles
Distance:192km
(32km per day)

Corbeny

Troyes

F R A N C E

Châlons-en-Champagne

La-Chaussée-sur-Marne

Reims

Verzenay

Vitry-le-Francois

Lentilles

Lentilles–Langres
Distance:168km
(28km per day)

Troyes

Brienne-le-Château

F R A N C E

Bar-sur-Aube

Clairvaux

Lentilles

Châteauvillain

Dijon

Mormant

Langres

5

Champagne Trail

IT'S EARLY MORNING and I'm walking with David through woodland paths camouflaged golden-green by sun shafts flickering through
the chestnut canopy of the Forêt de l'Orient. All this week, we've
been trekking through the little villages, lanes and field tracks of
the country between the Forêt and the Lac du Der, 'between the
woods and the water'. Between unruly hedgerows bustling with
blue cornflowers, hemlock lace and pink campion, past tumbledown
half-timbered Tudor barns and along pale dirt tracks through waving,
whispering seas of barley dotted with tall thistles swinging like
bobbing buoys, we've threaded a path from Outines to Lentilles,
through the villages of the ten timber-framed churches unique to
this region.

Leaning on rough wooden pillars cut from the Champagne forests
600 years ago, and clad like dragons in scaly skins of chestnut shingle
and *tavillon* battens, these little churches seem far older than they
are, like Saxon mead-halls or Viking longhouses, and here and there
shreds of ancient times are indeed woven into the fabric, as with
the Roman tiles recycled for the porch of L'Église de l'Exaltation-
de-la-Sainte-Croix in Bailly-le-Franc. A curious trio of altar
paintings in this church shows, on one side, St Helena, mother of
Constantine, digging up the True Cross from the hill of Golgotha
(thereby identifying the subsequent site for the Church of the Holy
Sepulchre) and on the other, the Virgin standing on the globe and
trampling the serpent of Original Sin underfoot, celestial radiance
streaming from her hands like water sprinklers. In the central
painting, an eighteenth-century anonymous work in poor condition,
the Emperor Constantine prostrates himself before the True Cross.

This fixation with holy sites and relics, the 'Jesus trail' of the ancient world, became a popular sport among the Roman aristocracy in the early Byzantine period, but it seems very strange here, in the idyllic hamlets of the Champagne-Ardenne.

Or perhaps not so strange. The mediaeval ruler of this region, Henry II, Count of Champagne, joined his uncles Richard the Lionheart and Philip II of France on the Third Crusade in 1190. After the mysterious murder of the Crusader king of Jerusalem, Conrad of Montferrat, by members of the Isma'ili *hashashin* sect (possibly put up to it by Richard), Henry of Champagne married Conrad's heavily pregnant widow Queen Isabella and assumed the rule of Jerusalem himself. This was more notional than actual, since Jerusalem and the Holy Land were now in the hands of Saladin, and the Crusader Kingdom had retreated to Tyre in Lebanon. Henry bankrupted the Champagne principality to finance his expedition and marriage and, after his death in 1197, falling from a first-floor window at his palace in Acre, a costly succession squabble ensued back home between his younger brother Theobald and his two daughters by Isabella. Apparently it wasn't the fall that killed him. His servant, a dwarf named Scarlet, grabbed hold of his master's sleeve as the balcony gave way, but didn't have the strength or weight to pull him back and so was dragged through the window himself and fell down on top of the Count, killing him instantly. Death by falling dwarf.

Sunlight streams in coloured shafts through the stained glass of Sainte-Croix, and draws the eye to a sixteenth-century *Pietà* window, the deep scarlet and blue of the Madonna's mantle draped in folds of tincture about the deathly white flesh of her prostrate son, limp and luminous between the leaded veins, the hollows of slumped muscle and ashen cheeks picked out in subtle threads of grey. Behind his golden hair, a halo sits like an upturned limpet. Beneath his feet spreads a roof of wooden scales not unlike that of the church itself. The simple humanity of the anguished tableau, set against a serene decorative backdrop in dark and pale greens of fleurs-de-lis and holly leaves, now slightly warped with the creeping flow of glass over the centuries, has only gained in poignancy with the passing of so many generations.

On an arch above the porch roof of the half-timbered church

of Lentilles, a sixteenth-century statue of Saint Jacques stands guard, cloaked and barefoot, staff in hand, traveller's bag slung over his shoulder and book tucked under his arm, and, stuck on his hat brim, the miraculous scallop shell of Galicia. Inside, rough timber pillars march down either side of the church, buttress beams arching like whale ribs into a ceiling latticed with wooden diamonds. Round windows above the choir bays shine the light of another world into the dim timber cavern, oculi of ancient glass like port-holes on to a sea of marvels – annunciations, visitations, *Pietàs* captured in brilliantly coloured lead-lined fragments stitched together like a glass quilt or a shattered vase painstakingly repaired, to refract the memory of ancient sacred scenes. I wonder what the sixteenth-century *paysans* made of it all, when they first saw the sunlight flood in beams tinged with lapis, emerald and scarlet through these oculi, illuminating the shadowy canopy of the church. They must have felt like the sailor in Heaney's poem, aboard a ship carrying them into the realm of the marvellous. *Que vous soyez, d'ici ou d'ailleurs, Quel que soit le pays d'où vous venez, Soyez les bienvenus dans cette église!* 'If you come from here or elsewhere, Whatever country you come from, Welcome in this church!' reads the pilgrim benediction at the back of the nave.

In every one of these warm, woody-smelling consecrated barns, we find a statue of Jeanne d'Arc, La Pucelle d'Orleans, visionary, warrior maiden, saint and martyr, a fifteenth-century Christian jihadi radicalised to become the liberator of her homeland. We're coming close to her birthplace in Domrémy. And in every church-yard we find the graves of more recent patriots, soldiers and resistance fighters from the two world wars, decorated with decom-missioned shells and helmets of gunmetal grey. Back in the WWI battlefields, near Reims, Arthur photographed a two-foot long shell lying in the path, one of the fruits of the annual 'Iron Harvest' thrown up from a newly ploughed field. In France alone, one ton of ordnance was fired for every square metre of the Western Front, of which a third never exploded, and, a century later, 900 tons of shells, bullets and barbed wire are harvested each year.

I read tonight in an email from my cousin Andy that my Aunt Rony, the youngest of my father's three older sisters, died today at 12.10 p.m., aged ninety-four.

Monday 10 July

It's 10 a.m. on a drizzly overcast morning, exactly one month since departure from London, and we're heading down eastwards from Baroville, after a wonderfully steamy, rainy, early-morning walk out of Bar-sur-Aube up into the forest, scrabbling up steep muddy paths over the hills into the champagne vineyards to the south-east. This has been the steepest section of the Via Francigena so far, bringing us up to 3,500 metres above sea level. Now we're walking a path through wheat and barley fields to our left and right, and, spread all across the hills to the right, neat lines of champagne grapevines march southwards in geometric grids. Away over to the north, through the mist, I can see the memorial cross to Charles de Gaulle, far off on the hill of Colombey-les-Deux-Églises, our base for three nights last week where we stayed at the most delightful country pub hotel, with roadside gardens overflowing with lavender and squadrons of magical pink and orange humming moths. De Gaulle's memorial, dedicated recently by Angela Merkel and Nicolas Sarkozy, is a 'Patriarchal cross', widespread in the Byzantine church, also known as the Cross of Lorraine, with two horizontal beams, twin symbols of resistance and victory, which the Free French adopted as their emblem. Colombey, where we saw the Tour de France pelting through last week, was de Gaulle's country retreat and final resting place. The story goes that, in 1960, the Old Man came to the roadside to see them all riding through, and every cyclist stopped to shake his hand and then continued with the race. Visiting his grave the other day, we saw a lavish bouquet of flowers with the tricolour of the French flag and a card expressing respectful greetings from the Tour de France. It seems that one of the cyclists has the job of diverting off the main drag through Colombey and up the hill to the churchyard to drop off the bouquet, and then presumably rejoins the race. During his exile in WWII, de Gaulle's London address, which subsequently became the HQ for the Free French, was 4 Colton Mews, previously the town house of . . . Arthur James Balfour.

At lunchtime we picnic in a tranquil clearing in the Clairvaux forest, dedicated to twenty-one 'otages' (hostages), civilians killed here by the Germans in 1941, in reprisal for guerrilla attacks by the French Resistance. Two buzzards cry in the woods behind us. Next to the clearing is the Fountain of St Bernard, maybe half a mile from the western perimeter of the gigantic Clairvaux Abbey, once the largest and wealthiest monastery in France.

At the end of the eleventh century, Robert of Molesme left his monastery in Burgundy with a small clutch of followers seeking a simpler, purer way of life. The Benedictine order had become enormously wealthy and powerful, with vast endowments and estates, its monks abandoning manual labour to serve as scholars. Robert and his followers sought a return to the simplicity of the Rule of St Benedict, and acquired a plot of marshland to the south of Dijon, called Cîteaux, where they began farming the land and building lodgings. They adopted traditional hermit garb – white habits of undyed wool – and dedicated themselves to manual work and prayer, underpinned by the twin goals of charity and self-sustenance. Their *Carta caritatis*, or 'Charter of charity', enshrined the ideals of a simple life of work, love, prayer and self-denial. So the Cistercian order was born. The order flourished, and their first 'daughter house' was established in La Ferte in 1113.

In the same year, a young nobleman of Burgundy named Benoît (Bernard) arrived at Cîteaux with thirty-five followers. Eloquent and strong-willed, Bernard would become the most influential and revered churchman of his era; within two years he was leading a band of twelve monks to found a new abbey in a wild tract of forest to the east of Troyes, a notorious haunt of robbers and outlaws, gifted by Count Hugh of Champagne. Undismayed, Bernard and his disciples began clearing the ground in an isolated glen known as the Val d'Absinthe to build a church and monastic dwelling, which they named *Claire Vallée*, the clear valley, corrupted over time to *Clairvaux*. Despite the extreme austerity of their existence, Clairvaux grew rapidly, attracting hundreds of disciples, including Bernard's own father and brothers, and spawning new monastic houses in the outlying dioceses within a few years.

Meanwhile, Bernard's writings and teaching were establishing his reputation across France and Europe as a visionary church leader of statesmanlike authority. When a schism erupted following the death of Pope Honorius II and the election of two popes, Innocent II and 'Antipope' Anacletus II, Bernard was called upon to judge between the rivals by Louis VI of France. He ruled in favour of Innocent, who was duly acknowledged as the true pope by the great powers, and over the next eight years Bernard used his influence and reputation to reunite the church in Europe, travelling from city state to province persuading statesmen and church leaders to support Pope Innocent.

When invading Seljuk Turks captured the Crusader province of Edessa, to the north-east of Antioch and Aleppo, in present-day Turkey, and threatened the kingdom of Jerusalem, Pope Eugene III commissioned Bernard to preach a rallying call for a Second Crusade, from Clairvaux Abbey. In the absence of any popular enthusiasm for a new crusade, the Pope granted the same indulgences as had Pope Urban III for the First Crusade in 1095. On 31 March 1144, Bernard preached to a vast crowd at Vézelay, in the presence of Louis VII of France, promising absolution for sins and the attainment of divine grace for all who took the cross. The entire crowd enlisted on this spot, so the story goes, and the recruiting monks ran out of cloth to make crosses, so Bernard gave his cloak to be cut up for more. Through his supreme gifts of oratory and unimpeachable reputation, Bernard turned a faraway territorial struggle in the Middle East into a popular cause, and the Second Crusade was born. Among the many nobility who rallied to the holy fray were Eleanor of Aquitaine, then queen of France, and Henry I, Count of Champagne, who carried a letter from Bernard to the Byzantine emperor Manuel I Komnenos, asking for his support. Bernard travelled to Germany, then Flanders, preaching the Crusade, miracles reputedly multiplying in his wake, and recruited to the crusader flag King Conrad III and his nephew Frederick Barbarossa, later king of Germany and Italy and Holy Roman Emperor. One of the unintended consequences of Bernard's preaching in Germany was the outbreak of a spate of attacks on Jews, vilified for supposedly failing to contribute sufficiently to the recapture of the Holy Land.

The miserable failure of the Second Crusade, ending with defeat at the disastrous siege of Damascus in 1148, was a crushing humiliation for Bernard which overshadowed his last years. He sent a letter of apology to the Pope, in which he sought to explain that the Crusaders' downfall had been brought about by their own sins. Monks in Germany meanwhile were writing that the Crusade must have been the work of the devil. Bernard flailed back and forth in an anguish of self-reproach, at first calling for a new Crusade, then attempting to dissociate himself from the whole enterprise. He died at Clairvaux five years later in 1153, at the age of sixty-three.

Since the abbey is now a maximum-security prison as well as a heritage site, our tour begins with showing passports and surrendering cameras and phones at the reception desk. The inmates include the infamous Venezuelan extremist Carlos the Jackal, once the world's most wanted fugitive, convicted of perpetrating multiple attacks on behalf of the Palestinian struggle and the cause of revolutionary communism in the 1970s and 1980s. During his 1997 trial in Paris, he said, 'When one wages war for thirty years, there is a lot of blood spilled – mine and others. But we never killed anyone for money, but for a cause – the liberation of Palestine.' How strange that he ended up at Clairvaux, launch pad for the Second Crusade.

The perimeter wall of the abbey and prison encloses a vast compound of courtyards, gardens, waterways, barns and *bâtiments de l'Abbaye*, with the Saint-Bernard Stream, a tributary of the River Aube, running most of its length east to west. As we wander across the handsome entrance courtyard, with its pointed turrets and magnificent blonde fortress walls, the guide explains that the old abbey was rebuilt in the eighteenth century, then an extremely wealthy foundation owning 20,000 hectares of farmland and forest and many forges for the production of iron and steel goods. It was the largest Cistercian abbey of the mediaeval period, housing between 800 and 900 monks and lay brothers known as *convers*, and the most powerful monastery in Europe, with lands producing a huge yield of agricultural wealth. Yet by the time of the Revolution, there were only twenty-eight monks and ten lay brothers still living at Clairvaux. The monastery was dissolved by the revolutionary government in 1791 and sold to a local architect, who set up a glassworks and paper mill within its walls. Then, in 1808, Napoleon's government set about converting the monastery into the largest prison in France, to house 3,000 prisoners. Amazingly, given the brutal conditions which prisoners here endured, Clairvaux Prison was conceived as a humanitarian initiative, to build a penal environment more humane than the dreadful galley-ships used by the French state hitherto.

Leading us through to the first enclosed courtyard, our guide points out a long line of *bâtiments* to our left – the flour mills and bakery ovens of the monks in the eighteenth century, with a top floor added for workshops where prisoners could practise arts, skills and crafts. To our right, lock-gates damming the Saint-Bernard Stream create a large moat on either side of a handsome mediaeval barn with a deep roof clad in acres of tiles. In the mediaeval period this lake provided the monks with their own supply of fish.

In the next courtyard we encounter the lay brothers' building, a Romanesque edifice dating from the first rebuilding of the abbey, under Bernard's rule, in 1135. Twelve giant arched bays run side by side along its western wall, with windows leading to twelve parallel naves seventy-four metres in length, each of which housed between 200 and 300 *convers*. The scale of operation back then, within just a few decades of the community's foundation, is astonishing.

We trudge up crumbling steps and round a small side courtyard filled with weed-strewn gravel and a busy community of starlings. Down one side looms a line of administrative prison buildings, similarly dilapidated. As we make our way into a huge ground floor hall of pillars, a cellar for food storage with a cobbled floor for carts delivering comestibles, the contrast between these lovingly restored monastic buildings and the self-evidently demoralised condition of the state prison across the yard is not lost on us. I get the sense that the ministry of culture is making a big push to restore these historic buildings but hasn't much idea of what to do with them. They're certainly not inundated with visitors. In the blonde ribbed vaulting overhead, we see a number of little carved crosses and compasses, signatures of individual masons in the twelfth century, marking the progress of their work and keeping a tally of payment due. Such 'Clairvaux marks' have been found as far afield as the grand Cistercian abbey of Alcobaça in Portugal, evidence that specialist itinerant stoneworkers were few and far between, and much sought after.

A short flight of steps leads down to the refectory, an impressive, many-pillared pale cavern of ochre-washed stone booming with the echoing footfall and chit-chat of a visiting school party just ahead of us. Arched windows high above head height on either side flood the blonde stone hall with light. I hang back, scribbling notes, and, as our group moves off across the refectory, the cacophony of echoes conjures a sense of the din with which this room must have reverberated with 300 *convers* at table. Six pairs of huge pillars spreading into ribbed ceiling vaults of the early Gothic period and twelve pairs of arched windows interspersed with iron sconces for large burning torches set the stage for an imaginary throng of lay brothers chomping and slurping, with the clink of cutlery and ale flagons, the scrape of wooden bowls on trestles and benches creaking on a stone floor strewn with rushes – and one hell of a racket. The guide tells me that, with rush matting on the floor, the echo would have been considerably less, but I don't believe it made much difference.

Upstairs, a huge chamber identical in structure provided the dormitory. It's incredibly plain: no paintings or statues, and no contact with the outside world, except through the grille of monastic seclusion. The Rule of St Bernard was ascetic devotion with no distraction. The original casements would have been much smaller than these large nineteenth-century windows, the guide tells us, and shuttered. Electric lights in wall sconces give an impression of the dim illumination the mediaeval brothers must have endured in this room, one of the largest to be found in any French Cistercian abbey.

Heading eastwards through a series of heavily secured gated courtyards, which our guide unlocks and locks again behind us, we find ourselves standing between a long prison wall to our right, topped with barbed wire, and to our left a line of eighteenth-century monastic buildings which in the Napoleonic period became the male prison. The watchtower at the far end is no longer in use, our guide says; this yard was an orchard in mediaeval times. I try to imagine avenues of apple trees in blossom, monks and lay brothers tending them, bees buzzing from flower to flower, and birdsong, but it's a stretch for the mind's eye against this dismal backdrop. We enter a long, vaulted cloister with grim grey iron cell doors in the right-hand wall, and, to the left, windows on to the cloister garden, a huge grassy yard sprouting dandelions and hemlock, getting on for a square kilometre, with a pitch-perfect acoustic, demonstrated as our guide's voice bounces off the far wall back to us. We're facing north across the square. Up to our left is the building which housed the kitchen and refectory for the monks. Over beyond the northwest corner was the abbey church, destroyed in the nineteenth century when the prison was established. According to the guide, there are plans for this dispiriting quadrangle, with its stalag-style cellblock lettering and numbers painted on the walls and weed-strewn scrub, to become an exercise yard for present-day inmates.

We traipse upstairs to the cloister gallery, now paved with the original stone slabs from the floor of the mediaeval church. Entering a low-roofed, dingy cell, perhaps thirty metres square, we're shocked to be told that this cramped space, with a single span of vaulting overhead and two deeply recessed barred windows on the south side, would have housed up to thirty prisoners. One small stone toilet built into the wall opposite the windows provided for their bodily functions. The extreme claustrophobia must have engendered a constant, simmering potential for violence. The guide tells us a tragic story which stirred public outcry in the 1830s. Claude Gueux was a pauper imprisoned for a minor crime, whose father had been incarcerated for vagrancy and begging at the age of sixty and died in his son's arms. Claude was a giant of a man, perpetually famished in prison, but when another prisoner took pity on him and shared his rations with Claude, a great friendship grew between them. A brutal prison warder, seeing this friendship, decided to separate them, which proved unbearable to Claude. He killed the warder and was executed for his crime on 1 June 1834. Initially reported in the *Gazette des Tribunaux* and retold in a short story by Victor Hugo written in three days and published within a month of Claude's execution, the episode provoked widespread condemnation of the cruelty of the French prison regime. Deeply moved by the case, Hugo described how Claude's fellow prisoners staged a 'trial' of the prison warder, found him guilty and sentenced him to death, after which Claude split his skull open with a hatchet. Writing thirty years later from his exile on Guernsey, Victor Hugo would bring his passionate anger against social injustice to its fullest expression in *Les Misérables,* the seeds of which can be found here at Clairvaux.

Up another flight of stairs, we're shown into a long, rectangular hall filled with wooden coops, *cages à poules*, each box maybe ten feet square and just over six feet high, gated with rusty iron cage doors, used for single-cell confinement of prisoners until 1971. These were installed in 1875 as an 'improvement' to the conditions downstairs. They're opened all together by one single sliding bolt overhead, which drags across a series of iron bars to release the doors. These individual hen-coops were perhaps an improvement on thirty men to a cell, but the lack of shared body heat left prisoners exposed to extreme cold, and many froze to death.

The nineteenth-century prison chapel, formerly the monks' refectory, feels quite beautiful after such grim exhibits. It actually reminds me in its proportions of the exquisite royal chapel at Versailles. It's the only room at Clairvaux in which the eighteenth-century wooden panelling is preserved, with elliptical medallions originally framing allegorical representations of the Virtues and the Seasons, which are exhibited now in a different part of the abbey. Ornate medallions in pale grey stucco on the ceiling represent aspects of monastic life, such as gardening, albeit with elegantly neo-Palladian quaintness, stucco spades and rakes crossed like heraldic arms, beneath a slender watering can surrounded by symmetrical garlands of roses, surmounting a wicker basket of flowers. The floor is white octagons of the local clunch stone, lozenges picked out at each corner with small black diamond shapes. Seven steps lead up to a high, wide marble chancel floor and a sanctuary with a marble altar and double pillars surrounding an altar piece of the Enlightenment-era Masonic-eyed triangle of the Divine presence – the 'Eye of Providence' – amid a golden burst of sun-rays. On the left wall is a pulpit, built before the refectory's conversion into a chapel, for the reading of homilies during the monks' meals, which otherwise were taken in silence. According to our guide, the chapel could accommodate 1,500 inmates standing.

As we retrace our steps to the entrance courtyard, I ask the guide about a little chapel which we spy to our left, from a staircase on the south side of the abbey.

'That was the chapel of the children's prison,' she says.

'The children's prison?'

'Oh yes, there were hundreds of children imprisoned here as well. In 1858, the records show there were 550 child prisoners, some as young as five years old.'

Five years old. Dear God. And this was supposed to be a revolutionary state, founded on the ideals of *liberté, egalité,* etc. This is the tipping-point in the scales of my revulsion for Clairvaux and everything it symbolises about our capacity for brutality, inhumanity and ignorance.

Wednesday 12 July

We set off from the beautiful mediaeval walled town of Châteauvillain in a damp early-morning mist, with skylarks pealing across fields of dripping dew and ghostly drifts of vapour curling over the strange skeletal thickets of oilseed rape, like great clusters of earthbound mistletoe or tumbleweed. What space do we make in the bright palette of our sleek, ergonomically designed world for this kind of penumbral beauty? The drizzly charm of dripping boughs, indeterminate greys and greens of wet bark and stem, leaf and twig, the melancholy of damp, murky skies? As the sun leaks irresistibly through the vapour, burning off the misty veil like a flame spreading beneath paper, we plunge into the Forêt de Châteauvillain through a canopied colonnade of beeches, planes, holm oaks and acacias, a broad avenue tracing the tramp of the Roman road from Reims to Langres of the famous cheese. Roman legionaries never marched in step, according to our Via Francigena guide – the synchronised impact of a thousand iron-shod footfalls would have cracked the roads – so they had to learn to march in varying rhythms, which is trickier than it sounds. Walking in small clusters of twos and threes, we synchronise our strides without thinking. Jude recounts the moody, misty haunts of the Crag Walk along Hadrian's Wall, which she did as training for this Walk, to limber up her newly replaced hip.

After a mid-morning stop in Richebourg, where Arthur quits for the day to rest his knee, and further mesmerising meandering through hypnotic sunflower fields, we arrive at the hamlet of Mormant for lunch beneath a chestnut tree next to what remains of the *Maison-Dieu de Mormant*, a fortified pilgrim hostel of the Knights Hospitaller of St John of Jerusalem. It starts to rain just as our driver Steve finishes laying out the lunch things against the crumbling stone steps, so we retreat with our lunch under the dripping chestnut. The higgledy-piggledy end wall of the *Maison-Dieu* is a hotchpotch of ancient clunch stones and breeze block repairs, many times patched and rebuilt. Once a mediaeval fortress, hospital and priory, then clearly a farmstead for several centuries, this ramshackle assortment of tumbledown barns and mediaeval *bâtiments* doesn't convey much sense of the reach and power of the Order of St John of Jerusalem at its height.

The history of this ancient religious military-medical order of knighthood is wonderfully strange. Their emblem, the white eight-pointed cross of Malta on a black background, has become an international symbol of first aid as the logo of the St John Ambulance charity, but it was worn first on the robes of the original Brother Knights in the Hospital of St John in Jerusalem, founded in the eleventh century to care for sick pilgrims to the Holy Land. After the Crusader capture of Jerusalem, they received official recognition from the Pope as a religious order and added a military dimension to their functions, to safeguard pilgrims travelling to the holy sites. At its height, the mediaeval Hospital of St John cared for 2,000 patients, including Jews, to whom the Hospitallers took the trouble to serve kosher food. The Hospital also became an orphanage for the many children who lost their parents to illness or injury in their travels to the Holy Land, many of whom were apprenticed to the Order. Today, the Hospital of St John in Jerusalem, with its sister hospitals in Gaza and the West Bank, is the only provider of ophthalmic care to Palestinians in the Occupied Territories.

The rise of the Knights of St John to become one of the great players in the mediaeval history of the Levant, their exile after the fall of the Kingdom of Jerusalem - first to Cyprus, then Rhodes, and at last to Malta, their metamorphosis from Crusader warrior-doctor-monks to corsair-fighting navy of the eastern seas, their incredible feats of valour in defending the islands of Rhodes and Malta against overwhelming odds in repeated Ottoman attacks by the forces of Mehmet the Conqueror and Suleiman the Magnificent in the fifteenth and sixteenth centuries and their final mutation into the medical charity and chivalric order of today – all this is the matter of many books. But the extent of the influence and wealth of the Knights of St John through Europe is perhaps less well known.

The *Maison-Dieu of Mormant*, we learn from a scruffy heritage sign, was sold to the Knights Hospitallers by the bishop of Langres in 1200, then reclaimed in 1227 by papal decree. In 1300 the Pope gifted the priory, 'ruined by the negligence of his abbots and canons', to the Knights Templar until the dissolution of their order in 1312. After the disbanding of the large and extremely wealthy order of the Templars, most of their assets were turned over to the Knights Hospitaller, including the priory and hospital of Mormant, which they proceeded to rebuild and fortify, piercing the outer walls with embrasures for cannons, and decorating the inner walls with frescoes, one of which apparently survives somewhere inside – a brightly tinctured fragment of a Deposition from the Cross. The old hospital is built over three arched tunnels leading into a low-ceilinged vaulted ground floor, now heavily propped up with reinforcing wooden beams and makeshift scaffold. Clearly the floor has built up over the centuries, so these vaulted caverns feel almost like a basement. The capitals at the base-juncture of adjacent spans, decorated with scallops, fleurs-de-lis and fruits, are almost at floor level, like strange branching trees mottled with moss and mould, erupting from a substrate of limestone, pigeon feathers and loose rubble. How much further down do the pillars go? Scrambling around this cobwebby cellar, it's hard to imagine that one might actually be just beneath the ceiling of a once vast atrium.

Arthur has been exploring the site while he and Steve waited for us to arrive, and has found the mausoleum of Pierre de Bosredon on the other side of a drystone wall, in the adjacent field. Born in 1424, he was a councillor and chamberlain of both Louis XI and Charles VIII, and an honoured Knight Hospitaller of Rhodes. From 1485 he was Commander of the Order in Romagna, Robécourt, Pontaubert and Bure, and here in Mormant, as a reward for his heroic service in Rhodes, he held the *commanderie* from 1506 until his death in 1513, arguably something of a mixed blessing. After the Hundred Years War (1337–1453) forced the Hospitallers to abandon the *Maison-Dieu*, its new commander was now required willy-nilly to undertake an ambitious programme of restoration and redevelopment to transform the old priory, erecting a vast new Eglise de Sainte-Marie with two chapels to Saint Marcoul and Saint Antoine. The old Roman road, now the Via Francigena, was diverted to run either side of the new Priory. Perhaps as a further reward, Pierre de Bosredon was appointed Grand Prior of the Order of St John in the principality of Champagne in 1511, at the age of eighty-seven. He died two years later, no doubt exhausted after such a mammoth renovation, worthy of several episodes of *Grand Designs*. By the beginning of the eighteenth century, the enormous church was in a sorry state of disrepair. The nave was pulled down in 1788 at the time of the dissolution of the Order of St John in France. Only the choir section of the church survived the Revolution, first to be sold as state property, then demolished shortly afterwards to make way for a quarry, with many ancient remains scattered about the site. At his death on 15 July 1513, exactly 504 years ago this Saturday, Pierre de Bosredon was buried in a vault in the middle of the choir of the new church he had built, beneath a stone slab bearing his coat of arms.

'It's just over that wall,' says Arthur, 'underneath an old pallet, down some steps. Mind your head.' I scramble over the wall and, sure enough, under a tangle of ferns and wild flowers is an old pallet balanced precariously over a hole in the ground. I heave it out of the way to reveal a dank, slippery staircase leading down into a dark catacomb. At the bottom I stoop to feel my way along a short, cramped passage, ending in the bricked-up wall of a tomb, into which four heraldic slabs are set. By the light of my phone I can just about make out the words, engraved in a runic semi-gothic script:

A été le tombeau de frère Pierre de Bosredon, qui fut fait, l'an 1506, Commander de Mormant Ponthaubert.

[Here was the tomb of Brother Pierre de Bosredon, who was made, in the year 1506, Commander of Mormant Ponthaubert.]

Below this slab I can feel the recess of the tomb-shaft, filled with a rectangular block which might be the end of a stone sarcophagus going back into the wall. It seems to be decorated with an engraved figure of the Knight Commander. To the right another slab frames his coat of arms, a shield divided in four with plain quarters top right and bottom left, and on the other diagonal, a pattern like a series of horizontal colonnades, which I believe is called *nebulée* – lines made up from bulbous protrusions supposed to resemble clouds. It's a strange feeling to crouch in this dank cave under a muddy field in eastern France and think that here in front of me lie the earthly remains of a man born before the fall of the Eastern Roman Empire, who stood with his brother knights in 1480 to defend the island of Rhodes against Sultan Mehmet, Conqueror of Constantinople, and in his lifetime saw the innovation of the printing press revolutionise Europe, ushering in the Reformation and a new era of history. *Imperious Caesar, dead and turned to clay, Might stop a hole to keep the wind away.*

Sunday 16 July

We're noticing a different style of church as we come closer to the Swiss border, mostly twelfth-century Romanesque strongholds with Norman arches, square towers and little gabled roofs, shingled in the Alpine style, and elegantly intricate wrought-iron weather vanes. And the countryside's becoming hillier, more undulating, with lots of rivers running through wide, flat-bottomed glacial valleys as we climb higher above sea level, approaching the mountainous country which eventually will become the Alps. These villages are known as the *Circuit des Lavoirs*, each boasting a proudly preserved ancient public bath or *lavoir* for washing clothes, built over a spring or village stream, a stone pool built on several tiers with a water channel running between, housed with pillars, arches and stone roof, and in these villages decked with brightly planted hanging baskets. Some of the oldest *lavoirs* date from the tenth century, the mediaeval forerunner of the laundrette.

As we march in sweltering sun from Champlitte to Courtesoult-le-Gatey to Dampierre, I'm struck by the incredible proliferation of life everywhere around us: the cut fields of wheat and barley strewn with stalks chucked out by the combine harvesters and the balers rolling up the bales; clouds of butterflies, wonderful red spotted and golden, brown and yellow and miniature blues and swallowtails; pairs of swifts courting on the wing and skylarks, starlings and swallows twittering. Fabulous heat pulses everywhere through the buzzing rhythms of crickets and combine harvesters, plums are beginning to ripen on bushes, and, on the horizon to the north, elegant bell-shaped church cupolas shimmer through the haze, rising above the skyline like Oxford colleges glimpsed across Christchurch meadows. It's *fecund*. The landscape is fabulously fecund. I'm walking under a scorching sun, with a chafing arse and blistered feet, and my eyes are stinging from a pungent cocktail of sun cream and sweat, but I'm absolutely loving this.

Later that night, after dinner in Dampierre, I'm sitting out on the front step of our farm bed and breakfast-gîte, scribbling notes and smoking, when a chubby little boy, Mateus, rides by on his bike and stops to chat. He's old-young, courteous in an old-fashioned way, interested in our walk, and raises his eyebrows when I say we've walked from London, and again when I mention Jerusalem. What time are you leaving tomorrow? *À sept heures.* How far? How many bags? Do you have a *tante*? An aunt? Yes, several, each with a *plume,* perennially poised. Why does he want to know that? After several more goes and a bit of mime, I realise he means tent. Ah yes, a *tente! Oui, oui, absolument.*

Later, a hedgehog comes nosing right up to where I'm sitting, raises beady eyes to gaze short-sightedly at me, then scuttles away.

In my pocket I'm carrying a small black pebble, which I picked up at the Good Friday service earlier this year at my home church, St Luke's, in Holloway. Our vicar Dave invited everyone as part of a meditation to pick up a pebble from a glass bowl and drop it into the font, symbolising something you wanted to let go of. I picked up a pebble, but for some reason I didn't want to let it go, so I'm carrying it to Jerusalem.

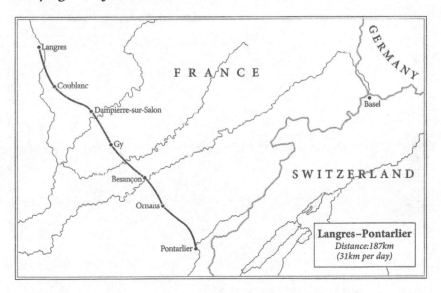

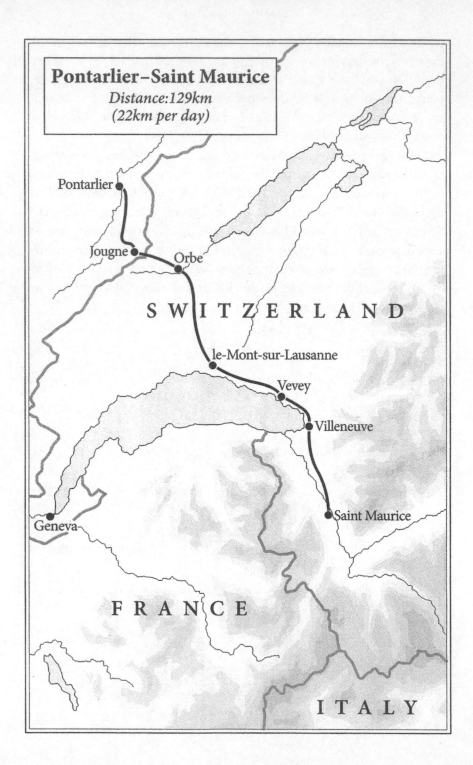

Pontarlier–Saint Maurice
*Distance:129km
(22km per day)*

Pontarlier

Jougne

Orbe

S W I T Z E R L A N D

le-Mont-sur-Lausanne

Vevey

Villeneuve

Geneva

Saint Maurice

F R A N C E

I T A L Y

6

À Piedmont à Pied

TODAY WE BEGIN our ascent into the Pennine Alps, from the ancient Gallo-Roman town of Martigny in the canton of Valais in Switzerland, burrowing up into the steep valleys and clefts on the path that will lead us, in Napoleon's footsteps, to cross the great ridge of mountains from Mont Blanc to the Matterhorn and Monte Rosa at its lowest point, the Great St Bernard Pass. This pass, leading from Valais down into the Aosta Valley in northern Italy, is named after Bernard of Menthon, patron saint of the Alps, skiing, snow-boarding, hiking, backpacking and mountaineering, of whom more anon. Martigny was built by the Emperor Claudius in his conquests to clear the route for his invasion of Britain in AD 43, methodically occupying the foothills of the Alps and the plain of the Rhone Valley, where he established a new town at the foot of the pass, on the site of the Celtic settlement of Octodurus.

After a stirring reading from Lynn first thing this morning, standing down in the circus arena of the Amphitheatre of Claudius, her voice ringing around the ancient stone tiers as she declaimed the words of hope and solidarity, we're walking east out of Martigny now. To our right is the little Alpine railway to Sembrancher and Orsières and, beyond it, the River Dranse, tributary of the Rhône at the junction where, running south-west into Martigny, the great river takes a right-angled turn to flow north-west into Lake Geneva. Dense pine forests stalk up the steep slopes of massive interlacing valley spurs ahead, clinging to the crags like giant thickets of moss, green and glorious in the Alpine sun.

After a dash back to London and a mad flurry of days attending my Aunt Rony's funeral, my youngest son Joey's primary school leavers' service and the recording of my play *The Devil's Passion* at the BBC with the mighty David Suchet in the title role, as well as having my sodding laptop stolen from my bag at Euston, I've returned to the Walk with my older three kids, Benedict, Eleanor and Jacob, to plunge them in at the deep end on 'the worst section of the whole Via Francigena', according to Alison Raju's *Via Francigena* guide. Dire warnings notwithstanding, this is spectacular walking, through almost impossibly verdant meadows shimmering lime and emerald green and speckled with gems of Alpine flowers, gossamer-bladed lilac crocuses veined with threads of purple filigree, cradling tiny stamens of brilliant yellow like treasure caskets of gleaming gold, waving wands of rosebay willow herbs stippling the slopes of reservoirs, feathery quills beaded with phosphorescent violet, Alpine thistles like pink porcupines riding on pineapple stalks. Rounding the valley shoulders splayed like giant fingers into the glen, thicketed with sweet-scented pines and marching vines even at this altitude, every new vista is a magnificent reward. Alpine streams cascade in mists of rainbow spray over shining crags, gushing down through rivulets of slime-green boulders, under timber footbridges creaking beneath our boots, as we wend our steps up the valley side on to the forest path, winding along woodland slopes mottled with sunlight through the trees. Massive boulders scabbed with lichen lie riven and wedged in huge tumbles at the twists and turns of the hillside path, rockfall shrapnel of ages past like fallen meteorites – surly, intransigent facts on the ground. The Roman historian Livy wrote that Hannibal blasted a path through such rockfalls in his crossing of the Alps, using fire and vinegar to shatter the rocks by thermal shock.

After an hour or so, we cross the Dranse for the second time and climb on eastwards and upwards, under the tiny railway line, to walk up into the mountain village of Bovernier, *le pays des vouipes*, the 'land of wasps', as a roadside sign announces, beneath a huge comic wooden model of a wasp. As always, there's a legend attached. Apparently, St Théodule, the first known bishop of Octodurus, was returning over the mountains from Rome sometime in the late fourth century, and on his way he fell in with an Italian merchant, who was really Satan in disguise (aren't they always?). As they descended from Sembrancher, the elderly saint grew more and more weary, afflicted with rheumatic pains and leaning heavily on his bishop's staff. Chatting away affably, Satan bided his time until St Théodule sat down to rest by a hot spring flowing from the mountain rock, to bathe his feet. As the old man set down his staff, Satan seized his chance, grabbed the staff and ran off with it down the valley. A peasant in a nearby field saw the merchant haring down the mountain, staff in hand. Thinking it odd that a merchant should be carrying a bishop's staff, the peasant chased after him, but his feet seemed to drag like lead and, try as he might, he couldn't catch up. As Satan approached the village of Bovernier, the peasant's wife was rolling empty wine barrels to the stream, to wash them before her husband delivered them back to Fully across the Rhône valley for refilling. Seeing Satan tearing down towards the village with the stolen staff, she rolled an empty barrel in his path to stop him. He crashed into the barrel, tripped and fell headlong, whereupon the peasant arrived on the scene and grabbed the staff, which Satan had let fall. The devil roared with rage and disappeared in a cloud of black smoke. At that moment St Théodule came hobbling down the hill and received his staff gratefully from the peasant, who was kneeling prostrate before him. The saint raised him to his feet and thanked him, saying, 'My son, I bless you and will reward you. From now on, rich vines will grow here in your village, and the barrels of Bovernier will be filled with fine wine from your house.' Just then a harsh voice cried from down the valley, thin and full of malice, 'And I'll send you swarms of wasps to devour your blessed grapes!' And sure enough, to this day, Bovernier's vines (at an altitude generally regarded in European viticulture as too high for ripening) produce grapes and fine wine in abundance, swarms of wasps notwithstanding.

After a brief pitstop, we slog on up into the mountains towards Sembrancher. It's a huge joy to have my kids with me, Benedict having just finished A levels and Eleanor her GCSEs, and to see them muck in with the group. Jack's delighted to have some companions his own age at last. Out of their earshot, I receive many compliments from the walkers about what affable company my kids are, how relaxed and personable, to which my standard rejoinder (having first checked we're talking about the right kids) is to take all the credit myself. Benedict has hit it off with Chris's brother Mike, a fellow physicist and another *Game of Thrones* nut, who's come out to join us for a stretch. He's a deputy head at a school in Hounslow with a mosque right next door, where 50 per cent of pupils are Muslim. In recent years, a number of bright A-level students from schools in West London (though not from Mike's) have gone off to Syria to join ISIS, so there is a distinct atmosphere of heightened vigilance these days. A number of new walkers have joined us for the crossing of the Alps: Chris and Joanna, retired missionaries from Devon; Bethan, an art therapist from Dublin; and Rachel from Hampshire, a nurse and former 'Ecumenical Accompanier' who's worked in Palestine with EAPPI, the Ecumenical Accompaniment Programme in Palestine and Israel, a human rights monitoring initiative created by the World Council of Churches in 2002.

Various signs along the route commemorate Napoleon's crossing of the Alps. It's strange to think of these idyllic mountain passes as a passage of war and conquest, in the footsteps of Charlemagne and Hannibal (and his elephants), as Jacques-Louis David's painting famously depicts Napoleon, in windswept golden cloak astride his rearing charger, right hand pointing the way to the conquest of Italy, with an army of 40,000 men at his back, and 10,000 horses. (In fact, he reached the Great St Bernard Pass riding a mule.) Stranger still to think of this whole region invaded by Moorish, Aghlabid and Fatimid invaders from Andalusia and north Africa – described generically as 'Saracens' in the Middle Ages – whose occupation rendered the pilgrimage route to Rome impassable.

Two days ago, back in London, I had a coffee with Ahmed, who was miserable, having taken a month off work to visit his family in Gaza and been unable to get there. His mum's unwell again and he's desperate to see her and all of them. He's been trying to secure permission to enter Gaza through an Israeli NGO which supposedly helps Palestinians abroad obtain visas to visit the Occupied Territories, but it's come to nothing, and now, he said, they're ignoring his calls. He even flew out to Egypt on spec, to see if he could get through at the Rafah Crossing, but as usual it was shut and he ended up stuck in Cairo, a city for which he's developed an intense loathing after countless ordeals of bullying and humiliation at the hands of Egyptian officials.

'And really, they're just dying by slow degrees in Gaza,' he said.

'It's like a slow death. They say it would have been better if they'd all just been killed in the war. This is a death by a thousand cuts.'

Next stop was my Apple Mac supplier, just down the road in Islington, to get a replacement for my stolen laptop. My contact there is a Jewish friend – we'll call him Benny – who has supplied and serviced all my Macs over the years. He's the kindest fellow you could hope to do business with, and, genuinely distressed to hear about the theft, he ran around like a blue-arsed fly to find me a replacement in just twenty-four hours, which was a tall order. He's a religious Jew and was just off to Israel with his wife and kids for a holiday. 'It's my nephew's Bar Mitzvah, and we'll all be staying together on a kibbutz,' he said. 'It'll be so wonderful to get the whole family together again after so long. My wife's a seventh-generation Israeli, so there's a huge family there – there's some I haven't even met yet.'

Lynn has a new granddaughter just born back home, Daisy Belle, whom she won't see for another month and a half, when we reach the end of the Italian leg of the Walk, but this is her choice, something she's agreed with her daughter in advance. I told Benny I was about to walk across the Alps with my kids, and he was enthralled. I didn't tell him we're on a pilgrimage to Jerusalem for Palestinian rights. I chickened out. I felt completely pinioned between the two encounters. Two guys, more or less the same age, living within half a mile of each other in London, both wanting the most normal and natural thing in the world: to visit their families back home. Trying to share Benny's enthusiasm for his holiday, I felt hollow, and horrible, as if I was betraying both him and Ahmed by not speaking. I wished I had the time and energy to broach the difficult topic with him, and vowed to find a moment in the future to do so.

My Aunt Rony's funeral was another regathering of the clan, an act of 're-membering' the story of her long and eventful life, which I found deeply moving and nourishing. It's a great sadness to me that, after the loss of my father and brother, for one reason or another I lost contact to some extent with my paternal family. Not for lack of effort on their part, and not because of any falling out, but simply because . . . well, because things drift and change. I've re-established contact more recently.

At one point, my cousin Max, who's a pilot with British Midlands but lives in the West Country, mentioned that he and his wife Sacha have been running the Padstow to Land's End Marathon for the past few years and have always made a point of stopping off at Zennor to pay their respects to 'Uncle Phil' and Matthew. I found myself unspeakably moved by this, completely taken off guard, learning that, despite the fragmentation of our family by tragedies which have blasted us far apart, my cousin has made such efforts to preserve and cherish the memory of my father and brother.

'When I came to our father's ancient tomb,
I saw a spring of fresh-poured milk flowed down
from the top of the mound, and all about, the tomb
was garlanded with all the flowers that grew . . .
and straightway my eyes were filled with tears of joy.

. . . Who in all the world would send
Such offerings and put them on our father's tomb?'[1]

[Sophocles' *Electra*, ll. 860-864 & 897-898]

The arbitrary cancellation of a Ryanair flight which prevented Rony's closest surviving relative, my Aunt Alison, from attending her sister's funeral, was a cruel blow, and reminded me of Ahmed's predicament. We reunite to share and complete each other's stories and are each enlarged, deepened, restored; the tribe is re-membered. But for Palestinians, exile, occupation and blockade leave them dismembered.

Sembrancher is a ridiculously picturesque village of timber-shingled Alpine chalets, replete with cuckoo clocks, garden gnomes, wooden flower tubs and hanging baskets bursting with geraniums, and antique iron implements hanging from the eaves. At any moment you expect to see Heidi skipping out of the pages of children's fiction with Uncle Alp and Peter the goatherd and the rest of them. Our new driver, Tony, has found, ingeniously, a chalet for our lunch, which is a kind of communal bakery for the village, where he lays out a smorgasbord of Swiss cheeses, bread, pâté, tomatoes, fruit and other goodies, which we descend on like a plague of locusts. Our host is a delightful young woman called Frederica who holds the bakery keys and seems very pleased to help us. Unsurprisingly, in this pristine mountain hamlet of sparkling meadows, glistening pine forests, immaculately rustic chalets and azure skies of air so fresh you can taste it, the village loo is spotlessly clean. After lunch, a group of us take the steep, challenging path over the hill, while the rest follow the road round for an easier stroll down into Orsières. We follow a set of Stations of the Cross up a knee-creaking staircase back and forth across the hillside through the pine forest. Jacob's not familiar with the tableau of Simon of Cyrene helping to carry the cross, and asks me about it.

Earlier today, chatting with Lynn about prayer, I found myself recalling my friend Mark Oakley's luminous book, *The Collage of God*, in which he shares the thoughts and illuminations of poets, thinkers, artists and theologians who have inspired him over the years. In one chapter, 'Praying', he explores some of the commonly held definitions and understandings of prayer – most of which he feels uncomfortable with. Then he puts forward an alternative: in the language of the ancient Assyrians, he says, the word for 'prayer' was the same as their word for the opening or unclenching of the fist. How would it be, Mark asks, if we were to approach prayer in this way ourselves? Not as the muscular action of the will, banging our clenched fist on the table, making demands, and not as a defensive shield, trying to protect ourselves from the 'slings and arrows of outrageous fortune', but rather as an unclenching, a surrender, a letting-go before God of all that we cannot carry.

Bethan talks about art therapy and the essence of her work, as we breast the pine ridge and begin the descent into Orsières. On the way down we're caught in a downpour, so a dozen of us cram into a tiny derelict timber cabin to shelter for a few minutes. The little wooden shack is perched precipitously by the roadside, with a steep drop away to the east down the mountain, so I suggest we all keep very still.

Orsières is a pretty little one-horse town with a fourteenth-century bell tower and an ancient bridge over the River Dranse, dating from Roman times, and, as in Martigny, the tiny Alpine railway runs through it. Records date from AD 987, when the town was known as *Pons Ursarii*, Bridge of the Bear-Trainers. The *Ursari*, or

Richinara, are a traditionally nomadic tribe or clan among the Roma people who specialised in animal handling, in particular the training of dancing bears and monkeys. As to what they were doing here in 987, if anything, history appears to be silent. In Old French, *orsière* or *oursière* means a bear's den, or an area teeming with bears, and the town's coat-of-arms over the centuries has been a bear in all sorts of positions, *rampant* in Jan Stumpf's *Swiss Chronicle* of 1548, *passant* (walking on all fours as you'd expect) in a local painter's crest of 1745, and, most recently, *salient* – standing on hind legs with forepaws raised, as if leaping. Or maybe dancing.

The chat over dinner with Jude, David and Arthur is of nudity in theatre (mine and other people's), life drawing, the naked form, the difference between men's and women's desires, etc. From desire we segue to love, romance, marriage. Is marriage a one-state solution or two? Do you have to be whole in yourself to be fit for relationship? Or do we complete each other? Conjoined units or missing halves? Jude thinks the former, David the latter. Jude describes an adolescent-style romance with her late husband Graham, even though they were both in mid-life when they met. Arthur talks about safaris and snakes.

After dinner, Benedict, Eleanor, Jacob and I have a wander in the balmy evening air through 'downtown Orsières', laughing about the day. We stroll round the corner from the hotel, suddenly off the pristine beaten track, and find a ramshackle bar, a spit-and-sawdust flea-pit filled with an amazingly battered-looking bunch of locals who all seem to have black eyes, cross eyes, missing teeth and knock knees. Maybe they're the bear trainers.

Monday 31 July

Today we have a guide, Sarah, to climb with us from Orsières to the Great St Bernard Pass. She's been working in these mountains for twenty-odd years, in the ski shop and guiding groups walking in the mountains. Today will be a heck of a schlep, she tells us, a 2,400-metre climb over a distance of 38 km. So, after our morning reflection, off we set, left past the little railway station and down some steps to cross the Dranse, then south along the *Route de Podemainge*, crossing the river again after a few hundred yards and

98

veering up on to a wide gravel track which zigzags steeply uphill towards the hamlet of Montatuay, and so on to a footpath through the pinewoods. Sunlight floods the slopes and rocky scarps across the valley, falling in great blotches and spots of radiance stencilled through the clouds. So much sky and space. Lizard-skinned pines and firs sway and sigh in the breeze, as tall and skinny as telegraph poles, feathered with twiggy quills and ragged bristles like scrawny brushes, waving floppy mops of foliage high overhead, and here and there a parchment-peeling silver birch glimmers baldly through unruly swathes of needle fronds. Rough timber-clad cottages sit high on stacks of stone and concrete, decked with strings of holed and pointed wooden clothes pegs like tiny clogs. Reservoir lakes ripple grey-green in the sun behind huge, curving dams of sculpture-smooth concrete, poised to flood the dry stream beds, signposted forbidden to walkers, at the opening of a sluice. Amazing insects bustle and patrol through the wildflower meadows, some kind of red-winged bee or wasp I've never seen before, and a hovering moth-shaped flying fortress with luminous green wings. Climbing a glistening meadow slope so steep I have to grab handholds in the grass, I come nose to nose with a small, white starburst of flower, bright yellow nuggets at its heart, a sea anemone probing the air with fingers of snowy floss, and realise with a thrill I'm seeing an edelweiss for the first time.

We fall in with Mateus, not the little boy from Dampierre, but a Flemish-speaking PhD student from Ghent who's researching new biochemical methods for analysing blood samples. He's walking the Via Francigena in stages with his brother, and is catching up a stretch which his brother did previously without him, before they resume the route together.

We eat lunch on a grassy knoll on top of a granite mound overlooking the thirteenth-century church of Bourg-St-Pierre, an idyllic mountain village 1,600 metres above sea level, where the original pilgrim hostel and monastery date from the eighth century, even older than the Hospice du St Bernard at the pass. Another superb picnic-spot find by our redoubtable new driver. Tony was an aerospace engineer for thirty years and used to live and work in Israel. 'That's why I support the Palestinian cause,' he says. 'I was there in '82, when the massacres of Sabra and Shatila happened in Lebanon.

That's what opened my eyes.' He drove a lorry on the aid convoy from Britain to Gaza in 2010. *And he doesn't snore.*

We sit, looking over the rooftops shingled with overlapping *lauze* tiles of Alpine slate, back down over the valley we've ascended, with the satisfaction of having earned our lunch. I 'catch' the lady bellringer sneaking into a small postern door in the church tower to ring the bell at noon, and photograph her in action. Do they really ring the church bell on the hour all through the day? And at night? Maybe they have a rota of bellringers. If so, it must be half the village population; the place seems pretty deserted, with just a few old folk to keep the bare minimum going. The rest of the houses, I assume, are owned by rich city dwellers as ski chalets for the winter season. The reason they're all elevated on stone stacks, Sarah tells us, is to raise the door and floor out of reach of mice and rats.

The mountain ridge marches up along the skyline, serrated like jagged teeth, with patches of snow now appearing here and there. Four hours to the pass. Trees are growing scarcer now, giving way to the bare grass-clad sinews of limestone and shale, heaved from prehistoric oceans by tectonic convulsion forty million years ago and writhen by the grinding ice of vast glaciers.

Sarah gives us a quiz, during a mid-afternoon breather, on photosynthesis and colour in plants and flowers at high altitude. Green, of course, is predominant; red grows scarcer as you climb higher; the highest flowers of all are blue. Onwards and upwards, with throbbing calves and twinging knees, feeling, like Rabbi Heschel, as if our legs are praying, or at least interceding 'with groans too deep for words'. The Melancholy of Anatomy. My kids are all doing valiantly. Benedict confides in me at one point that he's genuinely astonished at the hardihood of our redoubtable sexagenarians, and hopes he can keep up with them. It's touching to see how much younger, or perhaps softer, and less cynical my kids become in this very mixed company and in the glorious outdoors, away from the cut-and-thrust of London, playground politics, the social whirl and Snapchat/Instagram maelstrom. Touching also to hear them chatting away with the walkers, and to feel united with all three in this endeavour, and ordeal. Eleanor seems so young sometimes (even for sixteen), and wonderfully gentle, and restored.

I notice she and Jacob have brought drawing pads with them, quite unprompted. At one point today, probably around lunchtime, Jacob got out his pad and was drawing a detailed sketch of a meadow grass seed head.

At last, scaling an ever steeper rugged stony path between barbed peaks and vast rocky shoulders pooled with drifts of snow, we sight the cross on the skyline above us and ascend the old cobbled track of the *Combe des Morts* to the pass, 8,114 feet above sea level, where the 1,000-year old Hospice du St Bernard nestles in a cleft in the mountain ridge. After pretty much unbroken sunshine all day, we gain the pass in a grey, cloudy early evening, with many photographs, hugs and high fives. It's a great feeling of triumph and satisfaction at the end of a very long day. Hats off and medals all round, and a vat of cold beer for me. My man of the match award has to go to Jude, I reckon, who had a hip replaced less than a year ago and, at sixty-six, is a bloody amazing trooper. The Hospice, open all hours since the year 1050, straddles the road at the pass, the original chapels and pilgrim hostel housed in a long, sturdy, white-walled building to the east, with the more modern Hôtel de l'Hospice to the west, built in the early twentieth century as an overflow facility to accommodate increasing numbers of travellers, with a 'Bridge of Sighs' linking the two. On a rocky knoll to the east of the Hospice stands the ancient stone mortuary, burial chamber for unfortunate travellers down the centuries who lost their lives attempting to cross the mountains.

Bernard of Menthon was born in the early eleventh century to a wealthy family near Annecy in the County of Savoy in the kingdom of Arles and, according to popular legend, avoided an arranged marriage by leaping out of a window in the Chateau de Menthon the night before the wedding. Most helpfully, angels appeared to catch him and lower him, unhurt, to the ground forty feet below. Determining to enter the service of the church, he became an acolyte to the Archdeacon of Aosta, and was ordained priest. Outstanding in learning and virtue, as well as escapology, in due course he succeeded his master as Archdeacon and resolved to devote his ministry to the people of the Alps, still languishing in pagan beliefs and practices, and spent the next forty years travelling and preaching throughout the remote mountain villages, notching up a creditable score of conversions and miracles in the process. As Archdeacon of Aosta, he was charged with the care of the poor and also travellers, and so he founded a canonry and hospice at the highest point of the perilous mountain pass across the Pennine Alps on the pilgrim route to Rome. There he established a community of 'canons regular': not monks but priests with an active ministry in the surrounding locality, committed to the Rule of St Augustine, whose generous hospitality became renowned throughout the region.

As part of their mission, the canons would go out in search of travellers waylaid by snowstorms or freezing weather, accompanied by their dogs who were trained to find and rescue pilgrims lost, stranded or injured. These strong, loyal herding dogs of the Valois canton became known, at least as early as the seventeenth century, as St Bernards. The canons would offer food, clothing and hospitality to travellers in need, and bury the dead in the stone mortuary at the Hospice. The final approach to the pass, the *Combe des Morts*, is notorious for avalanches, and was the terror of travellers in times past. Giant walls of snow can accumulate at the head of the valley and on surrounding crags, blown by strong winds from the Swiss side of the pass, and reach such a perilous teetering mass that the slightest vibration can send the whole drift hurtling down the combe, obliterating everything in its path. No surprise they named this the 'Valley of the Dead', and our last approach up the old cobbled track to the pass, the 'road of the dead'.

The canons still keep St Bernards as pets at the Hospice and nearby *Chenil*, but they're no longer used widely for mountain rescue because they're extremely heavy and difficult to train, despite their friendly, loyal temperament. Nowadays, mountain rescue services use German Shepherds, who pick up the drill much more quickly and are light enough to travel two in a helicopter. One or two St Bernards are kept in training for avalanche rescue, where their massive strength equips them like no other dogs for pulling buried travellers out of deep drifts or rock slides. The unnamed 'faithful hound' in Longfellow's poem 'Excelsior' is clearly a St Bernard, who must have wished he'd got there sooner to avert the composition of one of the most mawkish flights of folderol in the Victorian era.

> A traveller, by the faithful hound,
> Half-buried in the snow was found,
> Still grasping in his hand of ice
> That banner with the strange device,
> *Excelsior!*

Excelsior. Onwards and upwards. 'That voice kept ringing in my ears,' Longfellow wrote to a friend, describing how the poem came to him late one night as he was trying to get to sleep, so he got up, lit a lamp and wrote it out. If only he'd had temazepam.

It's extraordinary to think that the Hospice du St Bernard has been open continuously, providing an unbroken ministry of hospitality to pilgrims for 1,000 years, never closing. After a beer or three in the hotel bar, we drag our throbbing feet and creaking limbs up to the pilgrim-house restaurant for dinner, chit-chat, good-natured gossip and ribaldry in a euphoric daze of bonhomie and exhaustion. Rather uncomfortably stuffed, I go through to the Hospice and across the 'Bridge of Sighs' with Chris, Tim, Denise and Bethan. The main chapel upstairs is an unexpectedly gaudy affair, with handsomely carved wooden stalls for the canons down either side, garishly painted panels in the domed ceiling illustrating the life and deeds of St Bernard, and someone up above playing the organ very badly, while visitors wander around laughing and taking photographs. I'm tempted to go up to the organ loft and play something half decent, but instead I follow Chris and the others down to the crypt chapel (I'm on sabbatical from church music, after all), to hear Buddhist chants and devotional poems, which somewhat wash over me. Indigestion and windy gut make it difficult to 'mean' anything very much in my prayers, so I settle for intellectual assent. That will have to do, God. It's a dark, spare, but welcoming catacomb chapel, with a deeply recessed sanctuary, cut back into the rock. After our little reflection, I decide to stay for compline, although I have to vacate the front row as the priests and nuns and members of the community file in and it's made clear to me that visitors' seats are at the back.

The priests wear white polo-necked tunics with pectoral crosses. Several of them carry tiny little prayer benches, tucking their calves and feet back underneath them and kneeling upright. Weirdly, someone is filming the service from a camera tripod set up in the top left corner of the chapel. Several priest-cantors lead the singing in French in rich baritone voices, and the assembled community and congregation sing beautiful plainsong cadences in reply, with much crossing and many obeisances. A young woman does a reading, frowning with concentration, and someone lets rip an enormous fart. No one reacts. We sing the *Nunc Dimittis* in French to a very pleasing, harmonised chant, the office hymn *Te lucis ante terminum* and the highly appropriate Psalm 121, 'I will lift up mine eyes unto the hills'.

Earlier this summer, at the funeral of Phyllis Harrison, the remarkable and inimitable mum of my dear friend Andy, the priest quoted the last verse of this psalm from the King James Version: 'The Lord shall preserve thy going out and thy coming in from this time forth, and even for evermore.' 'Pilgrims on the rough road to Jerusalem were encouraged to look up to the hills,' he said, 'and to trust that the God they sought in Jerusalem was also with them on the road.'

7

Aut viam inveniam aut faciam

'I shall find a path or make one.'

Hannibal

Saturday 2 September

I'M SITTING SCRIBBLING notes on a hotel terrace looking out over the busy ferry port of Ancona, on our last morning in Italy. A kaleidoscope of recollections revolves in my memory, a snapshot collage of a month walking across the northern neck of the Italian peninsula. After three months of blisters, my feet have recovered at last, following the (idiotically simple) chance discovery that one pair of socks, not two, is the way to go. The foot-lore fundamentalists are wrong; two pairs of socks make your feet hot and give you blisters. I've just come off the phone from wishing happy birthday to my oldest friend Max Jones, a historian at Manchester University and expert on Scott of the Antarctic. 'It's all about the feet, Butch,' he said, and quoted the fateful entry in Scott's last journal: '*My right foot has gone, nearly all the toes — two days ago I was proud possessor of best feet. These are the steps of my downfall . . .*'

Our hotel, auspiciously named *Fortuna*, is almost on top of the ferry port, right down in the thick of things, the multicultural maelstrom of Italy's eastern seaboard: dirty, busy, noisy and vibrant.

It seems a million miles since we set out walking down the Aosta Valley, but the presence in Ancona of many migrants from Somalia, Morocco, Sudan, Iraq and Syria, whom we've seen in increasing numbers, begging on the streets of every town along Italy's Adriatic Riviera, reminds me of the poem we heard read exactly one month ago, gathered in the cable car station at Pré-Saint-Didier: Brian Bilston's ingenious palindrome, 'Refugees'.

Back then, the refugee crisis seemed a million miles away, as we descended from the cloud-wreathed Olympian heights of the Italian Alps to the city of Augusta Praetoria Salassorum, Roman Aosta, where cafes and shops were coming alive at 9 a.m., wafting irresistible olfactory temptations from every pore and portal, glorious aromas of Italian coffee and freshly baked pastries of all shapes and sizes: cream-filled *pasticiotti* and sugar-dusted *panettoni*; tubular stalks of Sicilian *cannoli*, oozing a sap of sweet ricotta; almond *biscotti* and flaky shells of *sfogliatelli*, exquisite fluffy pastry parcels of delectable custard cream. Dawdling behind, I was the first to break rank. The other walkers, seeing me catch up sheepishly, loaded with pastries and coffee, unsurprisingly demanded equality. Chris yielded, far too fond of coffee himself to tell me off.

Second breakfast scoffed, we wrenched ourselves from the fleshpots of the old city and pressed on through elegant parkland, past guano-spattered statues of the Emperor Augustus and Victor Emmanuel II, *le roi chasseur*, the huntsman king, shotgun in hand, sporting plus-fours and jaunty Alpine hat, a dead ibex slumped at his feet. Apparently these gardens were planted to frame this statue of the first king of the newly unified Italy after the *Risorgimento*. On the plinth he's described as *Le Roi du Savoie*, King of Savoy, an independent county from mediaeval times, a territory of huge strategic importance and influence comprising the Valle d'Aosta and parts of the French Alps, the *Haute Savoie*, and Switzerland.

Onwards through Aosta, beneath the massive arches of the Roman city walls, nine feet thick at the base, and past the 'Leper's Tower', the *Tour du Lépreux,* and the ruins of the 4,000-seat Roman theatre, to the Arch of Augustus, a perfectly preserved 2,000-year-old *arc de triomphe* on a glistening grass-green roundabout outside the city walls. Built in 35 BC to celebrate the Roman victory over the local tribe of the Salassi, it led to the ancient road down the Aosta Valley to Chatillon, Pont Saint Martin and Ivrea, now the route of the railway, which we'll follow in parallel on the Via Francigena path. And so we climbed the northern slopes of the valley to follow the way to Chatillon, through Saint-Christophe and the Commune of Quart, with its castle and convent of the *Mater Misericordiae*, the 'contemplative centre of the Aosta Valley Church', as Pope John Paul II described it, run by the nuns of the discalced Carmelite Order, bless their non-existent cotton socks ('discalced' = barefoot, eschewing shoes). After a pitstop in the shady grounds of the *Castello di Quart*, we pressed on eastwards towards a late lunch in the village of Nus. With snow-capped Alps in the distance behind us and high slopes of sweet-scented conifers, fruit orchards, vines and meadows to either side of the valley, this has to be one of the most beautiful places to walk in Europe.

Listening back to voice memos on my phone, a record of my impressions as we jogged along, carries me back to those moments: walking along an idyllic series of paths cut in the valley side, with here and there a little bit of shady tree cover, and away down to the right, the distant noise of the big road running along the valley floor. You can never quite escape the noise of the main road in this valley, until you get really high up in the remote villages. There are lots of farmed fields down the slopes to the right, and swathes of dark-green forestry plantations over the far side of the valley, and up to our left, wild meadows thick with fabulous tall grasses, wild flowers and heather, strewn with rocks and wild holm oaks, vines and acacias, and fantastically noisy cicadas or similar insects in the trees overhead, squeaking and squawking away. All these paths have water channels gushing alongside, which gives a wonderfully refreshing, energising feeling to the walk, despite the heat. We've just seen a sign telling us that this network of irrigation channels and aqueducts across the valley is known as the *nus*, built between the thirteenth and fifteenth centuries, to channel the vast amounts of water coming down off the mountains into an ingeniously engineered system of micro-capillaries, preventing flooding and irrigating the slopes and terraces of the valley sides. Land which would otherwise have been too dry for cultivation has been transformed over the centuries into incredibly fertile terraces where we see an abundance of fruit and veg, and the vines of 2,000 years of wine production.

Passing a handsome farmhouse chalet at one point along the way, Chris and I meet Felippo, a charming, urbane fellow, now a viti-culturist and wine merchant, who worked in the past for Gilat, an Israeli engineering firm. 'One time, a few years ago,' he says, 'I was working in Egypt with two guys – one Israeli, one Palestinian – and

I said to the Israeli guy, "Can we not all work together?" and he said, "Well, the problem is, first we need to kill them all.'" I give him the spiel in Italian, a script I've learned which is becoming fairly fluent now: *Noi caminiamo di Londra a Gerusalemme, per i diritti di Palestinesi, per parita di diritti per tutti in Terra Santa*, etc. He's intrigued and inspired. 'Perhaps we can get something going here in Italy,' he says. '*Bene auspicio!*'

The Via Francigena runs through many farmyards, gardens and allotments on its route along the Valle d'Aosta, including an extraordinary house encrusted with dozens of pilgrimage murals, wooden plaques, wrought-iron figurines and totems: a shrine to globetrotting wayfarers curated by Marcello, a big fat fellow in a string vest with a week of white stubble, who emerges bleary-eyed, offering to make us coffee, at a price. *Grazie mille, Marcello, e molto gentile, ma non possiamo fermarci . . .*

A little later, we share our mission with an elderly peasant lady as she pushes fruit to us through her fence. '*E troppo longo camino!*' she exclaims, astounded, '*ma è meravigliosa . . .* everyone is always fighting and stealing (*rubare, rubare*) and we need peace, to bring people everyone together. *Io pregherò per voi.*'

That evening, after staggering into beautiful Châtillon around 7 p.m. and ordering every bottle of cold beer in the hotel, we

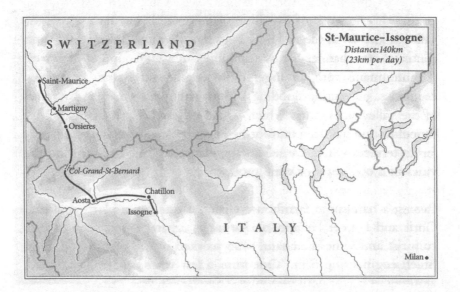

staggered up the hill for a pizza. Later still I staggered down to the hotel basement to join Eleanor and Jacob in the healing waters of the jacuzzi which they'd discovered down there. After soaking and bobbing for half an hour or so, wonderfully pummelled by magical fountains of bubbling jets, I peel grossly huge white and yellow blister flaps off the soles of my feet (sorry, dear reader), beneath which the skin shines pink and vulnerable, like a limpet out of its shell. My feet, to employ a medical term, are f★★★★d.

Flicking the snapshots, I recall walking from Châtillon to Issogne along a stretch of perfectly preserved Roman road, the *Via delle Gallie*, curling around the wall of the valley, wide enough at points for two carriages to ride abreast, with a retaining wall to the left and a drop away to the right, down a slope of fruit orchards and vines. This takes us through Montjovet, a district between the villages of Almas and Toffo, where an ancient Roman temple dedi- cated to Jupiter/Jove preserves a plethora of Roman remains. We've also walked through a number of villages abandoned in the early-mid twentieth century after the inhabitants found it impossible to make a living any more from farming. In previous centuries, the bulk of the valley's population had their permanent dwellings in the highest mountain villages where they grew wheat, potatoes, oats and barley, only descending to the hamlets on the lower slopes at certain times of year to cultivate their vines, fruit orchards and vegetable plots. The economic and social upheavals of the twentieth century led to the gradual abandonment of agriculture as the region's primary livelihood, and many villages were deserted.

We trudge at last into Issogne for a late lunch, where we're greeted by a bouquet of Roses – Chris's wife Sarah and daughter Millie, and Mike's wife Gill and son Nat, who've all come out to join us – with much sweaty hugging and back-slapping. We picnic in the town square adjacent to the castle, the church of St Mary of the Assumption and a bijou gallery and museum. Waiting for the second shuttle to the digs, Lynn and I explore the castle grounds, and the church, which we discover is decorated with striking murals by a contemporary Italian artist, credited as L. Bartolo, who has illustrated many parables and Gospel episodes in a gritty, magical style reminiscent of the mural art of Latin America, the frescoes of

Diego Rivera in Mexico City, and also of the graffiti art on the Wall in Bethlehem.

Astonishingly, there's a Nativity scene set in contemporary occupied Bethlehem. Just to the left of a Holy Family cocooned in a blaze of light, we see an angel welcoming a shepherd and beyond them, a watchtower, barbed-wire fence, tank and drone. It's Bethlehem today, under Occupation. Above the whole scene is a picture of Adam and Eve being driven from the garden of Eden – a walled garden on a high hill, very like a settlement – one scene of exile underscoring another, with a six-winged angel keeping them out; and there below is the Virgin Mary with Jesus, the eternal *Logos*, conceived in her womb. It's astonishing to come across such

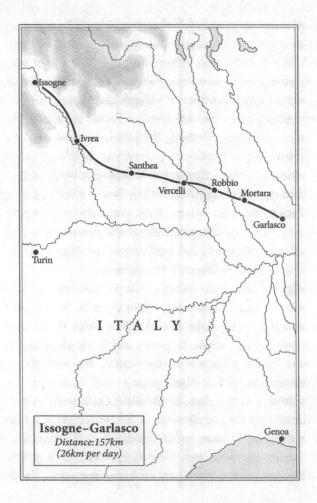

Issogne–Garlasco
Distance: 157km
(26km per day)

images by chance, in a pretty little church in a sleepy little town in the heart of the Aosta Valley, every spare bit of wall space covered with amazing murals testifying to a radical vision of liberation theology. It feels almost like an angelic visitation.

Clouds of yellow dragonflies flock across the memory viewfinder, a glittering swarm which assailed us on all sides one day, along the beautiful vineyard paths from Pont Saint Martin to Ivrea. It must have been hatching-day for the yellow dragonflies of Piedmont. A few days later, I'm sitting on the rickety wooden balcony of a fairy-tale Alpine cottage high up in the tiny mountain village of Persod, an idyllic *lauze*-shingled chalet lent to me and my family for a few days by a very generous friend of a friend. To our great joy, my wife Nancy and youngest son Joey have come out to join me and the older three, so for a few days all six of us will be walking together, 'commuting' from Persod to join the Walk each day.

There's been a downpour today in the Valle d'Aosta, an absolute deluge drenching the hills with rain, and I'm sitting looking straight across the valley at an almost unearthly view of the Italian Alps wreathed in mist and cloud, like the *Hithaeglir*, the Misty Mountains of Tolkien's Middle Earth, as if some vast cauldron was bubbling away, enveloping all the mountains with steam. There's rain trickling everywhere, but we're dry under the eaves of the balcony. Tall poplars dripping with water like a tropical rainforest block the view to one side, and down across the valley lush green meadows soaked with rain seem to pulse with the quenched heat of the last few days. Birdsong twitters through the streaming susurrus. I saw a hare loping across the meadow just now, and one or two birds flitting back and forth down there from one roost to another, probably trying to keep dry. The roofs of this little village stretching below us are shingled in Alpine style, interleaving slabs of slate and limestone shaped like shells, or scales on the skin of a giant lizard, perforated with little chimney stacks. This tiny hamlet's almost entirely deserted. Over to the left, a great welter of cloud is dispersing gradually, tearing wisps and wreaths of smoke rising and thinning through the treetops.

There was some lightning earlier this evening; the sky above is white and grey with vapour and, across the valley, the clouds are beginning to dissipate, settling like great drifts of cotton wool in the hollows of the mountains and curling around the shoulders of the hills. The tops of the mountains are shrouded in mist and, every so often, through the blanket of white, you can see crags peeping through, redolent of mystery and magic, great dark masses looming through the fog. The mists and clouds have different intensities – in some of the higher valleys and ravines it's a really deep, dense white, and then elsewhere it drifts across the lower slopes and foothills in wispy tendrils, teased out into spun flaxen fibres of gossamer. Over to my right there's a haze or veil of mist drifting westwards and beginning to shroud the conifers, wafting around the trunks, encasing them in obscurity. A forest of little chimney stacks poke up through the swirl from slate roofs to the right. It's an utterly magical and astonishing scene.

In Bologna, halfway point of our pilgrimage, a remarkable covered walkway shelters the path from the hilltop Monastery of the Virgin of San Luca down to the city. According to legend, an eleventh-century pilgrim brought an ikon of the Virgin Mary, painted by St Luke himself (patron saint of artists as well as doctors) from the Hagia Sophia in Constantinople to Bologna, where a hermitage was established on the hilltop overlooking the city, tended by two holy women, to shelter and enshrine the ikon. Over the centuries, the tradition of an annual procession developed, in which the ikon was carried down from the monastery to bless the city and its inhabitants. The walkway was built over the period of a hundred years, from the late seventeenth century, to protect the ikon from the elements in its annual procession. The beautiful triptych at my church, painted by the numinously gifted Edinburgh artist Paul Martin, has an image of St Luke (modelled on my friend and Arthur's neighbour Malcolm Doney) painting the first ever portrait of the Virgin Mary.

We marched the Roman-road route of the Via Emilia from Bologna, mostly along busy main roads, where the reflected heat of the tarmac scorches many ankles with rashes, through a landscape of ploughed fields, rippling red-brown seas of glinting furrows between green wooded hills, down to Castel San Pietro di Terme. Here, in this beautiful spa town, staying in a beautiful riverside hotel presided over by the beautiful Francesca, we said farewell to our wonderful driver and factotum Nick, and welcomed Fatima, a photo-journalist whom I'd met at a number of solidarity events back in the UK.

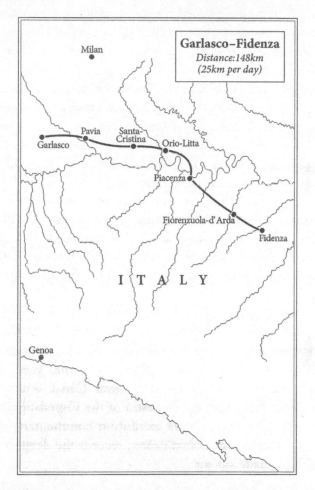

Fatima was born and grew up in Shatila refugee camp in Beirut, infamous for the 1982 massacre of up to 3,500 Palestinian refugees, Lebanese Shi'ites and other ethnic minority residents in the camp and the surrounding Sabra neighbourhood, perpetrated by Maronite Phalangist militias, under the eyes of the IDF, who surrounded the area to prevent residents escaping and fired illuminating flares to assist the Phalangists in their butchery. A subsequent Israeli government inquiry found that IDF personnel had been aware that the

massacre was in progress and failed to stop it. The enquiry held
Israel indirectly responsible for the atrocities and Ariel Sharon, as
Defence Minister, personally responsible, forcing his resignation.
Sharon had ordered the Phalangists into Sabra and Shatila, allegedly
to 'flush out terrorists' blamed for the assassination two days earlier
of Lebanon's President-elect Bashir Gemayel. But the only people
in the camps were defenceless civilians, refugees who'd lived there
in exile since 1948.

'Half of my family were killed in Shatila,' Fatima told me after dinner.
'My mother's sister, and all her immediate family. Her daughter was
pregnant, and the Israeli soldiers made a bet, for a can of beer – boy
or girl? Then they cut her open and killed the baby boy. They said,
"He would have grown up to be a Palestinian terrorist." Yes, the
Phalangists were there, but it was the Israelis who did it. Sharon was
watching the whole thing. My other cousin, who survived, told me
she saw Israeli soldiers outside her house, giving orders to the Phalangists,
in English. "Finish your work and come out," they said. Then the
women and children were all rounded up into a sports stadium and
killed. Some of us managed to escape through the alleyways.'

The next day a group of us made an unforgettable trip to Venice
to see an astonishing exhibition of paintings, 'Exodus', by Safet
Zec, a Bosnian artist, inspired by the current refugee crisis to transform La Chiesa Santa Maria della Pietà, the very beautiful
eighteenth-century church on the Royal Canal where Vivaldi
directed the all-girl choir and orchestra of the Ospedale della Pietà,
into a 'forest of wounds', as the exhibition commentary described
it. My voice memo, transcribed below, records the deep impression
the exhibition made on me.

I'm here in Venice, in the church of Santa Maria della Pietà, Holy
Mary of Pity, a wonderful little baroque church, and it's moving
to think that Vivaldi lived and worked his whole life here, director
of music for the Ospedale della Pietà, writing music for the
orphaned girl children of Venice. I've just wandered down from
St Mark's Square to see an exhibition of paintings by Safet Zec,
an extraordinary Bosnian artist exiled in the 1990s because of the
civil war and the siege of his home city of Sarajevo. He was my

age, forty-eight, when he fled Sarajevo in 1992 to come to Italy. He lost everything – his home, and all his work, which remained in his studio there in Sarajevo – and had to start again, rebuilding his life and career from almost nothing. Subsequently his work and home were restored to him, and he now lives between Venice and Sarajevo, but back then he was destitute. So he understands the refugee experience intimately. He has made this incredible exhibition of paintings called 'Exodus', here in the Chiesa della Pietà. And it really is almost overwhelming. They hang, unframed, on ragged great lengths of canvases made of collages, newspaper articles and photographs stuck together to create a kind of news footage papyrus of the refugee crisis; huge, hanging canvases actually fashioned from the media storm of images that assails us daily. He's painted a brown-green wash over each canvas, as a base, a backdrop for the most astonishing cycle of paintings of exile, flight, the plight of refugees, very much echoing and in tribute to the Pietà paintings and sculptures of Michelangelo, visceral images of limbs and bodies, sinews, hands hanging, arms embracing and clutching, feet and limbs bent, trailing, weary, haggard-looking adults, their sinews standing out, carrying infants or wounded adults into exile. Each figure is in white, almost like grave clothes, pyjamas. Even though some of the children wear sneakers or trainers, there's a theme of white in the clothes – rags, robes – and the figures are therefore timeless, universal and yet terribly contemporary. And here and there, headlines, photographs and snatches of newsprint glimmer through the dark brown and green wash.

There's a huge frieze to my right, on the south side of the church, a throng of figures on a raft, some slumped exhausted, limbs dangling over the edge, some looking in desperate hope towards the horizon, on an enormous, epic scale: five separate canvases hung side by side down the length of the church. The exhibition commentary tells me that the piece is, among other things, a clear homage to Géricault's 1819 painting, 'The Raft of the Medusa'. Some figures are sitting, some kneeling, some lying, cradling others in their laps.

Here at the western end of the church there's another huge frieze of three suspended canvases, bearing a painting which is almost overwhelming. It's very clearly based on the famous photograph of little Alan, the migrant boy, lying face down, drowned, on the shore of the Mediterranean at Bodrum. As the exhibition commentary reads, 'Zec presents this image with silence, after the great noise that the media attributed to it, and makes it re-emerge in all its truth. On the dark background of the beach, Zec chooses to give up a significant element: colour.' Also in white (not the red T-shirt of the famous photograph), little Alan has lost one shoe, so he has one white sock on his left foot and a little shoe on his right foot. One hand, his left hand, is turned upwards. He's face down, drowned on the shore of the sea. It's very dark, this painting – dark greys and greens – and there he is, this little, martyred, almost . . . angelic figure in white, and it's really very heart rending, against this dark collage of newspaper and magazine articles. A thin red lace at the bottom of the canvas, almost a trickle of blood, refers to the colour of the child's T-shirt (in the media image) and the severing of the thread of his life. Thin and almost imperceptible, the red lace runs around the little boy's sleeve and waist and, down in the bottom right corner, where a copy of the original photograph has been stuck, the red lace becomes script, in which the artist has written, 'caro Alan . . . non sei solo!?' – 'dear Alan . . . you are not alone!?'

This red thread also runs across all the characters on the raft, and in fact through every painting, as a leitmotif of lifeblood unifying all the characters, all humanity. Here, looking up the stunning east end of this church with its beautiful dark-red-draped pillars either side of the altarpiece, between them there is another painting of breathtaking poignancy by Safet Zec: bodies hanging, in a kind of double crucifixion, wrists bound with ropes and hanging, dangling and people lifting them from above and embracing them around the thighs, around the knees. Here in this painting the red thread becomes the trickle of blood running from the wounded flesh of Christ and down the back of the cross. The scene is very like a deposition from the cross scene, and the sinews standing out, the rib cages, the limp humanity are very, very reminiscent of Michelangelo. In this setting it's extremely raw but very, very beautiful.

Safet Zec has written in the exhibition commentary: 'I would like for my art to contribute to the growth of the necessary moral uprising, that only can tear apart this unbearable curtain of indifference.'

We set off really early the next day from Castel San Pietro after a fine breakfast very kindly provided at 5.30 a.m. by the hotel's ancient retainer (who I suspect might have been Francesca's grandfather), to continue down the Via Emilia towards Imola and Faenza. Gathering for our reflection in the shadowy dusk just before dawn, we shouldered our packs and strode out to commence the last stretch across Italy, a series of long, hot days of road walking, ultimately to strike the Adriatic coast at Rimini. All this schlepping along busy main roads in scorching heat is probably my least favourite stretch of the whole pilgrimage thus far, but the truth is that, apart from their cherished Via Francigena, from which we diverted eastwards at Piacenza, Italians don't have a culture of rural footpaths and country walks, and the great Roman roads of Emilia, Flaminia and the Appian Way, repaired and rebuilt over the centuries, have endured to become the asphalt highways of modern Italy, along which we were now trudging so many hot and relentless kilometres. Ah well. *Aut viam inveniam . . .*

Shaking the kaleidoscope, vignettes of these days on the Via Flaminia shift, scatter and constellate: popping into the beautiful sixteenth-century Convent of St Mary Coronata (the Virgin Mary in Glory, Queen of the Universe, if you please) one day just before a mid-morning mass, where an elderly lady, Maria Elena, wept when I told her about our mission. She had worked in refugee camps in the West Bank herself, and was bowled over by the arrival of a sweaty, suntanned bunch of Palestine activist-pilgrims in her church. She introduced us to Father Marco, an eighty-year-old priest who'd served his entire working life in the Philippines and Paraguay. 'Today, and tomorrow, at the mass, we will pray for you,' he said. Following a spiky, modern series of relief sculptures of the Rosary mounted on wooden posts along the roadside for a mile or so after the Convent, the Five Glorious Mysteries, Five Dolorous Mysteries, Five Luminous and Five Joyful — an education for me, Lynn and Naomi. Poaching in the plum and kiwi orchards of Imola, swathed under gauze canopies, presumably to keep the birds off, through long, straight rows of trees laden with boiling hot (and tasteless) fruit . . .

An oasis of angelic hospitality shimmered from mirage into reality one punishing day, after 24 km on the tarmac treadmill, not far from Cesena, where we sheltered at one point from the heat in the shade of a grassy verge and garden wall in front of an isolated homestead. *Would the residents be bothered by us?* I wondered. But then a chap came out with drinks and fruit and invited us into his garden for refreshments. His name was Lorenzo: a tall, slim, handsome, sandy-haired man who introduced us to his wife Simona and their seven children: the Montevecchi family. They're part of a Christian community, called something like the Heart of Jesus and the Virgin Mary, working for peace and justice, based in Rome, Palermo and Cesena, and they showered us with amazing kindness and hospitality – fruit, cake, cold water, Coke and toilets. They loved what we were doing, thanked us for our mission and said, 'God be with you on your journey.'

After the blessed relief of reaching the coast at Rimini, our final trek down the Adriatic Riviera of north-eastern Italy took us through the pretty seaside town of Cattolica and a glittering hullabaloo of early-morning harbour scenes: fishermen laying out their catch, glistening silver and wriggling, on the wharf sides; cafes opening up and brewing the first coffee of the day; elderly residents and holidaymakers cycling along the esplanade and walking their dogs; and tractors ploughing up the beach and smoothing it out into a fresh, pleasing plain of golden sand, flat as a bowling green.

From Cattolica we climbed over the wooded headland of Focara along the forest paths, vineyards and cornfields of the Monte San Bartolo national park, passing the Ospedale of Gabicce Mare, a hostel for pilgrims to Rome. Famed for its clifftop beacon-fires, lit to warn ships off the reefs, the headland had been engulfed by a series of wildfires a week or two before, which raged across the promontory leaving an aftermath of blackened, twisted stumps and stalks of immolated vegetation and charred earth slopes all across the clifftops and hillsides scorched by the blaze.

On Lynn's last morning, we gathered in the old Roman piazza of Fano, terracotta jewel of the Adriatic coast, where our current Roman road, the Via Flaminia, strikes inland towards Rome. Lynn reads an inspiring piece, 'To Be a Pilgrim', by Paul Haines, and Fatima teaches us a phrase in Arabic: *Al-Quds rahin hejazh bil malayeen!* ('We're going to Jerusalem, as pilgrims, and there are millions of us!'), an adaptation of a famous Palestinian slogan, asserting their determination to return to their home. By 7.30 a.m. we're on the move. There's a very bright sunrise across the sea, and fishermen on the breakwater, long rods perched taut against the current. We had a sumptuous fish dinner last night and wandered afterwards through the lovely cobbled streets of Fano, serenaded by a late night opera recital beneath the old city walls. Most of our walk today is straight along the coast, down to Senigallia, with the beach to our left and hotel after hotel to our right, through hot sun, sand and holidaymakers enjoying the tail end of the school vacation, kids running around on the beach and the shallows and beautiful young Italians playing beach tennis and volleyball. Everyone is tired after a 36 km walk yesterday, the longest day in the hardest week of the whole Walk, but it's great to be out at this time of day. There's a fabulous sun glittering across the Adriatic, the sea calm as shimmering glass, dotted with dozens of little boats. The white shingle beach is bounded by stretches of breakwater a hundred yards or so out to sea. Yesterday, from the cliffs of the Focara headland, David and I could see the Croatian archipelago, across the sea, but this morning, the horizon is murky with cloud and mist. Fishermen are hauling in huge bags of mussels in Senigallia, and in the harbour, where the broad green *Fiume Misa* flows into the sea, we study a chart showing all the different types of fish caught in these waters. Down on the beach, a little boy flaps his arms at a parrot on a perch, pretending to fly.

In the evening we meet up with Laura Mandolini, a friend of my friend Anders Bergquist, vicar of St John's Wood Church in London. Laura works for the Senigallia diocesan newspaper *Voce Misena* and she's hugely enthusiastic about the Walk. She's been to Palestine and visited Aida Camp in Bethlehem and Al-Arrub Camp on the Hebron–Jerusalem road. She recently set up a journalism course in the local prison, got the prisoners publishing their own newspaper, and then arranged to twin the prison with a local school, where the pupils now also publish their own newspaper. She takes us to a groovy beach restaurant with an extensive (and expensive) cocktail menu, and interviews us about the Walk. Laura's a lovely, bright, joyous character and a great boost to us all. Over a celebratory dinner for Lynn's last night with us (until Jordan), we toast her epic achievement, walking from London to Ancona with barely a blister, acquiring a new granddaughter (in absentia) and turning sixty-four along the way – a true sport, classy dame and all-round good egg.

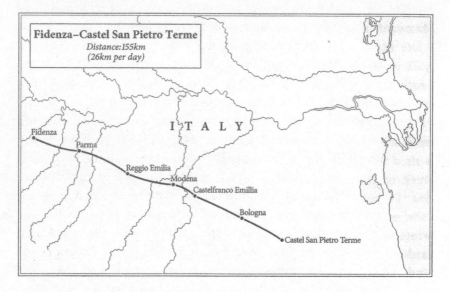

Fidenza–Castel San Pietro Terme
Distance: 155km
(26km per day)

ITALY

Fidenza
Parma
Reggio Emilia
Modena
Castelfranco Emillia
Bologna
Castel San Pietro Terme

Hannibal's maxim was tested to its utmost limits on the final day's walking in Italy.

We began with a reflection on generosity, led by Tim – not only the generosity of those we meet, but also the generosity embodied in the pilgrimage by all those taking part – and then we set off to walk to Ancona, the very last leg of our journey through Italy. A light, pleasant rain is pattering as we depart, and we're treated to amazing vistas of the rising sun across the Adriatic, blazing through the clouds to our left. The beach is shingly, scrubby and weedy and the sea is grey-green, reminding me nostalgically of seaside holidays in England. I really enjoy the griminess of the beach, the urban landscape and grey weather after so much Adriatic Riviera and sun. A coffee stop in a seaside cafe built of weather boarding and canvas is vividly reminiscent of beach huts on the Suffolk coast, making me positively homesick. Arthur's *skat* partner of thirty years, a German friend who (allegedly) cheats by memorising cards, is fond of nineteenth-century adventure stories by Karl May, a kind of German Kipling or Rider Haggard, many of them about scimitar-wielding Albanian brigands, and is apparently convinced we'll all be hacked to death in the wilds of the Balkans. Jack's heard there are wild dogs in Albania.

'I hope so,' I say heartily. 'It'll make a great chapter in the book – Jack single-handedly wrestling into submission a pack of wild Albanian dogs in pursuit of Arthur's trousers.'

'I'm not really a fighter,' says Jack.

'No, but if a pack of dogs were taking chunks out of my trousers, I'd trust you to do the right thing,' says Arthur.

'Oh yeah, if it came to it,' says Jack.

Around 9 a.m. it's still grey overhead and spitting with rain. A filthy old goods train rattles by, astonishingly long – something like fifty carriages, but just wheels and flatbeds of iron, with nothing on top, for containers, I suppose. We're walking now into Montemarciano, one of the dirty industrial areas north and west of Ancona. Over the other side of the railway line there are ruined warehouses and heaps of driftwood on the beach, amid the shingle and weeds and occasional scrubby trees, and here and there a beautiful tiny yellow flower. They've dumped a load of stone along the shoreline here as a sea defence, a long reef of blonde boulders heaped like a drystone wall. Beyond the breakwaters is an oil rig, which looks like a spaceship landed on the water. After the unbroken Riviera of pristine holiday towns, this grimy, driftwoody, shingly, dark stretch of coast, all a bit broken down and tatty, is tremendously stimulating. The sun is really tearing through the clouds now over to the south and east across the sea, glittering, shimmering over the water, making all the little billows of the waves sparkle.

The rain gets heavier as we slog on into Ancona along the Via Flaminia until mid-morning, when we meet up with Don Valter Pierini, another friend to whom Anders has introduced me, a parish priest and ecumenical advisor for the Archdiocese of Ancona. Don Valter is a gentle, generous man in his sixties, who greets us warmly and directs us to his church, an ugly, concrete hunk of brutalist architecture, next to a very hospitable bar-cafe, where we sit and steam in our wet clothes, and he invites us to order coffee and *pasticceria,* on his tab. We chat about our pilgrimage in mingled Italian and English, and at one point he says, 'But the Palestinians and the Jews don't want to live together.'

'Well, they used to live together,' I say, 'for centuries, before 1917.'

Then he says, 'Britain made a big error, a crime, in 1948, when they just left.'

I agree, of course, but interestingly it's the first time in our travels I've heard anyone else articulate this view.

Considerably restored, and warmer (if not dryer) after several rounds of coffee and pastries, we press on with many thanks, agreeing to meet Don Valter later at Ancona Cathedral, where he's offered to show us around.

The miserable weather seems to darken my mood as we trudge on into Ancona, and I find myself deluged with gloomy reflections on my failures as a parent - times when I've shouted at my kids, or failed to listen, been impatient, the usual stuff, but now, for some reason, 'all occasions do inform against me' and the rain seems to weep. I recall the prayer-image of the fist opening, and ask if perhaps I can let all this go now. Naomi is walking close to me, and for two pins I would tell her what I'm feeling, but I don't. But her presence alongside me is consoling.

Before long, the road becomes a dual carriageway, and walking along its narrow hard shoulder in pelting rain, with huge lorries thundering past and a high wall on our right, is becoming unpleasantly dangerous. Naomi and I decide to strike off, where a small slip road leads up and away, climbing steeply into a field high above the level of the motorway. We walk along this for a while, and then along the high wall above the motorway, with a twelve-foot drop to our left, but eventually we're forced off the wall by brambles growing over it, into a series of thickets of eight-foot high corn grass and bamboo. We beat our way, Indiana Jones-style, through this thicket for several hundred yards until eventually we manage to reunite with the main group. *Aut viam inveniam, etc.* As we emerge, scratched, hot, bothered and soaking wet from the undergrowth, Naomi's dad Quentin says, to my lasting delight, 'Dr Livingstone, I presume?' They also decided to strike off the perilous motorway, so we walk up into the fields above the road and end up in the garden of a little old Italian lady, who betrays not a whisker of surprise at seeing a dozen ragamuffins turn up in her orchard. She directs us through a vineyard up to a very sticky, muddy, ploughed field, where we pick up a ton of soil on our boots, and thence to a road which we follow down into Ancona.

Later the rain has gone and we walk in bright mid-afternoon heat to the cathedral, a magnificent blonde stone edifice on the hill above the ferry port, where Don Valter takes us down into the crypt to see the tomb of San Ciriaco, the fourth-century founder of the bishopric of Ancona. It's a beautiful, serene, 1,000-year old basilica, built in Romanesque style, and the crypt is magical. Don Valter explains the legend of San Ciriaco in faltering, uncertain English mingled with Italian, which I do my best to translate. Apparently, San Ciriaco was a Jew who lived in Jerusalem in the late third and early fourth centuries, the son of a noble family who were the keepers of a great secret. When St Helena, mother of the Emperor Constantine, travelled to Jerusalem, she met San Ciriaco and he revealed to her the hiding place of the True Cross and the location of the Crucifixion. She carried the True Cross back to Rome, where she established the Basilica di Santa Croce in Gerusalemme in AD 325, now one of the Seven Pilgrim Churches of Rome, although the largest fragment of the True Cross has been removed to St Peter's. Then in Jerusalem, based on San Ciriaco's identification of the site – underneath a temple of Venus built by the Emperor Hadrian in the second century to hide the cave in which Jesus had been buried – Constantine ordered the temple to be replaced by a church, the Holy Sepulchre. During the building of this church, Helena – with Ciriaco's help – is believed to have discovered the tomb of Jesus.

There is much confusion surrounding the legend of San Ciriaco, or Judas Cyriacus, but the version Don Valter tells us is that, after helping Helena find the location of the True Cross, he was baptised and consecrated as bishop of Jerusalem. Then he travelled to Ancona and established the church there (also built on the site of a former temple of Venus/Aphrodite), and became its first bishop. Ancona was a Greek city, founded on a Temple of Aphrodite. 'Ancona rests on the shoulders of Aphrodite,' Don Valter says. San Ciriaco returned on pilgrimage to the Holy Land, only to be caught in the persecutions of Julian the Apostate. He was arrested and tortured for his faith for several months, but he remained steadfast, and eventually died. (Tim mentions later that Ancona had a large Jewish ghetto. The Jews of Ancona were forcibly converted in 1555, and twenty-four who refused to convert were hanged.) In the legendary *Acts* of the martyrdom of San Ciriaco, he is depicted engaging in a dialogue with the emperor Julian, and suffers horrible torments, along with his mother Anna. The Empress Galla Placidia (AD 392–450) is said to have presented the city of Ancona with the relics of Judas Cyriacus after his death, although a relic purported to be the saint's head was brought back from Jerusalem after the Second Crusade by Henry I of Champagne to Provins, in France, where he built a church to enshrine it.

In front of the tomb of San Ciriaco is an elongated colour photograph, mounted on plywood, depicting the mummified saint in bishop's robes and mitre, after his remains were exhumed in 1999. Don Valter tells us that the saint's ordeals, as described in the *Acts* of his martyrdom, were verified by the exhumation, to the last detail. 'For example, the book of martyrs describes his torturers pouring *piombo* . . . *piombo* . . . er . . .'

'Lead?' I say.

'Ah, si! Lead . . . molten lead down his throat . . .'

Muted exclamations of disgust from the walkers, who prefer their saints unleaded, *senza piombo.*

'Yes, and they found lead in his throat when they exhumed the body – *piombo!*' he exclaims, delightedly. 'And there were wounds to his head and body, exactly as described; and they starved him, so there was evidence of malnutrition.'

He prays for us, taking our hands, and he says, 'I will pray for your dreams to God – *prego per vostri sogni a Dio* – and for your pilgrimage, and wish you many *auguri* to remain strong, walking all the way to Jerusalem, and for your cause of justice.'

And we join in the Lord's Prayer – in several languages – and in that golden crypt, hands linked in a shared hope for peace and justice, for our 'dreams to God', we are touched by a spirit of love and hospitality and deeply moved by the warmth and kindness of this gentle priest, and an awareness of how far we have journeyed. As he prays, the organist upstairs begins playing 'Jesu, Joy of man's desiring'. He shows us the original bishop's throne upstairs in the sanctuary, and we give him our remaining food for distribution to the migrants' refuge in Ancona. 'Every city in Italy has a refugee centre,' he says.

Afterwards we wander down to a beautiful square in the old city, named *Plebiscite*, for dinner al fresco, and enjoy local recipes and not-so-local fish.

Saturday 2 September, 10 p.m.

I'm sitting up on the top deck of the Ancona–Durres ferry, behind the funnel and main engine shaft, looking out on a dark, calm sea. There are stars overhead and, over on the starboard side of the funnel, the moon has appeared, three-quarters full. The three Albanian lorry drivers who were leaning over the starboard rail have just gone down, leaving me in undisputed possession of the deck. The ship's engine throbs and pummels the water with a steady rhythmic rumble, at a *basso profundo* pitch which makes my ears vibrate and my seat tremble. Away on the eastern horizon I've been treated to a spectacular display of sheet and forked lightning flashing through the clouds for the last half-hour. Brilliant glimmers fleeting across the sky, now and then concentrated with intense radiance in coiling forks, now diffused in yellow splashes spilling behind, along and through the clouds. It's a thrilling sight. It reminds me of the line in the 'Exultet' – 'This night shall be clear as day' – which we sing at our Easter Eve service at St Luke's every year, modelled on the eastern Orthodox Vigil of Fire.

Away to the starboard, the moon sheds a shimmering patch of radiance on the sea, a fleeting swathe of ghostly light rippling on the dark water, like a streak of white sand in a black expanse. Inky-dark clouds have engulfed the moon now, breaking up these pools of reflected radiance into one or two pale, shining streaks of moon water on a black sea. Cloud has covered the stars overhead and the lightning glow in the east has all but vanished. On the dark starboard horizon, I can see what might be the far-off lights of Brindisi.

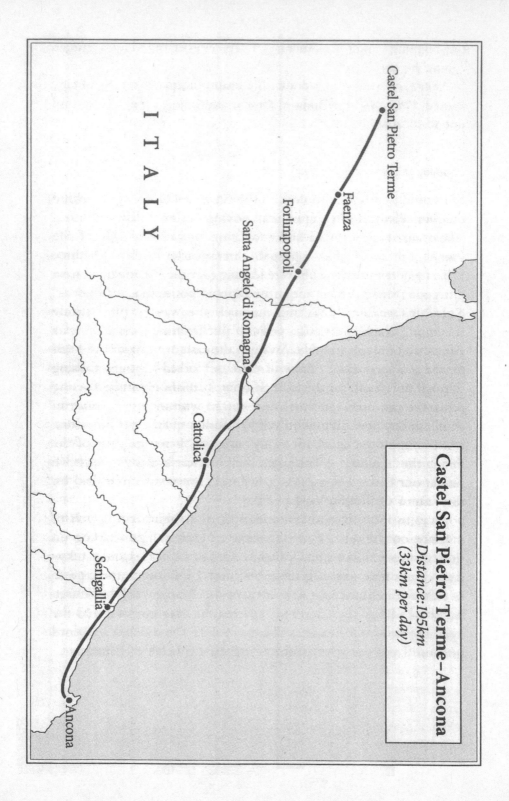

I T A L Y

Castel San Pietro Terme

Faenza

Forlimpopoli

Santa Angelo di Romagna

Cattolica

Senigallia

Ancona

Castel San Pietro Terme–Ancona
Distance: 195km
(33km per day)

8

Balkanisation

Viola. What country, friends, is this?
Captain. This is Illyria, lady.

Twelfth Night, Act I, Sc. ii

Sunday 3 September

IT'S LUNCHTIME, AND our ferry is pulling into the harbour at Durrës, on the coast of Albania, after an amazingly calm crossing. As we nose our way in past the breakwater, what do I see? Swarms of tiny naval boats, a great scattering of small fishing craft and, everywhere, hundreds of dockside cranes unloading huge piles of containers, the cargo of a busy port bringing goods to and from Albania in vast container ships named *Adriatic Liberty, Free Enterprise* and other good capitalist personifications. Forests of white, grey, yellow and orange tower blocks and multistorey carparks bristle up immediately behind the port; a space-age thicket of round orange storage silos sprouts amid much construction work, and everywhere the cityscape is dotted with new concrete marvels, emerging from thatches of scaffolding like hatching insects from chrysalis pods. A huge grimy ferry parps its twin red funnels, sun strikes the yellow dome on a little mosque, wooded hills stretch up beyond the city. It's a bright, warm day with a salt breeze blowing in from the Adriatic, and, as far as the eye can see to the south, is the sprawl of Durrës, Roman Dyrrachium in the province of Illyria, originally Epidamnos, founded by Ancient Greek colonists from Corinth and Corcyra, present-day Corfu. The harbour seems littered with detritus of dereliction and enterprise in equal measure, rotting hulks and collapsing corrugated iron shacks next to big piles of gravel, sand and shingle for new construction.

Foot passengers are a minority, almost an oddity on what is predominantly a lorry-route sea crossing, so we're waved through a kind of wharfside lorry park with much quizzical good humour by a massive pot-bellied Albanian Falstaff, with a fabulous walrus moustache and shiny bald head, walkie-talkie in hand, his enormous girth encased in luminous high-vis. We meet our cheery Albanian guide, Ardi, in the empty customs hall and set off south along the coast for the welcoming and cosily tatty hotel, most of us in a minibus, some walking. 'Homely' is probably the *mot juste* for this run-down *pension*, where a tacky film of local colour coats most of the surfaces and dodgy cabling connects the appliances perilously to ancient sockets, but the staff are delightfully friendly.

Later on, back in town, I wander round the historic sights with Cressey: the squat, round Venetian tower, a fifteenth-century survival of a brief period of rule by the Republic of Venice, when the city's Byzantine fortress was rebuilt as a defence against the Ottomans; the ancient Roman columns and city walls of the heyday of the Eastern Empire, built in the late fifth and early sixth centuries by the Emperor Anastasios I to repair the damage from a catastrophic earthquake in AD 345; and the huge Roman amphitheatre, the largest in the Balkans, built in the early second century by the Emperor Trajan, with seating for 15,000 spectators, 'whatching gladiators fight, beast fight and different artistic shows', as the quirkily worded sign puts it, until the Emperor Honor banned such displays in AD 404. Between these ancient remains, the city is a curious mix of smart shopping boulevards with spotless pavements lined with palm trees and neat municipal lawns, tatty tenement blocks festooned with great improvised tangles of electrical and telephone cabling, satellite dishes in every nook and cranny, and improbably lavish prestige projects evincing the inrush of new money from somewhere or other, such as the many-pillared glistening glass and cream-plaster edifice of the Albanian College Durrës, an international school opened in 2014. Colourful graffiti proliferates on every wall off the main drag (a ten-foot high 'F**K GREECE' slogan in blue and white horizontal stripes catches the eye), and many of the little cobbled streets and back alleys are decorated with some genuinely attractive and inventive murals, *trompe l'oeils* of children in sailor suits and dungarees playing with a cat around an open wooden *trompe l'oeil* door, next to a paradisal scene of a tree of life in an enchanted hippy garden twittering with doves, butterflies and angel-fairies, with the caption *Faleminderit Shqipëri!* – 'Thank you, Albania!' Boats, divers and tropical fish swirl dreamily across another wall above a fresco seabed of crustaceans, coral and waving weeds, into which a ground-floor window intrudes weirdly, its ledge lined with pot plants behind wrought-iron bars. *Shitet biznezi* reads a sign in a closed shop window. *Shitet*, to the undying amusement of the Just Walk cavalcade, means 'for sale' in Albanian, so there's *shitet* stuff everywhere. The most popular brand of Albanian chocolate bar is *Noblice*, which also unlocked a fountain of mirth.

The chapel built into the amphitheatre, underneath the *vomitorium* of the second elliptical gallery, probably in the seventh century, perhaps to baptise the site of so much bloodshed and licentious entertainment, contains the only surviving mediaeval mosaic in Albania, and the only mediaeval mosaic to be found anywhere in a Roman amphitheatre. One panel on the southern wall of the chapel represents St Stephen, clearly labelled *O Agios Stephanos* (the Holy Stephen), in martyr's garb of white tunic, with golden hands raised in prayer. The sign outside the chapel claims St Stephen as the 'martyr of the city of Durrës', which is the first I've ever heard of it. A larger panel appears to depict the Virgin Mary as a Byzantine empress, with crown, sceptre and orb, flanked by angels, the east-ernmost example of a 'Crowned Virgin', otherwise only found in Italy. Alongside her is a pair of female saints labelled Sophia and Eirene, a unique iconographical pairing of the saintly personifications of Wisdom and Peace respectively. The only other instance of such pairing is in the adjacent churches of Hagia Sophia and Hagia Eirene in Istanbul, which together formed the Constantinopolitan patriarchate. The stoning of St Stephen is believed to have taken place next to the Lions' Gate in Jerusalem, through which *insha'Allah* we will eventually enter the Old City. Known in Christian tradition as St Stephan's Gate, the site is revered by the clergy of the Armenian Church, who wear crowns once a year on St Stephen's Day to honour the first Christian martyr. By a neat coincidence, the first debating chamber of the House of Commons was St Stephen's Chapel, built in the reign of Henry III and largely destroyed by fire in 1834, and the clock tower of Big Ben in the new Palace of

Westminster was known originally as St Stephen's Tower, until it was renamed the Elizabeth Tower in 2013 for the Diamond Jubilee, so our journey began and will end on the trail of St Stephen. And our long road from Durrës to Istanbul, the mighty Via Egnatia linking the twin capitals of the Roman Empire, begins and ends with the symbolic marriage of Wisdom and Peace. May it be so.

We wander past a sadly dilapidated eighteenth-century Ottoman *hamam* (bath house) behind rusty padlocked gates, then up the hill leading back from the seafront to King Zog's Summer Palace. A pink and cream 1920s Bond-villain mansion, with strange round windows like portholes, the Royal Villa, built in the shape of an eagle with wings spread, looks out to sea from the scrubby wooded hilltop of Durrës, behind high graffitied walls, tangles of rusty barbed wire and wrought-iron gates chained shut. The only sign of life is an amorous couple entwined in the back seat of a car parked at the top of the drive. Previous guests have included Nikita Khruschev and former US President Jimmy Carter. The palace was restored to Crown Prince Leka of Albania, only son of the late King Zog, in 2007, but its current ownership is now apparently a matter of dispute between the State and the house of Zogu's new heir, Crown Prince Leka II, who has served as an official in several Albanian ministries and married a popular Albanian singer and actress last year, in Tirana.

On our way back, Cressey and I pop into the Catholic Church of St Lucia, beautifully and simply rebuilt in local blonde stone, a plain, neo-Romanesque basilica with white pillars and an eastern apse arched in a perfect semicircle, bathed in sunlight from round-arched windows to either side of the dome. The building was used as a puppet theatre in the communist era and allowed to fall into disrepair. The new incumbent is English: Father Martin, a friendly, jovial chap who's just arrived in post a couple of weeks ago, and makes us very welcome. Around 10 per cent of Albania's population are Catholic, he says, compared to around 7 per cent Orthodox and nearly 60 per cent Muslim, with the remainder made up of small faith communities, such as the Sufi order of the Bektashi, as well as those unaffiliated to any religion. He mentions the odd connection of the artist and nonsense poet Edward Lear with Albania and the Balkans. Apparently he arrived in Thessaloniki, or Salonica as it was known, only to find that an outbreak of cholera had closed off all other routes of possible exploration, so he set off travelling through Macedonia and Albania in 1848, painting and recording his adventures of a wild and unknown part of Europe never previously visited by foreigners. In his *Journals of a Landscape Painter in Albania*, amid vivid depictions of the environment, culture and politics, he describes 'luxury and inconvenience on the one hand, liberty, hard living and filth on the other' in this mysterious corner of the beleaguered Ottoman Empire at a time of seismic upheaval across Europe.[1]

Heading back out of town between the main road and the railway (where trains haven't run for years, by the look of the tracks), I'm harassed by snarling wild dogs who wander the roadsides and wastelands in between, scavenging for food and barking ferociously at anyone who comes within a hundred yards. Several dogs actually cross the road to come and pester me. I fill my pockets with pebbles and quicken my pace.

Back at the hotel, many beers and cordial greetings are shared in a garden of overgrown fig trees with the dozen or so new walkers who've come out to join us for the Balkans. There'll be more than twenty of us on this first stretch of the Via Egnatia, and they seem a convivial bunch of good eggs and good sports. *Ambulando solvitur.*

Edward Lear on the Occupation:

> There was an Old Man with a beard,
> Who said, 'It is just as I feared!—
> Two Owls and a Hen, four Larks and a Wren,
> Have all built their nests in my beard.[2]

Monday 4 September

Walking the Albanian Riviera as the beach cafes, shops and market stalls are just coming to life is an eye-opener. Viewed from the beach, this seafront of deck chairs and umbrellas, pink and cream hotels, restaurants and piers, swimming pools, volleyball courts and playgrounds could be anywhere along the Italian Adriatic coast. 'There's a lot of new investment in tourism,' says Ardi, 'and thousands of people coming on holiday here, from all over Europe.' And why not? Beautiful beaches of soft golden sand, lapped by a warm, glittering sea under a glorious sky – everything you need or want for a family holiday at a bargain price. But a street or two back from the seafront, the broken-down southern suburbs of Durrës are like an African slum, potholed alleys flooded with huge, stinking puddles from broken sewage pipes and water mains, chaotic jumbles of cabling slung any old how across the streets, and pockets of wasteland heaped with refuse between collapsing shacks and tenements. From Albanian Riviera to Albanian Kibera. Maybe this is why all the traders set up their stalls on the beach; there's a chance of meeting people with some money here. I've actually never seen fruit and veg stalls set out on the beach like this, alongside neat displays of magazines, newspapers and paperbacks laid straight on to the sand. It reminds me of the pavement traders in the slums of Nairobi, constructing neat pyramids of tomatoes and corn cobs on the roadside, with nothing more than a tea towel for a table. Presentation is everything.

Ardi points out a shiny pier leading out to a circular space-pod on stilts in the sea. 'This is a private club and beach houses,' he says, grinning broadly, 'where our president and his ministers can come at taxpayers' expense, when they're feeling a bit stressed, you know, 'cause they work so hard for the people of Albania. We're very happy they have a nice place to come and relax, you know, they deserve a rest.' Ardi is a stocky, well-built guy in his mid-forties with a perpetual grin and excellent English, and a great line in gallows humour.

We've struck away from the coast now and are making our way inland through the slum-belt of the last southern sprawl of Durrës and eastwards up steep hills through the commune of Golem. The name provokes much Serkis-Smeagol banter from various walkers, as to the precise location of the Via Egnatia path: *Where is it, my precious? We can't find it, we wants it, yes, precious, and we're hungry, yes, and hot, precious, oh yes, and where are we going anyway? Jerusalem? Where's that, precious? Nice hobbitses mustn't go to nasty places, no, precious, stay here in Albania,* etc.

After the Albanian Riviera and the Albanian Kibera, we're walking now through Albanian Tuscany, heading inland and eastwards through a landscape of very rough, primitive villages scattered between undulating hills of wonderful rich, red soil, terraced and planted with olive trees, plums, vines and figs. Everywhere across the hillsides we see the silver-green olive leaves glistening in the sunlight. It's cooler and greener and the hills are bigger, but otherwise it's very like Tuscany. We're walking a rough country track that follows the path of the Via Egnatia through little fields of wigwam haystacks which Arthur tells me are called 'stooks', with here and there a tumbledown cluster of farm buildings, barns and sheds with rickety roofs of corrugated tin and terracotta shells, each with its little orchard of fruit trees. There's a tomato patch here to my right, plants climbing up a forest of cane-supports and a couple of fig trees, with an old farmhouse behind. From time to time, smart, modern buildings pop up out of nowhere. Ardi says that people who manage to accumulate enough money in this extremely poor rural area always build smart new houses. Or they might belong to second home owners, he says – businessmen or politicians from Tirana. There's a bright-orange villa to the right, and over there to the left, across the valley, a very smart pink house, three storeys high, rising up from the fields, with a patch of forest behind it. Further along the brow of the valley to the left there's a yellow-ochre three-storey house of identical design, almost like some monstrous weird fruit popping up out the hills.

Now we're passing a flock of great big turkeys here on the right, gobbling and squawking with an extraordinary racket. There are dogs everywhere too, flaked out and flopped down in front of their sheds, basking lethargically. They've obviously had an exhausting morning. We've met several donkeys, ambling along doing their own thing, or carrying vast bundles of firewood and straw, chivvied along by peasant farmers or their wives, who look like extras from a period drama in white headscarves, patterned smocks and colourful shawls. They're invariably delighted to see us, their weatherbeaten faces cracking with amusement at this bunch of Brits walking through their land, and always offer us figs, plums and pomegranates. Their lifestyle, scratching a hand-to-mouth living by small-scale subsistence farming, is extremely basic, but their hospitality is as warm as any we've encountered along the way.

We're walking along a high ridge now, with a rather fetid lake away down to the left. It's getting pretty hot, despite a fair bit of cloud cover. Another huge gobbling flock of turkeys waddles by indignantly, grotesque pink snoods and dewlaps wobbling furiously. It's a beautifully green, fertile and very poor landscape, full of quirks.

Ardi comes from Deja, in north-western Albania, not far from the border with Montenegro. He likes being a tour operator, he says, but he'd like to spend more time at home. He's not married, though he has someone in mind. He played football for an important club when he was sixteen, before there was any state funding for football.

'If it was now,' he says, 'definitely I would have had a chance, you know, to try to play professionally. But then I had to join the army for two years, from age eighteen. My first year in the army was the last year of the communist regime. So, with the change of government, my second army year was easier. Still army, but not so strict. I mean, they still woke you up at 5 a.m. and made you run for forty-five minutes in boots, thin trousers and vest; you still had to do rifle training, learning how to dismantle and reassemble a rifle in one minute, you know, all that stuff.'

'And how is public life now in Albania?' I ask. 'What's the political culture?'

'Completely corrupt,' he says emphatically. 'After the fall of communism, the government and their cronies stole the public wealth, like, you know, the oligarchs in Russia. An average teacher's salary in Albania now would be around 300 euros a month; a doctor's, maybe 600 euros. The economy is broken. After the first elections in 1992, the government created these investment schemes, persuading everyone to buy government bonds, promising ridiculous profits, like 20 per cent, 25 per cent. But they were a fraud, like Ponzi schemes, just a front for money laundering and arms trafficking. Hundreds of thousands of people – millions – bought these bonds, two-thirds of the population; the government stole the money and in 1997 the whole thing collapsed. Some people sold their houses to invest in this. It was a massive crisis. There were huge riots, a revolution, they kicked out the government, it was a state of emergency. Other countries were taking their people out of Albania. Army tries to control the riots, but it was a civil war, really, looting and criminal gangs taking over. More than 2,000 people were killed. So after this, we have to start again to try to build an economy from nothing. You know, there was a Canadian fracking company who came to extract shale gas from a certain part of Albania, and they messed things up, they made a big mess, an environmental disaster. They left many people homeless and others having to flee to avoid the poisonous pollution. Some people died, many people lost their homes, and no one was held to account. The Canadian company sold the business for many millions to the Chinese and bribed the politicians.'

'Was there no campaign, no protest?' I ask.

'No, it's not like the UK,' he says. 'Here people are only thinking today about tomorrow's bread. Yes, you have stresses and pressures in the UK, but you are free to say what you like, you have some systems of social support, and you are smarter. You know how to organise these things.'

'And what about the press, the media?'

'Completely bought.'

'Bought?'

'Bought by the government and the oligarchs. There are no significant critical voices.'

'What would Albania need to move forward?' I ask.

'I think we need some kind of justice,' he says, 'some kind of accountability. We need to see politicians held to account, and not just in word – something from the pocket as well. It won't give me any satisfaction to see these people sent to prison for one or two years, like in Croatia. They need to pay.'

He talks about the different faiths in Albania, and the resentment many feel about the role of the Orthodox Church in massacres and ethnic cleansing in Kosovo.

'And what do people in Albania feel about the Palestinian struggle? Do they know about it?'

'Of course,' he says, and pauses for thought. 'Well, in Albania, we saved our Jews in Second World War. Everywhere else in the Balkans, in Europe, they were betrayed, but we protected them. Albania was the only country in Europe to come from the war with more Jews than before. Jewish population was very small before the war, just a few hundred, but King Zog's government gave Albanian passports to any Jews who wanted to come and live here, so they were escaping from other countries to Albania. King Zog was very clever; he wanted the Jews to come and live here to help develop the country, to bring prosperity, education, expertise. When the Italian occupation came in the war, the Albanian government made a deal with the Italians, that they would refuse to hand over any Jews to the Germans. Later, the Italians surrendered and the German occupation came, and we hid the Jews in the small villages, in the countryside, dressed them as Albanian peasants. We fed them and protected them. We have a thing in Albania, *besa*, the promise of hospitality you make to your guest. You swear to protect them, anyone who is your guest. We would prefer to die than allow anyone to harm our guest. And we have *kanun* – like a law of how you must be, you know, like . . .'

'A code?'

'Yes, a code. *Kanun* is our code. *Kanun* says that your house belongs to God and to your guest. So we managed to save the Jews in Albania. From 200, there were more than 2,000 Jews after the war. There is something in the Jewish museum in New York, I think, thanking Albania for what we did. And in Israel. Albania is named in the nations of the righteous. So Albania is quite friendly to Israel.'

'So King Zog was a good guy, then, a man of vision?'

'Yes, but he ran away to France, and then later to Britain, when world war came, so afterwards we got rid of the monarchy. He was regarded as a traitor and a coward. He should have stayed and fought. Afterwards he lived in Scotland. We get a lot of Israelis coming to Albania, in fact, for extreme rambling trips, especially in the north.'

'Israelis come here for walking holidays?'

'Yeah, and birdwatching, but they're always complaining,' he says, 'And they never speak to me if the air conditioning in their room isn't working properly, or some other problem. They always phone back to Tel Aviv, and then the travel company phones me to complain. Italians complain a lot too.'

Suddenly he stops and closes his eyes, in an effort to remember something. 'There is a beautiful Albanian poet,' he says, 'our national poet, Naeem Frashëri. He lived in the nineteenth century and was one of the big voices in the national movement for liberation, to get our independence from the Ottoman Empire. He wrote this poem, *O malet' e Shqipërisë e ju o lisat' e gjatë! Fushat e gjëra me lule, q'u kam ndër mënt dit' e natë!'*

'What does it mean?'

'It means, *O high mountains of Albania, O you tall oaks! The wonderful fields of flowers, Which I have in my mind in the day and the night!* And we have another great poet, Fan Noli, he was like a giant in Albanian history, modern history. He was a writer, a politician, someone making great speeches, a professor, a priest, and he was the creator of the Albanian Orthodox Church. He was leader of the revolution in 1924, and then became the prime minister and he was ruling the country. And he wrote his most famous poem, *Ku është toka më e ëmbël se mjalti? Në Shqipëri.* It says, *Where is the earth sweeter than the honey? In Albania.*'

Edward Lear on the Two-State Solution:

> There was an old man on the Border,
> Who lived in the utmost disorder;
> He danced with the cat, and made tea in his hat,
> Which vexed all the folks on the Border.[3]

Tuesday 5 September

It's 8 a.m. and we're walking out of Kavajë, after a distinct lack of breakfast at the hotel (it being apparently too early for the restaurant staff) – some stale bread, good jam, fruit juice and no coffee – and now we're heading eastwards towards Elbasan and Peqin. The latter was so named, Ardi claimed yesterday, after Albania's crazy Communist dictator, Enver Hoxha, decided that the Soviet Union had gone all soft under Khruschev and transferred his allegiance to Chairman Mao, whereupon Albania became a European outpost of Maoist China, surely one of the oddest alliances in modern history. 'Albanians back then had to wear Mao-suits,' he laughed, 'and carry the little red book.' I can't work out whether he's pulling my leg.

We're just passing a clothes-making factory. Women working away at sewing machines wave at us through the windows. It's an early start for them. Ardi says that Albania's becoming a big exporter of clothes and shoes. There was an article in *The Guardian* a few weeks ago, he says, about how British shoe shops were getting their supplies from Albania, charging a lot for them in the UK and paying a pittance to their producers.

The early-morning bustle of pavement commerce is cranking into life: lots of guys sitting at cafe tables busily drinking coffee and smoking; lots of vehicles, horse-drawn as well as motorised, out delivering melons and vegetables. There's a chap setting up his melon stall on the pavement. Again, it reminds me of African street scenes, with impromptu stalls being set out on every square inch of pavement: coils of hosepipe, brooms and brushes, flower pots and tools. A busy cluster of men in dirty overalls are debating something animatedly outside a mechanic's shop, jabbering and waving tools and gesticulating vigorously about how to fix a chainsaw. Scenes of industry and activity proliferate everywhere as we head out of town into the eastern hills of Kryezi, bordering the province of Tirana.

By mid-morning we're walking in a wide open country of green hills striped with olive and vine terraces, rolling scrubby rough grazing slopes, wooded valleys and arable pastures, becoming drier, dustier, yellower, always rising from each ridge of hills to the next as we trek inland towards the Skanderbeg Mountains, one of the many ranges that rear all down the length of the country from the Albanian Alps in the north to the Ceraunian and Pindus Mountains in the south.

As lunchtime approaches, we're walking down a steep track through olive groves and fig, plum and apricot trees. Dried thistle stalks, ferns and gorse rattle and rustle in a soft breeze. We've just passed a little Islamic cemetery, really right in the middle of nowhere, a remnant, Ardi says, of a time when these remote hills were more populated. We walk through another little homestead, with goats lounging in the shade of the wattle-and-daub farmhouse opposite a wicker compound roofed with plastic sheeting. The ruddy-faced smiling farmer and his wife greet us warmly, and a couple of other guys are arguing in a good-natured fashion about something or other, at top volume, with huge gesticulations. Ardi's younger colleague, Marcel, says, 'Oh yes, I know how these people speak, with too much energy, always very excited because they don't see people very often.'

The little grove surrounding the farmstead is a Tolkienesque glade of fabulously gnarled, ancient, twisted trunks of olive trees, with huge distended girth like baobabs, sprawling and stretching over the shelves of the hillside. All these hills were cut into terraces in the communist era, Ardi says, for the cultivation of vines and olives, although many of these trees are much older than that. More than anywhere we've been so far, it reminds me of Palestine, or maybe a cross between Tuscany and Palestine, though much greener. The trees are laden with olives; I suppose the harvest will be in a couple of months. But on the vines, the grapes are starting to wither. Maybe they're not harvested any more. Between the vegetation, where the mountain slopes are too steep for any cultivation, there are great pale escarpments, riddled and marbled with fantastical swirling rock formations. I didn't know what to expect of the Albanian Via Egnatia. It really is the most magnificent landscape, probably the best walking of the whole journey, alongside the Alps. It's a reasonable temperature, maybe 26 or 27°C, and there's a pleasant light breeze. Opposite us now across a little valley are some tilled pastures filled with those little wigwam stooks of dried cornstalks, green-grey and silver olive groves planted in neat rows, a little homestead with six houses, and another cemetery by the looks of it. The path criss-crosses its way down the slope and across the valley to the other side, where we can see mountains rising in the distance.

After picnicking in a woodland glade of giant olive trees, we follow the line of a high, narrow ridge running eastwards between steep slopes of open scrub, with the distant blue shapes of the Skanderbeg Mountains becoming clearer beneath cotton-wool strands of cloud on the skyline. Occasional barns roofed with terracotta tubes and abandoned rusty ploughs and harrows overgrown with tall grasses are the only trace of habitation. David, who's often at the front, seems to have a great talent for finding tortoises in Albania, roaming the wilds of the Via Egnatia as they have for thousands of years. His wife, Heidi, is working as a volunteer wildlife rescuer at the moment, back in Australia, and often sends him pictures of rescued koalas or convalescing kangaroos. As he picks his latest tortoise up to photograph, squirming and swimming indignantly in mid-air with its scaly legs out at full stretch, I tell him the comic legend of the death by tortoise of the playwright Aeschylus. Tortoises are sitting ducks for eagles in Greece, being so slow moving, but the eagles can't get inside their shells, so they fly up high, carrying the hapless tortoises in their talons, then drop them with deadly accuracy on a rock to split them open, after which they feast on the splurged innards. The story goes that the old man Aeschylus was enjoying a walk in the Athenian countryside one day, and sat down to rest in the sun. An eagle, flying high above with a tortoise in its talons, mistook the old man's shiny head for a rock and dropped the tortoise on him, thus bringing to an ignominious end one of the greatest literary careers of the ancient world. So put your hat on, Chris.

David and I chat about work, vocations and keeping on keeping on as we walk together. He's touchingly encouraging and enthusiastic as I describe some of my escapades over the years. 'It's fantastic,' he says. 'You haven't given up, you keep on going, following the vision, and you haven't sold out.'

'Well, I've tried to a few times,' I say, 'but no one wanted to buy me.'

He gives one of his trademark little chuckles. He got on to a roll designing shops and cafes in Queensland, and was offered a big job by a large shopping centre as their in-house designer, which he didn't want to do. They kept offering him more money, and he kept saying, 'Thanks, but you're not hearing me. I don't want to do it.'

Around mid-afternoon our path towards Elbasan coincides with an old railway line, long disused, cut into a winding shelf in a stretch of hills, and we stride along the sleepers for several miles. My thoughts turn to a sad recollection, almost unbearably sad, of the suicide of a dear friend's sixteen-year-old daughter a couple of years ago, back in the UK. After a protracted and agonising struggle with mental health problems, this lovely, bright, beautiful young girl took her own life by tying herself to a railway track. She'd written farewell messages to her family, thanking them for their great love and care, and assuring them over and over that no one could ever have wished for a more loving and supportive family. But somehow, it seems, for all the love, support and treatment she received, she couldn't escape from the despair that had overwhelmed her life. My oldest son, Benedict, was the same age at the time, and the tragedy knocked me sideways. I could hardly bear to imagine my friend's anguish. The memory punches me in the chest as I trudge along between the sleepers.

We strike off the railway line around 5 p.m. to sample our first stretch of genuine Via Egnatia: several hundred yards of gravelly track between farm buildings and fields, along which march the original Roman flagstones and slabs of the ancient road, laid in orderly lines, worn and beaten by the centuries, but unmistakable. It's just a farm track now; there are no heritage plaques or Ministry of Tourism signs, but this was the path on which Mark Antony and Octavian pursued Brutus and Cassius and their forces to Philippi after the assassination of Julius Caesar in 44 BC. This was the road of Constantine to Byzantium. It's a thrilling moment, and the thrill is enhanced a few minutes later by the discovery of an ancient Roman or Byzantine bridge to the left of the path, clearing a deep-cut stream bed in a single vault, the arch's rim of fanning stones slightly warped but still holding its span intact. Gobbling flocks of turkeys straggle across the road where Roman chariots once drove two abreast, as the sun begins to dip in the sky and we shoulder our packs for the last few miles to Elbasan. A beautifully generous lady farmer hails us over a fence, waving fistfuls of pome-granates. Her teenage daughter speaks good English, and we do our best to explain our mission, exchanging many bows, smiles and handshakes, and come away laden with fruit. I cut several of them open and share them round. The shiny red seeds are actually very chewy and sour, but I munch manfully through at least half a pomegranate before giving up, determined to be appreciative.

It's after 7 p.m. when we schlep at last into *Le Olive Hotel Bar Restorant* in Pajova, a village on the outskirts of Elbasan. The chef's gone home, because the hotel staff forgot to tell him we'd need dinner, so they scurry round to produce an improvised meal of pasta and salad.

Wednesday 6 September

Breakfast at 6.15 a.m. this morning. The butter had a distinct flavour of cheese, and the sweet young man serving took about twenty-five minutes to make one small cup of coffee at a time, each of which was then carried individually to the table with studious care. It was like watching Julie Walters as the superannuated waitress.

We drove to our starting point in Peqin, past the livestock market which Marcel told us is *the* place to buy donkeys or turkeys (€250 for a good donkey, which would have worked out at about a tenner each). Then, setting off from Peqin, I popped into a cafe to buy two coffees for me and Chris, both suffering withdrawal after the thimbleful at breakfast, and I explained, by way of mime, to the guys in the cafe – a lot of dark-faced old Albanian chaps sitting around drinking coffee and smoking, as you do, that's how you start the day – that we were walking to Jerusalem. Many raised eyebrows and expressions of astonishment, then one of them said, 'Wait, wait!' and got out an ancient mobile phone, insisting that I speak to his friend, who spoke English.

'Hello?'

'Hello!'

'Hello – your friend in the cafe wants me to tell you that we're walking to Jerusalem, for Palestinian rights.'

(Long pause.)

'I don't understand.'

'We're walking to Jerusalem.'

(Pause.)

'Oh.' (Pause.) 'Don't you think it's quite a long way?'

'Yes, it's a long way, more than 3,000 km, but we're OK.'

'Do you have a map?'

'Yes, yes, we have a map, and an Albanian guide. We're walking the Via Egnatia.'

'The Via Egnatia? And you have an Albanian guide?'

'Yes, yes, we're OK.'

'So you don't need anything?'

'No, we're OK, thanks. All OK, thank you.'

(Pause.)

'Oh. OK.'

'OK, thanks very much. Goodbye!'

'OK, goodbye! Good luck! Good journey!'

'Thank you! Bye!'

* * *

Horse-drawn vehicles are commonplace here; you often see a whole family loaded on to a horse and cart, trundling along the main highway, weaving between cars and flocks of turkeys by the roadside. Some people obviously feel they have to shepherd their turkeys, chivvying them along with a long stick, while others, seemingly more confident in providence or their turkeys' road sense, just leave them to wander. We're getting quite used to the sight of a dozen turkeys gobbling and pecking by the roadside as cars whizz by, mostly old Mercedes-Benz − everyone's favourite in Albania, it seems. At a brief cafe stop in another village we met a quartet of friendly builders, Amarillo, Fatosh, Karma and Krasis, who all spoke Italian, so I was able to explain our pilgrimage, which stirred interest, and they immediately demanded a photograph with me. In almost every village, when the local farmers and their wives − and particularly their children − see us striding through, they always come up to greet us, usually offering fruit, nuts, bread, and wanting us to take photographs.

Once again, we are walking through fabulous countryside, through a long flat-bottomed valley following the Shkumbin River from Peqin to Elbasan, with cornfields, olive groves and fruit orchards to either side. The weather is sunny and breezy, perfect for walking. At one point we scale the valley wall, plugging back and forth up a zigzag path which turns into a real scramble, on all fours at times, up a loose shale scree of wonderful red marble, to be rewarded with breathtaking views back along the Shkumbin towards the coast.

Edward Lear on the One-State Solution:

> Pussy said to the Owl, 'You elegant fowl!
> How charmingly sweet you sing!
> O let us be married! too long we have tarried:
> But what shall we do for a ring?'[4]

Thursday 7 September

We're walking from Elbasan today, following the Shkumbin River eastwards towards Librazhd, circumventing one of the most challenging stretches of the Via Egnatia, over a mountain pass, which would have kept us walking till around 10 p.m. tonight. We've just passed the most extraordinary folly, built like an imitation Swiss or Austrian fairy-tale schloss, overlooking the valley. We're striding out along a small country lane, with a lovely sunrise over the mountain to our left, fields, orchards, vines and haystacks to our right, and a cemetery up on the hill and a big breeze-block barn, lots of traffic on the road and dogs barking all around. Ardi can't get hold of the manager of the hotel where we're meant to be staying tonight and says he thinks he's been executed. This fellow was reputedly involved in lots of 'dodgy stuff'. Ardi's been ringing him repeatedly over the last week or so and eventually got the response, 'This number does not exist', so he and Chris are making alternative plans. I can never tell whether Ardi's joking or not. 'This guy was a criminal,' he says, chortling, 'executed or assassinated, for sure.'

He told us a great story yesterday, about the huge clouds of black smoke we'd seen the day before billowing up from a petrol station visible from the old railway line we were following into Peqin. Ardi was there, filling up the van with fuel, and he got a bit nervous when he saw a grass fire close by the petrol station and the flames spreading towards the forecourt. 'There were these two Macedonian truck drivers in the cafe,' he said, chuckling, 'and they were eating and drinking raki, and having a great time, with their two lorries parked up outside. They didn't care – they weren't bothered! I was very worried the fire would come and burn the van, so I decided to move it about 900 metres down the road.' He's giggling as he tells me, grinning all over his face. 'And then the fire came and went into the petrol station! And the next thing we saw was the fire engines whizzing along the road! *Nee-naw, nee-naw!* And huge clouds of black smoke because the tyres of these Macedonian lorries had caught fire! Then the firemen are shooting their hoses to put the fires out, and there's smoke everywhere! And then afterwards, I came back to have a look – and these two Macedonian truck drivers were *still* sitting there eating and drinking raki!' He's in paroxysms. 'Absolutely typical Macedonian! The trucks were burned out, the tyres destroyed, and they sat there and watched the whole thing and carried on drinking and eating!'

This morning we had our first serious encounter with midges, in horrible, thick clouds, but we're past them now. We're back on the Via Egnatia, walking a terrace path cut along the south side of the Shkumbin Valley. Down to the left the river meanders, braided in several streams around islets and spits of gravel and the scattering of vegetation across the valley floor. There's a little town over on the north side of the valley, and here and there the occasional farm building. The sun is away to our right, peeping over the brow of the hills. Down in a field to our left now is a regiment of little haystack stooks, made up from dried corn grasses. Huge swathes of blackberry bushes crowd all along the path to our right, and here comes a fellow very intrepidly riding his bicycle on this very stony, difficult path for cycling. What sounds like a huge flock of starlings is twittering away somewhere to the left, and cockerels in every barn and coop across the valley are crowing. Everyone seems to keep poultry in Albania, so we're never far from the sound.

In the late morning, we walk through a tranquil glade of maple trees around a small lake and fountain, an ancient woodland shrine to the pagan gods of spring. Philip tells me they celebrate the birth of the new spring here every year on 14 March with a feast and some kind of symbolic veneration of the pagan gods. The place is beautiful but horribly littered with rubbish. Philip tells me about the Bektashi, a Dervish strand of Sufi Islam, an ascetic order founded in the sixteenth century whose headquarters is in Tirana. He describes how the Bektashi venerate their *babas*, or holy men, who sometimes live as hermits on the outskirts of their villages. He and his wife met the local Bektashi *baba* in Gjakova once; he was extremely cagey at first, assuming they were up to some kind of mischief, but eventually relaxed and opened up to them.

Walking through disused railway tunnels after lunch prompts me to try to imagine what the tunnels from Egypt into Gaza must be like. I tell Naomi and several others how Ahmed nearly had to go through a tunnel to escape in 2009. Faint feelings of anxiety assail me around the middle of the dark tunnel (although there hasn't been a train for at least twenty years), equidistant between long stretches of darkness, with a tiny circle of daylight either end seeming a long way off. What if it collapses, or something falls off the ceiling?

Later in the afternoon, still walking along the old railway line, following the Shkumbin, we come to the magnificent Ottoman bridge not far from Librazhd. The old path down to the river runs through farmyards now, frequented only by chickens, but there at its foot stands the steeply humpbacked span of elegant sixteenth-century stonework vaulting the Shkumbin in two arches, over which soldiers and statesmen once followed the Via Egnatia to Istanbul.

A mile or so later, fed up of walking along the railway line, I scramble down the steep slope to walk along the riverbank, tread on a loose stone and fall spectacularly into a thicket of blackberry bushes. My shorts give up the ghost at last and rip open right across the crutch, so for the rest of the day I walk with billowing cloth around my knees, pants on display to all and sundry, to the great amusement of fellow walkers. When I rejoin the group, resting in the mouth of yet another tunnel, I spend twenty minutes picking thorns out of my calves, arms, hands and clothes. My long-ago white shirt is ripped and stained with blackberry juice, and my arms and legs are torn all over with scratches. I am a complete vagabond. As Robin says later, I'm cultivating the George Orwell *Down and Out in Paris and London* look. All these disused railroads and tunnels, with their rusty tracks overgrown with thistles, remind me of blues-album covers and the Coen brothers' fabulous film, *O Brother, Where Art Thou?* so I walk on, yodelling, 'I am a man of constant sorrow,' at the top of my voice, sending strange echoes of bluegrass reverberating up and down the dark tunnel.

Friday 8 September

It's 8 a.m. in Librazhd. Hung over from raki last night and a magnificent dinner in a fine garden restaurant. Now sitting drinking coffee outside a cafe next to what passes for the bus terminal – a motley line of assorted third-hand Mercedes buses, coaches and minivans with cracked windscreens and battered paintwork, with various destinations painted or printed on windows, or handwritten on bits of brown cardboard ripped from grocery boxes – Divjakë, Durres, Tirana, Vlore – parked up in a row in the middle of the town square. I'm returning briefly to the UK to act as celebrant at a Palestinian–Scottish wedding taking place at Pembroke Lodge in Richmond Park, childhood home of Bertrand Russell, where my friend Manal Ramadan, director of Zaytoun, will marry her fiancé

Ian White: the girl from Damascus and the boy from Dunblane. I've never been the celebrant at a wedding before, but I was touched to be asked. So now all the walkers and guides have gone, leaving me with a coach driver and a few thousand *lekh* in my pocket and some vague instructions as to where to find the bus for the airport once I get to Tirana, from somewhere outside the Vatican embassy. I will rejoin the Walk in Thessaloniki.

In the square, the locals are going about their business, men wandering about chatting and smoking, old ladies in traditional white or black headscarves, young women in jeans and dark glasses, families getting on and off buses. Vehicles pull into the gas station to fill up with the local brand of diesel, wonderfully named *Kastrati*; someone's trying to load some large plastic barrels into the back of one of the coaches; Balkan folk music plays in the cafe, while an old lady in Muslim headdress changes a little girl's nappy behind a large municipal rubbish bin. Hardware shopkeepers are laying out coils of hosepipe for sale on the pavements outside their shops. Opposite, the *Salonni* hairdresser advertises styling in glamorous poster images, with the promise of *Eleganca*, beneath which *pranojmë kursantë – we accept trainees*. As everywhere in Albania, a number of buildings are for sale, advertised with the ubiquitous *shitet* sign. Somewhere not far off a goat is bleating. One hears cockerels crowing almost everywhere in Albania.

Time to get on the bus. The driver sits slumped over the wheel, face in his hands, and seems not to hear my enquiry. Eventually he looks up, when I ask for the third time, 'Excuse me, is this for Tirana?' He mutters something grumpy and motions me to sit down, then slouches off the bus to exchange words with a chap on a motorbike. Across the street, old ladies in headscarves are greeting each other, fags in hands; a street stall seller is pegging socks for sale on a clothesline hung across the front of the *Salloni*, from which a nest of big, blue, empty water bottles dangles, strung together for resale.

This morning, Ardi said that the area around Librazhd, close to the border with Macedonia, or FYROM as the Greeks insist, was highly militarised in the communist era. He pointed out tunnels in the cliff faces above the Shkumbin River, former military installations. 'In the communist period, they were completely paranoid about an invasion from Yugoslavia. Nobody was allowed out, nobody in. They would shoot anyone trying to escape over the border. It was like prison.'

'No one was allowed to travel?'

'No. Only import–export lorry drivers, who were recruited from elite communist party members. And if you escaped, as a lorry driver, they would take your whole family – not just your wife and kids, but parents, brothers, sisters, everyone – and put them in one of the worst parts of the country, like one of the mining regions, or some poor rotten village somewhere, with no opportunity for work or anything. So anyone thinking of defecting must think about this, what's going to happen to their family back in Albania. They'd get a "bad biography" – that was the expression.'

With much tooting and manoeuvring, the bus pulls away. An ancient sign in French at the front of the bus says, *Porte obligatoire de la ceinture de securité*, but there's no sign of any seatbelts anywhere. The constellation of cracks across the windscreen is spectacular. Albanian pop music croons tinnily from coach speakers. After a long haul westwards broadly following the Shkumbin River back towards Elbasan, which includes some heart-stopping feats of white-knuckle driving around mountain road and river valley hairpin bends, we head north-west into Tirana county for the capital, our approach augured by a comforting logjam of rush-hour traffic.

Having paid just one euro for my ninety-minute bus journey, I decide not to bother searching for the Vatican embassy and the airport bus and splash out on a taxi instead, which will cost less than a tenner. The road to the airport is lined with derelict greenhouses. I notice two old ladies inside one of them, sitting on the grass. What are they doing at 9.30 on a Friday morning, sitting in a broken-down greenhouse on the main road? Sheltering? Sunbathing? Praying? Between the greenhouses many fields are advertised for sale – *shitet toka*. A smart new development in glass and steel, the Tirana Business Park, glistens in the sun as we approach the airport, nestling in the midst of a wide open plain commanding a fabulous panoramic view of the surrounding mountains.

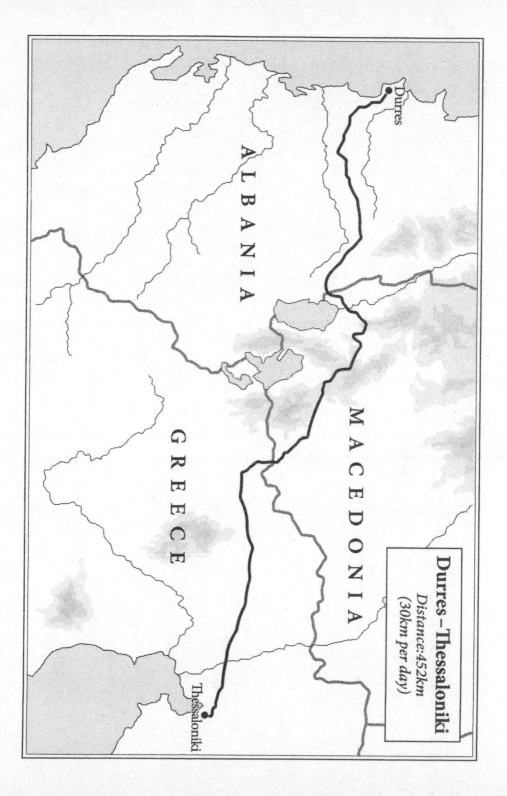

Durres

ALBANIA

MACEDONIA

GREECE

Thessaloniki

Durres – Thessaloniki
Distance:452km
(30km per day)

9

Refugee Road

Friday 22 September

I'M STANDING BENEATH the dome of the Rotonda of Hagios Giorgios (St George again) in Thessaloniki, an amazing early fourth-century round basilica with an astonishing acoustic, beautiful sunlight and wonderful Byzantine mosaics. Some Greek publications claim it as the oldest Christian church in the world. Built on the orders of the Emperor Galerius in AD 306, intended either for his own mausoleum or possibly as a temple for late pagan-era worship, it was converted by Constantine into a Christian church, originally dedicated to the Archangels, in AD 326, and that's certainly what it looks like now.

It's a bit like the experience of standing in the great Hagia Sophia in Istanbul, on a smaller scale, under a glorious empty dome, with quite a few surviving mosaics in gold and silver and bright colours around its bowl, in three concentric zones. In the lowest tier we see a very Roman-looking architectural backdrop, glittering golden pillars and columns of palaces and temples, with fabulous peacocks perched in every cranny. Through their portals, like space travellers in a psychedelic pop video, float martyred saints, or perhaps apostles and biblical characters, arms spread wide, palms open in benediction or prayer. Over the golden temple roofs and cupolas above their heads only a ring of sandalled feet survives the ravages of the centuries, traces perhaps of a convocation of worshippers revolving in a circular dance of veneration to – what? After a wide expanse of pale stripped tile-bricks contracting to the apex, a ragged halo of surviving mosaic reveals, almost comically, the faces of winged seraphs or archangels peeping above the desecrated bare patches, hands and outspread wings raised in acclamation, with eight-rayed stars blazing between each angel, the topmost tier of praise modelling the attitude of ecstatic prostration for everyone in the building to imitate, saints above and sinners below, in worship of . . . a tantalising bald patch at the summit. Whoever it is, only the fingers of his right hand, part of his halo and the end of his staff survive. A phoenix head in the midst of one of the eight-rayed stars suggests themes of fire, sun, death and renewal. The prevailing interpretation is that the central figure is Christ coming in triumph, the destroyed figures with dancing feet are prophets, saints and angels, and the praying men are martyrs floating before buildings which symbolise the heavenly Jerusalem. An alternative theory identifies the missing central character as the Emperor Constantine himself, basking in the adoration of every order of creation, by his emergence as sole emperor thanks to the divine favour of Christ. But might it not be both? *Christos Pantocrator* embodying the risen glory of the new dawn, the new faith, the new emperor and empire, Christ and Apollo and Constantine all rolled into one. Whether by the Byzantine iconoclasts of the seventh to ninth centuries, or Ottoman censorship of figurative art, or simply the mishap, wars and weathering of two millennia, today we are left only with what St Paul might have called 'a monument to an unknown god.'

Sponsored by the nobility and the emperor, these buildings provided ample opportunity for the mosaic craftsmen of this period to flourish their artistry. In the little arch leading to the west door, there's a wonderful set of what look like parrots and peacocks between bowls of fruit on consoles decorated with acanthus leaves, a scene of exuberant fecundity which can't decide whether it's a kind of pagan Bacchanalia or a Christian image of peace and plenty. These many paradisal birds, golden fleur-de-lis decorations and silver mosaics scattered like glitter in a child's collage all across the arch ceilings create the impression that this new faith must have been very jolly, a wonderful effervescence erupting from the fault line or cusp between the pagan and Christian eras. After Constantine promulgated the Edict of Milan in AD 313, which established permanent religious tolerance for Christianity in the Roman Empire, suddenly the artistry of craftsmen, mosaicists and architects was – as it were – baptised. Having produced images of Jupiter, Juno and Venus in temples and shrines for the many cults of the Roman pantheon for centuries, this vast industry of artificers suddenly transferred its energy to a massive outpouring of Christian art.

With me is my friend Julia Katarina, opera singer, oud-player and cellist, a fluent Arabic-speaker who taught music in the West Bank for more than three years and now runs Music with Refugees, a project taking Arabic music performances and workshops into refugee camps in Greece, Germany and other countries. She's joining the Walk for six weeks through Greece and Turkey, and is keen to visit one of the many refugee communities here in Thessaloniki.

From the Rotonda we wander down to the Arch of Galerius, straddling the Via Egnatia, a triumphal monument to beating up the Persians in Armenia in the late 290s and capturing their capital city. Right next to it, beneath the busy main Egnatia thoroughfare, we can see the caverns of a massive archaeological dig, fragments of the original Roman road nestling between the huge floating sewage pipes of more recent times. Next we pop along to the Church of Hagia Sophia, but it's all closed up. Then we get a call from a young French woman, a friend of a friend of Julia's, who works with refugees in Thessaloniki. We meet Liane in the *plateia* of the Rotonda and walk with her to a cafe, run by friends of hers, which may be a venue for Julia to sing later this evening, an alternative Bohemian joint, with a handful of grungy young guys smoking and drinking tea, a delightful young Greek woman who's training to be a singer and a gaggle of small children running around.

Liane has a busy, distracted air. She mentions a squat somewhere out to the west of Thessaloniki where a lot of migrants live. Julia's interested in just tipping up and playing some music, but it's not recommended to go alone. I'm fairly lukewarm about this idea, but steel myself to go along if need be. Then there's a refugee camp nearby, but apparently it's really hard to get in without a permit. 'I'm not allowed in there any more,' says Liane. 'It's a military-run camp and I have to go in and out illegally now.' Eventually it transpires that there's a young people's education project for refugees, called Arsis, on a nearby street called Ptolemeon, and a guy there called Bernardo will welcome us.

Eventually, as shades of dusk are settling after a good forty-minute trudge, we near the vicinity of Ptolemeon, and find that the street number Liane has given us is wrong. It's a dingy, unkempt street, with many empty shops with vandalised windows and overgrown trees rupturing the pavements and crowding overhead into a canopy shrouding the street in shadow, just one street up from the busy Egnatia thoroughfare. Having not found the place and unable to get anyone on the phone to establish the correct street number, we're on the point of giving up when I decide to explore back along the way we've come. Every doorway has a cluster of buzzers with sundry labels, crossed out, plastered over with new stickers and handwritten scrawl. Some doorways are open, leading to darkened derelict stairwells with broken lifts and odd assortments of detritus – rolls of carpet propped up against bannisters, piles of boxes, broken panes of glass leaning against walls. Not very promising. At last I discover a smartish-looking sign for the Arsis project, emblazoned with logos of Norwegian Aid and other charities. I hail Julia, struggling with her broken phone and useless Greek sim card down the street, and we prowl through another darkened vestibule and up the stairs.

We enter a beautiful enclave on the first floor, as far removed from the squalor of the street as you could imagine, and ask for Bernardo. He's not here today, we're told by the charming, smiley Bangladeshi–Greek assistant, but we're asked to wait. The place is light and airy, with plenty of daylight, smart marble and pine floors and classrooms and refectories opening off a pleasant atrium, with an aura of warmth, order and safety. Various children, teenagers and teachers pass through. A kindly faced, Bohemian-looking teacher arrives – Roana – who's Moroccan and fluent in Arabic, Greek and English. We introduce ourselves and our flimsy point of contact, and ask if Julia might sing to some of the kids. 'Why not?' says Roana. 'That would be nice.' She guides us to a classroom, set up with a round table and tiny chairs for nursery and primary school children, and Julia tunes her oud.

Initially, Roana brings in two teenage Syrian lads, Hosain and Mahmoud, who are both around fifteen and dressed in jeans, trainers and hoodies. Mahmoud has a kind of Rambo-style bandana on his head; Hosain has a tiny ponytail or topknot. They're really nice lads and remind me very much of my fourteen-year-old son Jacob. Julia chats to them in Arabic and plays and sings a number of Syrian songs. A kind of melancholy enchantment suffuses the room. They're mesmerised, these lads, thoughtful, sad, maybe a bit weirded out by the situation, but very appreciative, and there are many smiles. They clap after each song and sing along with some. Gradually, other kids start to steal into the room, of all ages – some Syrian, some Iraqi, some Kurdish, some north African. Maybe twenty kids all told, and three or four teachers. It's a beautiful, fragile moment of oddity and tenderness, conjured by Julia's music and the attention of these kids, uprooted from their homes and homelands, who've travelled by God-knows-what means from war zones and the perils of people-traffickers and the sea, and ended up here in Thessaloniki, in an all-but-failed state that doesn't want them, finding refuge in this warm and hospitable enclave. The teachers and volunteers are, quite simply, beautiful people.

Hosain and Mahmoud are both from Aleppo. Mahmoud, who's a really good-looking lad, came with his older sister and her husband. Hosain came with his parents and several siblings. In both cases, their parents decided it was time to go. The areas where they lived were too close to the bombing. Their schools were closed, in one case bombed, in the other turned into a hospital. Mahmoud's parents clearly felt that he had a better chance in the West, and of course he would have been very vulnerable to potential recruitment by one of the militias, or simply being murdered as a potential combatant. 'And your family are still there?' I ask him. 'Yes,' he says, 'and at the moment they're OK.' (This exchange is translated by Julia.) Mahmoud supports Barcelona, Hosain Bayern Munich. Here at Arsis, they're learning Greek and maths and other subjects. 'But I don't want to learn Greek,' says Mahmoud. 'I want to learn English and go to the UK, or Germany. There's not much for us here. But we understand it's difficult.'

What would they like to do when they grow up, I ask. They smile. They don't really know. They've missed out on four or five years of schooling, Julia explains. They'd like to get an education, go to the UK or Germany, be with their families. They'd like to go back to Syria. There's something that touches me about their 'western-ness' – their clothes, their faces, their manner and the open, unguarded gentleness of their demeanour, their whole mode of communication. It touches me very deeply. I have to hold it together. They're lost, and they're brave, and polite, and dignified, and they're really doing their best. They are lads I would be proud to have as my sons. They're lads I would be glad for my kids to have as friends. I so desperately want good things for these two lads, I feel almost overwhelmed with the grief and incomprehension and sheer bloody bad luck of their whole situation. I wish some of our UKIP voters and tub-thumping politicians back in the UK could be here tonight to meet them. We must open our doors and our hearts to these people and stop, stop, stop this abominable war.

Roana shows us around after the recital, to the common rooms, dining room, the school theatre space, with sliding doors to reveal a recessed classroom that can be used as a performance space. 'We do a lot of theatre,' she says, 'and then at lunchtime we can open up these three classrooms adjoining and make a long line of tables for all the kids to eat together.' She's a really lovely lady, with amazing warmth and positivity, and supremely encouraging about our pilgrimage. A great tangle of curly dark hair held off her face by a forehead band, T-shirt and checked shirt, jeans and trainers, packet of fags in her shirt pocket, a kindly, lined face and glasses perched on her nose – could be any age between fifty and seventy, petite, husky-voiced, lots of bangles and earrings. An angel in teacher's guise.

'We teach maths, physics, Greek, English, everything here – all the normal classes. A lot of the kids come at noon and spend most days here. It would be wonderful if you could come back and do a concert, and we'll get all the parents in and organise food, and everything. Thank you for what you're doing. It's wonderful. It's so important. It's beautiful.'

Not half as wonderful as what you're doing, I think. She hugs and kisses us, and we exchange high fives with Hosain and Mahmoud, and line up for a group photo. I want to hug these lads and never let them go.

Saturday 23 September

Today I am the driver, covering a gap between Fatima's stint and our new driver Ollie's arrival. And, sod's law having yet to be repealed, today turns out to be just about the hardest, longest and most perilous driving of the entire bloody pilgrimage. I drop the first group off to start their walk at the White (actually brown) Tower of Salonika, in the still dusky early-morning gloom after a 5.30 a.m. breakfast, then head back for the second group. Tim has real trouble navigating the drop-off point and we go round the whirligig three times until eventually we find a place to pull in off the motorway at the tiny woodland shrine and church of St George, which is also a travellers' campsite, by the look of it, and the walkers cross the road via a tunnel. I give Tim the beautiful book *Anam Cara*, by John O'Donohue, from which to read a reflection with the group:

> Humans are new here. Above us, the galaxies dance out towards infinity. Under our feet is ancient earth. We are beautifully moulded from this clay. Yet the smallest stone is millions of years older than us. In your thoughts the silent universe seeks echo. An unknown world aspires towards reflection. Words are the oblique mirrors which hold your thoughts. You gaze into these word mirrors and catch glimpses of meaning, belonging and shelter. Behind their bright surfaces is the dark and the silence. Words are like the god Janus, they face outwards and inwards at once.
>
> If we become addicted to the external, our interiority will haunt us.[1]

Humans are new here . . . an observation that could hardly be more prescient when it comes to finding functioning roads across the wild, remote countryside into which we're heading. After driving the second group successfully to a rendezvous point with the first, then driving back to the hotel to load up everyone's bags, load salad boxes and say farewell to one of our companions, Regine, who's off back to Germany, I head off to meet the walkers for a lunchtime rendezvous, where I surpass myself (though I say it myself) by finding a beautiful village cafe with a garden, where the proprietor Costas doesn't mind us eating our own food as long as we drink lots of his coffee. I supplement the very sweaty salad boxes supplied by last night's hotel with some delicious Greek bread from a local deli, taramasalata, tzatiki and olives. Most gratifyingly, the walkers all give me a big thumbs-up and say I've passed the Just Walk driver's exam and got the job. Then a long drive to find the extremely quaint little village of Peristera, where Cressey is already ensconced at the extremely rustic hotel, and one hotel staff member – a young girl with no English – is making up beds.

Then an epic drive over a mountain to meet the first group at the end of their walk, down in the village of Ardameri. A burly priest in a pickup truck at the top of the village directs me up the tiny road over the mountain: keep going, all the way to Ardameri. The little road soon becomes a concrete drive and then an extremely rough, steep, red mountain track, littered with enormous boulders and pitted with huge holes and trenches, slowing my progress to about five miles an hour, but my satnav points onwards encouragingly. Then, despite the clear evidence of a continuing track ahead, the satnav suddenly orders a sharp left turn, down a kind of stony gully sloping sharply downhill and back westward. With serious misgivings, I swing the van round and start to creep down the gully, which is barely wide enough for the wheels. After twenty or thirty yards I come to a sharp right turn, beyond which there's clearly no possible further path. I climb down from the van to explore on foot for a few yards. No. This so-called path is a feckin' stream bed narrowing to a steep ravine. I'll be lucky to get the van back out in one piece. Acutely aware of the time and the fact that there are two groups to be picked up, with palms sweating I inch the vehicle back up the gully, managing not to plunge it over the edge on the right, or crunch it into the rock wall on the left.

Back on the mountain track, mightily relieved and damning all satnavs to hell, I resume the rumbling crawl over the hill and, by a mixture of luck, guesswork and Providence, at last get the van down the other side into Ardameri, where the first group of walkers gape in disbelief at the thick shroud of red dust coating the vehicle roof to tyres. I drive them back over the mountain to Peristera; they are not disappointed. The potholed, shrapnel-littered road of ruin more than lives up to my description. After depositing them at the hotel and smoking a much-needed fag, I decide to go a different route, *around* the mountain, to pick up the second group, as it's now getting dark. It may be tripling the length of the journey, effectively driving round three sides of a square, but there's nothing else for it, so I hare off around hairpin-bend mountain roads for an hour or more, driving as fast as I dare, to pick up the second group from the village of Vasilika, then back the same way to Peristera. Fortunately the roads are well surfaced and completely deserted. After a day of driving that started at 6 a.m., I get the last walkers to a magnificent rustic village restaurant by 9 p.m., where a splendid spread of local vegetables, meats, salads and breads awaits.

What a day. Talk about a baptism of fire. Actually, I'm glad it was me and not one of our volunteer drivers.

Just across the field from our hotel, a handsome complex of traditional timber farm buildings, a flickering mirage of will-o'-the-wisp twinkles from the churchyard. I stroll over with Julia to explore, and discover that every grave and tomb has little candles burning, in glass lanterns and votive niches. Why do they light them? A Saturday night vigil before the Sabbath? Or is it a special occasion? It reminds me of *Dia de Muertos* festivities in Mexico. Very pretty, if not a little spooky.

Bed at last after a day like no other. *Humans are new here.* You can feckin' say that again, O'Donohue. So new they haven't built any roads yet.

Breakfast the next morning is followed by a comedy exchange with the proprietor's son about how to defraud Booking.com:

'You pay us in cash, so we don't have to pay the commission, yeah? Then we can say that you cancelled, you didn't stay here.'

'But why would we not stay here, if we booked?'

He scratches his head, then has a lightbulb moment. 'Well, you could make a complaint!' he exclaims delightedly, 'About the hot water?'

Yup, that's the way to fix a broken economy.

Tuesday 26 September

There is gloomy news this morning of the killing of three Israelis (two security guards and a border policeman) by a Palestinian gunman outside the settlement of Har Adar, north-west of Jerusalem. With brilliant congruity Ian reads Thomas Hardy's poem, 'The Darkling Thrush', as our morning meditation:

. . . a voice arose among
The bleak twigs overhead
In a full-hearted evensong
Of joy illimited;
An aged thrush, frail, gaunt, and small,
In blast-beruffled plume,
Had chosen thus to fling his soul
Upon the growing gloom.

So little cause for carolings
Of such ecstatic sound
Was written on terrestrial things
Afar or nigh around,
That I could think there trembled through
His happy good-night air
Some blessed Hope, whereof he knew
And I was unaware.[2]

Amid a cloud of flocking starlings, we walk along the coast towards Amfipoli. We eat our lunch in the shadow of a towering statue of an enormous lion in rippling limestone, with snarling jowls, whip-cord veins and deep-set stone eyes staring out from the ancient world, pointing the way to the Graeco-Roman city of Amphipolis. Unearthed by Greek soldiers in the Balkan Wars of 1912–13, the lion was discovered to be a fourth-century BC funerary monument erected in honour of the admiral Laomedon, from the island of Lesbos, a devoted companion of Alexander the Great, commander of a trireme warship and later Alexander's satrap of Syria.

Trekking on up the hill across muddy fields, we stumble almost by accident on the ruins of ancient Amphipolis, a windswept, neglected archaeological site on a deserted hilltop. Under a drizzly, misty mid-afternoon sky, we wander around the rocky crags of the Roman and early Byzantine citadel, gazing at the swirling geometric patterns weaving across mosaic floors of long fallen basilicas, deer and fish and birds framed in alternating circles and squares like creatures peeping through windows from another world, now blotched and faded with neglect. The city where Alexander the Great once directed his invasion of Asia and St Paul preached on his journey to Rome in AD 49–50 is now a deserted hillock, where the tumbled pillars of collapsed colonnades lie in the grass beside their pedestals and a few lines of foundations trace the walls of atriums and porticoes built in the high summer of the Byzantine world, abandoned to the elements.

Wednesday 27 September

Walking across the moors of Rodolivos with Jude, I pause to record a magical potpourri of sounds – tinkling goat bells and dogs woofing, bees buzzing, cicadas trilling and the silvery sliver of wrens and thrushes singing – a soundscape unchanged on these hills in 3,000 years. Then we have an intriguing chat about the Incarnation, which gets my thoughts whirring. Apropos of I can't remember what, I say something about the microscopic cellular reality of the Incarnation, the idea of God entering and becoming part of creation at the smallest level, in a woman's egg, creating a zygote in which God and human essence fuse.

Jude says, completely reflexively, 'What, do you believe that?'

'Yes.'

'Well, how could he? He wouldn't have the right genetic material. I mean, if you say that God caused her egg to start spontaneously dividing and developing into a foetus, a clone, then Jesus would have been a woman.'

Obviously, I don't have an answer to Jude's objection, but I flounder for a bit, then say, 'Well, I don't know how, but it kind of feels important to me . . .'

'*It's a mystery*,' says Jude drily, with heavy italics.

Running quickly into the long grass talking detail with a scientist, one is tempted to take the short cut to 'Mystery' – and this feels not good enough to me.

The poetic symbolism of God and human essence fusing as zygote in a woman's womb is *amazing* – like Dali's picture of the Ascension, in which he depicts Christ 'ascending' into the nucleus of an atom – and I want to hold on to it. I get that it doesn't make sense medically, and I very quickly run out of answers when interrogated by a doctor on this.

At this point a caveat looms: I'm aware of the early church and mediaeval queasy obsession with Mary's virginity, worshipping the

BVM as virgin goddess, cherishing her undefiled hymen, etc. – none of which holds any interest for me, other than anthropological. As Jude points out, there's something less-than-fully woman about this BVM – as if the early church fathers, who were very bothered about sexuality, could only cope with a woman in such a pivotal role at the heart of the faith if she were a meek, pure, immaculately conceived goddess – in fact, not really a woman at all. I remember once hearing the composer John Tavener speak about the Eastern Orthodox view of Mary as an extremely robust figure, Maria Theotokos, the God-bearer, and the pivotal moment of her choice, crucial for human history and the whole symphony of redemption. He spoke of the vital importance in Eastern Orthodoxy of Mary's 'yes', without which the Incarnation could not have happened. It wouldn't matter in the slightest to me whether Mary was a virgin or not; the bit I'm interested in is the divine conception.

Despite Jude's unanswerable objection, I'm not satisfied with simply reverting to the idea of Jesus conceived in the normal way with a human father, as a normal human child who somehow – what? – 'attains divinity' through his life. How? By some kind of divine 'hostile takeover'? Surely the whole point about our nature as creatures is that we're made *in the image of*, but *distinct from* God. Surely that's the miracle of God's creative love – being able to, and choosing to, make stuff *different from* himself, *other than* himself – like space, time, energy, matter, and other small achievements. The idea of a human being somehow attaining perfection and then *becoming* God doesn't work for me – it makes it sound as if our ultimate destiny is to be reabsorbed into the divine essence, a kind of *nirvana*.

I'm also not satisfied with taking a quick, easy exit sign to 'Mystery'. It's intellectually lazy, and when we hear religious leaders and clergy spouting this kind of flannel, it makes them sound condescending: 'Don't come pestering me with your petty scientific objections; I operate on a higher plane.' I'm not satisfied with two-tier descriptions of reality – on one level literal truth and on another level – what, a 'higher' level? – some kind of disembodied 'poetic' or 'mythic' truth? It sounds very dualistic to me, as if we can't find poetry or beauty in what *is* – so we have to escape to some kind of 'other' realm to invent it. I don't want to do that.

Why does it matter? Well, the thing is, my *experience* of Jesus is, I believe – albeit apprehended partially, falteringly, imperfectly, intermittently – of a rescuing Saviour bringing light, hope, warmth, strength and – above all, above all – his affirming, redeeming *love* into my life at the deepest level. However much I have despised or despaired of myself, however much I disappoint or dislike myself, I am somehow given the strength or hope to learn to value myself, care for myself, respect myself – one could in fact say, *love* myself – because he shows me the way. For the first thousand years of Christianity, this Saviour was known as *Christus Victor*, who rescues us from the pit of despair, like Dionysus descending to Hades to bring back Semele, the springtime of the earth, or Orpheus and Heracles in different legends entering the underworld to overthrow death, or the philosopher in Plato's simile of the Cave in *The Republic* who, having escaped from the shackles of illusion and unreality to attain the true light of day, chooses to return to the darkness of the Cave to liberate the rest of humanity.

Every year at our Easter Eve Vigil at St Luke's, in a darkened church lit only by the single flame of the previous year's Paschal candle (before it is extinguished to leave us waiting in darkness for the dawning of Easter Day), we hear the words of the ancient Orthodox homily for Holy Saturday:

Something strange is happening – there is a great silence on earth today, a great silence and stillness. The whole earth keeps silence because the King is asleep. The earth trembled and is still because God has fallen asleep in the flesh and he has raised up all who have slept ever since the world began. God has died in the flesh and hell trembles with fear.

He has gone to search for our first parent, as for a lost sheep. Greatly desiring to visit those who live in darkness and in the shadow of death, he has gone to free from sorrow the captives Adam and Eve, he who is both God and the son of Eve. (Ancient second century homily)

I understand that Richard Dawkins would probably say that what's going on here is an inner psychological game that has a biological or evolutionary explanation: the individual, experiencing negative emotions about self for whatever reason, needs for evolutionary purposes to feel better about self, so invents an external Saviour, an authority figure, to say nice things about said individual, which results in positive attitude about self, thus better health, wellbeing, etc. Or a psychotherapist might say we need to learn to do this for ourselves, and not rely on Jesus or some external Deliverer (because this 'infantilises' us, in psychobabble). But the point is that, for me, if we demythologise or demystify the whole thing and make it a kind of internal, antiseptic self-help exercise, it wouldn't work. I don't have the Saviour, the Strong Deliverer, already within my psyche; I need to invite him in. 'Behold, I stand at the door and knock.'[3]

So why not just believe in God? Or a Higher Power? Why trouble with all this complication of the Incarnation, all this Jesus stuff?

I guess what's so compelling for me about the Incarnation is God's incredible act of solidarity with us in *changing his own nature* to become part of his creation. God, who – according to Rowan Williams, we should imagine as 'sublimely and eternally happy to be God' and needing nothing to complete or fulfil his nature to any greater completeness or fulfilment than he already has – *merges his own essence* with humanity to take on our 'frail flesh', to experience hunger, cold, weariness, sorrow, desire, pain and, yes, even death. And he triumphs over all deathliness *from within the messy heart of his human existence* – and leads me, beckons me, strengthens me, shows me the way to do the same. He is our pioneer, our Orpheus, leading us out of Hades, our Dionysus restoring spring to the world, our Philosopher choosing to forgo the pure realm of light and truth to come and sit with us in the darkest place.

On one level, of course, our pilgrimage to Palestine is seeking to do this – to bring some hope, strength and love to people imprisoned in the darkness of occupation by a huge and dramatic act of solidarity. The paradox is, of course, that by seeking to be 'God-bearers' – *Christo-phers* – ourselves, we actually find God there in the place to which we seek to carry him. This is the paradox of our pilgrimage. 'I know we're doing this for the Palestinians,' said Jude at one point, 'but I'm also doing it for me.' And it doesn't seem to matter which way round you start. If you go 'for yourself',

seeking enlightenment, God, whatever – you end up doing something that has amazing significance to others. If you go 'for others',
you end up encountering God for yourself.

So, in theological terms, I need Jesus to be greater than myself
– not just a very enlightened but 'normal' human being who 'attains'
divinity, but *Christus Victor*, Strong Deliverer – *and* I need him to
be human, because everything I experience, in all its messy reality,
he has experienced too. He stands in solidarity with my humanity.
Calls me to a fuller humanity. So I need Jesus to be God *and* human.
I need the miraculous birth and the Incarnation. This is why I
needed to walk to Palestine, where it all began, where he actually
walked, breathed, worked, slept, swam, ate and drank, wiped sweat
from his brow, got blisters on his feet, shivered in the cool night
air, picked olives and dates, etc., etc. – and where the struggle of
Incarnation, the struggle to be born, the struggle to live – in the
place of impossible tension, the place of crucifixion – is still raging
torturously at the heart of the world.

Tuesday 3 October

I lead the morning reflection in the noisy hotel foyer, reading
Szymborska's poem, 'Nothing's a Gift', and off we set, eastwards
through the outlying districts of Xanthi, labyrinths of broken-down,
impoverished shacks and breeze-block houses, many with polythene
instead of glass in the windows. A Nissan people-carrier trundles
past with a dozen kids in the back and some kind of loudhailer
announcing the price of their cargo of fruit and veg, a common
sight round here. There's a very jolly Christmas star hanging from
the eaves of one house, an olive sapling planted outside another,
and washing lines everywhere. Apparently, this is a Bulgarian slum
or suburb; we've just met some kids who say they're from Bulgaria,
and several people have warned us not to go this way, shaking their
heads, wagging their fingers and pointing eastwards, saying 'Roma,
Roma.' It seems there's a pecking order of poverty here and the
Roma are bottom of the pile. But this way lies our route. We pass
an old Roma lady with one arm, headscarf and colourful shawl. I
smile and say, *'Kalimera'* ('good morning') and she reaches out, palm
extended, clearly asking for money. We've not experienced this

before on the Walk; normally, however impoverished, we've always found people rushing out to greet us or offer hospitality.

Eventually we make it out of the slums and shanty towns, through a horrible stretch of unofficial rubbish dump with towering piles of refuse on every side, and then cross a broad scar of industrial wasteland filled with vast lengths of plastic and fibreglass tubing, machinery and excavation works for tunnel digging, like a movie set for *The World is Not Enough*, which we learn is the construction site of the new Trans-Aegean pipeline, bringing natural gas from the Caspian Sea through Azerbaijan and Turkey into Greece. From here we pass into a beautiful area of National Park and a truly sublime morning's walk along a wooded dyke, with river and mountains in the north to our left, and the Thracian Plain running down to our right towards the sea, a patchwork of sunflower and tobacco fields, and cotton fields sprinkled with snowy daubs, with a line of pylons and cables marching eastwards. While the others walk the Via Egnatia along the dyke, I'm walking a parallel path along the riverbank, twenty yards or so to the north. It's a beautiful, vividly green, verdant path between holm oaks and pine trees, birches, poplars and hawthorn bushes and everywhere, wonderfully bright new grass is coming through. I don't know if it's been seeded or just seeded itself but the path is a glorious carpet of absolutely glistening, golden-green slender shoots in the sunlight between the trees. There are little lizards darting through the grass, and lots of frogs hopping around the muddy sward just to the left by the river-bank.

I follow a strange, low-pitched throbbing sound to the foot of a tall beech, bearded with huge growths of ivy, just about to flower, and absolutely swarming with bees. Hundreds and thousands of bees crawling over and under and in between the ivy leaves and mistletoe to gorge on the nectar, buzzing and humming and rumbling in the most amazing polyphony. It feels like a scene from one of the Alexandrian pastoral poets, Theocritus or Callimachus, or maybe the fourth book of Virgil's *Georgics*. The undergrowth around the beech roots rustles with snakes or rats, or maybe a pine marten hunting them.

There's a pilgrim prayer which I often recite inwardly, in rhythm with breath and stride, as a silent mantra while I walk:

Father Almighty, Maker of heaven and earth, build your kingdom
in our midst.
Lord Jesus Christ, Son of the living God, have mercy on me, a
sinner.
Holy Spirit, Breath of the living God, renew me and all the world.

I wander down towards the riverbank and, as I step just over the
brow of the bank, breathing these words, suddenly a kingfisher
flashes out down the middle of the stream, a brilliant, heart-leaping
spark of sapphire, streaking along the golden-green water. Amen.

After lunch at a river ford crossing, near the village of Amaxades,
where a pair of shepherds have corralled their sheep in the shade
of acacias and plane trees to rest out of the midday heat, we march
on to end the day's walk at a bizarre final destination – a vast,
gleaming out-of-town toy store, near Iasmos in the Rhodope region,
completely deserted except for a single store assistant. Ollie picks
us up in several loads and ferries us to beautiful lakeside apartments
near the village of Lagos. We wander to a spit-and-sawdust seafood
cafe in the lake harbour village, where the restaurateur claims the
card machine 'has a bad signal', which means he wants to be paid
in cash, like everyone in Greece.

Jude has told me about a teenage lad called Amir, a refugee
from Iraq, whom she met in Kavala Camp the other day, who's
now looking after his three younger siblings because his father was
killed in Iraq by Daesh/ISIS, and his mother has been arrested
recently, in a small town close to the Greek–Turkish border, the
frontier running along the River Evros. His stepfather is also in
the camp at Kavala. The story they've heard from Rasha, Amir's
mother, is that she was meeting a friend in the border town when
Greek police set on her, took all her money (around 2,000 euros),
her phone and paperwork and then dumped her in the no-man's-
land between the borders, whereupon the Turkish police picked
her up and took her to a detention centre or prison in Edirne,
not far from our route through Turkey next week. Jude was very
moved by Amir's obvious anguish and is determined to get Rasha
released and reunited with her family. According to her husband,
Amir's stepfather, Rasha's paperwork was all in order for her to be
received into Greece as an asylum seeker, as they were fleeing

persecution in Iraq, so the alleged behaviour of the Greek police is inexplicable in legal terms.

Terrible night's sleep, freezing cold and persecuted by nightmares. The one I remember is a kind of *Hunger Games* scenario in which I'm being prepared as a kind of quarry to be hunted by savage dogs – stripped down to a loincloth and sandals (oo-er) and having cuts inflicted on my arms and legs to give the dogs the scent of my blood. Hideous. I wake up and go to the loo and put on all the clothes I can find in the dark without disturbing my roommate, Ollie, and pass a fitful night between waking and sleeping.

Friday 6 October

A day spent slogging through the pine woods and forests of oak and acacia and heather-sloped hills of the eastern Aegean hinterland, the easternmost reaches of the Rhodope foothills. The first group left at 7.30 a.m. and the second around 8.45 a.m., or thereabouts. We drove out to meet the first group somewhere along the coast between the road and the railway and had to wait quite a while for them to beat a path to us. Eventually they made it through and we gathered for a reflection – me reading a poem by Edwin Muir which begins, appropriately, 'Friends, I have lost the way . . .'[4]

Then off we walked, striking off the road to hike over a series of huge, red-soil, shale-sliver fire breaks cut through the forests of the national park. Huge, tractor-cut gashes in the forest, broad and steeply undulating, completely exposed to the sun, the red shale slopes dotted with lumps of marble. Here and there the shale fragments into little shards and pebbles of oil-slick radiance, each as slick and shiny as pawa shells in New Zealand. After a hefty series of quite punishing climbs through these fire-breaks, around one o'clock we strike off on a path marked by the Via Egnatia Foundation as 'the way', although it swiftly becomes overgrown with pine saplings and gorse bushes, wild roses and rhododendrons. Above the tree line we see spectacular vistas of wooded hills on all sides. A series of steep, scratchy scrambles bring us slap up against a rusty old fence at the edge of the forest, beyond which a tantalisingly clear strip of ground runs as a path heading south-east. We can't cross the fence, despite the Via Egnatia Foundation's suggestion that we should, and the intermittent booms of Greek army artillery practice in the distance warn us to err on the side of caution. There's a sweet smell of pines everywhere. In the past twenty-four hours we've heard the tearing rumble of Greek warplanes across the sky, several low-flying military helicopters and numerous reports of tanks and troops massing on the border.

It's early October, but it feels like a hot English summer, walking in this bright sun, it must be 27 or 28 degrees. The cicadas have gone quiet now, obviously having their siesta. The rock is a kind of broken shale, which flakes off in thin slivers, and the steep gorge we're walking down now, parallel to the military fence, scattered with shale shrapnel, pine cones and pine needles, clearly must become a stream bed in the wet season. Beautiful thickets of pink heather tumble down the right hand slopes of the gorge. My white cotton shirt is soaked with sweat after our climb to 440 metres above sea level, so I'm carrying it like a flag on the end of a stick over my shoulder, trying to dry it out in the breeze and hot sun. Jokes fly back and forth about flying the white flag, to persuade the Greek and Turkish armies we're a peaceful contingent caught in the crossfire.

After our lunch stop, we plunge once more into the improvised path through woods and scrub and prise our way through the undergrowth to rejoin the fence and slog our way up it until, at last, we emerge in a high clearing with two dozen beehives and a mass of swarming bees. This in turn leads us to the road, where we encounter once more the Trans-Aegean gas pipeline being laid across the forest, sections of sturdy black plastic piping being sunk in deep trenches to either side of the road. Down the forest road we stride, and I end up at the back keeping Arthur company, who's struggling with knee trouble. Rasha's husband, he tells me, is emphatic that she was kidnapped and robbed by the Greek police. She had gone to a small town near the border to meet a friend or family member and was accosted by the police, who not only took her money but also ripped up all her paperwork before dumping her in no-man's-land. Why would the Turkish authorities agree to take her, under such circumstances? Well, Turkey receives payments from the UN for every refugee under their 'care', so Rasha's husband has surmised that this could be some kind of 'pushback' racket, whereby both countries get compensated for effectively shuttling the same person back and forth and the Greek police get to line their own pockets on the side. According to her husband, her right to reside as a refugee in Greece is not in dispute, and she is just waiting for the Greek authorities in Edirne to go and get her out of prison, so she can come back to Greece. We'll try and make some kind of representation on her behalf next Monday when we're in Turkey to hasten the process along.

Eventually we catch up with Robin and Naomi and phone Ollie to come and pick Arthur up from here. We leave Arthur and walk the final 11 km into Alexandroupolis. Beer and pizza, red wine and ice cream back at the hotel beach bar and then, after supper, I go for a swim, braving the dark, rocking waters of the Aegean by night. It's blissfully refreshing to laze in the buffeting waves under the moonlight, with stars peeping through the clouds in the south across the sea. Swimming free in the cool dark waves after this long, hot, scratchy day in the woods is exhilarating.

Sunday 8 October

I'm up at 6.30 a.m. for breakfast to ferry the first group into the lighthouse in the centre of Alexandroupolis to begin their day's walk. Then back to the Santa Rosa hotel. Standing on the beach just down from the hotel, looking across to Samothrace sitting wreathed in cloud like a volcano, I've rarely seen such a beautiful sea, blissfully calm after last night's hurricane. There's a great veil of clouds strung across the sky, with blue patches everywhere peeping through, and the moon over to our right, to the west, just fading (as my friend Nigel Forde would have said) like a boiled sweet dissolving on your tongue. Over to the east, the stunning sunrise over the sea is kindling the clouds on the horizon into gold. I've never seen this before: cloud sitting on the horizon in an unbroken hedge, like a great ice barrier. It looks like what I imagine the coast of Antarctica must look like – a fairy-tale seascape of glacier and ice. And between the clouds and the sea are the dark slivers of the islands stretching away eastwards towards Turkey. It's breathtakingly beautiful, all the more so because of that incredible storm last night, a great boiling sea with massive rollers, torrential rain, lightning and thunder. One can't bear to think of any refugee boats caught in that; nobody would have survived. This morning the beach furniture was all in disarray, tables and sun-loungers hurled all over the place, and apparently there was damage all down the coast. Our lady proprietor, Despina, said this morning that very bad weather has caused terrible damage on Samothrace recently, just across the water, and there's been an aid effort from all across Europe to help repair the damage.

Most of our 'day off' yesterday was taken up with arrangements for rental vehicles and taxis to get our gear and our walkers to the border, then over the border, then get the van back. Despina and her husband Dollis were hugely helpful, putting me in touch with Avgerinos, a local fixer who turned up to negotiate logistics. You can't walk over the border and you can't drive a rental vehicle across. It's a heavily militarised frontier at the best of times, but security's tighter than ever since the refugee crisis.

Avgerinos organises a nine-seater minibus for us, as Ollie has gone back now and returned the previous bus to Thessaloniki. When we arrive at the Kipi–Peplos border crossing on Monday, Avgerinos has arranged for his friend Lakis, a Turkish taxi driver licensed to go back and forth over the border, to ferry the walkers through to the Turkish side in several cars, to a point where Ivor the driver and a new volunteer, Alexandra, will be waiting for us with a Turkish rental vehicle. Then I will return the minibus to Alexandroupolis and Avgerinos will take me through to join the walkers in Turkey.

I have another breakfast with the second group (compensation for all this factotum-drudgery), then take them down the main road to meet the first lot. Our morning reflection (in the Shell gas station) is led by Joanna, part of a beautiful poem by John O'Donohue, 'For the Traveller':

> Every time you leave home,
> Another road takes you
> Into a world you were never in . . .

I return with Julia (who's taking a day off walking), load up the van with everyone's baggage, pay the bill and order a stack of takeaway sandwiches. Final farewells, thanks and away to meet the walkers for their lunch stop. We fly the Palestinian flag from the van.

After many wrong turns down muddy, off-road tracks in the countryside of the Loutros/Feres area, eventually we find the group and give them lunch, which gets a thumbs-up, then drive on to Hotel Isidora, next to Therma Loutri Traianopolis, the site of some famous Roman baths, where Maria and Elefterios greet us warmly. After dumping the bags, we set off for the pickup at a remarkable twelfth-century Byzantine basilica in the centre of Feres, the Monastery of Panagia Kosmosoteira, the (female) all-holy saviour of the world, a title for the Virgin I've never heard before. The first group tell me they've had a visitation from the Greek border police. I drive them to the hotel and return for the second group, to find a drone flying over the church. After a sneaky coffee in the cafe with Arthur, I ferry them to the hotel and my day's driving is done.

After a phone call to my daughter Eleanor, chatting over her history essay and dredging up everything I can remember about Robespierre, Danton, the *ancien regime* and the reign of terror, I wander along the track from the hotel to look at the ruined Byzantine church and the Roman baths. Julia arrives with her oud and sings an impromptu recital of Dowland and Arabic songs hauntingly in the echoing bath chambers. Outside, the sky is on fire with an amazing sunset, great drifts of fiery orange spreading across the horizon above a golden coppery sunset burning through the clouds with glittering radiance. A magical, almost numinous moment of the journey, our last night in Greece.

Monday 9 October

I rise at 6.45 a.m. and go down to breakfast, where Arthur and Jude are laying plans to go to the Greek Consulate in Edirne. Coffee, bread and jam. I feel weary and jaded, and 'coffeed out'. I drive the first group to the amazing church of Panagia Kosmosoteira in Feres. There's a glorious sunrise lighting the mist across the valley to the east as I return for the second group.

With both groups assembled, we gather for a reflection outside the church, where Joanna reads the second part of John O'Donohue's poem:

A journey can become a sacred thing:
Make sure, before you go,
To take the time
To bless your going forth . . .

We bless our going forth with a group photo against the ancient Byzantine walls of the monastery, the walkers depart, then Julia and I explore the fabulous basilica. It's a magical space, apparently modelled on the Haghia Sophia in Constantinople, and the most important Byzantine survival in the whole of Thrace. There are some magnificent twelfth-century Byzantine frescoes, probably of the Emperor and his family: four portraits of Byzantine princes, emperors or warriors, with swords and spears and armour, above a flock of saints glowering out at us. In the late 1300s the Ottomans seized the building and turned it into a mosque, damaged the paintings with hammers and then plastered over them. Fragments of this plaster remain, with traces of Ottoman decoration, patterned leaves and fleur-de-lis. The gold, blue and brown coppery colours of the frescoes were restored in the 1920s, when it was turned back into a church. It's a beautiful place to visit on our last day in Greece, a building which bears the marks in its body of the centuries-old conflict between Greeks and Turks, Islam and Christianity, Ottoman and Byzantine.

After their last morning's walking in Greece, we'll meet the group on the border and organise ferrying all the walkers and their luggage across. 'Take the time to bless your going forth'. This feels like the right place and moment in which to pray for blessing on our going forth. A beggar, Iannis, comes in and asks for a euro to buy some coffee. He smells and seems a little crazy, insisting several times that his parents are in Germany. We give him what coins we have and shake hands. Maybe he's Jesus in disguise. Then we sing several Alleluias and the Trisagion in the chancel, until a bevy of old Greek ladies come in to pray and light candles, and we beat a hasty retreat. 'No female voices allowed in Greek churches,' Julia reminds me. Off we set, having prayed for the pilgrimage, lit a candle, given alms and sung. Job done.

10

Walking Turkey

9 October, Kipi Border Station

THE BORDER CROSSING next to the village of Kipi is a fabulous slalom of DIY-improvised traffic control. There are lorries parked everywhere, higgledy-piggledy. You can drive up and down any lane in any direction. We came down a little slip road from the village, a little finger of Greece poking into Turkey, and found ourselves effectively on the Turkish side, so if we'd hopped over the fence there we could have avoided all this palaver. There's obviously a vast amount of furniture, textiles, timber, cotton and tobacco going back and forth. Ironically, every other lorry seems to have the word 'Logistiks' painted along the side. Humble foot passengers like us are the least of anyone's concern. I expect the main priority is searching the lorries coming from Turkey for migrants. It's a grey, overcast sky, with a bit of blue peeping through, over this slightly surreal *Mad Max* scenario. It's how I imagine the Gaza border at Rafah. There are one or two soldiers wandering around. Mind you, there are lots of army surplus shops in this part of Greece, so you don't really know who's a soldier and who isn't. I think the soldiers flog as much of their gear as they can to make a few bucks.

Lakis is a fantastic character, a dodgy Turkish taxi driver from Central Casting, in dark glasses, with a week's stubble, two or three chins and a massive belly, like a Turkish John Belushi. Together with a sidekick in a second taxi, he takes half the group and their luggage over the border.

While we wait for him to return, Joanna asks me about Orpheus, as this region of Thrace is his legendary homeland. So, sitting on the pavement in this strange in-between realm with my little band of travellers, I tell the story of Orpheus, the fabled singer of ancient days whose voice was so beautiful he could charm even animals, plants and rocks to rise up and follow the sound of his singing. How he sailed with Jason and the Argonauts to Colchis to win the Golden Fleece, and by the magic of his voice lulled to sleep the dragon of Colchis, the terrible guardian of the fleece. How he loved and married Eurydice, the most beautiful maiden of Thrace, and the bliss of their life together. How Hades, god of the Underworld, envious of their joy and desiring Eurydice for himself, pursued her in the guise of a shepherd into a glade where a venomous snake lay hidden. Bitten by the snake, Eurydice died in the arms of her grief-stricken husband. His sorrow was so deep, and his songs of lamentation so piteous, that the gods themselves were moved, and granted him leave to go down to the Underworld, while yet living, to appeal to Hades in person. Orpheus braved many terrors in this journey, spurred on by his undying love for Eurydice, but by his courage and the power of his voice, he came at last before the dreadful throne of Hades and his queen Persephone.

There he sang a song of lament which has become famous down the ages, set to music in the operas of Monteverdi and Gluck (and even Offenbach) and depicted in countless poems, vases, sculptures and paintings over millennia: the song of Orpheus which moved even the god of death to pity. Urged by Persephone, Hades granted his wish: Eurydice could walk free out of the Underworld, back to the world of the living, but Orpheus must walk ahead of her, leading the way, and never looking back. If he looked back, he would lose her for ever. Once more he set forth on the terrifying journey through the realm of death, soothing to sleep the savage three-headed hound, Cerberus, who guards the gates of Hades, and braving all perils until he came at last in sight of the light of day and the land of the living. Every step of this journey the temptation to look back tormented Orpheus. He could hear no footsteps following his. Perhaps it was all a dream, a mirage, and she was not following at all. Now, as he set foot on the threshold of the living realm, he yielded at last and turned. Overjoyed, he saw, just a few yards behind him, the shade of his beloved Eurydice, and their eyes met. Her feet had made no sound because she was still a wraith and could not be restored to life until she came into the light of day. As the spell broke, grief and horror filled her eyes, and she turned and fled back into the dark, Orpheus calling after her in anguish. For the rest of his life, he mourned her, singing songs of grief and longing which moved to weeping all who heard and stirred the hearts of gods and mortals. He tried to enter the Underworld a second time, but he could not. In his songs, he called for death to take him, so that he might be reunited with Eurydice. Some versions of the legend say that Zeus struck him dead with lightning, fearing he would reveal the secrets of the Underworld; others that the hapless Orpheus met his death torn to pieces by wild beasts or by the Maenads, the frenzied female followers of Dionysus.

Perhaps it's the awareness at the back of my mind of Rasha's ordeal, held in prison in Turkey and separated from her family, or simply the plight of all the refugees we've encountered in Greece, but I find myself ambushed by the story, taken unawares by its heart-churning sadness. The liminal setting of the border crossing could not be more apt.

After Lakis returns for the second group, I drive back to Alexandroupolis to dump the rental vehicle and meet Avgerinos. He's a tall, silver-haired fellow in his mid-fifties with a canny, battered face, excellent English and a flow of talk. All through the long drive to the border and through to Keşan in Turkey, he waxes lyrical about the corruption of Greek politicians and the Orthodox Church. 'All Greek politicians are bastards,' he says, 'there is no lighter word. And the church! They have so much money, and they pay no tax! Their wealth could have paid off our deficit, but they contribute nothing. They are selling the silver icons from the churches to make themselves rich – and, you know, so many of them are gay!'

'Really?' I say. 'I thought they had to be married, in the Orthodox Church.'

'This is just for show,' he says. 'Believe me, I have some know-ledge of this.'

He's very bothered about gay people.

'When I think about two men kissing, with the mouth, I feel sick! I don't want to think about it!'

'Well, you don't have to think about it, do you?' I say. 'I mean, I don't fancy it myself, but I don't have to think about it.'

'Ok,' he says, thoughtfully. 'I see what you mean. Like they don't have to think about what you are doing with your girlfriend, your wife. I mean, two women together, for spice, you know, that's different.'

'Ah, yes.'

'But then, you know, you must join in.'

'Of course.'

'It's completely different. But two men . . . please!'

'Hmm.'

'You know, I had a guy in my taxi once who told me he was gay.'

'Oh yes?'

'I told him, "Keep your hands to yourself!"'

'Quite right.'

'"Keep your hands where I can see them!"'

'I have a lot of gay friends,' I say, 'in the UK, in my church, and also I work in the theatre, and you know there are a lot of gay people in the theatre.'

'For sure,' he says, knowingly. 'Of course.'

'Well,' I say, 'I don't think anyone chooses to be gay. Why would you?'

'Well, some people . . .'

'Well, OK, maybe, but most gay people say that they knew from an early age that they were different. They didn't choose. Why would anyone choose? You have to suffer so much, so much . . . persecution.'

'OK.'

'So everyone has to live as well as they can. So, if someone's gay, isn't it better for them to live in a stable, loving partnership, rather than having to live in secret, and maybe being very promiscuous, because they're living a lie?'

'Hmm, I don't know. Yes, maybe. You know, there was one time I went to a football match with my son. I was a bit worried about him, because he didn't have a girlfriend and I wasn't sure. So we went to this match, our team against Athens Olympiakos, and he said to me, "Dad, there are two things you will never have to worry about: I'll never be gay, and I'll never support Olympiakos." He turns to me. 'It was the happiest day of my life!'

We get through the border crossing without mishap – a long stretch of no-man's-land, across the bridge over the River Evros and through to the Turkish checkpoint, where they want to look in my bag, but are satisfied immediately and wave us through. As we drive into the plains of eastern Thrace, we see immediate signs of Turkish industry, piles of building materials with construction teams and diggers busy widening the motorway. Avgerinos is full of admiration for Turkish graft. 'When they start something, they never stop until they finish.' He's cautiously positive about Erdogan, and tells me how he was courting the Russians' favour recently, trying to acquire S-500 rockets from Putin. NATO put a stop to it, since no member state is supposed to purchase weapons from Russia. This is one of the oddest aspects of the enmity between Greece and Turkey: they're both members of NATO, so if either attacks the other, the rest of the alliance are obliged to defend the injured party against the aggressor.

As the motorway bends southwards towards Keşan, Avgerinos points away down to the right, where the coastline stretches to the extreme north-eastern corner of the Mediterranean. 'There is Gallipoli,' he says, 'and the Dardanelles.'

Tuesday 10 October

Hotel Linda is a tatty affair, a dirty, broken-down motel on a Shell petrol station on the edge of a roundabout under a motorway flyover on the outskirts of Keşan. One could almost describe it as a squalid dump, but for the effusive good nature of our young host, Jagla, and his colleague, Sigun, who are at pains to make us welcome. Jagla is a really sweet fellow who works here 364 days a year as night porter, and tries to get some sleep each night on the sofa in the reception area. He earns 2 Turkish lire an hour – 46p. I feel bad asking him for anything on that pay. He's studying computer programming and watches Netflix to improve his English. He can't quite get his head around what we're doing, or why we want breakfast at 7 a.m. each day, but he steps up manfully to the challenge. I feel rather sorry for him, abandoned to run this dump single-handed. There's a ludicrously glamorous young woman with long blonde hair who lives here as a permanent resident and apparently goes out every evening in a taxi to a strip club, where she dances for several hundred lire a night and the men, she says, are not allowed to touch her. This I gleaned from Brian, a fellow walker, who had a chat with her one night.

After the border crossing on Monday, Arthur and Jude took a taxi with Lakis to Edirne, where they arranged to visit Rasha, who was well enough physically but very miserable and psychologically in a bad way after three months in a detention centre. The Greek Consulate in Edirne have refused to help, so I've written to a barrister friend in London, who specialises in asylum law. He in turn has written to several lawyer friends working for refugee rights in Greece. Jude has the bit between her teeth.

From Ipsala, with its fine old mosque and tower, we set out on a long, bright day of walking across Turkish farmland, green rolling hills, harvested fields and rough grazing land for sheep and goats. Tim leads a reflection in the Shell station yard on 'slowing down', raising his voice above the roar of traffic to impart sublime insights of Buddhist teaching. We're assailed by clouds of flies and midges throughout the day, and see hundreds of little frogs hopping in and out of every puddle in our path. We encounter several groups of jovial Turkish farmhands, who are completely mystified by the sight of twenty-odd Brits walking across the fields. When we say we're walking to Istanbul, they point away south to the main Egnatia highway and say, 'Asphalt! Asphalt!' And we laugh and say, 'No, we like the fields.' And they point at our bare legs and mime bad things vigorously, pulling pained expressions. They're obviously worried we're going to get scratched and dirty. Much hand-shaking, grinning and waving.

We catch up with Cressey, who's put on trousers out of caution, as a woman walking (mostly) alone through Turkey. She's worn shorts all the way thus far. We discuss media opinions of Erdogan, and stories about human rights abuses in Turkey and the 'creeping Islamicisation' of what is supposed to be a modern secular state. We certainly see huge numbers of mosques, with gleaming minarets, vastly oversized and overblown for these humble rural villages. These enormous new mosques are the legacy of Erdogan's former political partner, Fethnullah Gülen, a multi-millionaire property magnate and Islamic guru who was the leader of a movement, almost a cult, which had widespread support throughout the country, and owns a huge empire of banks, media and construction companies across Turkey, Africa, Central Asia and Europe. Having been Erdogan's closest political ally, he's now in exile in the USA, suspected of involvement in last year's attempted coup. I wonder how many of these giant mosques and numerous new-build towns are financed and built by his companies.

Wednesday 11 October

Rachel (from Wolverhampton, not Hampshire) leads the morning reflection in the Shell station forecourt with an inspiring poem by Mary Oliver, and we walk off, straight from base this morning, through the industrial wasteland behind the hotel and into the countryside. An eerie mist hangs over the woods and hills to the east of Keşan; is it smog from the city, smoke from burning rubbish or just a mist of dew? Either way, it makes for some magical effects of light in the morning sky over the plain and the valleys, with this veil of mist hanging over them and the sun shining off the domes and minarets of village mosques. I walk at the back with Julia, and before long we are all schlepping up steep forest paths and fording streams and scrambling down precipitous slopes of compacted mud, with Julia singing 'Climb Every Mountain' in her best comedy-soprano warble. Although the farms seem quite primitive and ramshackle, with extremely pungent livestock, there are new tractors and harvesters everywhere, evidence of an active rural economy. Generous villagers greet us with almonds as we pass through, which have a delicious marzipan flavour. Dogs greet us snarling in every village, so we fill our pockets with pebble ammunition.

Today's walk ends in Malkala, a dusty, noisy new-build town with construction sites everywhere, workmen on perilous-looking scaffolding waving cheerily as we pass and posing for photographs. I'm relieved to see they're wearing harnesses.

Ivor ferries us back to Keşan, where I become acquainted with Alexandra, our new driver. She was a social services professional, working with disadvantaged kids and their families, who turned activist in response to the 2008–09 attack on Gaza. Her extraordinary adventures include driving a truck in the 2010 aid convoy to Gaza, sailing with the ill-fated *Mavi Marmara* flotilla later in the same year, and producing a play about WWI at the Leith Theatre, Edinburgh, for the Armistice centenary. She's the most easy-going and unflappable character imaginable, an indefatigable petite activist-hero with a huge mane of red hair and a self-taught working knowledge of Turkish, who seems to relish stepping up to any challenge.

Sunday 15 October

A few nights later, I'm up late chatting with Alexandra once more in the hotel garden in Marmara Ereglisi, a beautiful enclave of palms and little chalets stretching down to the Sea of Marmara, run by a delightful proprietor, Ahmet, whose son has come back from driving lorries in Greece to give him a hand hosting such a large group. Alexandra has a remarkably no-nonsense attitude to human rights activism. 'Governments and security services seem to think of us as troublemakers,' she says, 'but it's not the case. I enjoyed my work in social services enormously, and I only gave it up because I felt the convoy to Gaza was so important. What they don't understand is that ordinary people like us don't particularly *want* to put them-selves through potentially getting involved in activism. It's because governments and international bodies fail to sort out these terrible situations of injustice. Ordinary people have to get involved.' I feel the same. The provocation or trigger for me has always been a sense of a violation of values, a feeling that one can't stand by and do nothing. A couple of mornings ago, leading a reflection in a misty field up in the hills somewhere to the east of Keşan, I found myself, almost on the spur of the moment, re-enacting the story of the demolished house at Al-Khader, and the walkers were startled, transfixed. It reminded me of the extent to which the Palestinian story has got inside me.

Monday 16 October

Today, we passed dozens of swanky new seaside villas, second homes and holiday lets in the inexorable expanding sprawl of the megalop-olis of Istanbul, as we hiked across the strange hinterland of the Marmara coast. Walking through a more traditional area, we met a lovely old couple who stripped their front garden bare to load us up with tomatoes and cucumber and warmly invited us to stop for coffee, but we had to press on, thanking them with many a *Teshekur* and regrets for the coffee not tasted.

Wednesday 18 October

This morning, we set off on the last day's walking before we reach Istanbul proper, through seaside villages and new-build villas, harvesting figs from roadside trees as we walk, and accepting gratefully the bundles of fruit pressed on us by wonderfully generous locals. We trek through pretty waterside esplanades and some not-so-pretty stretches of motorway. David, Julia and I walk as much as we can down on the beaches, in parallel to the main group, through wharfs and wharfside cafes, rubbish dumps and sewage pipes, over rocky headlands and around the feet of low cliffs and bluffs, always with the shimmering blue of the Sea of Marmara to the south. We catch up with the rest of the group down at the Guzul harbour, from where we walk on eastwards through a simply enormous street market, an alleyway souk stretching for miles, with canopies overhead and stall after stall of fruit and veg, pomegranates like a Frida Kahlo painting, spices, nuts and dates, pastries and cereals, olives, olives, olives, jewellery and hairbrushes, women's clothes, children's clothes, leather goods, woollen goods, haberdashery, hardware and wallpaper. Wednesday is obviously market day, and the traders all want their photographs taken, posing and cheering and laughing at each other, calling, 'International superstar!' and pressing free food on us, always with the refrain, 'Welcome to Turkey!'

In a far-flung outer suburb of 'Greater Istanbul', Büyükçekmece or Batikoy, we find an astonishing gold-plated BMW, which necessitates much posing for daft photographs, and then orchestrate a group photo, flourishing my Palestinian flag, beneath a vast highway statue of the father of modern Turkey, Mustafa Kemal Atatürk, whose image is everywhere. From here down a resplendent grass verge in the middle of the motorway we march all the way to the bounds of the ancient city, where the monumental Büyükçekmece bridge of Suleiman the Magnificent, built in 1566, spans the lake in three bounds. It's a fabulous feat of engineering from the heyday of the Ottoman Empire, wide enough for two chariots across, to welcome and impress travellers from the West in equal measure. Beyond, there's a beautiful sculpture park with fountains and elegant formal gardens around an old Ottoman hall known as the 'Leaded Han', a lodging place for visitors to Istanbul in Ottoman times. After lunch at the next-door cafe, run by Kurdish exiles who have a nuanced view of our pilgrimage, we walk on, across motorways and new-build suburbs, into the western fringes of Istanbul, passing quite close to the famous sky tower, through more markets and past what seems to be a huge sculpture exhibition under construction, where several sculptors are working away with machine tools on huge white blocks of marble underneath tarpaulin covers.

The virtuosity of the refuse collectors is a sight to behold, as they manoeuvre huge, one-ton sacks of rubbish, mounted on wheels and a metal frame, at top speed from dump to dump, performing death-defying feats as they whizz along the edges of major roads, posing for photos and grinning and waving, even holding up the traffic for us so we can cross.

At the end of the day's walk, we arrange taxis to ferry the group through Istanbul-Cumhuriyet out to a hotel at Mayis-Fatih, a slightly tatty seaside resort – maybe the Turkish equivalent of Romford – where we berth down in a slightly tatty hotel, with mildewy taps and shower heads and door handles that come off in your hand.

Thursday 19 October

Bread, honey and instant coffee for breakfast, then Joanna reads Constantine Cavafy's marvellous poem 'Ithaka' for our morning reflection:

> Keep Ithaka always in your mind;
> to reach her at last is your destiny.
> But do not hurry the journey at all –
> better far that it lasts for years
> and you reach the island in your old age,
> wealthy with all you have gained on the way,
> not expecting Ithaka to make you rich.
>
> Ithaka gave you this journey of marvels;
> without her you would never set out.[1]

Alexandra and Ivor drop us in the grubby half-built suburb where we ended yesterday, to begin our final day's walking in Turkey, indeed in Europe, into the old city of Byzantium. I cut a stick from a dead sapling on a patch of wasteland and fly the Palestinian flag for our last day. We walk on into town, with many toots and waves for the flag as we stride over motorway bridges and along hard shoulders and verges. Many people ask us, 'What is the flag? Iraq?' and we say, 'No – *Falasteen*!' and they smile and touch their hearts. 'Beautiful. Thank you.' At one point, a car pulls into a forecourt where several walkers are visiting the toilets in a cafe, and two young men get out and approach us. They say they're Turkish policemen and ask us about the flag, all in the most pleasant, friendly manner you could wish. I explain about the pilgrimage and give them a 'Just Walk' card each and off they go, with handshakes and bonhomie.

One passer-by, a Turk from Berlin who speaks good English, asks me about the flag and I explain, wondering if he's also a plain-clothes cop. At one point, a cafe owner seems so touched that he invites us all over for Turkish chai, which we accept gratefully, sitting at pavement tables outside his spit-and-sawdust establishment. He serves chai to everyone, then produces a broomstick, to which he pins a Turkish flag, and wants to pose for a photograph with me. 'Only Turkish flag!' he says, grinning. I let him hold the flag and smile somewhat queasily for his friend taking the picture. He insists that I hold the flag as well. I really don't want to hold the Turkish bloody flag, but we've drunk his chai, so it feels rude not to humour him. Hmm.

We press on through pleasant tree-lined suburbs to the last stretch. Later this afternoon we're due to meet a young photographer, Isinsu, whom my friend Ben Hopkins has organised very kindly to film our final approach into the old city. I call to update her on our progress and then try, for the umpteenth time, to get hold of the young Palestinian activist who's supposed to be organising some kind of reception for us outside the Hagia Sophia. It seems he's taken fright and gone to ground; apparently the Palestinian Consulate in Istanbul has been asking around about him: what his group is, what groups he's in contact with, and so on. He's sent me a message saying he's very sorry, but he can't be involved after all, and now

I can't get hold of him. It all seems rather unfortunate, if one group of allies has frightened off another. I call Chris, who's now in Jordan, to consult. 'Don't worry about it,' is his typically calm advice. 'He might just be a bit of a fantasist.' I mention to him that one of the walkers has told me he's unhappy about me carrying the flag, and feels that I'm putting the group at risk. 'No, it's the opposite,' says Chris, whose idea it was. 'If people thought you were on a Christian pilgrimage, you might run into trouble. The flag's your protection.'

For the sake of harmony, I dump my sapling and furl the flag for the final approach, through the mighty Land Walls of Theodosius, last defence of the Eastern Roman Empire in 1453, and down to the university, where we meet Işinsu. She's a lovely, enthusiastic young photographer, hugely excited to welcome and film us. 'I can't believe that you've walked here, to my city, all the way from London!' We pose for stills on the grassy slopes in front of the main campus and quickly choreograph the grand finale, as the light's fading fast. And so we tread the last steps of our European journey, down past the Hippodrome of Constantine and the Blue Mosque of Sultanahmet, to the greatest church in Christendom, the Hagia Sophia, Church of the Holy Wisdom, crowning jewel of the Eastern Roman Empire, built in the AD 530s by the Emperor Justinian in the greatest city of the greatest empire on earth. Gathering the walkers beneath the monumental walls, minarets and magnificent dome, I congratulate them with a full heart.

We gather in a circle to say the Just Walk liturgy, filmed by Isinsu, and then a euphoric carnival erupts of cheering and group hugs, high fives and a million daft photos. The walkers celebrate with chai and ice creams in the cafe next to the church, while Jack and I film interviews with Işinsu. After one last group shot in front of the magically floodlit bejewelled splendour of the Sultan Ahmed III Fountain, in the piazza between Hagia Sophia and the gates of the Topkapi Palace, I say a fond farewell to Işinsu, who has taken us to her heart. 'Your interview wet my eyes,' she said. 'It's so beautiful, what you're doing, so amazing.' People like Isinsu and another film-maker friend, Melih, whom I'm due to meet tomorrow, are part of a dwindling elite of artists, journalists and writers in Istanbul, who are leaving in droves, finding it harder and harder to make a living in the increasingly repressive and sterile atmosphere of Erdogan's reign. Many of them go to Berlin, where a thriving Turkish intelligentsia in exile has found an audience for their work. I'm marshalling the troops for the long tram and metro journey out to our hotel, somewhere close to Atatürk Airport, when Alexandra says, 'Oh hang on a minute, my friend Shaza's just coming to meet me. I want you to say hello to her.'

I sense a tremor of impatience ripple through the group but they stand to with pretty good grace. Alexandra explains to me that Shaza, who was on the *Mavi Marmara* with her in 2010, comes from Idlib in Syria and moved to Istanbul after the civil war began and her fifteen-year old son was killed fighting for the FSA. Now, just in the last couple of weeks, Shaza's sister and niece have been murdered here in Istanbul, in mysterious circumstances. What. I heave an inward sigh and think, selfishly, how are we supposed to say a 'quick hello' to someone who's just been through all that? Shazer is a warm, wise-faced Syrian lady in her forties, in hijab and traditional Alawite dark floor-length dress, accompanied by her brother Maen, a handsome, silver-haired man a few years older in a leather jacket, a dissident journalist in self-imposed exile because of his outspoken political views. A few of us exchange greetings and expressions of sympathy, while the rest wait to one side. I apologise that we can't stay. 'We're so sorry for your loss,' I say, 'and this terrible situation, and please be assured of our prayers for you, that things will improve. God be with you.'

'*Shukran*,' Shaza replies. 'We are praying for your journey to Palestine, and for your cause. Thank you for everything you are doing for the Palestinian people, for peace and justice.'

The next day I lead a group into Istanbul for some sightseeing, catching a ferry across the Bosphorus from Bakirköy to Kadiköy and then another smaller ferry back over to the old city. Seeing the fairy-tale domes, minarets and cupolas from the glittering Bosphorus is as thrilling as ever, reminding me of the famous encomium of the twelfth-century Byzantine diplomat, lamenting his absence from the city of wonders: 'O land of Byzantium, o thrice-happy city, eye of the universe, ornament of the world, star shining afar, beacon of this lower world, would that I were with you, enjoying you to the full! Do not part me from your maternal bosom!'[2] Then one of the passengers points out the *Mavi Marmara* moored up on the north side, a startling reminder of why we're here, and of Alexandra's experience in the disastrous flotilla to Gaza in 2010. The haunted ship is still here in Istanbul, awaiting its destiny. The passengers' dispute with Israel over the murders that took place during the takeover of the vessel in international waters has not been resolved, and so the ship is arguably still Exhibit A in a trial that the survivors vessel hope one day to see. When she eventually made it back into Gaza two years later (through a tunnel from Egypt), Alexandra says, her friends there showed her the memorial statues to those killed on the *Mavi Marmara* which the Palestinians have erected on Gaza Beach. Apparently there's talk of using the ship as some kind of floating human rights exhibition, but it's an expensive business. Just keeping it moored in Istanbul is expensive.

First stop in the old city is the Rüstem Pasha Camii, a little sixteenth-century mosque between the Golden Horn/Eminonu wharf and the Grand Bazaar, which my friend Anders Bergquist has recommended as having the most wonderful blue tiles. We wander up an alley and through a dark restaurant basement to access the mosque, and climb the stairs past workmen sanding and chiselling the beautiful blonde Ottoman stonework, to a reception desk where a uniformed chap says it's closed for restoration, but he allows us to have a quick peek at a couple of tantalising glimpses of blue between the plastic sheeting and scaffold. We forge on through the heady kaleidoscope of the Grand Bazaar, a sensory overload of gaudy extravagance, and on to the Hippodrome, where I show the walkers the obelisk of Theodosius, with its relief-sculpted racehorses pulling chariots like bathtubs, and foppish imperial bodyguards with their long hair and 1970s fringes, memorably described in William Dalrymple's *From the Holy Mountain*. Dating originally from around 1450 BC, the obelisk was one of a pair erected outside the Temple of Amun-Re at Karnak by the Egyptian pharaoh Thutmose III; it was brought first to Alexandria by Constantine II, and subsequently to Byzantium by Theodosius I in AD 390, to adorn the *spina* of the hippodrome in the new imperial capital.

After milling and gazing with the crowds in the Blue Mosque of Sultanahmet, we stroll through to the Fatih piazza between the mosque and Hagia Sophia for a brief ice cream break, where we sit and listen to the antiphonal calls to prayer ululating and rasping back and forth between the minarets of these two mighty buildings. It's a disturbing new development to hear the call to prayer from the minarets of Hagia Sophia, deconsecrated by Atatürk in 1934 and established as a cultural museum, neither church nor mosque but treasure-house of both traditions. With the increasingly strident Islamicisation of public life in Turkey, there's a vocal popular contingent agitating to have the building turned back into a mosque, to the dismay of many in the academic community. Having visited several times before, I give a potted summary of what I know about this 'sacred mountain of a building, vast and elemental', as historian Dan Cruikshank described it, to David, Denise, Jenny and Jude as we head through the outer precincts, at the feet of the soaring buttresses and lofty minarets, to queue for tickets.

The sway of the eastern Roman or Byzantine Empire under Justinian in the sixth century traced a gigantic circle of the known world, centred on the Mediterranean, extending from Spain in the West through to the Black Sea in the East, right down through the Levant and all across north Africa. It was quite simply the greatest empire in history, and materials were brought from its furthest reaches for the construction of this architectural marvel, which was to be the greatest church in the world: marble, porphyry, basalt and copper from Egypt, Lebanon, Sparta and Gaul, and temple columns from Baalbek, Heliopolis, Ephesus and Delphi. It's a miracle of engineering, built on a geological fault line, which has withstood the stresses of nearly 1,500 years of earthquakes, invasions, rebuilding, fires and neglect to stand here still, battered but intact, a breathtaking portal to the lost world of Byzantium. In essence one huge dome, 110 feet from east to west and leaping 180 feet from the marble floor to its apex, its structure was to remain unrivalled in architectural history for nearly a thousand years after its construction. Not until the fifteenth century would any other building in the world enclose such a vast floor beneath a single roof. How its architects or *mechanikoi*, Anthemius of Tralles and Isidore of Miletus, gauged the maximum tension the dome would support, how they calculated the precise balancing of thrust and counter-thrust to divert its unimaginable weight through four pendentives, curved triangles of vaulting at the intersection points with the supporting arches of an outer circumference of adjoining domes, or *exedrae*, and thence into the ground, is one of the mysteries of that lost world. And how they achieved this in less than six years, when the construction of Notre Dame in Paris took nearly a hundred, beggars the imagination. 'I say, renowned Roman Capitol, give way!' wrote the contemporary poet Paul the Silentiary. 'My emperor has so far overtopped that wonder as great God is superior to an idol!'[3]

Beneath the dome, forty windows flood the interior with light. Describing their effect, the art historian Victoria Hammond writes, 'The sunlight emanating from the windows surrounding its lofty cupola, suffusing the interior and irradiating its gold mosaics, seemed to dissolve the solidity of the walls and created an ambience of ineffable mystery. On the completion of Hagia Sophia, Justinian is said to have remarked, "Solomon, I have outdone thee".'[4] The domed ceiling was studded with millions of golden glass cubes, covering a surface area of four acres, to create a dazzling canopy, a firmament scintillating with refracted sunlit radiance and, at night, with each golden cube set at a fractionally different angle to catch the reflected glow and flicker of light from oil lamps and candles below, the awed visitors must have felt they had been transported into Paradise.

Or, as the sixth-century historian Procopius put it:

> So bright is the glow of the interior that you might say that it is not illuminated by the sun from the outside, but that the radiance is generated within. Rising above is an enormous spherical dome which appears not to rest upon a solid foundation, but to cover the place beneath as though it were suspended from heaven by the fabled golden chain.[5]

When the pagan ruler of Rus, Vladimir, Prince of Kiev, sent his emissaries in 987 AD to explore the beliefs of the neighbouring peoples of Bulgaria, Khazar and the Byzantine Empire, the ambassadors to Constantinople described their experience, attending a Greek Orthodox service in the Hagia Sophia:

> We were led into a place where they serve their God, and we did not know where we were, on heaven or on earth; and do not know how to tell about this. All we know is that God lives there with

mortals and their worship is better than in any other country. We cannot forget that beauty, since each person, if he eats something sweet, will not take something bitter afterwards; so we cannot remain any more in paganism.[6]

'Hagia Sophia summed up everything that was the Orthodox religion,' writes historian Roger Crowley. 'For Greeks, it symbolised the centre of their world. Its very structure was a microcosm of heaven, a metaphor for the divine mysteries of Orthodox Christianity. Hagia Sophia was the mother church – it symbolised the everlastingness of Constantinople and the Empire.'[7]

I slip to one side as we enter the narthex and sit down on a bench to compose myself and to offer up a prayer for a friend who, I've learned in the last few minutes, has been diagnosed with cancer. Feeling troubled and very far from home, I sit and breathe and pray. I also want to recall the first occasion when I stepped into this astonishing space, many years ago, and felt the thrill, almost dizzying, as the marble floor seemed to rush away from me in all directions. No one in the gaggle of sightseeing crowds was unaffected; everyone fell silent. The sensation of standing in the midst of such a huge space, beneath that soaring golden dome, gloriously empty but pregnant with numinous presence, is something I've felt only once elsewhere, in Regent's Park of all places, in London, where the wonderful horizontal expanse of table-top green seemed also to rush away from me across an ocean of grass like billiard-baize under a bright spring sky.

Entering the nave, I'm shocked to see that fully half the floor is covered in scaffolding, so high that it has a motorised lift, whizzing up and down with a high-pitched whirr. There are restoration works everywhere and a constant tap-tap of workmen's tools. With its mysterious emptiness so torn, the vast basilica seems sadder than ever, less a numinous vessel than a broken shell, through which crowds of tourists run hither and thither, laughing and chatting and posing for selfies, oblivious to the ghosts. Before long, I escape to the comparative calm and quiet of the galleries. White protective hoardings cover up much of the walls, and acres of mustard-yellow paint has been slapped over the vaults and arches from which the dark-eyed mosaic saints and angels of Byzantium kept vigil for a thousand years. But Christ in Judgement is still there, with John the Baptist interceding at his left hand for beleaguered humanity, surely the most wonderful and heart-piercing mosaic in the whole treasure-house, his shaggy hair and beard and anguished, haggard face seeming to embody the suffering of the world, eyes staring out at you with a poignancy that leaps across the centuries in a flash, as if he were looking directly into your eyes with an infinite compassion, knowing and empathising with your sorrows and interceding directly for you with the Saviour. So he has gazed out from this wall since the twelfth century. I wander and photograph through the ancient gallery until it's time to go and meet the Turkish journalist who's asked to interview me about the Walk.

Betül Berişe is a shy, bookish young foreign affairs correspondent for a left-leaning Turkish broadsheet, *Cumhuriyet* ('Republic'), Turkey's equivalent of *The Guardian*, and she loves our project. She's dressed in a smart trouser suit, western-style with no headscarf. 'So how do you like Istanbul?' she asks, as we sit down in the outdoor cafe and order chai. 'Well, I love it,' I say. 'I've been quite a few times, and it's always wonderful, magical. I love this city.'

'I don't,' she retorts, and laughs wryly.

'Oh, really?'

'No, I'd like to leave Istanbul. Our country is going backward, not forward.'

'Where would you like to go?'

'Germany, maybe, or London, I don't know. But this is my home, and my work is here. It's not so easy to leave.'

'Do you have problems with the government, as a left-leaning, independent newspaper? Do they try to censor you?'

'We are just journalists. Yes, of course, there's huge pressure from the government. But we will never bow down to pressure.'

'Well, let's see what they think of our Walk to Jerusalem.'

I field two hours of questions as best I can: should Britain apologise for the Balfour Declaration? Is the proposed Fateh-Hamas reconciliation a good thing? Is Donald Trump the saviour for Palestine?

Unexploded ordnance lurks on all sides of such questions, and I cannot risk saying anything that could be twisted or taken out of context to undermine the Walk or Amos Trust. Not that I mistrust Betül; she seems genuinely supportive, but years of involvement in this arena have taught me to be careful. Equally, if I'm dull she won't print it. At one point, discussing Britain's colonial history in the Middle East, an impulse stirs me and I exclaim, 'You know, if you want to talk about an apology, I think Britain should apologise to both sides, to the Israelis as well as the Palestinians, for getting them into this mess. We led them into an impossible, unworkable scenario. The British government should never have made those promises to the Zionist leaders, Weizmann and the others, a hundred years ago. They didn't have the interests of the Jews at heart. A responsible power, acting disinterestedly, would never have preferred the rights of one people over another. Of course the Zionist leaders were desperate to create a safe homeland for the Jews, after centuries of horrific persecution, most recently in Russia. But Britain used them to advance its own agenda.'

I actually wonder whether this might be a missing element in the necessary paradigm for a just peace; whether a proper acknowledgement by Britain of the deceitful and unjust actions of Lloyd George's government and subsequent administrations might actually liberate Israel, to some extent, from its role as the 'bad guy' and rebalance the narrative. Jews, along with Palestinians, were victims of Machiavellian *realpolitik*, and perhaps acknowledging this publicly might – possibly – take some of the heat out of Israel's furious hypersensitivity to any criticism. This episode, of course, is merely one in a long line of failures in its dealings with the Jewish people for which Britain could or should apologise.

There was probably some genuine sympathy for the centuries of Jewish suffering. Weizmann, who had inherited the mantle of Zionist leadership after Theodor Herzl's death, relates how, when he met with Balfour in December 1914 and explained to him the 'Jewish tragedy' in Europe, the British aristocrat and statesman was 'most deeply moved – to the point of tears'.[8]

Maybe there was even some sense of contrition for the role Christianity had played in persecuting Jews down the ages, or for the persecution and expulsion of England's Jews in the Middle Ages – although nothing I've read actually suggests this. Lloyd George and Balfour were both brought up as devout evangelicals, and were influenced by nineteenth-century Dispensationalist teachers such as John Nelson Darby, who believed the re-establishment of the biblical kingdom of Israel was a precondition for the return of Christ and therefore supported the Zionist ideal. As a Welsh nonconformist, Lloyd George felt a natural affinity with the struggle of a marginalised and persecuted race for freedom and equality, and, reared on the biblical stories of Moses and the Israelites, his imagination was fired by the aspiration of a valiant enduring people returning at last to their ancient land. Interestingly, the Anglican mission in Jerusalem was established in 1833 as a mission to the Jews, anticipating their return to Palestine. The first Anglican bishop, a converted rabbi named Michael Alexander, was appointed in 1841, and eventually St George's Cathedral was built in 1898 by the fourth bishop, George Blyth.

On the *realpolitik* side of the ledger, it's clear the British cabinet wanted a British-friendly buffer state in Palestine to strengthen our control of the Suez Canal. We wanted to 'get the Jews on side' in World War I, vastly overestimating the 'global reach' of 'the Jews' as some kind of ubiquitous (and monolithic) network of influence, wealth and power which could swing either our way or Germany's. This notion of 'world Jewry' as the secret power behind Bolshevism, the Ottoman Empire, the international banks, the press, etc., was itself an anti-Semitic fantasy, replicated subsequently in Nazi propaganda and elsewhere, with lethal consequences. We believed Jewish influence in the USA could help to bring the Americans into the war, on our side. Perhaps we believed Jews from German-occupied Europe would flock to our banner at the promise of a British-sponsored Jewish state.

Widespread anti-Semitism among the British aristocracy and Cabinet certainly played a part in British support for Zionism. As Prime Minister in 1905, Balfour himself had supported the Aliens Act, the first-ever legislation limiting immigration to the UK. Its primary aim was to prevent Jews fleeing the pogroms in Eastern Europe and Russia from entering Britain. The Pale of Settlement was the western region of Imperial Russia within which Jewish permanent residency had been allowed until recently. The assassination of Tsar Alexander II in 1881, for which anti-Semitic elements in the Russian press blamed 'foreign influence', coupled with the new Tsar Alexander III's fierce antipathy to Jews and the passing of new anti-Semitic laws, unleashed a wave of devastating anti-Jewish riots, or 'pogroms', across the Pale from 1881 to 1884 and again from 1903 to 1906, involving widespread destruction and looting of Jewish property and countless brutal attacks on Jews, with more than 2,000 killed and many more wounded. Following the arrival in London's East End of tens of thousands of Jewish refugees from the Pale, a rash of popular anti-Semitism had erupted, with marches, petitions and sporadic outbreaks of violence, some inflammatory articles in the press, and even the formation of a proto-fascist group, the British Brothers' League. Balfour believed it was ultimately impossible for a person to be fully Jewish and fully British, that the Jews were 'a people apart' who 'not merely held a religion differing from the vast majority of their fellow-countrymen, but only inter-married among themselves.'[9] So his support for a Jewish home-land was the direct corollary to his misgivings about Jewish integration in British society. As Herzl predicted in 1895, 'The anti-Semites will become our most dependable friends.'[10] It was for this reason that Edwin Montagu, the only Jewish member of the Cabinet at the time of the Balfour Declaration, regarded Zionism as a 'mischievous political creed' that would result in 'Jews hereafter [being] treated as foreigners in every country but Palestine.'[11] Strikingly, his *Memorandum on the Anti-Semitism of the Present Government*, submitted to the Cabinet on 23 August 1917, concludes,

> I would say to Lord Rothschild that the Government will be prepared to do everything in their power to obtain for Jews in Palestine complete liberty of settlement and life on an equality with the inhabitants of that country who profess other religious beliefs. I would ask that the Government should go no further.[12]

And then, of course, there was cordite, of which more anon.

Apparently there's a classic Friday night log-jam between Fatih and Taksim Square, so after the interview I scratch the plan to meet Melih and head up to the tram stop. The overhead electricity is out, so the platform attendant is herding everyone out on to the pavement. 'Go! Walk!' he spits, grabbing my arm and shoving me back. 'Next tram – walk!' he says, pointing up the hill away from Sultanahmet. And so a crowd of us, thirty or forty passengers, set off marching on to the next stop, walking five or six abreast along the pavement. I fall in with two Syrian guys, Jamal and Morhaf, and get chatting. Jamal is from Homs, Morhaf from Hama, and speaks English pretty well, acting as translator. They've been here four years, they say, and are both working in a clothing and shoe sales internet marketing company, down a dirty, dark alley which they point out to me along the way, across the far side of the main road. Jamal is a thickset, well-built fellow in his thirties with a fine beard and warm smile, a gentle bear of a man. Every so often he claps me on the shoulder and exclaims, 'Justi! Nice to meet you!' Morhaf is a tall, gangly, smiling fellow, also in his mid-thirties, gauche and awkward with his height, with a broad, slightly embarrassed grin at all times, and seems always about to break into a nervous laugh. When I tell them about the Walk, Jamal reflects for a moment and speaks in a measured, considered fashion, while Morhaf translates: 'He says, he feel your humanity, and he says he is very happy to meet you.'

Tram stop after tram stop is shut, with staff and engineers trying to fix the overhead electric rail, so we walk on and on in a growing crowd of hundreds. At one point we pass a large courtyard cafe, where my new friends invite me for chai. It's a fantastic, Arabian-nights *narghile* den, just off one of the big junctions, a courtyard alley leading to a lofty-vaulted indoor cafe with big open ovens heating charcoal for the *narghile*, hubble-bubble smoke puffing through the air in fragrant wafts and hundreds of mostly Arabic chaps sitting smoking and drinking chai. We find a table, order chai and discourse on the state of the world. They want to know my opinion about everything: what is the solution to Syria, the Middle East ('Arab-stan' as they call it), to the wider world? 'What is your opinion about our people, from Syria, coming to Europe, as the refugee?'

'Well,' I say, 'I think it's really tough to have to leave your home, and that no one would choose to become a refugee unless they were in great danger. I think that we people in Europe are very lucky to welcome you, because you bring many beautiful things, beautiful qualities from your country and your culture, and you come because you want to work, to make a life for yourselves and contribute.'

Morhaf relays my words to Jamal, the vizier translating for his sultan, who listens, reflects, then smiles warmly and replies. Morhaf says, 'He thank you because you say such a beautiful thing. We are very happy to come to Istanbul, and very grateful to have a home here, and to work. We want to work hard and give something to this country.'

At one point, Jamal wants to know my opinion of Assad. I say that I know the situation's fantastically complicated, that some of the country support Assad, that there are many factions and external forces involved, and that Syria's problems start way back, stemming from the French colonial mandate.

'Our President – *tee-hee* – is a foolish man,' Morhaf translates, grinning all over his face. 'He have not the answer to Syria's problems, only fighting. When your president is a foolish man, you cannot make the peace, the good life.'

They walk on with me, all the way to the metro station, where we part as brothers, with many embraces and warm greetings.

The next morning we say goodbye to our wonderful drivers, Ivor returning to his wife and his bees back home, and indefatigable Alexandra off to visit friends in Diyarbakir, in south-eastern Turkey, which has in the previous two years experienced a sharp increase in government repression and violence under the auspices of marital law, and we head off to Atatürk Airport. We say goodbye as well to the lovely Joanna, artist from Ullapool, who's staying on in Istanbul for a few days, and Julia, who plans to rejoin us, *insha'Allah*, in Palestine.

There's no alcohol in the desert, reads an urgent text from Chris, in Jordan, *and beers v expensive at hotel bar. Please pick up some whisky for me, Bushmills or single malt*. I'm in the duty-free shop comparing whisky prices when the phone rings. It's Chris. 'Hey fella, everything OK?'

'Yup, all fine, we're all here, waiting for the flight.'

'Excellent. You got my text?'

'Yup, don't worry, padre, I'm attending to the essentials.'

'Excellent. Belt and braces.'

Bushmills for Chris, Jameson's for me, and off to the desert.

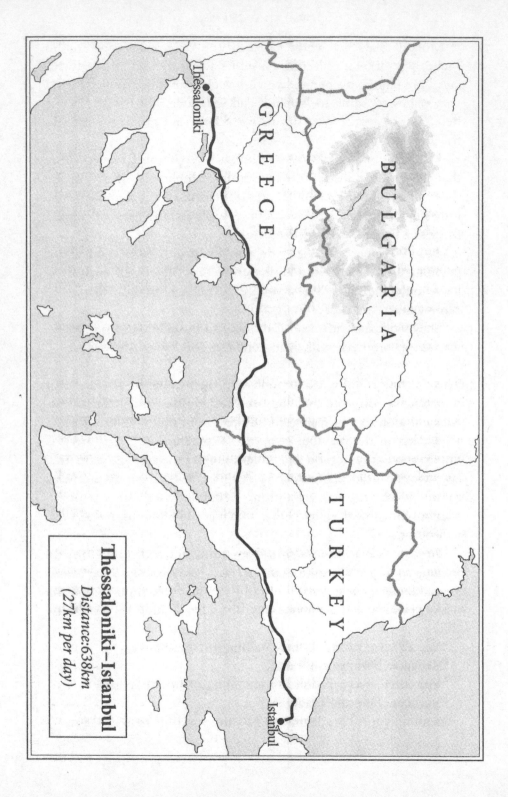

Thessaloniki–Istanbul
Distance:638km
(27km per day)

GREECE

BULGARIA

TURKEY

Thessaloniki

Istanbul

II

Crossing Jordan

WE'RE FLYING OVER the bare hills of southern Anatolia, a bony landscape of rocky escarpments, valleys and crags scored and pitted with deep grooves sharply etched in the bright sunlight. A fairy-tale view of clouds stretches westwards like the floor of heaven through the window to my right, with little dots of water, rivers and desert tarns, shining gold here and there between the hills. I've never flown to Jordan before. It's quite a small plane, just single seats either side of the aisle, and flying quite low, so we get a magnificent perspective of this rugged, riven landscape. It feels luxurious to be drifting for a few hours, free of the responsibility of logistics – routes, meals, hotel rooms, tickets and head-counts – after the barrage of intense experiences over the last forty-eight hours in Istanbul, which flash through my mind as the hills of Anatolia roll beneath us.

A year ago, when we were still planning our route, Ian Brodrick was all for us continuing on foot down through Turkey to Antalya – 'Fantastic country for walking,' he said – and then travelling by boat either to Cyprus (and thence by ferry to Haifa) or to Lebanon, to walk down the country into Israel. There were one or two problems with these options, such as adding another month by walking through Anatolia, the ferry from Cyprus to Haifa no longer running, and the small matter of the 'Blue Line' between Lebanon and Israel being effectively a war front. More important, we felt that to exercise the privilege of our British passports by travelling through Israel, which Palestinians are forbidden to do, would be an odd conclusion to a pilgrimage of solidarity. So we decided to follow the route by which Palestinians are required to travel, through

Jordan and across the King Hussein/Allenby Bridge crossing, into the West Bank.

We're met in Amman by Ibrahim, from 'Experience Jordan', a jovial fellow, short, sturdy and bald-headed with a piratical grin and gravelly laugh, who will be our guide for the next few days. He steers us through customs and out, beneath the giant Jordanian flags rippling over the terminal plaza, and soon we're speeding along the highway through the desert plain of the East Bank plateau, towards the twinkling lights and skyscrapers of Amman, Philadelphia of the ancient world, the 'city of brotherly love'.

It's a joyous reunion at the hotel with Chris and lovely Lynn from Southport, newly granddaughtered and fighting fit, Rowena the magic lock-keeper from Oxford and jovial Phil from Preston with his booming *basso profundo*, as well as a host of newcomers: Doug, Ralph, Anne, Mel and Ron, a taciturn Dutch chap with whom I'm sharing a room. One of the newcomers is Carol, a British-Palestinian whose family was originally from Yaffa. In the *Nakba* they fled to Lebanon, where she was born, and moved subsequently to the UK. This is her first attempt to go back to visit her ancestral home. 'I don't know what will happen at the border,' she says, 'whether they will find out somehow that I'm Palestinian, and stop me. But I have to try.'

After dinner and a briefing with the whole group, around thirty walkers altogether, I find a quietish outdoor table to write my journal. After a while, Ron comes out to join me. He used to work for several different airlines in airport management, he says, but a few years ago, his long-term battle with alcohol reached crisis point, his marriage came to an end and he had a breakdown and a spell in psychiatric care. I apologise for the large bottle of Jameson's on my table. 'God, don't worry!' he laughs, 'I'm used to it now. This is part of what you have to deal with. You have to operate in the real world.' He now works for the NHS in hospital management and as a support counsellor in mental health services, and he's heavily involved in Alcoholics Anonymous, running four meetings a week and mentoring people going through the Twelve-step Programme. He's easy-going and disarmingly honest, with a droll sense of humour, which bodes well for sharing a room.

Sunday 22 October

The only way to walk from Amman to the Allenby Bridge, our enquiries have ascertained, would be along the main highway, Prince Faisal Street, with traffic thundering past and Jordanian police outriders front and behind. Which, while it would be something to tell the grandchildren, would also be noisy and unpleasant, extremely hot and dusty, and dull. The border region between Jordan and the West Bank is so heavily militarised, patrolled from air and land by Jordanian and Israeli forces, that walking through the desert to the bridge is out of the question, not to mention the real danger of treading on a land mine. Even when you get to the bridge, you can't walk across. The three border authorities involved require travellers to cross in a series of coaches through the labyrinth of customs points and stretches of no-man's-land that bring you eventually, *insha'Allah*, through to Jericho in the West Bank. So we've decided to spend three days doing an equivalent amount of walking in some far more interesting parts of Jordan: the ancient Nabataean site of Petra in the south, the Wadi Goeer in the Dana biosphere reserve and the hills of the Transjordan Plateau above the Dead Sea.

And so the next morning we drive for three hours down the main Desert Highway, broadly following the route of the King's Highway, the 5,000-year-old desert road that meanders north–south through Jordan down to the Gulf of Aqaba and the Wadi Rum south of Petra, the Valley of the Moon where David Lean filmed his 1962 epic, *Lawrence of Arabia*. Following the King's Highway along the rolling hills above the Dead Sea rift would have been picturesque but much slower. Trade route and battle frontier since prehistoric times, the ancient road tracks the line of maximum hilltop rainfall, linking springs, settlements, Crusader castles and monasteries from Madaba to Karak to Shobek. The book of Numbers relates how Moses was refused permission to travel on the King's Highway by the king of Edom, whose capital was at ancient Raqmu, later known as Petra:

'Let us pass, I pray thee, through thy country: we will not pass through the fields, or through the vineyards, neither will we drink of the water of the wells; we will go by the King's Highway, we

will not turn to the right hand nor to the left until we have passed
thy borders.'   (Numbers 20:17, KJV)

But the king of Edom evidently didn't fancy 600,000-odd men
(plus women, children and livestock, according to Numbers 1:46)
passing through his domain, so transit visas were denied: 'Thou
shalt not pass by me, lest I come out against thee with the sword'
(Numbers 20:18, KJV).

Ibrahim is a seasoned raconteur, chatting away in his husky rasp
through a microphone at the front of the bus. 'Jordan is the
Switzerland of the Middle East,' he says, 'neutral, stable and
welcoming to everyone. Of our ten million population, 3.4 million
are Palestinian refugees from '48 and '67. The majority of Jordan
is Sunni Muslim; Christians make up 8 per cent of the population,
and relations between the faiths are good. It's not a huge economy
– we have no oil, except olive oil! We export fruit and vegetables
grown in the Jordan Valley, olives and olive oil, medicinal potash
from the Dead Sea and phosphate, for cement. We're supported by
the USA and Europe and by the Gulf States, to be a stable country,
and we give shelter to all the refugees from across the Middle East.
In 2003, a million Iraqi refugees came to Jordan; in 1990, half a
million from Kuwait, and in recent years, more than two million
have come from Syria. Tourism in Jordan is very unstable, because
of the many wars and crises in the wider Middle East, but our
currency is very strong.'

His family came originally from Bethlehem, he says. 'I have nine
brothers and sisters, and all of us have university degrees!' Humorous
applause ripples through the bus. A railway track runs between the
sand dunes and low-lying scrubby wasteland to our left. 'This is
the Hijaz Railway,' says Ibrahim, 'from Saudi Arabia to Aqaba, which
Lawrence of Arabia attacked, famously, in World War I, and it runs
all the way from Damascus to Medina. It's no longer used in Syria;
here in Jordan we use it for transporting phosphate. You see these
hills of sand? These are slag-heaps, from phosphate mining, and
over there, beyond, you can see a big phosphate factory, built with
a lot of investment from India.'

Along the roadside, we see many clusters of half-built houses
behind high compound walls, with concrete pillars rising at the

corners above completed ground floors, but no upper floors. 'These are Bedouin communities,' says Ibrahim. 'They build one storey and then, when a new generation arrives, they build a second. They like to build behind high walls, for privacy. Eight per cent of Jordan's population is Bedouin, but only a small number live in traditional desert dwellings now, maybe 1 per cent. The rest have jobs in the police, the army, and so on. Over to the left there you can see they're building a new pipeline. They've found water in the desert here recently.'

Nancy and I are trying to decide, via texts and emails, whether our daughter Eleanor should come out to join me in the West Bank. Unusually, Nancy's much more gung-ho than me. What happens if I get turned back at the Allenby Bridge? Or if the Israelis pull her out of the line at Ben Gurion airport and subject her to a gruelling interrogation? Even if I were outside the airport, waiting with a taxi, I'd be powerless to intervene. It could be a traumatic ordeal, followed by deportation and a ten-year ban in her passport. And she'd be on her own. 'That's the worst-case scenario,' I say, 'and as long as you and she are clear about that, and she's still keen to come, then great, let's do it. It'll be an amazing experience for her, and wonderful for me to have her here with me at the end. Of course, you also need to think about the risk when she's here.'
'What risk?'
'Well, you know, if things get hairy.'
'What do you mean, hairy?'
'Well, we're here to make a noise, right? To make as much noise as we can, about the Balfour centenary, the Occupation, denial of Palestinian rights, etc. The whole thing is a massive stunt, to grab as much attention as possible, and we can't shy away from that.'
'So what could go wrong?'
'Well, hopefully, nothing. But think about it. We could get arrested – possibly. Or get attacked by crazy settlers. Or end up in the middle of a riot. I'm not trying to be alarmist. It *should* be fine. Everything's been planned, very carefully, with Holy Land Trust and the Amos partners on the ground and, *insha'Allah*, everything should be fine. But it's a military occupation, and the Balfour centenary's a hot potato. You never know.'

Later, I text her, saying, 'I need your wisdom. I miss you and I feel weak and fearful and I don't know how to decide.'

As we approach the mountainous region of Petra, the hills to either side are cleft with ancient terraces planted with olive trees and vegetables; rocky, twisted hills scantily stubbled with grassy scrub. 'Petra is known as the Wadi Musa,' says Ibrahim, 'the place where Moses struck the rock and water gushed out, and it's said that his brother Aaron was buried here on Jabal Haroun, the "mountain of Aaron", to the south of Petra.'

It's a miraculous setting, no question. No wonder Spielberg chose it for the climax of his 1989 swashbuckler, *Indiana Jones and the Last Crusade*. Passing gift shops stuffed with Indiana Jones hats and whips, we begin our descent to the fabled Valley of the Siq. An astonishing lunar landscape of writhing desert stone rears up on either side of the broad defile leading down into the gorge, pockmarked with fantastical troglodyte dwellings and tombs, bubbles of blonde rock hewn out of the bluffs, scarred with ancient carvings and pierced with dark sockets, windows on to black recesses, like eyeholes in faceless masks. Here and there between the rippling shoulders of sandstone, strange freestanding cubes of masonry ribbed with beige pillars pop up arbitrarily – 'djinn blocks' as the Bedouin call them, carved monoliths inhabited by capricious spirits - in fact, memorials to the dead erected by the first-century Nabataeans. Gaping rectangular hollows in the rock walls house rough-hewn cave tombs, stone alcoves where the poorer classes laid their dead. Sprigs of desert thorn, broom and juniper cling in the crevices and fissures of the undulating boulders, and over the smooth-swept surfaces of sun-bleached rock, lizards bask and skitter.

Mounted Jordanian archaeology police in spiked helmets stand guard close to the dark mouth of a huge tunnel, a phenomenal feat of ancient world engineering, bored eighty-eight metres through the mountain rock to divert flood waters away from the Siq into the nearby wadis Al-Mudhlim and Al-Mataha – a massive drain to protect the citizens of Petra from the potentially lethal flash floods not uncommon in the desert. And so we plunge into the Siq itself, an astonishing natural gorge of sandstone that winds gently down between towering rock walls of fabulous hues and fantastical shapes, to the heart of the ancient city of Petra. Or, in Spielberg-land, the Valley of the Crescent Moon, leading to the lost city of Alexandretta, legendary resting place of the Holy Grail.

A triumphal arch (which collapsed in the late nineteenth century) once spanned the entrance to the enchanted chasm, flanked by busts of the Nabataean king, welcoming friends and warning foes, and water channels, lined with clay pipes, on either side of the gorge, carried fresh spring water to the city below. The milling throng of tourists all around us and the rattle and clip-clop of carriages drawn by nimble Arab ponies is probably pretty much how it would have been 2,000 years ago (apart from the selfie sticks) – a bustling, populous city that welcomed a constant procession of visiting traders, dignitaries, pilgrims and sightseers walking this same path. The votive niches and *baetyls* ('god-blocks') scattered along the ancient road suggest that this approach to Petra may have had some cere-monial or ritualistic significance, a literal rite of passage cleansing or preparing the visitor for an encounter with the sacred shrines of the Nabataean gods and the monuments haunted by ancestral spirits. *Only the penitent man will pass*, as Indiana Jones knew.

The wrinkling hollows and ridges of the red and amber rocks seem almost to melt and slither down the cliffs as we wander, awestruck, along the mesmerising ravine. Grooves and creases of lambent golden stone slump and fold in transfiguring shafts of sunlight sluicing the gorge, bathing shoulders and hillocks of crum-pled rock in magic radiance. Rivulets of pink and ochre pigment stream and eddy in congealed strands, patterning the cliffs with tapestries of coloured veins. The opposing rock faces seem almost to shiver and sway together, giant flanks and haunches of animate stone conjured into life by the beating sun. Here the blind artistry of rushing water and sifting sediment outshines any work of human hand, in fantastical hollows scooped and twisted from the lemon-gold flesh of the precipice walls, framed and fluted with paper-thin flanges of sculpted sandstone, like tunnelled holes though a gigantic cheese. Orange-ochre scarps rise like lumps of giant dough, sun-baked boulders swelling into pitted loaves of stone. Soaring columns scored and gashed with rust-red grooves, like scorched bark of some monstrous tree, lean and whisper close, almost blotting out the sliver of white-gold sky.

It's a bewitching landscape, and the best is yet to come, glimpsed thrillingly around a corner of the chasm for an instant, then hidden once more from view, until we emerge into the vast natural atrium at the heart of the mountain to stand before the miraculous rose-blushed splendour of the fabled Treasury, Al-Khazneh, mausoleum of King Aretas IV. Talbot Mundy captures the exhilaration of this moment in his 1922 novel, *The Lion of Petra*:

> Exactly in front of us, glimpsed through a twelve-foot gap between cliffs six hundred feet high, was a sight worth going twice that distance, running twice that risk, to see – a rose-red temple front, carved out of the solid valley wall and glistening in the opalescent hues of morning.
>
> Not even Burckhardt, who was the first civilised man to see the place in a thousand years, described that temple properly; because you can't. It is huge – majestic – silent – empty – aglow with all the prism colours in the morning sun. And it seems to think.[1]

Johann Ludwig Burckhardt, the first modern European to visit Petra, was a Swiss explorer and orientalist who travelled in disguise through Jordan in 1812 in search of the legendary city. On his way to Aqaba, he heard tales of some ancient ruins in a narrow valley near the purported site of Aaron's Tomb and persuaded a local guide to lead him here. His journal conveys his astonishment as he stumbles upon the hidden recesses of the lost city:

> *August 22nd* . . . directly opposite to the issue of the main valley, an excavated mausoleum came in view, the situation and beauty of which are calculated to make an extraordinary impression upon the traveller, after having traversed for nearly half an hour such a gloomy and almost subterraneous passage as I have described. It is one of the most elegant remains of antiquity existing . . . its state of preservation resembles that of a building recently finished, and on a closer examination I found it to be a work of immense labour.
>
> . . . Several broad steps lead up to the entrance, and in front of all is a colonnade of four columns, standing between two pilasters. On each of the three sides of the great chamber is an apartment for the reception of the dead . . . The doors of the two apartments opening into the vestibule are covered with carvings richer and more

beautiful than those on the door of the principal chamber. The colonnade is about thirty-five feet high, and the columns are about three feet in diameter with Corinthian capitals.[2]

A frieze of winged griffins writhing between vases and scrolls crowns the six Corinthian capitals, above which the central sculpture of the goddess Isis stands triumphant, framed between pillars on a cylindrical pedestal topped by an ornately carved rose-pink cupola and flanked by gyrating female warriors, Amazons with axes whirling above their heads. The giant vase, or urn, surmounting the cupola like a huge pineapple, is pockmarked with bullet holes, where local Bedouin tribesmen, believing it to be a treasure trove of the Nabataean kings, fired salvos to shatter the vessel and spill the gold. Despite their disappointment, the name Al-Khazneh stuck, the 'Treasury' of the lost city of Petra, and so it stands today, a marvel of the ancient world sculpted from a single vast block of rose-red sandstone, 'a brilliant display of man's artistry', as Edward Dawson writes, 'in turning barren rock into a majestic wonder.'[3]

It was here at Petra, precisely one hundred years ago, in October 1917, that T. E. Lawrence raised a Bedouin rebellion forcing the Turks to divert troops from Palestine just as Allenby was preparing his attack on Ottoman positions at Beersheba to unleash the Third Battle of Gaza, which would break the six-month stalemate and open the way to the British conquest of the Holy Land. First Lawrence sent his spies to the fortress of Shobek, to win over the Ottoman garrison which, being composed entirely of Syrians, changed sides overnight to join the revolt. The next day he led his combined Arabian, Bedouin and Syrian forces in an attack on the Damascus–Medina Railway. Although the Turks managed to hold the terminus against Lawrence's forces, the attack had the desired effect. The American academic-turned-war-reporter Lowell Jackson Thomas followed Lawrence's desert campaign closely. His description of the Turkish attack on Petra reads like an episode straight out of Kipling or Buchan:

> After the desertion of the entire Shobek garrison and Lawrence's bold sortie against the railway terminus, Djemal Pasha, commander-in-chief of the Turkish armies in Syria, Palestine, and Arabia, decided,

against the advice of Field Marshal von Falkenhayn, then German generalissimo in the Near East, that before he could hope to recapture Gueirra and Akaba it would be necessary to retake Petra. Djemal transferred a crack cavalry regiment, an infantry brigade, and several organizations of light artillery from Palestine down the Hedjaz Railway to Maan.

This was a clever strategic coup for Lawrence. First, the Germans and Turks had to diminish their forces opposing Allenby in the Holy Land. Secondly, they were walking into the trap which had been set for them; because it was Lawrence's belief that if a battle were fought by his irregular Bedouin troops in the mountain fastness of ancient Edom, the superior mobility of his army would eventually enable him to defeat any division of methodically-trained regulars in the world.

. . . [Lawrence] permitted at least a thousand of the enemy's troops to push headlong into the gorge before he gave the order to fire. When he had the Turks wedged into the narrowest part of the gorge, near the entrance to the city, one of his aides fired a rocket into the air as a signal for the Arabs to attack. A moment later pandemonium broke loose in the mountains of Edom. The Arabs poured in a stream of fire from all sides. The crack of rifles seemed to come from every rock. With shrill screams the women and children tumbled huge boulders over the edge on the heads of the Turks and Germans hundreds of feet below. Those stationed behind the columns of the Temple of ISIS kept up a steady fire . . .

A few minutes before the sun declined behind the rose-coloured mountains, Lawrence and Malud Bey sent up a second signal to their followers.

'Up, children of the desert!' shouted Malud.

Crouching figures sprang from behind the rocks on all sides. 'Allah! Allah!' came the answer from the throats of hundreds of Bedouins as they swept down the ridges into the valley.[4]

The Arab forces captured the entire Turkish transport, together with a complete field hospital and hundreds of prisoners, killed several hundred more and routed the rest. The Battle of Wadi Musa, one hundred years ago to the day, was a triumph of guerrilla warfare for the Arabs, a humiliating defeat for the Ottoman and German forces and yet another exploit of daring and brilliance in the growing legend of *El Orence*, this quiet, shy scholar and most unlikely soldier who had taken the Arab peoples and their struggle to his heart. As a diversionary tactic, it tipped the balance in Allenby's favour in the Third Battle of Gaza and contributed directly to British victory over the Turks in Palestine, along with everything that followed.

After photographing the fabulous façade of the Treasury from every possible angle to capture its astonishing variations of tone and texture in sun and shade, I can't resist a brief ride on a camel called Wifi, to my companions' weary amusement, led back and forth across the huge natural atrium by a Bedouin in kaftan and combat jacket. Then on we go, past further splendours of the sprawling ancient city, tombs and temples and astonishing caves of marble veined and striped with pink and pearl and ochre yellow strands swimming like an oil-spill prism. Past the enormous amphitheatre of Petra to the remains of the Byzantine Church of the Virgin Mary, with its riotous floor mosaics of rabbits and fish and dancing devils, dogs and peacocks and wild boar capering in a cartoon Bacchanalia around overflowing urns and ewers of fruit and wine, with chaps in mosaic miniskirts leading camels laden with riches and leopards sporting beneath pineapple trees - a jostling menagerie swarming across the 1,600-year-old floor in an exuberant jumble of pagan and Christian imagery, conjuring a snapshot of the lost world of the Byzantine Levant. Papyrus scrolls discovered in 1993 in a room to the north-east of the church, carbonised in a fire and thus preserved by happy accident, reveal a tantalising snippet of monastic life in sixth-century Petra. Written in Byzantine Greek, the twenty lines of text in the only completely preserved document read:

> List of things which I, Epiphanios, have lost − and I suspect the most reverent Hieros, son of Patrophilos: the big key of the upper floor, two cypresses from the double-roof, six birds, a table. When he emptied his apartment, I gave him two rooms to move into, and he did not give those back. Priest Epiphanios, son of Damianos − I have accepted the oath from the most reverent Hieros himself.[5]

The other documents range from real-estate transactions, disputes and divisions of property to marriages, dowries and inheritances, revolving around the affairs of Theodoros, son of Obodianos, deacon and later archdeacon, and his extended family and peers, Arabic-Nabataean Christian subjects of the Byzantine Empire.

Onwards, past the remains of the old hotel and restaurant in the valley of tombs where Agatha Christie lived for three months in 1933 writing her novel, *Appointment with Death*, and up and over the wonderful mountain staircase of the Nine Hundred Steps of Ad-Dayr. At each twist and turn of the path, Bedouin women with stalls set out on brightly patterned rugs sell jewellery, trinkets and cotton *keffiyehs* in black, white and red barbed-wire mesh designs, and press us to stop for almost undrinkably sweet Bedouin tea, brewed in blackened kettles on charcoal campfires. Every so often one meets a donkey clopping down the steps under its own steam, presumably heading back to its owner at the bottom.

Words exhaust themselves in straining to convey the desert splendours of this landscape of wonders. Every vista is a film poster or an album cover; around every corner is a film location for *Lawrence of Arabia* or *The English Patient*. Over the massive bouldered scarps of the Nine Hundred Steps and through the shrapnel of tumbled stone littering the mountain slopes we press on, as the baking sun declines across the western horizon, until we arrive at last in our Bedouin encampment, an amazing caravanserai nestling in the desert hills of Dana'a, run by a Bedouin called Atif who's dressed as Captain Jack Sparrow from *Pirates of the Caribbean*. Around a roaring fire crackling in the middle of a large circular divan decked with Bedouin rugs, Captain Atif and his crew of unlikely lads, Bedouins dressed as jolly Jack Tars, serve us a fine chicken casserole under the stars. After dinner, Ibrahim leads a raucous a cappella chorus of Arabic songs, while Atif and his pirates prepare *narghile* pipes.

We sleep in dinky little camping cabins perched up and down a labyrinth of sandy pathways planted with palm trees and cacti, sheltered beneath a low bluff of sandstone hills, a miniature Ayers Rock, which Atif has hung with twinkling fairy lights, the finishing touch of delightful kitsch to this enchanted caravanserai.

Tuesday 24 October

After a day of walking through the spectacular beauty of the Wadi Goeer in the Dana Biosphere Reserve and a night sleeping under the desert stars, we bid farewell to our Bedouin hosts and set off in Toyota pickup trucks on a bumpy ride through the dried-up river bed and desert tracks to the nearest stretch of road, where we rejoin the coach and head off towards the Dead Sea. As we turn right on to the King's Highway, we see huge empty trucks coming up from Aqaba in the south, having delivered their loads of potash to the port, 'for making fertiliser and ladies' make-up', says Ibrahim.

We're driving north now, parallel to the border with Israel; just a few kilometres to our left we can see the green hills of Israeli farms. 'All this desert area along the frontier, for 300 km up to the Syrian border, was mined after the '67 War,' says Ibrahim, 'but the Jordanian army has mostly de-mined it because so many Bedouins were getting killed or injured, particularly their children. The mines become very sensitive with age – even wind and dust can set them off. You know, it costs ten to fifteen dollars to lay each mine. How much do you think it costs to remove a single mine? Two thousand dollars. The Bedouin have sheikhs, tribal leaders who govern according to traditional Bedouin law, which interweaves with Jordanian law. They bury their dead very quickly, within four or five hours, sometimes within two hours, maximum twenty-four. It's difficult for doctors to get out to examine the bodies in time.'

Mel tells me that yesterday, after most of us had walked on from the Bedouin tent where we were having tea, Carol suddenly felt faint and dizzy. Immediately the Bedouin wife, who had been very much in the background previously, stepped forward to take charge and look after her. It was a touching moment, Mel said, being looked after by people whose life appears to us so vulnerable and impoverished.

An hour or so later, we reach our hotel at the north-eastern end of the Dead Sea, close to where the Jordan River flows in. On the far side, almost two-thirds of the shoreline lies within Palestinian territory, where the south-eastern corner of the West Bank meets the north-western beaches of this strange salt lake. It's the closest most Palestinians ever get to a sea of any description, but they are turned back regularly at the Beit Ha'arava checkpoint on Route 90, their only point of access. An *Independent* article of 2008 quotes the testimony of Doron Karbel, an Israeli army reservist, who said that his unit was told at the beginning of their tour of duty that the purpose of the checkpoint was to 'prevent Palestinians coming from the Jordan Valley to the Dead Sea beaches', and·quoted the IDF Jordan Valley brigade commander, Colonel Yigal Slovik, as saying that 'when Jews and Palestinian vacationers were sitting on the beaches side by side it hurt the business of the surrounding *yishuvim* [Jewish communities, ie settlements].' In other words, as the Association of Civil Rights in Israel (ACRI) asserted in its petition to the Supreme Court, 'We are dealing here with travel bans and entry prohibitions to public places in occupied territory which are tainted with discrimination and characteristic of colonial regimes . . . preventing the protected population of the occupied territory from using its own resources, while the very same resources are put at the disposal and enjoyment of the citizens of the occupying power.' The same article quotes a Palestinian bus driver, Mohammed Ahmed Nuaga'a, describing being turned back by the military with a party of children, aged between six and twelve, on a school trip from Hebron, officially coordinated and planned with the Palestinian Authority: 'I tried to explain to them that these are young pupils who came from very far to fulfil a big dream – to see the sea. But the soldiers were aggressive, and started shouting at us that Palestinian passage is forbidden, whether children or adults. The pupils begged the soldiers to let them go for even ten minutes just to see the sea and return, but nothing happened.'

Israel's refusal to allow Palestinians to access the mineral and energy resources of the Dead Sea costs the Palestinian economy nearly $1 billion a year, according to a statement by the Palestinian Authority's Ministry of National Economy in 2015. If Palestinians were allowed to establish investment projects along their Dead Sea shoreline to exploit its rich resources of shale, sand, asphalt, bitumen, oil and natural gas, the statement reads, as well as tourism and agricultural opportunities, they would be able to establish sustainable economic development. To add insult to injury, Israel licenses companies such as Ahava Dead Sea Laboratories, located within the illegal settlement of Mitzpe Shalem in the West Bank, to mine raw materials from the Palestinian shoreline, to supply its annual global sales of $150 million. According to the Palestinian human rights organisation Al-Haq, 'the appropriation and exploitation of Palestinian land and natural resources in the occupied Dead Sea area by Israeli settlers and companies . . . meet the requirements of the crime of pillage.' The Israeli foreign ministry's statement claimed that, under the Oslo accords, Israel has territorial jurisdiction that includes land, subsoil and territorial waters in Area C (Palestinian Territory under full Israeli military and administrative control, 63 per cent of the West Bank), and therefore 'would be entitled to license a company to excavate mud in that area if it chose to do so'.

Over on our side of the shore, the beachside hotel is a surprisingly snazzy joint, with grand glass and marble atriums and gold furnishings, swimming pools and huge terrace bars out the back, and a plush aquatic leisure complex of gyms and spas advertising sundry penitential ordeals. Some of the walkers vote selflessly to stay put, to immerse themselves in Dead Sea mud treatments, massages and saunas, while the rest of us shoulder our packs and set off across the desert hills to the east.

It's an astonishingly desolate wilderness of pale boulders and parched, scratchy soil, with the scantiest shreds of dusty grass and desert scrub fitfully stippling the bleak hills and gullies. Every so often one sees a tiny Bedouin encampment perched, seemingly arbitrarily, in the lee of one of the broken ridges, with a few scrawny goats nibbling at tussocks. In one valley, quite bizarrely, a single irrigated patch of land appears in the midst of a huge expanse of sun-bleached waste, half a dozen neatly ordered fields and orchards planted like an outpost on the surface of Mars. Otherwise, almost nothing. It seems the emptiest landscape I've ever set foot in. And yet, 'with that deep hush subduing all', one's attention is focused with deepening intensity to the particularity of this or that contour of the path, this pebble, this boulder, this blade or tuft of grass. Why is it, I wonder, that so many of the scattered stones seem to have split away from their substrate with sharp, square edges, almost geometric in their precision?

I look westwards across a deeply cleft, arid valley surmounted on the far side by a road running along the highest ridge, climbing steadily south above massive rocky shoulders outflung from the valley wall like huge buttresses, each striated with parallel wrinkles as if a great spill of lava had solidified in mid-flow down the slopes. Back behind the road sits a long, low white caravan or tent, tiny at this distance, and beyond it a further ridge dotted with two or three tiny nodules, buildings against the skyline. Borne on a whisper of breeze through the valley, we hear the far-flung mournful cry of a muezzin ululating the midday call to prayer across the barren slopes. But where is the mosque? One of those tents or huts, maybe? Or just the open sky? Spellbound, I use my phone to record a few seconds of this extraordinarily evocative soundscape, which hasn't changed in more than a thousand years: the far-off tinkling of goat bells, the fragmentary cadences of the muezzin's call rasping faintly over the stony ridges, and the desert wind whipping and whistling round these desolate hills.

Back at the hotel, I make a forlorn attempt to wash my once-white linen shirts, hang them out to dry on the enormous terrace outside my room, then head down to the beach for the obligatory dip in the Dead Sea. It's an eerie, oily experience, floating first on my back, then tipping forward on to my front in the pearly, waxy salt water, with every blister, scab and graze stinging like fury. I'm careful not to get any in my eyes, after David's anecdote about diving in blithely on a trip years ago and being almost blinded by the salt, then rushing in agony to the nearest shower to wash out his eyes. I clamber out of the slimy shallows on to the weird grey mud of the beach, like Neo emerging from his amniotic pod in *The Matrix*, and shower myself clean with some relief.

At dinner, to my great delight, we're joined by my friend Dan Beasley, an Amos trustee currently working for the UK Department for International Development (DfID) office in Amman, who tells us about the desperate situation in Yemen. The challenges of channelling emergency relief aid into this largely unreported humanitarian disaster zone, he says, are almost insuperable.

After dinner, in a deserted bar area down by the pool, Chris briefs the group on the Allenby Bridge crossing tomorrow, instructing us to 'clean' our phones – delete any incriminating photographs (such as me carrying the Palestinian flag into Istanbul) and archive our WhatsApp group chat – and talks us though our fake itinerary, the 'Ancient Pathways Pilgrimage' leaflet, which has been issued to everyone. Chris will be dusting off his dog collar tomorrow to assume his habitual disguise of Anglican priest, the innocuous vicar of St Clement's Eastcheap leading an innocuous Christian pilgrimage to swoon at the sites of the Holy Land. 'The more Christian you play it, the safer you'll be,' he says shamelessly. '*Oh yes, we're going to see the holy sites, the places where Jesus walked, the Sea of Galilee, the Nativity Church, Jerusalem. It'll be so wonderful, we can't wait, we're so excited, all that guff . . .*'

As ever, he's as cool as a cucumber, but I know this is a much bigger deal than usual. There's a high concentration of seasoned activists in the group, several of whom have done three-month stints in the West Bank as EAPPI volunteers. Moreover, the King Hussein /Allenby Bridge crossing, the only route by which Palestinians are allowed to travel internationally, is subject to much more intense scrutiny than any other border crossing.

After the briefing, I go off in search of a WiFi zone to try to FaceTime Nancy and my oldest son, Benedict, without much success, then head down to the terrace bar to look for Dan and Chris. In the lift, I find myself closeted with a glamorous dark-haired maiden clad in a long, black cloak spangled with silver stars and glitter. She looks a bit like Morticia from *The Addams Family*. As she sweeps out, I realise that she is none other than Anastasia the Belly Dancer, advertised enticingly in posters on every other wall in the hotel. I follow the trail of her perfume out to the terrace bar, where she disrobes for the crowd of Russian oligarchs and their girlfriends and performs vigorous gyrations to a tinny soundtrack of electro-Arabic pop. Dan and the others are nowhere to be seen. I don't hang around.

After writing my journal and pulling in my dry washing, I sit out on the terrace with a glass of whisky. Across the Dead Sea, the lights of Jericho twinkle through the night. The Promised Land, across the Jordan. Tomorrow, *insha'Allah*, we will be there.

After a last breakfast in the Free World, we load bags on to the coach, say a fond farewell to Ibrahim and his fellow-guide Joad, and set off north for the crossing. To our left through the coach windows the land stretches flat towards the northern tip of the Dead Sea and the central rift of the Jordan Valley. A dirt beige wasteland in the foreground, broken with patches of scrub and the occasional succulent, recedes across the river plain to a pale-yellow prairie dotted and pitted with hummocks and fissures, a weird lunar landscape pocked with craters where subterranean salt has shifted to create sinkholes in the collapsing top soil. Here and there submerged brakes of palm trees peep out of deep hollows in the plain, almost like soldiers lurking in foxholes. It's a bleak, forbidding borderland, where the devastation of this unique eco-system, the lowest river plain on earth, 1,410 feet below sea level, speaks eloquently of the slow asphyxiation of the Palestinian people and their culture. Throughout its 223-mile journey from the springs of Mount Hermon in Syria to here, where the strangled dregs of the once mighty Jordan (now less than 15 per cent of its former torrent) trickle into the Dead Sea, Palestinians are denied access to any part of the river in which Naaman was healed and Jesus was baptised.

Tension mounts as the coach swings westwards on Route 437 for the final approach to the border. Some of us try to laugh it off, joking and concocting daft scenarios about the imminent ordeal. 'I'll be blaming everything on Jack,' I say, 'and obviously David, 'cos he's Maltese and up to no good.' Most sit silent, gazing out at the surreal landscape stretching either side, fields of pale grey rocky hills with their tops chopped off, just like an upturned egg carton, interspersed with deep, dry ravines. I've never seen anything like it. The hills look as if they've been cast in concrete. Can this possibly be a natural landscape? Or is it a purpose-built no-man's-land of concrete hills, a tank-proof warren of impassable crevasses, to confine any possible approach to the Jordan River into this narrow corridor? And, presumably, to render a land invasion in either direction virtually impossible. Either way, it's a wretchedly bleak terrain. Follow the Jordan rift 2,000 miles south and you'd be wandering in the glorious open savannah of the Lake Nakuru National Park in Kenya, marvelling at the teeming flocks of pink flamingoes and herds of giraffe cantering in dreamlike slow motion across the fabled Rift Valley, where Karen Blixen lived and loved, and Mary and Louis Leakey found some of the earliest human remains. If that was the birthplace of humanity, this hideous wasteland feels like its cemetery.

The coach slows as we approach the Jordanian border control depot, a low complex of gateways, buildings and car parks fringed with palm trees, flagpoles flying the Jordanian flag, satellite towers and fences topped with coils of razor wire. It looks relatively innocuous, but still the approach to the actual border feels like sitting in the dentist's chair, palms sweating. *What if they confiscate my journal? Oh bugger, I hadn't thought of that. Hundreds of pages of handwritten scrawl, none of it transcribed yet, my sole record of this journey. What will I say to my publisher? Disaster. Ah well. Too late now . . .*

A uniformed Jordanian official is on the bus now, gathering in our passports. He seems a nice enough chap. He takes the stack of passports and gets off the coach. This feels more vulnerable than ever. We might as well be naked. We're completely at their mercy now, in the middle of the Middle East, in a horrible wilderness with no passports. Thinking back to a conversation weeks ago, a thousand miles back, in Albania, walking through a disused railway tunnel, our voices echoing around the black void . . . that's it! Of course – that's where we sang 'Cwm Rhondda' . . .

From the back of the bus, I start singing, 'Guide me, O Thou great Redeemer, pilgrim through this barren land . . .' Voices join in around me: Naomi and Cheryl and Ralph, and Phil from Preston, in his rolling *basso profundo*. This is the place and the moment this hymn was made for: *When I tread the verge of Jordan, bid my anxious fears subside. Death of death, and hell's destruction, land me safe on Canaan's side . . .*[6]

The Jordanian official returns our passports, all fine, no questions asked, and we drive on through the border controls and across the famous bridge, built first by Allenby in 1918 over the remnants of a nineteenth-century Ottoman bridge, rebuilt in the 1930s, destroyed in 1946 by the Palmach, the elite fighting force of the Haganah, then rebuilt, destroyed again in the Six-Day War of 1967, replaced with a wooden truss bridge the following year, then finally rebuilt after the Oslo Accords in 1994. Blink and you'd miss it; maybe fifty yards of tarmac road between thick beige concrete barriers across a gorge of yellow rock filled with a thick tangle of greenery. Photographs are not permitted at any point through the crossing, we've been warned. I look in vain for a glimpse of water to either side as we speed across, but the height of the concrete barriers and the broad swathe of bushes pretty much block any view of the river.

Now we're in Israeli-controlled territory, a short stretch of road through more concrete hills and another border terminal, where the coach pulls up and we all dismount and heave our luggage out of the hold for the next ordeal. We carry our bags into the customs building and submit passports for inspection at the first window, then we're waved through to a further checking stage where we feed our luggage on to a conveyor belt for X-ray, and then have to walk through a metal detector. This is where Ahmed was turned back last year. Chris goes through first, in his grey suit and dog collar, leader of the Ancient Pathways Pilgrimage. I hang back to make sure everyone gets through. If anyone's denied entry, we don't want to leave them stranded in no-man's-land or sent back to Jordan on their own. Some heart-related piece of shrapnel in Doug's chest sets off the alarm, and Jude and Jennifer and Mike all have metal hips, so they're all asked to step aside and wait for a body search.

We wait around for what seems ages while a female staff member goes off to get plastic gloves. 'Are you carrying a weapon?' the border policeman lurking nearby asks Jude.

She's not amused. 'No,' she says, fixing him with a steely glare, 'I have a replacement hip.'

He slouches off.

'What's the music like in your church?' I ask her, a propos of nothing, in an effort to keep spirits light.

'Oh, well, the minister does it with a machine,' she says. 'I still worship in the hospital chapel where Graham received his final care. The minister's very precise with the timing, cueing it up to come in at the right moment. We sing traditional hymns, sometimes, but every so often he throws in a wild card, a song by Bette Midler or someone, to keep us on our toes. I always look forward to those.'

At last the female officer returns and ushers Jude and Jennifer towards an adjacent private room, to conduct a body search.

'What are you waiting for? Why don't you go through?' the border policeman asks me.

'I'm one of the group leaders,' I say. 'I just want to make sure everything's OK.'

Eventually hips and hearts pass muster and we all go through. I get through the metal detector without a blip, then past the first passport window and then to a final window to get a sticker on my passport. I'm busy sorting out my bags so I barely look at the guy through the window as he scans my passport. It appears not to elicit any alarm bells, although for a moment while he surveys the screen my heart is in my mouth. Then he puts a green sticker on my passport and hands it back to me. Apparently green is the 'mildest' colour, according to activist folklore.

I manage to smash a bottle of orange juice on my way out – a spectacular mess all over the floor. I apologise profusely and offer to help clear it up, but all the staff reassure me it's fine, don't worry, we'll sort it out. They're really quite friendly.

We head on through to the next bus, load our bags into the hold and climb aboard to drive on to the Palestinian border control, once more through a no-man's-land of bare, tortured hills. At the next depot, a Palestinian official comes on to the bus to take our passports and disappears. Smiles break out all round. Chris is sitting slumped at the back of the bus, his long legs splayed out, dog collar torn aside, the picture of exhausted relief. Minutes later the Palestinian official returns, all smiles, and hands out our passports, calling out our names: 'Mr Douglas, Mr Ralph, Mr Justin . . . welcome to Palestine!' Glory be. We've made it.

After the official gets off, Doug, who's worked extensively in the region in development research, describes this as a 'humiliating formality – not for us, but for the Palestinians – to take our passports, essentially for appearance's sake, go off and do who knows what with them, having virtually no power to stop or detain us, and then return them like that.' We drive the last few kilometres on into Jericho, pointing out the half-built breeze-block houses and black rooftop water tanks like old friends, then pile off the bus at the border terminal, walk out through the concourse and, as we stride through the last gate, chatting away and laughing, suddenly a huge fanfare of whoops, cheers and applause breaks out on all sides – from all our friends waiting to meet us!

I had no idea they'd all be here – the entire Amos Trust group of thirty who came through Tel Aviv with Nive Hall on Monday. Here they all are, a great crowd of friends all cheering, clapping and grinning – Nive and Nick Welsh and Chris's wife Sarah and their daughter Millie, Bethan and Joy and others who walked with us earlier along the way, and here's Sami Awad with his sunglasses perched on his head giving me a bear hug, and Elias Deis and all our friends from Holy Land Trust in Bethlehem . . . and tears are rolling down our faces and a great love-fest breaks out of hugs and kisses all round. Then the Mayor of Jericho turns up at the head of a civic delegation to welcome us, a burly gentleman around my age in suit and tie, a black Palestinian, one of the small population descended originally from Muslim pilgrims from Africa. His speech moves me to tears, as much as anything else because of the recognition our walkers are receiving at last, in Palestine, from Palestinians, especially those who've never been here before, like Arthur, Cressey, Jude and Tim, who've given months of their time and walked all this way in faith, no doubt wondering whether we'd ever get here and, if we did, whether it would mean anything to the Palestinian people. Here at last is their reward.

One of the Mayor's staff translates as he speaks. 'This is the oldest city which was inhabited by mankind,' he says, 'and here was discovered the first of mankind, as human settlement, 10,000 years old. We are jubilated to receive you here in our city, and to recognise the city, all its ins and outs, you could talk to people and you will discover how much we are humans, and how much we are appreciating other people, other communities – and peace also. So we submit our deep thankfulness to you, as you endured this exhaustion of all the travelling, and you cross long, long distances to arrive here to Palestine, to express your opinions, your beliefs and by rejecting the hated Balfour promise.

'This promise, which has been cut years ago, we are still suffering from it, until this moment. You cross all borders and barriers. Your existence here, actually, we hope that it would be a message to break the barriers for us as Palestinians. We know that your visit is a kind of standing in solidarity with Palestinian people. We thank you for those noble feelings. Once we noticed such solidarity groups with Palestinians, we feel that our case is still alive, particularly when we see delegates from the UK, the place of that promise. And, of course, we never blame the communities and people, as we know very well what is in your hearts. We wish such visits here to have a kind of positive reflect on the political rhythm, and to be repeated more and more in the future. We hope one day there should be a global or national rejection of all nations against this. We know that your visit here is submitting a kind of apology for that promise, and we wish of course for the UK government apology, and to translate it on the land. To put policy aside, first of all we are humankind, with the whole variety of our beliefs, names, nations, religions, we are shared in the humanity and seeking together, for the sake of stability and peace for all people. One more time we really thank you for those nice feelings, and this is a mental support to the Palestinian people. We wish you a pleasant stay in Jericho. Looking forward to the future, maybe a delegation from Jericho goes to London by walking!'

Laughter, cheers and applause break out at this last comment, and as we all line up for photographs with the Mayor, a huge gaggle of Palestinian schoolchildren races into the concourse to welcome us, carrying placards decorated with peace doves, images of the Wall, watchtowers and swirling ribbons in red, green and black. Another heart-stirring moment, bringing tears to the eyes once more. Wildly over-excited and beaming with Cheshire Cat grins, they present us with Palestinian scarves, shouting, 'Welcome! Hello! Hello!' and posing for photographs, getting the giggles, exchanging high fives then running away, embarrassed and chuckling to each other. Nick stage-manages us all into a huge phalanx, sixty walkers and fifty-odd schoolchildren plus friends from Holy Land Trust and the Mayor's office, and we walk forth together, with Amos Trust film-maker Mark Kensett filming our approach to Jericho from a car.

A modern sculpture of a crescent moon in shining steel above a fragmented stone wheel stands at the entrance to the city between the Blue Domed Mosque and the Latin Cathedral. On the sculpture, in Arabic and English, reads the caption, 'Jericho – city of the Moon.' The Arabic name of the oldest city on earth, *Ariha*, is derived from *Yarikh*, the Canaanite god of the moon, hailed as the provider of nightly dew. Wedded to the goddess *Nikkal* in Canaanite mythology, *Yarikh* provides the moisture that enables her orchards to bloom in the desert. From the same root comes the Canaanite *reah*, 'fragrance', and in modern Arabic *Ariha* unites both meanings, city of fragrance and the moon god, not only the most ancient but also the lowest city on earth, at 230 metres below sea level, between the mountains of Moab and Jerusalem, the oasis of Palestine. We march in a chaotic cavalcade through the dusty streets into the old town of Jericho for more speeches, photographs and TV interviews in the city square next to the town hall and municipality offices. Palm trees, lawns and flower beds surround the fountain on the central piazza, and as we wander into the square, suddenly foaming jets of white water leap and cascade in welcome, as the fountain bursts into life.

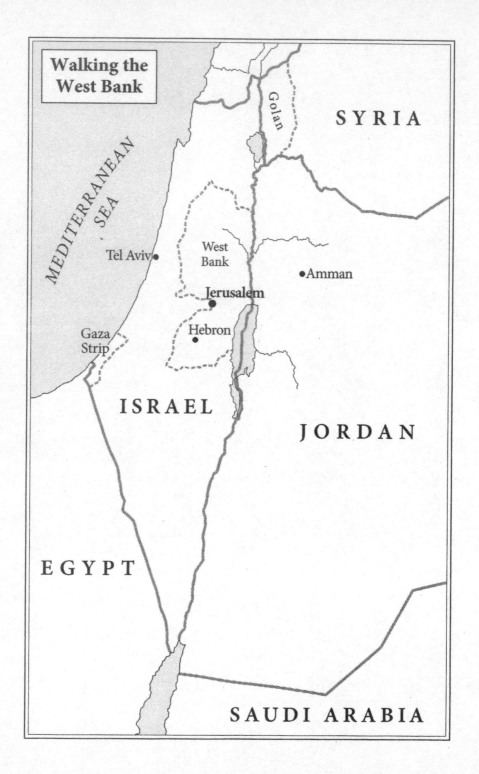

Walking the West Bank

MEDITERRANEAN SEA

SYRIA

Golan

Tel Aviv

West Bank

•Amman

Jerusalem

Gaza Strip

Hebron

ISRAEL

JORDAN

EGYPT

SAUDI ARABIA

I2

Jerusalem Syndrome

So he passed over, and all the trumpets sounded for him on
the other side.

> John Bunyan, *The Pilgrim's Progress*

Friday 27 October

WE'RE WALKING A spectacular wadi through the Judaean wilderness,
not far from Beit Sahour, with a group of 100 young Palestinians
and internationals from an organisation called Right to Movement,
organisers of the annual Palestine Marathon. We're being led by a
group of guides from Masar Ibrahim-al-Khalil, a Palestinian walking
association who in the last ten years have created a walking route
from the north to the south of the West Bank, known as the Abraham
Trail. As well as Palestinians, there are many young Germans, Danes,
Swedes, Czechs and other nationalities in the group. The great
convoy of walkers is a thrilling sight, ranged along the magnificent
desert wadi with its high walls and beetling crags, slopes strewn with
thorn and gorse, and sleepy camels basking in the already hot sun.
At our rendezvous this morning, at the village of Tuqu'ur, we had
a riotous reception on a hillside above the wadi and a gloriously
chaotic reading of our Just Walk liturgy in English and Arabic.

Now I'm walking and chatting with John Atick, the lead guide
for Masar Ibrahim-al-Khalil, a wiry Palestinian athlete in his late
twenties with a neat beard and a sunhat like a stetson. He's a charismatic young man who speaks very good English with a husky
trace of American which lends his voice a faintly Bostonian quality,
almost like Cary Grant.

'We're walking the Wadi Jihar,' he says. 'It comes from the Arabic *juhor*, which means a hole, because this valley has so many holes, for small animals like foxes. We're making our way towards a Bedouin village called 'Arab ar-Rashayida, where you'll see some of the wilderness of Jerusalem. I love going out to explore nature. Masar Ibrahim-al-Khalil, the trail we're walking now, the Abraham Trail, is 330 km from Rummana, north-west of Jenin, down to Beit Mirsim in Hebron. The trail is fantastic because it offers the diversity of Palestinian landscapes – the mountains, the plains, the Jordan Valley and Rift, and the wilderness of Jerusalem, all in one trail. Palestine is unique, in the centre of the world, and the corridor for migratory birds. We have more than 500 million birds migrating through Palestine every year. Migratory birds prefer to fly over land, and what connects Africa to Europe to Asia – is Palestine. As for the flora, we've recorded more than 2,700 species of plant in Palestine, even though it's such a small area, which also makes Palestine unique. Not to mention the people! Palestine is rich in history, but it's also rich with its people, famed for our hospitality. We love to see guests, and we always greet them with a warm heart and invite them to be part of our community and let them experience how it feels to be authentic, away from the tourist sites, which have so many people over and over again. Palestine has so much to offer – yet to be discovered.

'When Prophet Ibrahim came to this land, he must have walked through the Canaanite kingdom, and the beginning of this trail was in Rummana, one of the villages in the Jenin governorate, which was part of the first Canaanite kingdom. Then we traced all the Canaanite kingdoms towards the south, following the trade routes that potentially were taken by Prophet Ibrahim when he came to Palestine. So that's the idea of the trail. We started in 2006 and have been working on this trail, developing the infrastructure and giving training and workshops with local communities, and in 2013 we were officially registered as a union. In a few days we will finish way-marking the whole trail from north to south, following the European system, using red and white. We have all the topographic maps ready online, and trail descriptions if you don't want to read maps, or you can download all the GPS files and put it on your own device. We do a through-hike twice a year, in November and then again in March: twenty-one days continuous walking, starting in Rummana and ending in Beit Mirsim, near Hebron. Anyone is welcome to join us, locals or internationals; the trail is there for everybody to hike with us and enjoy this unique natural environment.

'Our national bird is the Palestine sunbird; it's very tiny, one of the most amazing birds you've ever seen. It's black, and on its back there are wavy, rainbow-mixed colours. We also have the red fox, the hyena, wolf, ibex, and the Palestinian deer, very beautiful, and the leopard.'

'Leopard? Really?'

'Yes, in one of the nature reserves, in the southern part of Palestine, it still exists, like an Arabian leopard, yellow and spotted, but indigenous to Palestine. I've never seen it. I wish to see it, but it's very rare.'

'It feels very hopeful, talking about this with you; it's a celebration of your land, culture and history, and it's about bringing people from all over the world to come and experience the Palestinian landscape, hospitality and nature. Does it make you feel hopeful?'

'Well, it does, because going out and being in nature makes me feel free. I'm not facing anything; I'm just walking. I'm not just a guide, I'm also a Palestinian adventurer – like one month ago, I was in France, climbing the Alps and raising the Palestinian flag on one of the highest summits. The message I send is to show the world the good image of Palestine: people looking forward, that we are peaceful, and we have capacities and talents and people with potential and skills. My plan is that I'm going to climb, hopefully, all the seven summits in the world, ending with Mount Everest – and there is no true Palestinian that's ever done that. By true Palestinian I mean born here, with a Palestinian mother and father. My next adventure, maybe, is going to be Mount Kilimanjaro in Africa, and I'm going to raise the same flag that I raised on the Alps on the top of Kilimanjaro and tell the people, here we are, here we stand, this is Palestine.'

'What's the impact of the Occupation on your work?'

'Well, that's one of the things we had to consider. Masar Ibrahim is the first trail that crosses all the Areas A, B and C in one trail, with no obstacles or anything. So you're always in the mountains, the valleys, away from any checkpoints or something that might stop you. We're trying to make the best of our lives. Maybe it's hard for us as individuals to change the situation; we can't change it back in one night, it's a big process, but we try to make the best of what we have right now, and people are encouraged to go out and hike and explore, and this didn't exist before. People used to say, "Why are you going out? Going hiking? Are you crazy? What's wrong with this guy?" But now they want to hike with me. It's very positive. One of the negative impacts of the Occupation is that people can become depressed and not want to go out or do anything. We're offering something positive. If people are stressed, it doesn't help anybody, but when you take them out into nature, they are more relaxed, they have inner peace – and that changes their life.'

'Do you feel you find God out here in the wilderness?'

'Well, I'm a Christian and I'm a believer, and I feel that going out, connecting with nature, there's also a higher bond of connection with that greater power which founded all this, which is God, and you can maybe seek silence. Some people just want to be by themselves, with themselves, so it can heal you, and maybe if you're into religion and you want to get closer to God, this is the perfect place for you.'

The walk ends at a Bedouin cafe/tent on the edge of Deir Rashaida in the Judaean wilderness, where we feast on hot flatbread pancakes soaked in olive oil and *za'atar*, washed down with super-sweet Bedouin tea. They show us their zaab-chicken oven, a kiln door in the ground leading to a dark recess, from which they're pulling casserole dishes, baked in the ferocious heat which the desert sand and stones have absorbed. Suddenly we hear a huge cheer from the Right to Movement crowd, roaring their congratulations to one of their friends who's shown up to meet them, having just returned from completing the Chicago Marathon and beating his previous year's record of two hours and forty-four minutes. He shows us his 2016 T-shirt, printed with the words, 'Right to Movement – we run to tell a different story. Fastest Palestinian Marathoner, Chicago Marathon 2016, 02:44:33.'

With many fond farewells, we head off to Beit Sahour, past clusters of settlements sprawling like Costa del Sol hotels across the outlying hills of Bethlehem. I'm in a group of eight, staying in the family home of a delightful schoolteacher called Reema, who serves up a superb Palestinian dinner. She's taught in Hebron for twenty-four years, since she was twenty. Seventy-two per cent of Beit Sahour is Christian Palestinian, she says. The three cities of the Bethlehem region – Beit Sahour, Beit Jala and Beit Lahem (Bethlehem) – are the heartland of the Palestinian Christian community, now a tiny minority in the West Bank. Palestinian Christians, always a minority, are mostly from the more affluent tiers of society, and as the Occupation has intensified more and more have left to seek a better life elsewhere.

After dinner, a number of us head off to the local bar to sink a few Taybeh beers (the local brew) and puff the *narghile* pipe under the Bethlehem stars. I share with Philip my still-unresolved dilemma about Eleanor possibly flying out to join us tomorrow, along with Julia Katarina and Gemma Bell, an Amos trustee. The prospect of her being subjected to a gruelling interrogation and possibly deported, with me powerless to intervene, has me very anxious.

'Yeah, OK,' says Phil, 'but that probably won't happen, and just think what a life experience this'll be for her, at sixteen, to come out and join you for this amazing adventure, the last few days of a five-month pilgrimage, on the Balfour centenary. Come on! That's gotta be worth the risk. I'd do it, if it was my daughter, or granddaughter. And even if the worst case happens, that's still a valuable life experience. Go for it, Justin!'

I decide to go for it.

Saturday 28 October

The entrance to Aida Refugee Camp in Bethlehem is an empty gateway or portal sculpted to resemble a vast keyhole, above which sits a giant bronze sculpture of a key, the famous Key of Return, a bitter-sweet emblem representing the cherished heirloom of every Palestinian refugee family – the key of the house they fled or were driven from in 1948. As Abdelfattah Abusrour told us on my first visit here in 2012, 'Aida' means 'she who will return', and so this camp, established as an emergency measure by the UN in 1950 – then just a collection of tents and temporary shelters which has

grown over the decades into a permanent shanty town – is founded
on the promise of UN Resolution 194, upholding the Palestinian
right of return, which has never been fulfilled. To the left of the
Key and gateway stands the UNRWA office which administers
essential services to residents of the camp. Mounted against one
corner of the office building is a poster of a bright-eyed Palestinian
teenager with a toothy smile and sticking-out ears. Above his
photograph the caption, in English and Arabic, reads: 'My name is
Aboud Shadi, a 13-year old Palestinian refugee. I was standing just
right here hanging with my friends when an Israeli sniper shot me
dead. My soul will remain here chasing the killer and motivating
my classmates. I wonder whether the international community will
bring justice to Palestinian children.'

As we pass beneath the arch, I notice a poem painted on the
right-hand inner wall of the keyhole frame:

> They are beyond numbers, rising
> through the sky proud and steadfast.
> They are the tales of the medows our
> seized aspirations, Determinedly
> leading our struggle towards freedom
> and dignity.

It's raining this morning, for the first time since our arrival in
Palestine, the grey sky and drizzle matching the mournful setting.
A few yards inside the entrance, the Wall looms up to our right,
its hateful grey slabs jostling like a row of uneven teeth, broken
only by a watchtower, charred by the smoke of burning tyres piled
against it in countless demonstrations. As everywhere in Bethlehem,
the Wall is a canvas for a smorgasbord of protest art. Next to the
sooty column of the watchtower, a large *trompe l'oeil* shows a vista
of the Dome of the Rock in Jerusalem, framed by the crumbled
remnants of the Wall, its copper dome resplendent against a blue
sky. Beyond the watchtower spreads a huge, coloured panorama of
the Second Intifada: in the foreground a Palestinian man, handcuffed
and blindfold, is arrested by three Israeli soldiers against a backdrop
of billowing smoke and burning buildings. On the right, Palestinian
youths in *keffiyehs* throw stones, swing slingshots and cradle their
wounded comrades as soldiers open fire from the left of the picture.

Against the swirling smoke the caption reads: 'WE CAN'T LIVE
– SOME ARE WAITING FOR DEATH'. Overflowing skips and
piles of refuse in front of the Wall complete the picture. Here they
live still, the refugees of 1948, in Aida, Beit Jibrin and Dheisheh,
the camps of Bethlehem, and in refugee camps up and down the
West Bank, and in Gaza, and in Jordan, Lebanon and Syria, the
exiles of more than 500 villages destroyed in the *Nakba*. And here
in the harsh fist of the Occupation, right in the shadow of the
Wall, people like Abdelfattah and his colleagues at Alrowwad strive
tenaciously to foster hope where there seems to be none.

Having worked so closely with Alrowwad last year on their UK
tour, it's a warm reunion with Abdelfattah and his associates Ribal
and Manal, and many of the teenage performers. Charismatic as
ever, Abdelfattah holds the walkers spellbound as he describes the
work of Alrowwad and their vision of 'Beautiful Resistance'. Dan
Beasley, who has travelled across from Jordan to join us for a few
days, introduces me to his friend Akram, a freelance film-maker
and journalist. At their request, I go up to the roof of Alrowwad
to record an interview against the jumbled Bethlehem skyline of
Palestinian rooftops crowded with water storage tanks, white settlement apartment blocks rising like Benidorm penthouses from every
patch of high ground, and the ridiculous, tragicomic Wall-enclave
of Rachel's Tomb smack bang in the middle of everything.

Inspired by Abdelfattah's talk and their visit to this haven of calm
and creativity, the walkers march on with a new spring in their
step, accompanied by a cavalcade of local kids, and with perfect
timing the sun comes out, as we wander through the maze of
alleyways lined with posters of teenage martyrs and graffiti murals
of a future land of justice and peace.

Dheisheh Camp, regarded by the IDF as a hotbed of resistance, is
the most hard-pressed of all the camps in Bethlehem. We're
welcomed in a large UNRWA community hall, where murals of
exile adorn the staircase walls: desert fields crowded with lines
of grey UN refugee tents marked with dates spanning the century of
dispossession – 1917, 1948, 1956, 1967, 1982 – framed with a jagged
cordon of barbed wire, hung with countless keys. Our guide in the
West Bank is the redoubtable Husam Jubran, a burly, deep-voiced,

erudite chap in his mid-forties with a droll, grumpy cast of countenance and great talent for gallows humour. His twin passions,
he says, are tourism and nonviolence. As well as guiding National
Geographic Expeditions, he provides training in conflict management and nonviolence and facilitates the Hands of Peace Program
each summer, which brings Israeli and Palestinian teenagers together
for a three-week experience of building dialogue and friendship.
After a generous lunch in the UNRWA hall, Husam introduces
Farid Al-Atrash, a human rights lawyer whom he describes as a
personal hero of his.

'You do a good, wonderful humanitarian job,' says Farid,
addressing us all. 'As Palestinians, we thank you, because you come
here with a humanitarian message to be sent to the whole world.
Three weeks ago, I was in the UK, invited by Amnesty International
to talk about violations of human rights by Israel. We were the
guests of the Palestine Solidarity Campaign and we attended the
Labour Party conference in Brighton. I tell all my friends here in
Palestine that we have so much support from England, against the
Balfour Declaration. We are so grateful, and really thank you from
the depths of our hearts for your amazing action and support for
Palestine.'

Warm applause fills the room. 'Farid is an amazing, brave, hard-
working lawyer,' says Husam, 'who challenges not just the Israeli
occupation but also local corruption here in Palestine.'

Next up is the magnificently named Jihad Ramadan, a dashing
young activist with a raven-black mane of hair and elegant *Mephisto*
goatee. 'I have the best name,' he grins, 'because it means in Arabic
"Holy War–Holy Month". You couldn't ask for a better name than
this, right? So, Dheisheh Camp was established by the UN in 1949
for 3,000 refugees from forty-six destroyed villages of western
Jerusalem and the area west of Hebron. Now there's around 15,000
people living here, on 0.33 of a square kilometre, so it's very crowded.
My family was from D'reesh Village, near Jerusalem, destroyed in
1948. Now they've planted forests there and they call it a "national
park". The Israelis have been "in the camp" twenty-four hours a
day since 1967, imposing a harsh regime of collective punishment.
We had thirteen martyrs killed here in Dheisheh during the First
Intifada, just for being out of curfew. The Israelis have been torturing

us, but we started to educate ourselves, to defend ourselves. Settlers used to make picnics here, coming from their settlements in Hebron. One guy came and stood in front of Dheisheh as a signpost, to direct settlers to come and attack us, but we defended ourselves.

'Here are the main problems we suffer: continual night raids from the Israelis, sometimes three nights in a row, turning everyone out of their houses and arresting young people; shortage of water – we only get water twice a month, then we must use the water tanks on the roof; massive overcrowding – like I said, we have such a huge density of population, it really makes life very difficult; and finally, our right of return – no one believes in it except us. Why do Palestinians remain in these refugee camps, some people ask. Because we are stateless persons, refugees for whom the UN has responsibility because our homes were taken from us. If we move out, go and live somewhere else, even if we could afford to, it's like we're saying, OK, forget about our homes, where we came from, our right of return, you can keep what you stole from us and we have no more right.

'At least three times a year the Israelis invade the camp – and we're in Area A, supposed to be under full Palestinian control, right? – and ten or eleven young people have been martyred in the last year or so. The Israeli commander came here and announced that he doesn't want a camp full of martyrs; he wants a camp full of invalids. So they have shot many of our kids in the left kneecap and now they are walking on crutches, or carried on stretchers, or having legs amputated. They are targeting Dheisheh Camp as a centre of resistance, since the First Intifada.'

I'm so stunned by this information that I have to double-check with Husam afterwards, as we're gathering outside the hall to move on. 'Husam, did I hear this right? What Jihad said about the IDF deliberately shooting kids through the kneecaps?'

'Yes,' says Husam, 'that's right.'

'This is unbelievable.'

'It's the truth,' says Husam, 'and in the last two years, more than 100 kids from Dheisheh Camp have been shot in this way.'

'And when he came and made these threats, did anyone record him saying it?'

Husam smiles bitterly. 'Every time we tell the residents of

Dheisheh about this, people from the UK, the USA, they ask the same thing. Think about it. This guy, this IDF commander, comes with his body-guards, with guns, to intimidate and threaten the elders of the camp. You think someone's gonna get out their phone and start videoing him? Ask him for an interview?'

From Dheisheh we set off across the terraced hills, olive groves and little villages to the south of Bethlehem, heading eastwards round towards Beit Sahour, with a huge throng of kids from Dheisheh Camp, for whom this is a rare opportunity to wander through the countryside in comparative safety. I hope they'll be alright getting back. Husam says that a number of their youth workers will supervise their transport home. Right at the top end of Dheisheh Camp, on the furthest south-western outskirt of Bethlehem, we pass through the village of Artas, overlooking a beautiful, cultivated hillside with planted terraces, Roman-era stoneworks and olive orchards stretching down into the Khreitoun Valley. Here the nineteenth-century Convent of Hortus Conclusus, 'the enclosed garden', marks the site where Solomon supposedly wrote the Song of Songs, now inhabited by an Italian order of nuns from Uruguay.

> You are like a garden enclosed, my sister, my bride;
> A garden enclosed, a fountain sealed.
>
> *(Song of Songs* 4:12)

On the far slopes a settlement sprawls, encroaching into the valley. Locals fear that it will expand across the whole of that far hill, at which point, Husam says, Bethlehem will be completely rimmed by settlements and the Wall. Walking down through the valley into the next village, a little hamlet named Tuqu, I meet an elderly Palestinian farmer who stops to shake hands. I say, '*Marhaba, keef halek?*' ('Hello, how are you?').

He shakes his head and says softly, 'What . . . what we can do with Balfour?'

'Well, we need to change it,' I say.

He shakes his head, eyes downcast, and says, 'Theresa . . . Theresa is no good.'

'I know, I'm sorry,' I say. 'She doesn't speak for us. We're here because we support you.'

'Thank you, thank you, my friend,' he says sadly, nodding. 'You are welcome here in Palestine.'

He's referring to Theresa May's announcement in Parliament last Tuesday, in which she stated, on behalf of the government, 'We are proud of the role that we played in the creation of the State of Israel and we will certainly mark the centenary with pride.' This coming Thursday, the Balfour centenary, she will be attending a celebratory dinner in London with Israel's Prime Minister and the current Lords Balfour and Rothschild, a dinner to which Jeremy Corbyn has declined his invitation. 'We must also be conscious of the sensitivities that some people do have about the Balfour Declaration,' she conceded, 'and we recognise that there is more work to be done.' Presumably these are the same people as the 'existing non-Jewish communities' which Balfour, with equal coyness, couldn't bring himself to name. I wish she were here now, to meet some of these 'people'.

While the rest walk on to Beit Sahour, Elias picks me up to drive to Ramallah for a TV interview. Eleanor's flight should be landing at Ben Gurion Airport about now. Heading along the main road from Al-Eizariya (or Bethany, site of Ivor's bakery), we pass an exit pointing to the settlement of Geva Binyamin, where Elias points out the barrier where they open the road specially to let settlers through. Earlier, heading north from Beit Sahour, our driver pulled off the main drag because there was an accident up ahead, with soldiers everywhere and a log jam of traffic. He called his friend to alert him while I sat stewing with nerves, thinking, *The longer we sit still, the more likely one of those soldiers is to come over and start giving us trouble, come on, let's just go, let's get moving!* By this stage, of course, I've got myself convinced that every Israeli soldier in the West Bank will have seen my TV interview in Jericho and be scanning the roads for a sight of me. I made a point of recording these wild fears on a voice memo, to remind myself of the state one can get into, driving in occupied Palestine at night.

As the administrative centre of the Palestinian Authority, Ramallah is the most modern and developed city in the West Bank, and the Palestinian Broadcasting Corporation (PBC) studios are a smart complex, with a grand glass and marble atrium leading to many floors of studios and production offices, all built with international development money in the 1990s, but now weirdly half-empty. No money to pay staff or make programmes, I presume. The interview is pre-recorded, for broadcast an hour or two later, which takes the pressure off somewhat. The programme host asks me lots of big questions about international affairs: will Theresa May apologise to the Palestinian people for Balfour? Will Britain support a Palestinian State? Can Britain's influence in the international community save Palestine? I have to wear an earpiece and speak in bite-sized chunks, with pauses for simultaneous translation. Confining myself to short, pithy phrases is a challenge, as readers of this book will be aware. Faced with such big questions, obviously I want to be upbeat and encouraging and project a strong message of support and solidarity, but at the same time I don't want to conjure unrealistic hopes.

Quoting what Sir Vincent Fean, former British Consul-General to the OPT, said last year at a conference on Balfour, I say, 'Britain has more political power than we like to admit. It's too easy for British politicians to say, "We can't do anything, Britain doesn't count any more, it's all up to the Americans." Actually, if Britain were to recognise a Palestinian State and call strongly for an end to the Occupation and the siege of Gaza, call for Israel to dismantle its illegal settlements, tear down its illegal Wall, address the right of return of Palestinian refugees, call for an end to the theft of water resources – in short, call for equal rights for everyone in the Holy Land, from the river to the sea, well – if Britain were to do this, other countries would follow.'

The programme host says, 'Your Prime Minister Theresa May has said she is proud of Britain's role in creating the State of Israel, that she will be celebrating. What do you think of this?'

'I think it's incredibly crass, and along with many other British people, I'm embarrassed by her.' I tell him about my encounter with the elderly farmer in Tuqu today. 'Her remarks are offensive and deeply insensitive to the one hundred years of suffering that Britain's actions have caused to the Palestinian people, but I can tell you that there is a growing popular movement in the UK in solidarity with Palestine. The British people support Palestinian rights. Our government does not speak for us, and part of what we're doing here, why we've walked all the way across Europe to Palestine, is to express our sorrow, our apology, on behalf of our country, whose governments continue to fail the Palestinian people. Theresa May says she'll be celebrating in London next Thursday with Israel's prime minister, but we are here, in solidarity with the Palestinian people, and we represent the British people, not the British government.'

Well, there's no going back now. This is why we've come, to make as much noise as possible. Chris and I have agreed to do the lion's share of the TV interviews between us, so that if there's any trouble at the airport when we leave the two of us will take the flak. Obviously a ban in his passport would be a major headache for Chris, but Amos Trust has other projects in other countries, and other people who could pick up the baton here. For me, it would matter less. I don't fancy a gruelling interrogation and possible detention, I really don't, and I don't want things to be unpleasant for Eleanor, but keeping the Israelis sweet is not the object of the exercise.

After my ten penn'orth and more, talking about various initiatives for Palestine, plays, concerts, festivals, replica Walls, etc., the host chats with Elias in Arabic about Holy Land Trust's work and their partnership with Amos Trust and the reception we've been getting from Palestinian communities everywhere. Afterwards, we line up with the translator for photographs on the studio stage, and then, with many warm handshakes and effusive thanks, we're on our way.

Outside, Elias bear hugs me. 'Thank you, that was such a beautiful interview,' he says. 'Everything you said, so generous and so true.'

'Oh, good,' I say, taken aback. 'Well, you know, just wind me up and let me go. Glad it came across.'

One of the remarkable projects in which Holy Land Trust participates is called Roots, a forum where Palestinians meet with settlers to try to build some kind of dialogue. 'We've taken part in discussions to see what kind of vision for peace and justice might emerge in the aftermath of the failed Oslo Peace Process,' Sami Awad told me. 'When seeing the land as one with all those who live in it, not divided by borders, it's important to understand all the communities here, including those motivated by religious belief – and to challenge them to adhere to their core teachings of justice and righteousness. With the failure of the Two-State solution we need to redefine who is my enemy and who is my partner. Those who do not recognise Palestinians as having full equal rights are the ones we need to challenge, no matter where they live, just as those who believe in our rights are our friends – no matter where they live.'

I mention the Roots forum to Elias, as our taxi heads south from Ramallah. Ultimately, Elias says, Jews, Christians and Muslims have to share the land. He doesn't so much want to see a political solution as a religious solution. It could be one state, he says, everyone with equal rights, open to all faiths, and just call it The Holy Land. If, as a Christian, he can go to Nazareth and walk by the Sea of Galilee where Jesus walked, if Jews can access the Tombs of the Patriarchs in Hebron, and if Muslims can visit the Al-Aqsa Mosque in Jerusalem, everyone would be happy. It's about rights of movement. Yes, it's also about land, employment, the economy and, of course, water, but fundamentally, in his view, it's about equality of religion. This is a view I've heard expressed by some Orthodox Jews, that they don't care what passport they carry as long as they can pray in Hebron and on the Temple Mount in East Jerusalem.

We get through the various checkpoints between Ramallah and Beit Sahour, where Elias's car is parked, without mishap, *hamdullah*. Wait till that interview's aired, I think; my card'll be properly marked then. We're staying in Hebron for a couple of nights, so Elias will drive me down there. I speak to Eleanor, who's made it through customs – *alhamdulillah!* – with Gemma Bell, and they're now looking for Julia. Having lived previously for three and a half years in the West Bank, when she was married to a Palestinian, Julia often gets the Israelis very confused at passport control.

Elias is very worried about his dog, who's been missing for several days. He's put an ad on Facebook, offering a 500-shekel reward.

'I didn't know people kept dogs as pets in Palestine,' I say.

'Yes, quite a few of us have dogs,' he says, 'and, in fact, here in Beit Sahour we've established the first Palestinian dog rescue centre.' Elias has been elected recently to Beit Sahour city council. 'We've twinned with a dog sanctuary in Canada,' he says, 'and if the dogs here aren't reclaimed, the centre in Canada will find them new homes over there.' Clearly, Elias's dog has had enough of the Occupation and decided to lie low for a few days, in the hope of a trip to the Yukon. I find it rather wonderful, in a bonkers kind of way, that Palestinians have found the time and energy to build a dogs' home. It reminds me of the zookeepers in Gaza, who smuggled an anaesthetised crocodile through the tunnels to restock their reptile house.

Remembering that Hebron is virtually dry, being 99.9 per cent Muslim (except for the settlers) and quite conservative, we've stopped again to pick up some beers, when Elias's phone rings. He has a long chat in Arabic, raising his eyebrows a few times to me, smiling broadly and giving a big thumbs-up. What's afoot?

'That was the aide to the President,' he says, coming off the phone.

'Abu Mazen?'

'Yeah!' he says, laughing. 'He says the President was watching the interview just now and absolutely loved it, everything you were saying. He phoned the programme because he wanted to greet you live on air, but they had to explain it was pre-recorded so he couldn't. He wants to meet you, and all the walkers, and thanks you for everything you're doing, and he said, "Please give the President's special greeting to Justin."'

Wow. Big thumbs-up, then.

'Well, that's great news, right?'

'Yeah!' he says, 'it is great. It's a fantastic recognition.'

'I mean, we were always clear in our minds that we wanted to plan everything here, all the meetings, receptions, activities and so on, with you guys, with Holy Land Trust, as a grassroots community organisation, that we weren't going through political channels, because we know the PA is not necessarily everyone's favourite . . . well, you know what I mean.'

'Yeah, yeah,' he said, 'that's right, but still, this is great, it will give us a much bigger profile.'

The Palestinian Authority is not well-liked or trusted by most Palestinians, regarded widely as a corrupt, self-appointed clique firmly in Israel's pocket, part of the problem, not the solution. The fact that our pilgrimage is an independent project will certainly have increased our appeal across the West Bank. But we should embrace this opportunity.

Sunday 29 October, Sa'ir, near Hebron

We're eating lunch in the village hall of Sa'ir, near Hebron, with the mayor and civic delegation, tucking into chicken and vegetable wraps, falafels and flatbread. This morning we visited Al-Arrub Camp, on the main Hebron–Jerusalem road, where 10,000 Palestinian refugees live on a quarter of a square kilometre. After an anarchic football match at one of the camp's two schools, we walked out to visit a family whose house was rebuilt in 2015 by Amos Trust volunteers, organised by Holy Land Trust. The demolition of this family's house had been utterly devastating, Chris said, the overnight ruination of all their aspirations and endeavours, as years of hard work and careful saving were crushed to rubble in minutes. Rowena and Cheryl from our group had been volunteers on the rebuild, and it was touching to see their reunion with the family, thriving in their new home. They produced endless cups of tea for us, and proudly showed us their new baby, their fruit garden and olive orchard and solar panels on the roof, where they plan to build a second storey. Julia sang a blessing on the house and family, the old Palestinian national anthem, *Mawtini* ('My Homeland'), sung in the open air to the buzzing of bees, and then we walked on, through terraced hills of olive groves to the ancient Roman reservoir of Al-Arrub. Known in Arabic as *Birket esh-Shatt*, the pool was dug in the procuratorship of Pontius Pilate to gather the waters of the three springs of the Wadi Arrub, which then were channelled by aqueduct to Solomon's Pool south-west of Bethlehem. The writer Nicholas Blincoe describes the Al-Arrub aqueduct, built in ancient times and still in use until 1967, as 'the most important man-made structure in all of Palestine, judged by its impact on the course of history.'[1] In the Byzantine era, it carried water to Bethlehem and Jerusalem by gravity alone, falling by about eight inches for every 120 yards. The Ottomans transformed it from a watercourse into a pipeline, and the British added a pumping station during the Mandate, but until the Israelis decided to bypass the reservoirs by drawing water direct from the aquifer at the settlement of Kfar Etzion, the Al-Arrub aqueduct had been in continuous use for more than 2,000 years. On from the reservoir we hiked the long path up and down many steep hills through farm fields and orchards, village roads and dirt tracks to Sa'ir.

A whistle of feedback through a rough and ready PA system announces that the mayor is about to address the assembly, flanked by the usual phalanx of older men in suits, seated along trestles at the front of the hall. From the wall above, a portrait of Arafat beams down, propped on top of an empty noticeboard. Our guide in Hebron is Marai, a tall, gentle man in his fifties with a deep, husky voice, who stands up now to translate the mayor's speech.

'You are welcome in Palestine, and especially here in Sa'ir, from the depths of our heart, with this initiative that you carry from London. Even though you have old people in your company, I call them young people because they are similar to me! *(Laughter and applause.)* We thank you all, especially the young who carry the flag of freedom and democracy because they are the messenger of the future. Nobody can feel what is the meaning of injustice except the man or the people who live under that injustice. You are feeling the situation that the Palestinian people live, the unjust situation, you are our supporter. Palestinian people suffer from injustice a lot of years. We achieve now one hundred years of suffering.

'Sorry to say that the reason of this injustice is the policy of your government in that time. Britain was a colonial country before and she colonised a lot of states around the world. When Britain was here it was a mandate, which means for a limited time – five years, six years – then she will give back the land to her owner. A mandate means permission for the British government at that time to improve the situation of the people, to teach them a lot of things, to achieve an independent state. But, sorry to say that the British government really only established and did so many things that make it easy for the Jews to establish their state. This State was established by the Balfour Declaration and was the cause to take a lot of Palestinians off their land. And there comes a lot of refugees out of Palestine to Jordan, Egypt, Syria, Lebanon. And, from that generation, I have seen by my own eyes the Palestinian women carrying her children, crying, to live in camps in that time, when it was so cold without anything, without essential things. Hungry. This was all seen by our eyes and we still see it. Everyone created by God misses the place that he was born in. Even the bear goes back to his place again.

'We find a lot of states agree about what happened to the Palestinian people, but even the United Nations still refuse to let the refugees go back to their villages. As a very civilised people, we love life, and we accept others. We are a people who like to live in peace, really; from the depths of our heart, we like and love to live in peace. But not the peace that will take me off my land. Your presence here, your walking here gives us a big hope. There is still hope in the world. Someday the world will wake up and support the Palestinian people and deny every injustice. You are welcome, and thank you again.'

Chris thanks the mayor, then Julia sings a traditional Palestinian lament, *Sanarjaa Yoman Ila Haiana*, holding the hall spellbound. The panel of old men at the front are dumbfounded, eyes glistening, humming along under their breath, fingers caressing the air, hearing the song of their homeland sung so hauntingly in their language by a stranger.

We walk the five miles into Hebron at a fair lick, running late for our reception with the governor and city council. Together with local activists Youth Against Settlements, the governor's staff have prepared a huge arsenal of flags and placards for us to carry into the Old City. The rally on the steps of the city hall is exuberant, with speeches from the deputy governor, the director of housing and engineers from the chamber of commerce, with much cheering and waving of flags.

For Chaim Weizmann, who would become Israel's first president, balancing his career as an academic chemist with his long campaign to bring the Zionist dream to birth was a constant struggle. It was his wife Vera who advised him, with extraordinary prescience, to pursue both goals with equal determination, for she was convinced they were more closely connected than he realised. As Robert Cohen related at the Southwark Cathedral conference last year, Vera turned out to be 100 per cent right:

> For men like Weizmann, Zionism was not about stealing land and destroying an indigenous people. Weizmann firmly believed that he was embarked on a project that was just and high-minded. And it meant far more than finding the Jewish people a safe home free

from anti-Semitism . . . In *Trial and Error* he writes about Zionism's 'inner significance' and its 'constructive moral-ethical-social character' for Jews as individuals and as a nation. This is Zionism as a psychological as much as a territorial issue.

Weizmann first came to the attention of the British government through his laboratory work at Manchester University. He'd been working on a way of producing Acetone through a fermentation process that used carbohydrates like starch and glucose . . . Acetone was important because it could be used to make cordite. Cordite is what's called a 'low explosive', like gunpowder, that can be used to propel a bullet or a shell to its target without destroying the barrel.

So if you could work out how to mass produce Acetone you could be of great service to the British War effort. Weizmann was at pains to say that the Balfour Declaration was in no way a gift to him from a grateful nation at war. And I would agree that would be far too simple a way of telling of the story. But in my mind there is a link, at least a metaphorical one, between Weizmann's chemistry and his Zionism.

After all, what is Zionism if not a process of mixing elements together to create a propellant with explosive potential? Take a pinch of Judaism, a dose of anti-Semitism, a dollop of European nationalism and a sprinkling of communal psychology and start a fermentation process. Out of the other end comes Zionism. And it's a pretty potent concoction.[2]

Weizmann's ground-breaking research gained him the ear of the British War Cabinet and opened the door to the Zionist cause which, mingled with Britain's colonial ambitions in the Middle East – proved an explosive cocktail indeed. And nowhere is this illustrated more graphically, or experienced more egregiously, than in Hebron.

In 1968, a group of Orthodox Jews visiting the Tombs of the Patriarchs rented rooms in the main hotel in Hebron and then refused to leave, effectively establishing the first settlement. Ever since, the city has been the powder keg, flashpoint and madhouse of the Occupation, with more than eighty heavily guarded Orthodox Jewish families living literally on top of the Palestinian residents in the heart of the Old City, where they subject their neighbours to a ceaseless vendetta of intimidation and attacks. This reached a horrific climax with the Hebron massacre of 1994, when Baruch Goldstein, an American-Israeli GP from Brooklyn, opened fire in the Cave of the Patriarchs, the ancient Ibrahimi Mosque, killing twenty-nine worshippers and wounding more than a hundred others before the survivors overcame him. Twenty-four more Palestinians were killed by Israeli police in the ensuing riots. The massacre was condemned by the Israeli government, but the settlements in and around Hebron have continued to grow and the city and surrounding area have witnessed continuous clashes ever since.

'There is no other neighbourhood like this one,' wrote Israeli journalist Gideon Levi in *Haaretz* in 2005, describing the area around the Tel Rumeida settlement in Hebron. 'Not a day passes without the throwing of stones, garbage, and faeces at the frightened (Palestinian) neighbours cowering in their barricaded houses, afraid even to peek out the window. Neighbours whose way home is always a path of torment and anxiety. All this is happening right under the noses of the soldiers and police, representatives of the legal authorities, who merely stand by. For the average, reasonable Israeli, to visit Tel Rumeida for the first time is to have your picture of the world turned upside down. This is the gutter of the settlement enterprise.'

I remember vividly my first visit to Hebron in 2012, wandering through the beautiful Ottoman streets of the Old City, roofed over with chicken wire to protect Palestinian residents from the missiles hurled down by their settler neighbours: bricks, soiled nappies, faeces and kitchen waste flung from upstairs windows. Deserted Palestinian shops line the old market street, now divided into two corridors separated by a barrier. The majority of the street is reserved for settlers, with just a narrow alley behind the barrier, on the far side from the shop fronts, left for Palestinian residents. The boarded-up entrances of the Palestinian shops have been daubed with offensive slogans in Hebrew and English – 'Gas the Arabs' and 'Die, Arab pigs' are two I recall – and, even worse, the Star of David spray-painted as an emblem of hate.

Certainly there has been violence committed by Palestinians as well, dating back to the 1929 Hebron Massacre in which sixty-nine of the ancient Sephardic community and the more recent Ashkenazi community were killed by Palestinian rioters, incited by rumours that Jewish settlers were planning to seize control of the Temple Mount in Jerusalem. The massacre, part of the wider 1929 Arab Riots, or Buruq Uprising, in which 110 Palestinians and 133 Jews were killed, led to the reorganisation and professionalisation of the Haganah, the Jewish paramilitary organisation which later formed the core of the IDF. However, Hebronites are proud that more than 400 Jews survived because they were sheltered by Palestinian families. In response to the 1994 Goldstein massacre, the Palestinian mayor of Hebron called in the Christian Peacemaker Teams, an international body committed to opposing any form of violence through direct action, human rights documentation and non-violence training.

Against this backdrop, it's no surprise when we run into trouble, more than a hundred of us with flags and placards marching in a colourful cavalcade down the main road into Hebron. A number of TV stations are here, filming our approach, as well as our own film-maker Mark Kensett, and several EAPPI human rights observers with cameras. Suddenly we become aware of angry voices up ahead. Army trucks and police jeeps are screaming up the road behind us, and Israeli soldiers on foot approaching from several directions. At the front of the parade, a city councillor named Mahdi Moreb is standing chest to chest with a big burly man wearing a skullcap, black T-shirt, combat trousers and army boots, with a pistol on his hip. He's screaming abuse in Hebrew and jabbing his finger in Mahdi's face, holding his phone overhead in his other hand, filming the whole exchange. He keeps pushing Mahdi, flourishing his fist in his face, barging with his chest and yelling. Mahdi is standing his ground, refusing to be pushed back, and now there's an Israeli policeman, also wearing a skullcap, and several soldiers half-heartedly urging the settler to calm down. They usher him a pace or two back, but make no serious attempt to stop him when he barges forward again, yelling and pushing.

I gather Eleanor and Millie close beside me, all of us now wedged between the steep fenced bank to our right and the soldiers and vehicles hemming us in from the road. The governor's delegation and the young activists are chanting, 'Free, free Palestine!' Many of the walkers join in. More army jeeps race up, sirens wailing, blue lights flashing, disgorging more soldiers. Now we're being herded along the main road, separated from Mahdi and his colleagues still standing their ground as the settler blocks their way, screaming and pointing. A number of TV crews remain behind, filming the row, despite the soldiers' orders. We're corralled into a tight throng on the right hand side of the road by a cordon of soldiers. At one point, with an open palm, Mahdi pushes the man's fist away from his face and suddenly a scuffle breaks out. Immediately the soldiers grab Mahdi and, seeing him pinned, the settler lunges forward, kicking and punching him. Still the soldiers do nothing to restrain the settler, despite the clamour of protest from Mahdi's companions. They're dragging Mahdi towards one of their jeeps now, TV cameras following every move as the settler pursues them, still screaming abuse and lashing out at Mahdi whenever he gets near him.

The soldiers are herding us off the road now, up some steps to the right, leading through a checkpoint into the Palestinian quarter, designated H1 to distinguish it from the Tel Rumeida settlement in the Old City (H2), adjacent to the Cave of the Patriarchs. Since the Goldstein massacre, the Cave has been divided, half-mosque, half-synagogue, with the Tombs of Isaac and Jacob in the middle, bisected by a sheet of bullet-proof glass. Down by the roadside, other settlers have gathered to watch our enforced exit. 'What about human rights abuses in the Yemen and Saudi?' yells one, an Orthodox Jewish man with a strong Brooklyn accent. 'Why don't you go and protest there? Where you don't have soldiers to protect you, huh? Anti-Semites!'

Our hosts ask us to wait for a few minutes while some of the governorate staff try to negotiate Mahdi's release. 'He could be held for eight days and then face a military trial,' one of them tells me.

'Does it help that he works in the governor's office? Does that mean he has a better chance?'

'We hope so. No Palestinian has immunity. We have Palestinian legislative members who are in Israeli prisons, sometimes even former minsters in the PA.'

After a few minutes, an Israeli police jeep deposits Mahdi in front of the barrier. Amid much cheering, he rejoins us and we resume our approach to the city centre, through the courtyards and colonnades of the old town, led by the Youth Against Settlements coordinator, Esa Amro, who's late joining us because he had to appear in an Israeli military court this morning in Ramallah. It seems that, with such a clear demonstration of settler aggression, witnessed by a large international delegation and many TV cameras, the Israelis have released Mahdi to minimise further embarrassment.

'This man is notorious for his attacks on Palestinians in the Hebron area,' Esa says. 'In the last two years, many Palestinians were killed by the Israeli Occupation forces, and this settler is a paramedic, and he has delayed the arrival of ambulances and treatment to the wounded on several occasions, resulting in their deaths. The best example is Hadil al-Hashlamun, an eighteen-year-old Palestinian girl who was shot many times at a checkpoint; he delayed the treatment for forty-five minutes, which made her die. With Fadil al-Qawasmeh, the same thing. He delayed the ambulance for around one hour. And many, many other examples. When Elor Azaria, an Israeli soldier, shot a Palestinian who was injured in Tel Rumeida, and he was completely disabled on the ground, this settler said to the soldier, "That dog is alive and somebody should deal with that." Then the soldier shot him. So he was the one who incited the soldier to shoot the injured Palestinian, which is considered a war crime. This same settler attacked me personally many, many times. He attacks all the tours, all human rights defenders, without any kind of accountability from the police and the soldiers.'

'And what happened to the soldier who killed that Palestinian?'

'The soldier was sentenced to fourteen months in jail. Only. For shooting an injured Palestinian on the ground, which is a war crime.'

'So he was sentenced in an Israeli military court?'

'No, in an Israeli civil court. Now, Ahmed Manasrah is a Palestinian child, fourteen years old, he tried to stab Israelis, which is wrong, and when he was twelve, he was sentenced for nine years and a half in prison. I'm a human rights defender, all my activities are non-violent, I'm on trial now, I have eighteen military charges against me for non-violent resistance and civil disobedience. They may put me in jail for two to three years for civil disobedience and for peaceful resistance, and a soldier who is a war criminal got only fourteen months. So there is no justice.'

One of the governor's staff, Nidal al-Jabari, points out a building behind a school playground where some Palestinian children are playing. 'That was my home,' he says, 'until five years ago. They forced me to leave it because they create a corrosive environment. They create these inhuman circumstances, and after that you will find that you should leave because your duty is to protect your children. And even with all these soldiers here, you still cannot protect your children. As a father, to my children I'm a hero – like any father around the world – so when the soldiers took me for two hours and just moved his finger, and told me by his finger, you can move, my son will look at me and he will say, "No, you are not a hero any more." This is touching our dignity; this is touching our heart. And we are Palestinian, we are proud people, we prefer to die with dignity than to stay without dignity. Your walk from London to Palestine is highly appreciated, highly appreciated from our side.

'Our message for Miss Theresa – we are suffering too much from this inhuman decision taken by Mr Balfour. All the Palestinian case is created by this Declaration. You should consider the Palestinians as human. We have the right to live independently, with equality. We are human, that's our message. By your celebration with the Balfour Declaration, Miss Theresa, you expressed that you consider the Palestinian as human no more. We express our thanks for you who have walked. We can understand that you as a British people refuse this attitude, that you want to deal with the Palestinian as a human, but Miss Theresa expresses by celebration that she agrees with this unfair, inhuman, unacceptable, illegal Occupation. It's so difficult to understand why she celebrates with this decision. Our great poet Mahmoud Darwish wrote, "We will not stop dreaming no matter how much we fail and we are broken." We are still dreaming.'

Monday 30 October, Umm al-Khair, south Hebron hills

I'm sitting in a flapping Bedouin tent on a windswept scarp in the south Hebron hills. The desert wind whips around the makeshift dwelling, billowing dust and rattling canvas. At one end of the tent, a young Palestinian-Bedouin man is showing us a series of aerial photographs lashed to wooden poles set in the ground. Tariq is educated and articulate, a charismatic young man in his early twenties, stocky and handsome, clean-shaven with a neat haircut, and a lot smarter in his checked shirt, jeans and trainers than most of our group, with our dusty boots and tattered walking clothes. Weather-worn, travel-stained, sunburnt and unshaven, myself and several others heavily bearded, our delegation is a ramshackle bunch.

To Tariq's left stands his uncle, Sheikh Suleiman, an elderly Bedouin farmer with a bristling grey beard, wild eyes glaring from under his white headdress, worn somewhat incongruously over a neatly pressed blue-and-white striped shirt. Uncle Suleiman is given to frequent impassioned outbursts, always prefaced with the oblig-atory '*Allah-hu-akbar!*' bellowed in a hoarse, prophetic rasp, arms flung high in imprecation. Uncle Suleiman is a little bit crazy, and Tariq has had to quieten him down a few times. You don't need to speak Arabic to get the gist: '*Allah-hu-Akbar!* God is great! Israel is . . . [something bad in Arabic]! America is also [something bad in Arabic]! They are choking our life! They are strangling us!'

'Not now, Uncle Suleiman, OK? We have visitors, please! Let me speak to them, calm down, shut up!'

Outside the tent, a cockerel crows. Goats and sheep bleat in their pens. Tariq reaches across to reattach one of the pictures blown loose by the wind. Taken with the assistance of the Belgian Development Cooperation, Oxfam and BIMKOM, an Israeli NGO, these pictures tell the story in microcosm of Israel's fifty-year mili-tary occupation of the Palestinian Territories. Tariq is a dynamic speaker, with a powerful, husky voice.

'So these aerial photographs show my village, Umm al-Khair, from 1969 until 2016. We were expelled by the Israelis from the Al-Arad desert, our original land, with our tribe Al-Jehali, and my grandfather and his cousin chose this area, Umm al-Khair, to live. The owners of this land were the people of Yatta, a Palestinian village near here; they welcomed them in the first years, then later on they forced them to buy the land. My grandfather bought his land here for one hundred camels. Why these mountains? Because Bedouins depend on grazing their goats and sheep. This mountain was green then, but now it's desert – this was from God, not the Occupation. But in 1980, an outpost started on the other hill. So this settlement of Carmel started like this: slowly, slowly, they brought settlers, with caravans, then concrete houses, and they took our land for settling, by force of weapons.

'And now these people are living here, these settlers – I want to say neighbours – for more than thirty-seven years. And we never attacked them. The only thing we want is to live in peace and quietness. But these settlers made it difficult for us. They shot my brother, and now he's disabled; they shot my stepmother, but she survived. We lost people, we lost animals, we lost the land, and this is continuous. I don't blame the settlers themselves; I blame their State. My war is with their State, because they are here to do the plans of their State. Maybe it's very satisfying for them to live here, because they have electricity, water, streets, buildings – for free! We, the owners of the land, we don't have the right to build. And the settlers – they have the right to do anything. This is the reality of the Occupation. It's nothing to do with "Israel has the right to defend itself". It's not like the propaganda which is spread in the western media – they say Israel is innocent, they have the right to defend themselves, but you can see here is the reality.

'And you know, the "old" settlers, living in the first neighbourhood of Carmel, they're quiet people, and they want to talk, they want to live, to be honest with you. But the settlers in the new neighbourhood, they came from Gaza, and they're so violent. They attack the people and it's nothing for them. Last year we were ploughing our land on the mountain, and one of the settlers came and attacked the guy who was ploughing, and he stole the donkey. And we were filming this, there are photos, we have a page on Facebook, you can see everything I'm talking about – I will not tell you something with no evidence. Afterwards, we will be walking together to At-Tuwani, and we will see the new extension of the settlement, and we will see where the bulldozers are working, with the army, on our private land.

'They started destroying our houses in 2007. They came in February and destroyed eight houses, when the weather was raining. In 2008 they did the same. They came in October, the beginning of winter, and destroyed the houses in this community – and you know, each time they destroy your house, you should move thirty metres away from the old site to rebuild your house, or they will come again *immediately* and destroy your house.

'In 2011 they came back and destroyed five houses. In 2012, they came and saw a house here – it was my mother's house, she was a widow, in the middle of winter – and I remember how they threw our furniture out of the house, and it rained, and how we slept the whole week after the demolition in a tent, with strong winds and rain. Last year, 2016, this guy here, my friend Zaeed – they destroyed his house four times in one year. So now he's living in my brother's house. So everyone here is suffering. In 2013 and 2014 they came and destroyed six houses in addition to the oven.

'You saw our *taboun*, our traditional bread oven, outside? It works with animal manure, as a fuel, and it's a natural system –, that's how we bake our bread. It's more than fifty years old – you saw the old stones, a traditional *taboun*. And the settlers complained, they said the smell of the smoke irritated their noses and was damaging their health. One of these settlers –' he mentions his name - 'came to live here in 2008, and he made a complaint against us in the court; he wanted us to pay him $100,000 compensation. So we appealed to the High Court of Justice to stop the demolition. So this settler was coming during the night to turn it off with a bucket of water. Then this takes us three days, with no bread for your family, to rebuild the system. So the Israeli military commander came to this oven – my Uncle Suleiman was talking with him, and the commander said, "Suleiman, we want to make a peaceful solution for this."

'My Uncle Suleiman told him, "I'll give you three suggestions: the first – give me electricity from the settlement for an electronic oven; the second – give me planning permission for a small room, I could fix it very well, and then bring an oven, and put it inside; the third: bring me bread every day as you bring the settlers, and that's fine."

'He refused all these suggestions, and in the end they destroyed the oven to satisfy the settler. We rebuilt the oven the second day. The third day they came back with their bulldozers, and they destroyed it again. The fourth day we rebuilt it, and the fifth day they came and destroyed it again. Three times in one week! And the last occasion they told us, "If you keep rebuilding the oven, we will come and destroy a bunch of the houses here, as a punishment." So this is the story of this oven. So now we have to buy our bread from Yatta village every day. This costs us a lot.'

He points up to the curved ribbing of timber and scaffolding overhead, to the shadow of a large stone sitting on top of the canvas, on the outside. 'From seventeen nights before, until last night, we were sleeping here with my friend Kulti in this tent, and they were throwing stones *every* night at this tent. Each time we go outside, we shout at them, and we phone the Israeli police, and they do nothing. See the stone, here? And there are three stones on the other part, there.

'We are not allowed any electricity, water, nothing. We are not allowed to build, and we're not allowed to have anything. We dig the soil by our hands; we are hard workers, we are shepherds. We wake up, and we work in the morning, we take the goats to the grazing land. My Uncle Suleiman, he's a symbol of the strong Bedouin people – he's seventy years old, but he's very tough and very strong. And each time they come to destroy the houses here, first they come and find my Uncle Suleiman, put him in a vehicle and take him away, because he keeps shouting at them.

'And this is the situation in Umm al-Khair. And we welcome you. Thank you for coming. The only request that our people want from you: tell our story as it is. Tell the world. We will not carry weapons to fight, but we will keep resisting in a non-violent way against the Occupation until we end it. And we will end the Occupation, I promise you.'

Apropos of nothing, Uncle Suleiman's cry rends the air: '*Allah-hu-akbar wa Lilah El Hamd!*'

Tariq turns to speak in Arabic to his uncle, asking if he wants to say something to our group. Uncle Suleiman is momentarily flummoxed, having been shushed so many times this morning.

'*Aah! . . . Ana Agoul . . . BriTania . . . sulTa BriTaniya . . . Hiya El Mas'oula Aan ma'anatna . . . Wa'ad Belfour . . . min Miyat Sana . . .*' His voice erupts in cracked cadences, as he shakes his arms, wringing the air with leathery hands.

'I will translate for him,' says Tariq gently. 'He says, Britain, the State of England – they are the ones responsible for our suffering. And they made the Balfour Declaration, and they gave the right to the Israelis to have a State in here. And now we are one hundred years from that Declaration, and our people are still suffering.'

Suleiman lets fly with another outburst, more anguished than ever.

'So now he's saying that Theresa May, she said that she's proud of the Balfour Declaration, she's very proud of giving the Israelis the right to have their State.'

Embarrassed murmurs rumble through the gathering. 'We're not proud,' pipes up one voice. 'She doesn't speak for us.'

'Yeah! We know!' says Tariq. 'Because of that you are here.'

And now Chris approaches Uncle Suleiman, holding out his hands. He speaks slowly, allowing Tariq to translate each phrase.

'Please tell him that we have walked from London to here – 3,300 kilometres – to say sorry for the Balfour Declaration, and to say sorry for what Britain has done.'

As the words translated sink in, a change falls across Uncle Suleiman's face. This crazy old man, overflowing with the unheard anguish of his people's dispossession and innumerable griefs, suddenly stops in his flow. His wild eyes dart back and forth from Chris to his nephew to all of us, sixty walkers sitting hushed in his tent, watching. Suddenly he grabs Chris's hand and yanks it skywards with a great rasping cry, '*Shukran! Thank you!*' Tears fill my eyes. He barks out a speech of thanks, intoning in stuttered bursts, as Tariq translates.

'So my Uncle Suleiman is saying that Theresa May, instead of saying like . . . to apologise to the Palestinians, because of the declaration of Balfour, she says that she's proud, so . . . so now my Uncle Suleiman says . . .' – he waits as the old man belts out another staccato volley – '. . . so we're taking off our hats to you, and we are so . . . we respect you. We don't listen to the governments, they are unjust always, but we listen to the people! We have the people! There's a power in the people!'

Uncle Suleiman broadens his address to the whole tent, spreading his arms expansively.

'He's thanking all the countries,' says Tariq, 'all the people who are standing with us . . . in this time. He says we need a solution for our peace . . . our president Abu Mazen went to America and said, "We want a peace, we want to live in peace."'

Chris says, 'Please tell him, we will remember your story, and tell people in the UK about you.'

'*Shukran!*' bellows Uncle Suleiman in his hoarse croak. '*Thank you!* Thank you so much because you walked all this way! Such a long way to come here, to stand with our people!'

Applause and laughter burst out as he grabs Chris's hands and raises them high. Cameras and phone-cameras click and flash across the gathering; many of us are wiping our eyes. '*Allah-hu-akbar! Allah-hu-akbar wa'd al-raheem!*' yells Uncle Suleiman over and over, capering and prancing, clinging to Chris's hand and waving it back and forth, punching the air and holding up two fingers in the victory-sign.

Mission accomplished.

At the village of At-Tuwani we're met by Sami Awad and Ben Jaeger, a former Israeli soldier who's now UK coordinator for Combatants for Peace. From here, David and I go by taxi to Ramallah for a radio interview on PBC, while the rest walk on with Sami and Ben to the Sumud Freedom Camp in Sarura, where former residents evicted from their traditional village in 1998 are joining with Israeli, Palestinian and international activists, including the US-based Center for Jewish Nonviolence, to rebuild their community. Along with Sami and Ben and activists from the five collaborating peace organisations, the walkers join the residents for supper in one of the cave dwellings of this extremely traditional desert village, after which they plant an olive tree on behalf of the Just Walk pilgrimage. Chris later describes the whole experience as 'ridiculously moving'.

Back at last at our hotel on the outskirts of Hebron, Elias tells me we've been invited to join President Abbas for lunch in Ramallah on Thursday. Wow. Then Chris mentions later, for my ears only, that the President's office is trying to arrange for us to complete the pilgrimage, after the presidential banquet in Ramallah, by walking down the Mount of Olives into the Old City of Jerusalem, ending in the compound of the Al-Aqsa Mosque, the single most contested site in the Holy Land. Double wow. If we could actually achieve this, on the centenary of the Balfour Declaration, it would be the most astonishing stunt, a massive PR coup and, of course, provocative beyond belief. . . Boris Johnson and Emily Thornberry yesterday both called for a sovereign, viable and geographically contiguous Palestinian State based on the 4 June 1967 borders. I've drafted an open letter to Theresa May on behalf of the Just Walk, and later this evening Chris and I refine the text with Gemma Bell,

Nick Welsh and Robert Cohen, who's flown in to join us for the last few days, with his wife Anne. We've asked for a meeting on Thursday with the British Consul-General to the Palestinian Territories, Philip Hall, at the Consulate in East Jerusalem, where a group of us plan to present him with a new version of the Balfour Declaration, which Robert has composed, closely modelled on the original sixty-seven words, but with a very different emphasis, which we will ask the British government to adopt.

Tuesday 31 October, Sderot, western Negev

After a morning walking across the Negev Desert visiting some of the Bedouin villages deprived of water, electricity, health care or building permits because they are officially unrecognised by the Israeli State, we're driving north to Sderot, the nearest Israeli town to the Gaza border. After the extreme poverty of the villages in the Negev, Sderot feels like an LA suburb, with its lush tree-lined avenues and smooth tarmac roads running between irrigated lawns and neat flower beds. It's hard to believe that just 2 km from here, the other side of the Gaza wall, nearly two million people are living in a vast open-air prison, the most densely populated patch of earth on the planet, with barely any water, electricity or medical supplies. Photographing a neatly landscaped roundabout planted with palm trees and marigolds, David says, 'It's like *Alice in Wonderland*.'

We pass a sign pointing south to Erez, the border crossing, through which Chris has entered Gaza several times to visit the Al-Ahli Hospital in Gaza City, which Amos Trust supports. He described the crossing as a horrible experience, a long, empty corridor through no-man's-land, bounded by metal walls and barbed wire, like a portal into the underworld.

Now we're turning off the main drag to the gated community of Netiv Ha'Ashara, an Israeli *moshav* immediately adjacent to the northern perimeter wall enclosing the Gaza Strip. Passing through a heavy iron gate strung with razor wire, we drive through an innocuous toy town of nondescript new-build houses, for all the world like a Milton Keynes housing estate, were it not for the watchtower that rears suddenly around a corner of shrubbery to our left, beyond which we see the grim silhouette of the Wall, domino slabs of concrete marching above the tidy hedges, each topped with its hallmark perforation.

The Paths to Peace Centre is a studio and gallery surrounded by a pleasant grove of olive and fig trees, run by a ceramic artist called Tsameret Zamir, a smiley, fair-haired woman in her forties who welcomes us warmly and invites us to help ourselves to tea and coffee. The terraces of her garden are adorned curiously with installations of rocket fragments, sections of charred metal tubing, tail fins and nose cones planted up with herbs and decorated with purple and green ceramic flowers, with signs in English and Hebrew reading 'Iron Dome and rockets'. Tsameret ushers us into her gallery to give her presentation. Display cases of ceramic hearts and butter-flies and colourful cartoon murals create an uneasy impression of a primary school art room. Speaking through a hand-held mic, Tsameret welcomes us once more and tells us her story. She speaks with a sing-song lilt, with that blend of American and Eastern European intonation characteristic of many Israelis speaking English. Her adult daughter appears with a video camera to film us from the front.

This village is named Netiv Ha'Ashara, Tsameret says, after ten Israeli soldiers who were killed in a helicopter accident. 'They wanted to make something peaceful, something beautiful out of this sad thing, so they built this village here in their memory. We were so happy to come and live here, my husband and our four children, and we thought, this is our beautiful new home. And for a long time we lived in peace with our neighbours, but then after three years, the life here started to change.' The unreal atmosphere conjured by the sentimental murals and Tsameret's sing-song narrative deepens the collective unease as we hear how she and her children and their friends were terrorised by a ceaseless rain of rockets, explosions and red alerts in the middle of the night, running to bomb shelters with only five seconds to respond, by the hatred of Hamas 'who want to kill us', by terrorists coming through tunnels and kidnapping people, how traumatised everyone in their village was, and how they had to bond together to be strong, to carry on a normal life and encourage their children to go out and play as usual.

At one point her microphone pops and she jumps, then laughs, 'I'm sorry, I'm very sensitive to loud noises.'

She started making art, she says, as a way to recover from the trauma. 'Sometimes, when I'm working in my studio, we hear the alarms and we have to run to the shelters, but always, afterwards, I'm trying to go back to my studio, to create another flower, another butterfly, and that's healing for me. I don't believe in violence. I believe we need to look for the solution in civilised ways, and about five years ago I decided to use some of the good energy of this special community we have here to create happiness. Very close to our village, just next to the houses, was a grey, scary wall, and it just reminds us of the danger, and I want to change it, to bring happiness to the people. I started to paint a white dove on that wall, and I wrote "Paths to Peace" in English, Arabic and Hebrew.'

Now she has many visitors from all over the world, and she helps them to make ceramics of hearts and flowers on the wall, as a message of peace to the Palestinians in Gaza. She would like us all to glue some ceramic stones on the wall later, she says, to send our message of peace. A ripple of unease murmurs through the group. She finishes her presentation, we applaud politely and she asks if there are any questions. One of the group asks what she thinks about the fact that in 2014, 2,000 adults and 500 children were killed in Gaza by the Israeli onslaught.

'I think when we are at the edge and we don't find any other way to deal with the problem, sometimes we give up and then a few choose the violence way. I believe that if they will keep trying to look for peace in a civilised way, we could be in a different place now.'

At this point Carol, the only Palestinian in our group, explodes. 'Gaza is a concentration camp – and people are being killed, and I've been at the tribunals and watched how they've slaughtered these kids. It's sick!' she exclaims, and storms out of the gallery.

Sitting next to me, Kevin is almost boiling over with frustration, despite his wife Jenny's whispered entreaties not to make a fuss, 'Kevin, there's sixty of us, she's on her own, please, don't . . .'

'Look, Jenny, I'm not going to shout at her,' he hisses, and raises his hand. 'May I ask you something?' His voice is shaking with emotion. 'Listen, I really appreciate the talk you've given us, and the honesty you've shown, and I accept utterly everything that you've said – including that some in the leadership on the other side of that wall, as you put it, choose the path of violence. The one thing that's missing, though, in the picture you paint, and it disturbs me, is not what their leadership have done, but what *your* leadership have done. The response has been so utterly disproportionate that the number of people killed – children, families, mothers just like yourself – on the other side of that wall, is massively, massively greater, and continues, because, as that lady who left said – and, you know, her family were driven violently out of Palestine way, way back – what I want to say is, I would like to hear you recognise that the violence of your leadership was utterly excessive, utterly inhumane, utterly in breach of international law, in fact was a war crime. What that is on the other side of the border is the violence – Gaza and the Wall is an expression of the violence of the Israeli leadership, in creating a concentration camp – remotely controlled – but still a concentration camp.'

'I want to feel safe,' says Tsameret.

A few minutes later, we're walking up a rough track on the outskirts of the village to a patch of high ground where we can look down into Gaza. The view is heart-rending. It's around half past four and the sun is beginning to set, a fiery orb on the western horizon over the tortured skyline of Gaza, spreading a blast of yellow radiance through the blood-red sky. Immediately below us is the outer barrier, a massive steel fence at this point, beyond which a wasteland of low sandy hills dotted with trees and scrub stretches towards the trapped enclave. Far away, almost on the edge of sight, is the inner wall, and beyond it a distant jumbled cityscape in an orange haze beneath the spreading sunset. I think of Ahmed back in London, and his family down there in that imprisoned land, his mothers and sisters and his mum Fat'ma, who just a few years ago was sitting at my kitchen table back home.

We passed several Israeli soldiers on the way up here, patrolling the path in a desultory fashion. After the awkwardness just now, one might have thought that Tsameret would leave us to experience this moment in silence, but she continues her commentary, explaining that this area is heavily patrolled because there was a huge tunnel here, with lights and air-conditioning, through which Hamas terrorists could come on motorbikes to kidnap Israeli civilians and abduct them back into Gaza. Chris thanks her once more and says that Nive is going to read a poem, by a Gaza poet, which feels appropriate for this time and place. We gather round, our faces bathed in the setting sunlight stealing across no-man's-land, as Nive stands on a pile of breeze-block to read:

> Oh rascal children of Gaza,
> You who constantly disturbed me with your screams under my
>   window,
> You who filled every morning with rush and chaos,
> You who broke my vase and stole the lonely flower on my balcony,
> Come back –
> And scream as you want,
> And break all the vases,
> Steal all the flowers,
> Come back,
> Just come back . . .[3]

This evening, from our hotel in Beit Sahour, we publish my open letter to Theresa May on the Amos Trust website and send the link via Twitter to the Downing Street press office and our entire press list.

To: The Prime Minister, The Rt Hon Theresa May MP
House of Commons
Palace of Westminster
London, UK

31st October 2017

Dear Prime Minister,
We are writing to you from the Occupied Palestinian Territories on the West Bank, where we, a group of sixty British pilgrims aged between 16 and 79, are nearing the completion of the Just Walk to Jerusalem, organised by Amos Trust, a 3,300 km journey on foot from London to Jerusalem to mark the centenary of the Balfour Declaration.

Departing London on 10th June, we have walked through England, France, Switzerland, Italy, Albania, Macedonia, Greece, Turkey and Jordan, and will arrive in Jerusalem this Thursday 2nd November.

This walk also marks the tenth year of Israel's land, sea and air blockade of Gaza and the fiftieth year of the military occupation of the West Bank, East Jerusalem, Gaza and the Golan Heights. Our company also includes walkers from America, Australia, Ireland, Lithuania, Malta, the Netherlands, New Zealand and Palestine.

We have undertaken this walk ...

– in penance for Britain's failure to ensure the Balfour Declaration promise – 'that nothing shall be done which may prejudice the civil and religious rights of existing non-Jewish communities in Palestine';

– in solidarity with the Palestinian people, who have experienced 100 years of dispossession, injustice, conflict and suffering, and with peace activists from both communities on the long road to peace and justice;

– in hope, that one day, all people in the Holy Land will live in peace, as neighbours, with full equal rights.

You have stated publicly that you intend to celebrate the Balfour Centenary this week 'with pride', attending a celebratory dinner with Israel's Prime Minister, and that Britain should be 'proud' of its role in creating the State of Israel. Well, some of us feel differently.

Walking across Europe, we have received heart-warming encouragement from countless people inspired by our journey, who have welcomed us and gone out of their way to offer us hospitality and support. Here in Palestine, there is a mood of widespread dismay and astonishment at your announcement of your intention to celebrate the Balfour Centenary.

On Saturday, as we walked through the remote village of Tuqu, to the south of Bethlehem, we were welcomed by an elderly Palestinian farmer, who shook his head and asked us, 'What can we do with Balfour?'

'We have to change it,' we replied.

He shook his head again and said, 'Theresa . . . Theresa . . . is no good.'

This, in a nutshell, is what Palestinians think of your recent announcement. We have been welcomed in every city, town, village and refugee camp by Palestinian governors, mayors, councillors and community leaders, who have expressed their deep pain and disappointment at your desire to celebrate the centenary of the Declaration which has caused them so much suffering over the past one hundred years.

Yesterday, the Mayor of the town of Sa'ir, near Hebron, welcomed us at a civic function and said,

'To hear from the Prime Minister of Britain that she is proud – is very shameful. I cannot understand, really, that the Prime Minister of a great country like Britain, which has a history of civilisation, a state that we can look to, to teach civilisation, teach history, teach poetry, she is a civilised state – I cannot understand that her Prime Minister can say this.

Because of the Balfour Declaration, a lot of Palestinians were expelled from their land, and became refugees in Lebanon, Syria, Jordan, and I saw with my own eyes, a lot of women and children refugees leaving, crying and living in camps, where it was so cold, without the essential, basic necessities in those camps. This I saw with my own eyes.

Everyone created by God misses the place where he was born. I would like to say that the Palestinian people are a very civilised people, who love people, who love the other and like to live in peace, really from the depth of our heart, we love to live in peace. We give you all our thanks for this initiative, which gives us hope for a better life.

This gives us hope that one day, all peoples will stand with us to give us justice and a return to our land. You are so welcome here and we thank you.'

We have seen the dispossession experienced by the Palestinian villages in the South Hebron Hills and saw the shocking intimidation and confrontation in the city of Hebron by illegal settlers against our Palestinian companions walking with us.

Israeli soldiers and police reacted by arresting the Palestinian official who was the victim of this intimidation. In contrast to the dismay provoked by your announcement, our arrival in Palestine has been met with effusive welcomes everywhere, and profound satisfaction that a group of British pilgrims have walked so far to express penance, solidarity and hope.

We can even say that there is a widespread feeling of joy and relief that their suffering is not forgotten. May we urge you, on behalf of the pilgrims of the Just Walk to Jerusalem, to reconsider your recent statement and make a suitable apology to the Palestinian people for your insensitivity to their suffering, in which Britain has played such a lamentable role and bears the lion's share of responsibility.

May we also urge you not to attend this grotesque celebration of a declaration which a British Foreign Secretary had no right to make, in which – as Arthur Koestler wrote memorably in 1949 – 'one nation solemnly promised a second nation the country of a third'.

At this historic moment, we welcome your Foreign Secretary's reiteration in yesterday's *Daily Telegraph* of the Government's position. However this is not enough without seizing this moment and the unique opportunity that lies before you to galvanise the 'best endeavours' of the British government to the achievement of what has been so chronically lacking for so long in Israel-Palestine – full equal rights for everyone who calls the Holy Land home, recognition of the State of Palestine, and calling on Israel to end its illegal occupation of Palestinian lands, and the inhuman blockade of Gaza. This would be a worthy celebration of the Balfour Centenary.

Yours sincerely

Justin Butcher and Chris Rose

On behalf of all those who have taken part in Just Walk to Jerusalem, and together walked for over 50,000 km between 10 June and 2 November 2017.

Justin Butcher is a writer and originator of Just Walk; Chris Rose is Director of Amos Trust, who have been responsible for Just Walk to Jerusalem.

Wednesday 1 November, Bethlehem

11am. We're standing wedged between a crowd of press photographers and local Palestinian activists at the end of the narrow street between Banksy's Walled Off Hotel and the Wall, in Bethlehem. In front of us, a kind of Mad Hatter's Tea Party with a Balfour theme is unfolding – Banksy's distinctive contribution to the Balfour centenary. Some of his most famous works, including the flak-jacketed Peace Dove and the little girl, carried by a bunch of balloons, are close to or on the Wall in Bethlehem, and earlier this year he opened this hotel next to the Wall as a satirical interactive installation which he describes as 'a three-storey cure for fanaticism, with limited car parking' boasting 'the worst view of any hotel in the world'. On the front steps beneath lettering picking out the hotel's name in glitzy lights against a wall pockmarked with bullet holes, a model chimpanzee dressed as a bellboy in white gloves and red tunic perches on a pile of luggage, one hand dangling a little gold bell, the other dragging an old-fashioned hatbox spilling its contents on to the steps. Inside, the hotel's delights include a lavish presidential suite with a hot-tub showered by streams of water from a bullet-strafed Palestinian water-tank, a foyer decorated like a gentleman's club with potted palms and leather sofas, where the fire in the grate flickers under a pile of rubble and paintings of seaside views are marred by discarded lifejackets scattered across the beaches, while a self-playing piano stutters out a ghostly accompaniment to the exhibits. A classical bust is shrouded with a mask against wreaths of tear gas spiralling from a canister next to the pedestal.

'Walls are hot right now, but I was into them long before Trump made it cool,' read Banksy's statement at the Walled Off launch in March. 'It's exactly 100 years since Britain took control of Palestine and started rearranging the furniture – with chaotic results . . . a good time to reflect on what happens when the United Kingdom makes a huge political decision without fully comprehending the consequences.'

The scene in front of us is pure genius. Beneath shredded Union Jack flags and charred bunting, a line of trestles is set with white tablecloths and cakes, cupcakes and balloons in red, white and blue. The guests are Palestinian children from Aida and Dheisheh Camps, all wearing soot-tarnished Union Jack helmets, gas masks and night-vision goggles. Between table displays of singed miniature flags and jugs of orange juice, a huge, lopsided Union Jack cake teeters, topped with a miniature crown. Entertained by a juggler, the kids are drawing pictures of Banksy's Peace Dove for a competition, while a Palestinian MC in top hat and tails welcomes the world's press – a great bank of photographers crammed on to the hotel terrace – with wildly over-the-top enthusiasm. Martial brass band music plays at wonky speeds, the *Dam Busters* and Sousa marches veering off key as the tempo slides. The narrow street is so jammed that most of us have to perch behind a barricade of sandbags between the hotel steps and the Wall, all stuck with flags.

A dinky red velvet curtain has been rigged up on the Wall, covering the new Banksy work about to be unveiled.

'We are so pr-r-roud to welcome you ALL on this auspicious occasion!' shrieks the MC, grinning manically, 'and now, ladies and gentlemen, boys and girls, we are so honoured and delighted to welcome . . . *Her Majesty the Queen!*'

Everyone applauds and the kids giggle as the 'Queen' appears – an actor dressed in sky-blue overcoat, white gloves and floral headscarf, wearing a cardboard party mask of HM, complete with glasses and trademark frown. 'God save the Queen' plays at varying speeds as she waves daintily to her subjects, ascends the podium and pulls a cord to unveil the new Banksy. Framed by a *trompe l'oeil* plaque, the royal crest is engraved above the letters 'Er', followed by three dots leading, on the line below, to a large 'SORRY' carved in foot-high capitals in the concrete.

Er . . .
SORRY

An awkward silence falls, broken only by the clicking of cameras and the occasional giggle from the bemused kids, and then, marvellously, the tea party is invaded by a crowd of activists from Aida Camp, waving flags and shouting, 'Free, free Palestine!' In a glorious finale, the ringleader jumps on to the table and plants the Palestinian flag in the cake. All of us present are quite clear that this is part of the script, the perfect coda to a biting and hilarious performance, but the world's press, including *Haaretz* and *The Guardian*, all report this as a hijacking of the event, an expression of Palestinian displeasure at Banksy's satirical piece. I'm quite certain they're wrong.

After a number of press interviews next to the Walled Off, we trek down to join a big demonstration, which will march up the main Hebron–Jerusalem Road through Bethlehem to the section of the Wall next to the Intercontinental Hotel (and the Wi'am Conflict Transformation Centre), where the infamous iron gate and watchtower shut off the road to Jerusalem. Assembling the walkers amid noisy crowds, gridlocked traffic, waving flags and TV cameras, Chris and our friends from Holy Land Trust ask the group to keep to the right-hand side of the march, and in the event of tear gas or soldiers appearing to head up one of the alleys off to the right. I make sure Eleanor, Millie and Jack are together and ask them to stick close to me. This is a fast-track education for them in political activism.

'How do you feel?' I ask Eleanor.

'I feel really . . . important!' she laughs. 'It's quite exciting. I don't want to get teargassed, though. I feel kind of nervous, but it's exciting because I feel like I'm part of something really important. I feel like I've got a role, making a difference.'

There's a buoyant atmosphere as we set off, hundreds of Palestinians around us in the crowd, all greeting us and shouting, 'Welcome to Palestine!'

Also happening this morning is something potentially momentous: Hamas handing over control of the Rafah Crossing to the PA, as a prelude to the Hamas–Fateh reconciliation. As reward, Egypt has promised to open its border with Gaza indefinitely from 21 November, effectively bringing the blockade to an end without Israel's say-so. Egypt will host negotiations in Cairo between Fateh and Hamas to form a national unity government, and facilitate the handover of ministries in Gaza to the PA. Despite many previous failed attempts at reconciliation, everyone seems genuinely optimistic that they might actually pull it off this time – which, of course, would be the last thing Netanyahu's government wants.

Suddenly we're choking and coughing with an acrid stench in our noses and sharp stinging pains in our eyes and throats. I didn't hear the canisters detonate, but up ahead I can see white plumes of tear gas arcing down the road. 'OK, let's move!' I splutter. 'Over this way!'

The march had seemed to be heading along very peacefully. We scurry to shelter beneath a garage awning. Covering his nose with a scarf, Chris ventures further up the road to check our group's all together. Eleanor, Millie and Jack are sheltering in an adjacent shop, where a little Palestinian boy led them. It was touching and sobering all at once, Eleanor says later, because this boy, maybe ten years old, knew exactly what to do as soon as we smelt gas. He tugged her by the wrist and led her towards the shop, saying, 'Come on! Gas! We have to go this way now, in here.' It was just part of normal life for him.

As we retreat to a safe distance further back on the right-hand side of the street, I find myself standing with Abdelfattah, director of Alrowwad, and ask him about what's going on.

'Well, the Israelis are starting shooting, so some of the people are saying we should advance and sit in the middle of the street, but the younger people are not easy to control, so probably they will opt for more direct confrontation, and you can see the jeep at the end of the street and the soldiers lined up. People are trying to make it smooth because of the cars going in and out . . .' – a tear gas cannon booms in the background – 'but as you see, it's started to accelerate.'

A queue of cars is jammed along the Hebron–Jerusalem Road behind us, horns honking, unable to advance any further because of the clouds of tear gas and the demonstrators blocking their path.

'So now, it's just soldiers shooting, but if their cars, their jeeps start shooting, it will be very intense.'

An elderly Palestinian man staggers past, coughing, 'The gas . . . it's an abomination!'

'Yes,' says Abdelfattah, 'really the effects are very powerful.'

'So, on a scale of one to ten,' I say, 'how worried or relaxed do you feel now?'

'Well, you know, most of the time it's like cat and mouse, a game. I mean, if the people go up to the Wall and the watchtower up there, by the Intercontinental Hotel, and throw stones, after half an hour, one hour, probably, they will get fed up and return, but the Israelis are making sure it's a direct confrontation and you see tear gas and maybe . . . This morning, I don't know if you heard, they were in Dheisheh Camp and they were using real bullets.'

'So have people been wounded this morning?'

'I don't know. I was just chatting with somebody from Dheisheh, because I spent the night in Jerusalem with my wife and children. But almost on a daily basis there's incursions like this, provocations, and they are on high alert.'

'So, regarding Israel's killing of seven Palestinians in Gaza on Monday night, the story I've heard is that they were farmers, there's a lot of water in that part of the Gaza Strip and they were digging for water, for irrigation, or something like that . . .'

'Yes, that's what I heard as well,' says Abdelfattah. 'I mean, it's completely besieged, Gaza, so attacking continuously and destroying homes and property and killing people – it's a violation of every human value.'

'Do you think that the attack on Gaza was timed deliberately?' I ask. 'There's a lot of noise about the Balfour centenary, people asking when are the Palestinians going to have their state, Boris Johnson saying he supports a sovereign Palestinian State, etc. Is that attack timed to demonstrate to the world, look, you see what the Palestinians are like . . .?

'Well, I guess they're always mixing things so that we become the wrong person . . .' – a tear gas canister explodes in the background – '. . . every time, they try to mix the cards and show the Palestinians as the violent ones, the Israelis are just defending themselves or defending democracies in the West, and so on.'

'It strikes me that, if the Israelis succeed in provoking some rocket fire from Gaza, that would enable them to say to the world, "Look, they're not ready for a State, they're terrorists, they want to kill us etc."'

'Well, I would say also that *they* are not ready for a State,' says Abdelfattah, provoking a burst of laughter from the small crowd that's gathered round to listen. 'Until today they don't have any fixed borders or defined constitution, so how the world are recognising such a State – it's complete hypocrisy from the international community. They treat the Palestinian Authority as a government for an independent state, while we have no authority over anything, on any level – except what's dictated sometimes from the international community, or even from Israel itself. So, I guess the governments who decide to partition a country that they do not own, and give it to foreigners, since they made those promises, they should also find the solution, and if this criminal state which was given the right to occupy us and destroy our homes and make us refugees continues to violate UN resolutions and human rights and create apartheid systems and apartheid laws, it's the responsibility of the international community to marginalise it, isolate it, punish it, one way or the other.'

I describe our visit to the Gaza border yesterday and the Paths to Peace Centre. 'I can't work out whether the whole thing was a propaganda exercise, or whether she was for real.'

'Well, I guess it's both,' says Abdelfattah. 'Israel tries to use different means to present a human face, and the media brainwashing, you know, "Everybody wants to kill us", whatever. I mean, for me, the Occupation is rape. So victims of rape can resist the Occupation, and of course they want to kill the rapist, or at least stop this rape, and every time people who are the victim of this rape try to defend themselves, it's presented as, "They want to kill us.'" He laughs wryly. 'Well, make justice, and then hopefully you will win the dignity and respect of people and nobody will kill you. But if you are continuously killing people and violating their dignity and humanity and you think they should appreciate it and throw flowers to you . . . that's why, when Palestinians call for boycott, divestment and sanctions – it was partly directed against this machine of propaganda, conducted through beautiful human beings who make a beautiful face for the Occupation. "Look, they are just like us, they are artists, they want peace," but peace while violating and legitimising the rape of a people and their dignity and so on. So it's important that this hypocrisy stops and people be aware that, even if the soldier at the checkpoint is the nicest person in the world, he is still a bastard of a soldier at an illegal checkpoint controlling my life, whether he gives me a cookie or whether he's stopping me with a gun. They shouldn't be there – that's it. People can live together, but can live together as equals. People can make peace, but can make peace on the basis of justice and equality. Other than this, it's complete hypocrisy.'

The demonstration seems to have come to a complete standstill so, thanking Abdelfattah, we head off the Hebron–Jerusalem Road, up through the maze of old Ottoman streets to our right that leads to Manger Square.

After lunch in Manger Square, Elias and I take a group of six walkers off to Ramallah for yet another interview on PBC, this time a kind of TV *Question Time* special on the Balfour legacy. We're seated in the studio audience with other delegations, while an introductory film sets out a montage of 100 years of Palestine in pictures, from the Balfour Declaration through to the present. A programme host and a sober-faced panel, made up of a Palestinian politician and two Palestinian academics, set forth questions arising from the Declaration and its legacy. Elias gives me a digest of what's being said. 'Israel uses the Holocaust to elicit world sympathy while trampling on the rights of Palestinians,' says one panellist. 'So Germany has apologised; why won't Britain apologise?'

Then we're invited to join the discussion. They question us closely: 'What is the popular opinion in the UK? Can the British people influence their government? Are young people interested in the Palestinian struggle? What could the British government actually do?'

As before, I'm wary of conjuring false hope. The solidarity movement is strong in the UK, we say, and growing, particularly among young people, especially after the wars on Gaza. As I start to express the aims of the Walk, I find myself ambushed by a sudden surge of emotion. 'We have walked for five months,' I say, 'from London to Palestine to express our sorrow, our apology for the actions of our government 100 years ago,' – my voice is starting to shake – 'for the 100 years of dispossession, injustice, suffering and conflict which we visited upon your people . . .' and then, with a choking gurgle, I grind to a halt. 'I'm sorry, I . . .'

For the first time, the programme host smiles and says in Arabic, 'It's alright.'

'I beg your pardon,' I say. 'We have also walked in solidarity with the Palestinian people, whose right of return is denied, and in hope, that one day . . .' and you know the rest.

I feel such a fool. How unseemly. Exhibiting my sentimental luvvy emotionalism in the face of their measured discussion of their ongoing nightmare. Pull yourself together, Butch.

But that's all my stuff. As it turns out, they're hugely appreciative. One of the panellists says, further along in the discussion, 'The obvious strength of emotion comes from being well informed about the Palestinian situation. What can we do to inform the world better about our story and our condition?'

Several of us reply that, in our experience, exporting Palestinian culture is the best way to inform the wider world – through literature, film, theatre, even cuisine. Then, at the programme break, suddenly, as one, the panellists crack broad smiles and bound down from the studio stage to greet us. All those grim demeanours were simply their broadcast manner. We walk away considerably buoyed.

We return to Bethlehem to join a beautiful candlelit vigil in

Manger Square, at which Sami invites the Mufti of Bethlehem and the local Orthodox and Melkite clergy to join him on stage for prayers of blessing 'on all the peoples of this Holy Land, sacred to the three faiths'. We're all invited to stand on and around the stage with Sami and the magnificently bearded and robed clergy for photographs and a special blessing of thanksgiving for the walkers, humbling and intensely moving. I have a snapshot in my memory of looking across to Eleanor at this moment, her face lit from below by candlelight. She was right: it feels important to be here, at the heart of the struggle, sharing the hope for justice and freedom with so many dear friends.

In the line-up, I notice a little Palestinian girl standing next to me, on the left end of the line. She wants to be part of the action and is standing proudly, grinning broadly for the cameras. She reminds me of my middle son Jacob aged three or four; he's always had a great sense of occasions and how to subvert them.

Elias is overjoyed with the impact of the Walk throughout the Middle East and flings an arm around me during the singing of the Palestinian anthem *Mawtini*.

After interviews with BBC Arabic, CNN, Sky Arabic, Al-Jazeera and other channels, we pack out Afik's catacomb restaurant, just off the square, the best cafe in Bethlehem, for a raucous dinner with many falafels and much Taybeh, while Chris runs through tomorrow's packed programme. 'We will not, after all, be ending our pilgrimage in the Al-Aqsa Mosque,' he announces, to much astonished laughter. 'Yes, it was under consideration for several days, but the Jordanian authorities who – weirdly – still control the site, were worried we might cause an international incident. We said, "Don't worry, we're very happy to cause an international incident," but they decided otherwise. So tomorrow, we'll say our Just Walk liturgy on the Mount of Olives then walk down to enter the Old City through the Lions' Gate, and end with a special service in St George's Cathedral, led by Garth and Canon Naeem Atik.'

Being the small world that it is, at Afik's we meet a group of olive-harvest volunteers from Bristol, led by a chap called Dan, who runs a small charity supporting farmers in the West Bank, and what do you know, they're connected with a church in Bristol, where we have a number of friends in common. Bethlehem's the place to meet.

Thursday 2 November, Jerusalem

It's Thursday evening on the day of the Balfour centenary. I'm standing with Eleanor in front of an ancient olive tree in the cloistered gardens of St George's Cathedral, Jerusalem. The Walk is complete. Our revels now are – nearly – ended, bar the final celebratory dinner back in Bethlehem. I have one thing left to do before we leave Jerusalem. As I mentioned thousands of words and miles back, I've carried a pebble in my pocket all the way from England. In a Good Friday meditation at my church in London, our vicar Dave invited everyone to take a pebble from a glass bowl and drop it into the font, to symbolise something we wanted to let go, to be free of, to release. I found that I couldn't let go of it, or didn't want to, so I carried it all the way here. Now I will let it go, here in Jerusalem, where our Walk ended. At the suggestion of one of the canons, I've decided to place my pebble, or post it, in the huge olive tree in the St George's Garden of Gethsemane. It looks very old – far older than the cathedral – its massive limbs knobbed and pitted with the twists and turns of centuries, the chance snaking trails and angles of mutation where the sunlight fell or the rain dripped, where the sap rose and the pruning hook clove to shape the contours of this ancient tree. Poised to drop my pebble into the deep hole at the heart of the tree, I think back over the weeks and months that led us here, and the wild flurry of impassioned words and encounters that whirled us through this final day.

8.30am. In the genteel tranquillity of the British Consulate in East Jerusalem, the heat and fever of Occupied Palestine seems a world away. Eight of us are sitting around a handsome dining table set with coffee and pastries, looking out through French windows on to a verdant lawn, the guests of the British Consul-General to the Palestinian Territories, Philip Hall OBE, who, as you might expect, is the most charming host. After a super-early start, and a brief detour to the Spanish Consulate, we found the right building and passed through dungeon portals and turnstiles, depositing our phones en route, to make our way up to the tastefully furnished interior, an oak-panelled enclave of old-world British elegance, where the Consul-General, his staff and his wife and daughter welcome us warmly in our walking rags, boots and beards, without batting an eyelid. After the early start, the coffee and pastries are mighty welcome.

The Consul-General, immaculate in suit and tie even at this hour, is genuinely friendly, insisting on first names and genuinely interested in the Walk, which we describe in brief stages, each taking a turn, country by country, to trace our route from London. He listens with attentive politeness and the occasional smile.

Then Robert Cohen presents our new Balfour Declaration, saying that here in Palestine we have heard many of the stories of Palestinians up and down the West Bank, and expressed our message of penance, solidarity and hope, but now, at the culmination of our pilgrimage, we also have things we would like to say to our government. Passing a copy across the table, Robert says, 'I would like to read this now to you, if I may, as we present formally our new Balfour Declaration, on behalf of those who have walked all the way from the Foreign Office in London, where the original declaration was penned, to be with you here today on the centenary.'

He reads:

'We request that the Consul-General pass this document to the Foreign Secretary, Boris Johnson, and to the Prime Minister, Theresa May.

We have walked more than 3,400 kilometres to be here today. We have walked in penance and in solidarity. We have walked in recognition that the Balfour Declaration led to one people's freedom and another people's oppression. We have walked with our Christian, Muslim and Jewish partners in the Holy Land to hear their witness to the consequences of Balfour. Today, one hundred years after the original Balfour Declaration was made, we propose a new declaration. We offer a 'new Balfour' to Her Majesty's Government, a new sixty-seven-word declaration written in the belief that peace will only come through justice and reconciliation.

The New Balfour Declaration
'Her Majesty's Government view with favour the establishment in Palestine/Israel of a safe and secure home for all who live there.

The nations of the world should use their best endeavours to facilitate the achievement of this objective, it being clearly understood
that nothing shall be done which may prejudice the civil, political
and religious rights of Palestinians or Jews living in Palestine/Israel
or any other country.'

Philip thanks him and says, 'I will, of course, pass this on to the
Foreign Secretary.'

'Justin also has a letter to present to the Prime Minister,' says
Chris, 'on behalf of the Just Walk.'

After the genteel tone of the opening exchanges, my letter seems
to tear the atmosphere. I manage to read it with some passion, but
without choking up, to my relief. I sense Philip blench at certain
points. Handing the letter to him, I thank him once more for his
time and attention. Now it's his turn to respond. He's unexpectedly
on side.

'The British government does believe that the Occupation should
end,' he says, 'and that it is illegal. We have said that and we do
say that. We also believe that the blockade of Gaza should end and
that it too is illegal, and all our diplomatic efforts in that arena are
directed towards supporting the reconciliation between Hamas and
Fateh, with a view to ending the blockade. If they can achieve this,
with a transition of power, transformation of the governing arrangements in Gaza, and the surrender of arms, then that would present
the circumstances for the end of the blockade.

'We do endorse your calls for solidarity and hope. We do feel
and express solidarity with the Palestinian people, through our
diplomatic efforts and our DfID programmes, funding the salaries
of teachers in Gaza, for example, as well as other initiatives, and
yes, we do feel hope, despite the challenges facing the Palestinians.
So there is much in your letter which we can agree with and
support, although I have to say, there is a difference in tone.' He
turns slightly pink. 'The sticking point is penance. Penance is not
something the British government can agree with and, in fact, we
don't feel. I do not feel that the entire responsibility for the suffering
of the Palestinian people rests on my shoulders. Some of it, yes,
and we should recognise that. We are proud of our role, historically,
in helping the State of Israel to come into being. We should also

remember that there were many steps between the Balfour Declaration and the creation of the State of Israel, not least the UN resolution of 1947. We support Israel, we regard Israel as a friend and, within its pre-1967 borders, as a country that we like and find admirable, and a democracy in the region, which we support.'

Lynn pipes up. 'We've walked through the Negev,' she says, 'within Israel proper, and seen the unrecognised Bedouin villages where people are living in extreme poverty, denied basic essential services like water and electricity, having their houses demolished and property destroyed by the Israeli military. I don't see that as an admirable country, a democracy to be proud of.'

'Of course,' Philip concurs, 'we would agree, and we understand that Israel's not perfect, but if you compare it to many surrounding countries, it treats its citizens a lot better.'

'What we feel,' says Chris, 'is that the voice of the victim should be listened to, and that Palestinians have been the victims of this 100 years of history. And that if they feel abused and dispossessed, the victims of injustice, they should be the ones to determine whether an apology is due.'

'We've spent the last week or so walking up and down the West Bank,' I say, 'through the Jordan Valley, the south Hebron hills, the wadis of the Bethlehem hills, visiting refugee camps, schools and Bedouin villages, and we've really enjoyed walking through the countryside and meeting Palestinian communities on the ground. I don't know if you've had the opportunity yet to walk through Palestine – I know you've only arrived recently in post here – but I can really recommend the experience. It's a great way to meet people at the grass roots. We want to be their messengers to the British government, and the message we're carrying to you from them is of disappointment, dismay and incomprehension that Britain can be celebrating this centenary with pride. And therefore there is a profound disjunction of perceptions here.'

'Yes. I would agree that there is indeed a disjunction of perceptions, as with almost every aspect of the challenges which this region faces.'

On to Ramallah, to 'A Century of Injustice' at the Carmel Hotel, an international conference hosted by the Fateh International

Relations Committee on the theme, 'A hundred years of the Balfour Declaration'. A glitzy ballroom full of men in suits, who rise to their feet to applaud us, in our rough-and-ready walking gear, as the conference chair introduces Chris.

'We apologise that we are not dressed so smartly as all of you,' Chris says. 'We only have the clothes we walked in, for 3,300 kilometres, through eleven countries, over 147 days, to express our deep sorrow for the Balfour Declaration and the disastrous impact it has had over 100 years of dispossession and suffering. We had no right to promise this land to anyone but you. We have walked to show our solidarity with Palestinians, denied their freedom of movement, on the long path to peace and justice for Palestine.' He invites all the walkers to stand, amid renewed applause. 'We want not only to remember the past, but also to look forward,' he says. 'Our organisation supports many Palestinian projects here seeking to build hope and opportunities for the future, such as the Al-Ahli Hospital in Gaza and the Near East Council of Churches scheme for young people's vocational training. So many young people in Gaza ask, "What future do we have here? We don't want aid; we just want a chance. Open the borders; we will prosper." We have met schoolchildren in Bethlehem whose teachers say that, after the age of ten, all they paint is the Wall and images of the Occupation. We have had the most wonderful times here, rebuilding demolished houses in Al-Arrub and elsewhere, and working with the children of Arrub Camp to build playgrounds and gardens.

'In Palestine, I'm very proud to call myself Abu Jack, and my son Jack is here today.' Chris points him out. 'He has walked all the way from London.' Jack stands, blinking shyly, to acknowledge the outburst of warm applause. 'We're calling on governments and solidarity movements across the world to unite for a just peace for Palestinians, to commit to non-violent means, such as boycott, divestment and sanctions, to work for a future for these children of Palestine. We will never give up the struggle, because we know that nobody is free until the Palestinian people are free. One day we will walk together to Al-Quds, to Gaza, Yaffa, Nazareth, to Istanbul, Thessaloniki, Macedonia, Italy, France and England, all the way to London!'

The audience are on their feet before he finishes, cheering him to the echo. The conference chair presents Chris with a memorial plaque and asks us to carry their greetings to Jeremy Corbyn, 'because we know that when there is a Labour government, they will recognise the State of Palestine.'

Today we're on the front page of *Haaretz*, featured in a story about the Banksy Tea Party as 'a group of 70 Britons [who] attended the party after marching from London to Bethlehem in a call on the British government to fulfil the second part of the Balfour Declaration – the promise to ensure the rights of non-Jewish minorities within the Jewish state.' *Sic*. Oh well. On we go, to the mother of all demonstrations in the city centre, where Chris has asked me to speak for the Walk. We plunge into a crowd of thousands, Palestinian marching bands, boy scouts and girl guides, cavalcades of schoolchildren, banners and flags and streamers flying, klaxons and horns blasting, and, where the main roads converge, a phalanx of press, cameras, tripods and microphones clustered, amid the vast swirl of humanity thronging the streets. Goodness knows where the demo's meant to begin or end, or where the speakers' platform might be. A wild thought has been growing in my mind that today, here in Ramallah, speaking in front of a huge crowd and global media, I'm going to be shot by a crazy settler or an Israeli sniper . . . the guy who had the big idea for this Walk, the ringleader, will get his comeuppance, assassinated like MLK or Gandhi or . . . Jesus. Clearly, I must have Jerusalem Syndrome, 'a delusive condition affecting some visitors to Jerusalem in which the sufferer identifies with a major figure from his or her religious background', as Collins' Dictionary defines it . . .

And here comes a chap in a red fez, with scarlet and orange tunic and trousers and, slung on his back, one of those fabulous Arabic samovar contraptions, a huge brass flask for brewing tea with a spout which pours when he tips forward, and he's handing out sweet Bedouin tea left, right and centre. *Shukran, habibi*, much obliged . . .

Now I'm walking along interviewing a fierce little man with a white beard and smart black suit, a former general in the PLO, stabbing the air with his finger and declaiming pugnaciously in Arabic, as Elias translates.

'His name, he says, is Mohammed, and he's sending a message to the British government from Palestine, the place where the three monotheistic religions started. From here we sent to the world the message of Jesus, he says, and we sent you the Bible, the message of peace, and from here also we sent the message of the Virgin Mary, the mother of Jesus, and in every place where you walk in this land, you can see this message of peace. As a Muslim, I believe in Jesus and the Virgin Mary, and you will find this message of peace also in the mosques here. So we sent this message of peace from the Holy Land, 2,000 years ago, to the world, to the British, and what we got back from the British government was just killing and war and injustice.

'Jesus was crucified once, in this land, but every day the Palestinians are crucified by the international policy and the injustices happening here. You have learned peace from this land. Why do you send back war to this people? We are asking the international community to come with a solution, any solution that brings peace! Let the American and British governments come and observe the nuclear weapons which Israel has, and let them put the fear of God before their eyes. It doesn't matter whether you believe in God or not, but please support the Palestinian rights.

'You who are walking all this way for our rights, God appreciates what you are doing, and all the prophets. Not me – I don't need to appreciate it. You are completing Jesus' message by coming here, and he's calling you to continue this mission, to continue the message of God and the message of Jesus, by coming here to support the Palestinians.'

He grips my hand and shoulder fiercely, then grabs my face in his hands and kisses me ferociously on both cheeks.

After an hour or so of marching, milling and multiple TV interviews, it's time to head off for lunch with the President, so my assassination will have to wait for another day, it seems . . .

The presidential banquet is magnificent, in a huge, brightly lit conference room-cum-sports hall, several hundred guests lining tables set with sumptuous food and flowers, *maftoul* and *freekeh* and tender lamb, roasted vegetables, salads, hummus and flatbread and pine nuts and *za'atar*, the best of Palestinian cuisine. No phones or cameras allowed, so all is from memory. We all feel extremely scruffy in such lavish surroundings. Julia plays and sings *Mawtini* and other wonderful bitter-sweet melodies. President Abbas, who in the flesh reminds me strikingly of Trevor McDonald, speaks a stirring vote of thanks to all the walkers, translated by Sami:

'Thank you all, dear friends, and welcome. You have travelled thousands of miles to express your solidarity with the Palestinian people, and to convey your rejection of the infamous Balfour Declaration. Your visit is a message of hope for the Palestinian people, that you support their struggle for freedom and independence. We are convinced that you represent the British people. We appreciate the noble action that the House of Commons has taken in asking the UK government to recognise the Palestinian State. We are still committed to the Two-State Solution. The alternative is apartheid, similar to that in South Africa. We are already under apartheid. If the Two-State Solution fails, it will be a full apartheid.

'We count on you to support our struggle – our peaceful struggle – for freedom and independence. We are the only people in the world still under a foreign military occupation, occupying us for the last fifty years. In the last few days, you have been travelling in Palestine and had the opportunity to see how our people are suffering under the Israeli Occupation. Nevertheless, our people are determined to resist the Occupation peacefully. I welcome also the delegates from the USA and Turkey here today. Dear friends, you are all most welcome and I thank you very much.'

Sami replies in Arabic on our behalf, and introduces Chris, who asks us all to stand and, once again, spontaneous applause bursts forth from all the guests and staff. We bow and smile and *salaam* and *shukran* and shake hands with those around us, and then we're invited to line up, each to have our photograph taken with the President. 'This is Justin,' says Sami in Arabic, 'a good friend of Palestine, and the creator, the originator of the Walk.' The old man's eyes widen and he smiles, taking my hand in his right and Eleanor's in his left as I introduce her, and we pose for the camera. Quite a week for a sixteen-year-old: settlers in Hebron, tear gas in Bethlehem and lunch with Abu Mazen to round things off . . .

Husam entertains us with the story of the cows of Beit Sahour on the bus from Ramallah. 'In the First Intifada,' he says, 'the Israelis held a complete monopoly on milk production and distribution, so the farmers of Beit Sahour decided to purchase some cows and started to produce Palestinian milk. The Israelis were very upset about this, and wanted to put a stop to it, so they banned the cows, and issued a warrant for their arrest. The cows of Beit Sahour, they said, represented an existential threat to the State of Israel and had to be eliminated. But first they had to find them, and the farmers kept moving them. Whenever they thought they'd got them cornered, the farmers found somewhere else to hide them, and so this game of cat and mouse began, the hunt for the outlawed cows. We kept it up for several months, always finding new places to hide the cows, in caves, in barns, in people's houses, churches, schools, sports halls . . . and they never found them! What became of the cows of Beit Sahour? Well, in the end, the farmers knew they wouldn't be able to hide them for ever, so they slaughtered them and ate them. There's a very funny film about this, in fact I'm acting in it, playing one of the kids . . .'

A golden haze lies over the city as the sun starts to sink in a fiery glow across the horizon, bathing all the west-facing contours of tombs and mosques and churches and walls in a blonde early evening light. Along the city walls of Suleiman the Magnificent the crenellations shine like glistening teeth across the Kidron Valley, and beyond the Al-Aqsa Compound, burnished by the sun-shafts slanting across the rooftops, the Dome of the Rock shimmers in coppery radiance like a mirage. I'd forgotten how many trees there were all around the Temple Mount and up the far side of the valley. Down the steep slopes of the Mount of Olives before us stretch the myriad grave slabs and tombs of the Jewish Cemetery and the Silwan Necropolis. Across to our right is the little teardrop-shaped church of Dominus Flevit, marking the place, they say, where Jesus looked down and wept over the city, foreseeing its destruction.

'As he came near and saw the city, he wept over it, saying, If you, even you, had only recognised on this day the things that make for peace! But now they are hidden from your eyes.'

(Luke 19:41–2, NRSV)

Here, at the top of the Mount of Olives, we say our liturgy together for the last time, and photograph the walkers against the world's most famous backdrop before setting off down the Palm Sunday path to the war-torn city of peace. Eleanor, Julia, Naomi and I hold a 'walking choir practice' as we wend our way down, for the piece that I've been teaching them in odd spare moments over the last few days – the trio for female voices from Mendelssohn's *Elijah*, 'Lift thine eyes'. No better place to sing it than here. I'm hoping there'll be a moment for it in the service at St George's.

> Lift thine eyes, O lift thine eyes to the mountains, whence cometh
> help.
> Thy help cometh from the Lord, the Maker of heaven and earth.
> He hath said, Thy foot shall not be moved, Thy Keeper will never
> slumber.
> Lift thine eyes, O lift thine eyes to the mountains, whence cometh
> help.

And so, at the end of a life-changing journey, 3,400 km through Europe and the Middle East, crossing eleven borders, three seas, countless rivers, mountains and soul-stirring landscapes from the green fields of Kent to the desert dust of Jordan, we walked at last down the Mount of Olives and through the Lions' Gate into Jerusalem, through which Ottomans 500 years ago and Israelis fifty years ago conquered the ancient city, and so on to the Via Dolorosa. Our companions clapped and cheered us through the gate, Palestinian drivers tooted their horns in welcome and high fived us through car windows – and a great tide of relief and joy swept us up and into each other's arms. We laughed and hugged and cried and whooped our way scandalously down the Via Dolorosa to St George's Cathedral, drunk with hope's euphoria.

Our preacher at St George's this evening was the great Naim Ateek, founder of the Sabeel Ecumenical Liberation Center in Jerusalem and one of the pioneers in shaping the liberation theology of the church in the Holy Land through decades of war, upheaval and occupation. Nearly seventy years since his family's expulsion from their town of Beisan (now called Beth Shean) two days before the declaration of the State of Israel, Naim's spirit is undimmed. At the heart of his magnanimous vision of a shared Jerusalem and a shared Holy Land are the words of the prophet Micah, foretelling the future glory of the holy city restored:

> In the last days
> the mountain of the Lord's temple will be established
> as the highest of the mountains;
> it will be exalted above the hills,
> and peoples will stream to it.
> Many nations will come and say,
> 'Come, let us go up to the mountain of the Lord,
> to the temple of the God of Jacob.
> He will teach us his ways,
> so that we may walk in his paths.'
> The law will go out from Zion,
> the word of the Lord from Jerusalem.
> He will judge between many peoples
> and will settle disputes for strong nations far and wide.
> They will beat their swords into ploughshares
> and their spears into pruning hooks.
> Nation will not take up sword against nation,
> nor will they train for war any more.
> Everyone will sit under their own vine
> and under their own fig-tree,
> and no one will make them afraid,
> for the Lord Almighty has spoken.
>
> (Micah 4:1–4)

Hope swelled from the hearts and voices thronging the cathedral this evening, in Naim's ringing prophetic words and the passionate and subversive songs and prayers of Garth and Zoughbi Al-Zoughbi, in the soaring female harmonies of Mendelssohn and the joyous Arabic melodies of the Bethlehem Choir, who made it through Walls and checkpoints to join us in the end, and in the hands clasped high as the chorus of 'We shall overcome' rose and filled the lofty vaults. Hope shone forth like an ocean of stars, like a sea of blazing flames, kindling every heart.

'I'm so glad you're here with me, darling,' I say to Eleanor, holding my pebble over the deep hole at the heart of the olive tree, 'to finish the journey with me.' The journey began for me in the ruins of Ali Salim's house in Al-Khader, the village where George the Palestinian saint, they say, was imprisoned, and it ends here at the cathedral that also bears his name.

'This pebble can be our prayer for Palestine,' I say, 'all the way from London. One small fact on the ground.'

'Come on, Dad,' says Eleanor, smiling. 'Let it go.'

I drop the pebble into the dark recess. We stand together in silence for a few minutes, then walk away. Above the floodlit cloister walls of St George's, the night sky spreads black over the Jerusalem hills.

Epilogue

MEMORY OF THE *Cactus* is an award-winning 2008 documentary by Palestinian film-maker Hanna Musleh which tells the story of three Palestinian villages in the Latrun Valley expropriated by Israel in the 1967 War. Between heart-rending testimonies of elderly Palestinian former inhabitants describing their expulsion and the destruction of their homes, the film follows a group of young Israelis visiting the site, now a recreational area called Canada Park, financed in 1973 by the Jewish National Fund of Canada. Led by Eitan Bronstein, the director of Zochrot, an Israeli NGO that promotes knowledge of the *Nakba* in Israel and supports the return of Palestinian refugees, the visitors observe how telltale stems of cactus plants, used for centuries by Palestinian villagers as boundary markers between plots of land, stubbornly return despite repeated attempts to uproot and eradicate them. Canada Park is presented by Israel's tourist industry as an archaeological site rich in Roman ruins, but the cactus plants are tenacious witnesses to the lost villages of Beit Nuba, Imwas and Yalo which cannot be suppressed.

'How profoundly ironic it is,' said Robert Cohen at the Southwark Cathedral conference on Balfour, 'that we are happy to dismiss the claims of Palestinian refugees to "return" to their land after seventy years. We want them to get over it and move on, not move back. We on the other hand have turned our idea of "exile" and our "right of return" after 2,000 years into our chief claim to majority rule in the land. Maybe in 2,000 years the Palestinians will have a more convincing case. They just need to be more patient. They haven't waited long enough.'

Some people reading this book (if they get this far) may ask, 'Well, OK, this is all very well, but why are *you* so interested in this conflict?

What's *your* stake in the plight of the Palestinian people? What does it matter to *you*? There are any number of answers. As a Brit, I inherit a shared responsibility for the consequences of Britain's actions one hundred years ago. As a Christian, my faith connects me umbilically to the Holy Land, as an inheritor of the spiritual tradition which flows from Christianity's Jewish roots, but I must also acknowledge the heavy burden of the violence perpetrated by Christians against Jews and Muslims down the centuries, which defiles the history of my faith. Or I could talk, as I have not previously, about my dear godmother Karla, a German Jew born in Palestine in the 1920s who emigrated subsequently to England.

But in fact, the answer is much simpler: I am interested in the Palestinian struggle because I have *been* and I have *seen* the reality of the Occupation, the Siege of Gaza, the refugee camps, the settlements and the Wall. And while Israel and its supporters continue to expend every effort to obscure or falsify these realities, it behoves people of conscience everywhere to keep on telling the truth, on behalf of those whose voice is silenced. As we said to Ali Salim and his family in the ruins of their home in Al-Khader, 'We promise to use our voices to tell your story.' If it were me and my family, my people, suffering such oppression, I would want people from other countries to come and see, and to speak up for me and my rights. And sometimes, the difference it can make is palpable – as when the news came through in January of this year that Rasha had been released at last from detention in Turkey and reunited with her family in Greece, largely thanks to Jude's and Arthur's intervention.

On the eve of the Balfour centenary, Robert Cohen published an article on the *Patheos* blogsite, in which he wrote movingly about the 'second Balfour century' which had just begun:

'We know we cannot turn back the clock to a time before Balfour. Whatever the second Balfour century looks like it will include Jews and Arabs living on the land. The question is: will they live as equals and in peace or will they live, as they do today, as oppressed and oppressor? The slogan for the Just Walk has been "Change the Record"; change the record of injustice, end the soundtrack to oppression. Our call is simple, but frustratingly it is also highly contentious: Equal rights for all who call the Holy Land home. Is that a dream? Naive? Impossible? Foolish? Or is it the only possible response to what we are seeing?

. . . Nothing tells me that the future looks better than the past. Nothing tells me that a second Balfour century will not end with more celebrations. When hope is so difficult to find there is only one thing left. We can choose where to walk and who to walk alongside. Each day of the Just Walk to Jerusalem has begun with Words of Hope which end with this thought:

Ambulando solvitur – It will be solved by walking.'[1]

Nine months on, the blisters have gone but hope also seems to have vanished from the horizon. From the Trump administration's opening of a new American embassy in Jerusalem to the horrific massacres on the Gaza border fence of unarmed civilians massing in the Great March of Return, to the Knesset's passing of the widely condemned Jewish Nation-State law, described by *Haaretz* as 'making discrimination constitutional', among other things downgrading Arabic as no longer an official or indigenous language of Israel – this past year has been an *annus horribilis* for Palestinians, a litany of shame and disgrace to mark the 70th anniversary of Israel's creation.

When hope is so difficult to find there is only one thing left. We can choose where to walk and who to walk alongside. I would like to record once more my undying thanks to Amos Trust and to all those – Palestinians, Israelis, Brits and all the other nationalities involved, people of all faiths and none – whose stubborn, generous hope in walking, driving, giving or supporting at close or long range collectively turned the Walk imagined into a reality.

We did put some new facts on the ground: we walked a bloody long way, the apology was made, the solidarity expressed, the hope celebrated – in the teeth of all likelihood.

'Hope,' wrote Walter Wink, 'imagines the future and then acts as if that future is irresistible' and no act born of hope is ever pointless, I believe, in the economy of God. Who knows in the end what 'facts on the ground' our journey will change? Where the reverberations of so many footsteps will finally be heard? Whether mainstream media or official histories bother to record what we did, Palestinians will remember us – a motley band of pilgrims who chose to imagine a better world, a new Jerusalem – and walk towards it.

Acknowledgements

In recognition of the companionship and compassion, courage and dedication, generosity, hope and humour of all the pilgrims of the Just Walk to Jerusalem
10 June – 2 November 2017

Those who walked all the way –
David Cuschieri, Tim Hagyard, Denise Lepore, Naomi Message, Robin Message, Judith Nash, Arthur Pooley, Jack Rose and Cressey Wallwork

And those who walked much, some or a bit of the way, or drove support, or otherwise participated –
Alicja Barton, Hugh Barton, Gemma Bell, Caroline Bone, Peter Bone, Shari Brown, Tracy Buckland, Benedict Butcher, Eleanor Butcher, Jacob Butcher, Joachim Butcher, Nancy Butcher, Liz Cannon, Chris Cant, Jo Cant, Philip Carlin, Phil Davenport, Ann Davison, Annie Delahunty, Jenny Derbyshire, Mary Dobbing, Gaynor Drew, Nick Finlay, Jean Fitzpatrick, Lauren Fitzpatrick, Bruce Francis, Simon Fuller, Anthony Gratrex, Carol Hage, Paul Haines, Jackie Hall, Nive Hall, Ollie Harding, Fatima Helow, Ian Hempshall, Mary Hempshall, Jane Henson, Rev Canon Garth Hewitt, Gill Hewitt, Ronald Hoogland, Neil Irving, Julia Ana Katarina, Quentin Keeling, Sue Keeling, Ralph Keene, Mark Kensett, Steve Kinneavy, Cheryl Kipping, Bridget le Huray, Ingrid van Loo, Alexandra Lort Phillips, Jennipher Marshall-Jenkinson, Lynn McAllister, Rowena Millard, Lilli Miller, Diana Mills, Carol Munro, Regine Nagel, Rachel Nassif, Mel Neale, Brian Newman, Bethan Parkes, Neil Parkinson, Rachel Parkinson, Peter Parsons, Vanessa Pooley, Ben Powell, Ann Pratt, Elisabeth von Rabenau, John Randall, Marie Randall, Stephen Raw, Mike Rose, Millie

Rose, Sarah Rose, Anne Russell, Giedre Sabonyte, Douglas Saltmarshe, Nigel Seaman, Sally Seaman, Lindsey Sharpe, Rod Sharpe, Ivor Sperring, Steve Strong, Brian Wadman, Kevin Warner, Ben Warren, Nick Welsh, Tessa Wilson, Paul Winchester, Helen Woodall and Peter Woodall

With special thanks to the Amos Trust staff and trustees who worked with such belief, generosity and hope to turn the Walk imagined into a reality, and, for his hours, days, weeks and months planning our routes, Jim Stewart

And my particular thanks to my friend and collaborator Chris Rose, Director of Amos Trust, who knew it would be OK

My deepest gratitude also to all our friends in the Holy Land: Sami Awad, Elias Deis and our friends at Holy Land Trust; Dr Abdelfattah Abusrour and our friends at Alrowwad; Jeff Halper and our friends at ICAHD; Daoud Nassar and our friends at Tent of Nations; Dr Zoughbi Al-Zoughbi and our friends at Wi'am, and all the many others whose extraordinary courage, compassion and hope inspire me to seek to emulate their example.

My heartfelt thanks to all those whose extraordinary kindness, belief and generous support have sustained me throughout the Walk and the writing of this book, from conception to completion, even – and perhaps especially – when I felt my feet slipping and my courage failing: All Saints Eco Prayer group; Ascot Community Environment Network Core Group; Ascot Quiet Garden; Ella Bahaire; Rev Dr Anders Bergquist and St John's Wood Church; Rachel Blackamore; Harvey Brough and Clara Sanabras; my mother Rosemary, for her lifelong belief, encouragement, example, love and support; Robert Cohen; Martin Evans; Peggy Guglielmino; my dear pal and partner-in-crime Andy Harrison; Garth Hewitt, whose pioneering example first set me on the road to Jerusalem; Crispin Holland; my two oldest friends Ben Hopkins and Max Jones; Rick Leigh and the Choir of St Luke's Church, West Holloway; Ahmed Masoud and Heather Gardner-Masoud; Ellen Lykke Myrup; Kinross Playreaders; Manal Ramadan and Iain White; Adrian and Judy Reith, with particular thanks for the shoes, which saw me all the way; Tim Richardson; Steve Shaw, whose love and wisdom have been a light on my path over many years; Alan Smith; Deborah Stuart; Caroline Trevor, Peter Phillips and the Tallis Scholars; Bernadette and Paul Burbridge; John Feehan; Rev Dave Tomlinson and Pat Tomlinson and my whole community of St Luke's Church, West Holloway; James Vergis; Peter Wilson; Rev Lucy Winkett and the community of St James's Church, Piccadilly; Alistair Wood; Anne Yarwood of The Imagination Acts; for their great kindness and encouragement in reading my manuscript, Yasmin Alibhai-Brown, Adjoa Andoh, Dr Swee Ang, Patrick Cockburn, Frank Cottrell-Boyce, Brian Eno, Pen Hadow, Jeff Halper, Jeremy Hardy, Simon Mayo, John McCarthy, Rosalind Nashashibi, Rev Canon Mark Oakley, Rev Peter Owen-Jones, Barnaby Phillips, John Simpson, David Suchet and Rev Lucy Winkett; for his extraordinary generosity and hard work in transcribing weeks of my voice memos and his insightful and inspiring encouragement, my dear friend and collaborator Rupert Mason; for his joyful, endlessly buoyant creative vision and unfailing support to me over so many years, my dear friend and mentor Martin Wroe, who has 'had my back' and never stopped believing in me; for her unfailing generosity and belief, keen interest and wonderfully inspiring encouragement and support, my dear friend and collaborator Julia Holden; for their huge support and encouragement, my literary agent Charles Walker and colleagues at United Agents Nicki Stoddart, Christian Ogunbanjo and Florence Hyde; for catching the vision and believing in me through many travails, and for her unfailing patience, forbearance, kindness and hugely heartening encouragement and enthusiasm, my editor Katherine Venn at Hodder and Stoughton, and her whole team, in particular Jessica Lacey; to anyone whom I've inadvertently forgotten to mention, my heartfelt thanks; to all my family, living and dead, for everything you are and have been; and last, beyond words, to my wife Nancy and our children, Benedict, Eleanor, Jacob and Joachim.

Notes

Chapter 1

1. Balfour's memorandum to Lord Curzon, 11 August 1919, file FO/371/4183 in the Public Record Office, cited in Doreen Ingrams, *Palestine Papers 1917-1922: Seeds of Conflict* (London, John Murray, 1972), p.23.

Chapter 2

1. Howard Zinn, *You Can't Be Neutral on a Moving Train: A Personal History of Our Times* (Boston, Beacon Press, 1994, 2002), pp.279-280.

Chapter 3

1. Jonathan Jones, 'Why Rodin's sculpture is Britain's best work of public art', *The Guardian*, 23 March 2010.
2. When I asked him about it, months later, David laughed and said, 'Yes, I was a bit embarrassed about this. Before I left Australia, I'd read on the internet that, if you soak your feet in mercurochrome (iodine), it helps to prevent blisters. The golden reddish tinge disappeared from my skin after a few days, but it took some time for this colour to wear off my toenails! Not sure if it worked but it may have done – as I got my first and only blister in Greece!'

Chapter 4

1. Captain F. Clive Grimwade, *War History of the 4th Battalion The London Regiment (Royal Fusiliers) 1914–1919* (London, Headquarters of the 4th London Regiment, 1922), pp.265–6.
2. James C. Bradford (ed.), *International Encyclopedia of Military History*, (London, Routledge, 2006), p.42.

Chapter 6

1. Sophocles' *Electra*, ll. 860–98, trans. Robin Bond (Christchurch NZ, University of Canterbury, 2015), p.23.

Chapter 8

1. Edward Lear, *Edward Lear in Albania: Journals of a Landscape Painter in the Balkans* (London, Richard Bentley, 1851), p.102.
2. Edward Lear, *The Book of Nonsense*, (London and New York, Frederick Warne and Co. Ltd., 1846).
3. Edward Lear, *More Nonsense, Pictures, Rhymes, Botany, etc.*, (London, Robert John Bush, 1872).
4. Edward Lear, *Nonsense Songs, Stories, Botany, and Alphabets*, (London, Robert John Bush, 1872).

Chapter 9

1. John O'Donohue, *Anam Cara* (London, Bantam Press, Transworld Publishers, 1997), p.14.
2. Thomas Hardy, 'The Darkling Thrush', 'The Graphic Newspaper', 29 December 1900.
3. Revelation 3:20, KJV.
4. Edwin Muir, 'The Way' (*The Labyrinth*, Faber, 1949).

Chapter 10

1. Constantine Cavafy, 'Ithaka' author's translation τα Ποιήματα 1897-1933, (Athens, Ἴκαρος 1984).
2. Cited in Cyril Mango, *Byzantium: The Empire of New Rome* (London, Weidenfeld & Nicholson, 1988), p.74.
3. From a panegyrical ekphrasis on the Hagia Sophia, *Descriptio Sanctae Sophiae*, 11 150-155, by Paulus Silentarius, a poet and official of the imperial court of Justinian, delivered in December 562 or January 563, transl. Peter Bell, *Three Political Voices from the Age of Justinian* (Liverpool, Liverpool University Press, 2009), p.197.
4. Victoria Hammond, *Visions of Heaven: The Dome in European Architecture* (New York, Princeton Architectural Press, 2006), p.165.
5. Procopius, *De Aedificiis*, 1, 1, 11.30, 45-47, translation from William Dalrymple, *From the Holy Mountain: A Journey in the Shadow of Byzantium* (London, HarperCollins, 1997), p.40.

6. *The Russian Primary Chronicle Laurentian Text*, transl. and ed. by Samuel Hazzard Cross and Olgerd P. Sherbowitz-Wetzor (Cambridge, Massachusetts, The Medieval Academy of America, 1953), p.III.
7. Roger Crowley, 'Fading Glory', *Smithsonian*, December 2008, Vol. 39 Issue 9, pp.54-64.
8. Chaim Weizmann, *Trial and Error: The Autobiography of Chaim Weizmann* (New York, Harper, 1949), pp.152-3.
9. *Hansard*, Aliens Bill, HC Debate 10 July 1905, vol. 149, col.155.
10. Theodor Herzl, ed. Raphael Patai, transl. Harry Zohn, *The Complete Diaries of Theodor Herzl*, Vol. 1 (New York and London, Herzl Press and Thomas Yoseloff, 1960), pp.83-4.
11. Edwin Montagu, *Memorandum on the Anti-Semitism of the Present Government*, submitted to Cabinet 23 August 1917, Public Record Office, Cab. 24/24.
12. Edwin Montagu, *ibid.*

Chapter 11

1. Talbot Mundy, *The Lion of Petra* (London, Hutchinson & Co., 1932), p.212; first published in *Adventure* magazine (New York, Ridgeway Company, 1922).
2. Johann Burckhardt, *Travels in Syria and the Holy Land* (London, John Murray, 1822), pp.424-5.
3. Edward Dawson, *Travel through Jordan* (Leominster, Day One Publications, 2010), pp.91ff.
4. Lowell Jackson Thomas, *With Lawrence in Arabia* (London, Hutchinson & Co., 1924), pp.182-6.
5. Petra papyrus transl. Marjaana Vesterinen (Collection of the American Center of Oriental Research, Amman, 2002).
6. *Guide me, O Thou Great Redeemer*, original text by William Williams Pantycelyn, first published in *Mor o Wydr* (Sea of Glass) hymnal, 1762, translated and adapted by Peter Williams, *Hymns on various subjects*, 1771; melody *Cwm Rhondda*, John Hughes, premiered at the Cymanfa Ganu festival, Pontypridd, Wales, 1905.

Chapter 12

1. Nicholas Blincoe, *Bethlehem: Biography of a Town* (New York, Nation Books, 2017), p.57.
2. Robert Cohen, 'Reclaiming the lost Jewish voices of the Balfour Declaration', paper at the Balfour Project conference 'How will we

mark the centenary of the Balfour Declaration?', Southwark Cathedral, London, 5 November 2016.

3. Khaled Juma, 'Oh Rascal Children of Gaza', *Nothing Walks in this Dream* (Amman, Al-Ahliya for Publishing, 2015); originally published on Facebook, 24 August 2014, during Israel's 'Protective Edge' offensive on Gaza, in which 2,251 Palestinians were killed, of whom 1,492 were civilians and 519 were children.

Epilogue

1. Robert Cohen, 'For the children of Palestine the second Balfour century has already begun,' *Patheos*, 1 November 2017.

Index

47Soul, 9, 15

'A Century of Injustice' conference,
    Ramallah, 274–6
Abbas, Mahmoud, President of the State of
    Palestine and the Palestinian National
    Authority and Chairman of the PLO,
    aka Abu Mazen, 17, 239, 253, 254, 278
Abbaye de Notre Dame, Wisques, 49–55
Abusrour, Dr Abdelfattah, 22, 229, 231,
    266–8
ACRI (Association of Civil Rights in Israel),
    212
Adriatic, 105, 117–20, 127, 131
Aeschylus, 139-140
Afghanistan, 41
Al-Ahli Hospital, Gaza, 32, 255, 275
Aida Refugee Camp, Bethlehem, 22, 229–31
Albanian Orthodox Church, 130, 135, 137
Aleppo, 78, 155
Alexander III of Macedon, 'the Great', 160
Alexandroupolis, 170–2, 177
Allenby Bridge, see King Hussein/Allenby
    Bridge crossing
Allenby, Sir Edmund, General, Head of
    British Third Army, Western Front
    (1915-17), Commander of Egyptian
    Expeditionary Force (1917-19), later
    Field Marshal and Viscount Allenby
    of Meggido and Felixstowe, 70-1,
    207-9, 217
Alps, Albanian, 138
Alps, French, Swiss and Italian (Pennine), 88,
    91-104, 106, 107, 111, 139, 227
Alrowwad Cultural and Arts Society, 22, 33,
    34, 231
Amaxades, 167
Amettes, 36, 58-9
Amman, 12, 200-1, 214, 224
Amnesty International, 32, 232
Amos, ancient Hebrew prophet, 13-14
Amos Trust, 2, 3, 9-13, 20-1, 28, 32-4, 193,
    203, 214, 219-21, 229, 237, 240, 255,
    259, 262, 285
Amphipolis, 160-1
Amro, Esa, 246-7

Anatolia, 199
Ancona, x, 105, 120-5, 126
Antalya, 199
Anthemius of Tralles, 189-90
anti-Semitism, 10, 14, 194-5, 243, 293
Aosta, 101, 102, 106, 108
Aosta Valley (Valle d'Aosta), 91, 105, 107,
    108, 111
apartheid, 27, 267, 278
Appian Way, 117
Aqaba, 201, 202, 206, 211
Aquitaine, Eleanor of, 39, 78
Arab Spring, 61
Ardameri, 158
Armenian Orthodox Church, 129
Arras, x, 36, 54, 63, 64-8, 70-1
Al-Arrub aqueduct, 240
Al-Arrub Refugee Camp, Hebron-Jerusalem
    Road, West Bank, 119, 231, 240,
    275
Arsis (refugee project), Thessaloniki, 153-6
Artas, 234
Ashdod (largest Israeli port), 11
Atatürk, Mustafa Kemal, founder of
    Republic of Turkey and first
    President (1923-38), 183, 189
Ateek, Canon Naim, 280-1
Atick, John, 225-228
Al-Atrash, Farid, 232
At-Tuwani, 250, 254
Aube, River, 79
Augustus, first Roman Emperor (BC 27 - AD
    14), 106
Auschwitz, 31
Avignon, Popes of, 57-8
Awad, Dr Mubarak, 30
Awad, Sami, 24, 28-32, 34, 220, 237, 254,
    270, 278

Bailly-le-Franc, 73-4
Balfour, Arthur James, MP for Hertford,
    Prime Minister, Foreign Secretary,
    later 1st Earl of Balfour, 4, 6, 13-14,
    71, 76, 193-5, 235-6, 248, 262, 268,
    283-4, 292
Balfour Declaration, 3-8, 13, 14, 234, 235-6;

apology for, 192, 193, 253, 264, 273, 275;
Arthur Koestler comment on, 3, 163,
    262;
'Balfour Tea Party', *see* Banksy
Boris Johnson comment on, 6;
celebration of, *see* May, Theresa;
centenary of, 3, 5, 203, 229, 252, 254,
    259-60, 262, 267-8, 271, 275, 284,
    285;
Edwin Montagu's opposition to, 195;
failed promise of, 260, 276;
impact of, 3, 4, 241, 248, 252, 261, 268,
    272, 274;
inherent inequality of, 6;
new Balfour Declaration, 255, 272-3;
Palestinian attitude to, 5-6, 220, 232, 241,
    248, 252-3, 260-1, 268, 278;
parallels with Plantation of Ulster, 7;
text, 4-5;
Theresa May's celebration of, 248, 252-3,
    260, 262;
Weizmann, cordite and the Balfour
    Declaration, 243;
where penned, 6, 8;
Balfour, Roderick, 5th (current) Earl of, 235
Banksy, 262-4, 276
Barghouti, Dr Mustafa, leader of the
    Palestine National Initiative, 33
Baroville, 76
Bar-sur-Aube, 72, 76
BBC (British Broadcasting Corporation), 4,
    5, 92, 270
'Beautiful Resistance', 22, 24, 231
Becket, St Thomas, Archbishop of
    Canterbury, 39-40
Bedouin, 24, 203-4, 207-11, 213, 226, 228,
    248-9, 252, 255, 274, 276
Beersheba, 207
Beit Jala, 229
Beit Lahem, *see* Bethlehem
Beit Mirsim, 226-7
Beit Sahour, 225, 228-9, 234, 235, 238, 259,
    278-9
Bektashi, 130, 145
Bergquist, Rev Dr Anders, vicar of St John's
    Wood Church, London, 119, 121, 188
Berişe, Betül, foreign affairs correspondent,
    Cumhuriyet ('Republic') newspaper,
    192-3
besa (traditional Albanian duty of hospitality),
    136
Bethany, *see* Al-Eizariya
Bethlehem (*Arabic* Beit Lahem), 2, 17, 20-5,
    27-9, 31-2, 110, 119, 202, 229-31,
    234, 240, 260, 262, 264, 269-71,
    274-6, 278, 281, 294
Bethlehem: Biography of a Town, 240, 294
Bethlehem Choir, 281
Bethlehem Unwrapped festival, 21-2, 28

Bet Lahem Live festival, 17, 27-8
Birket esh-Shatt (Al-Arrub Reservoir), 240
Black and Tans, 7
Blue Mosque of Sultanahmet, 186, 188-9
Bologna, 112, 120
Borough Market/London Bridge terrorist
    attack, 2, 55
Bosredon, Pierre de, Commander of the
    Order of St John, Mormant, 86-7
Botswana, 57
Bourg-St-Pierre, 99
Bovernier, 92-3
'Brexit' (British exit from European Union),
    6, 7, 35, 41, 46
Brindisi, 125
British Mandate in Palestine, 4, 7, 240-1
Brodrick, Ian, 34, 199
Bucknall, Harry, 34
Burckhardt, Johann Ludwig, Swiss explorer
    and orientalist, 206-7
Burghers of Calais (Rodin sculpture), 42-3
Buruq Uprising (Arab Riots), 244-5
Butcher, 2nd Lieutenant Clarence Edward,
    63-4, 65-70
Büyükçekmece/Batikoy, 183
Byzantine/Eastern Roman Empire, 74, 76,
    78, 87, 128, 129, 130, 141, 151, 152,
    160-1, 172, 173, 185, 186, 187-92,
    209-10, 240
Byzantium (original name of Constantinople,
    later Istanbul), 141, 185-92, *see also*
    Constantinople, Istanbul

Cairo, 71, 94, 265
Calais, 36, 42, 43, 46, 47;
    Pas-de-Calais, 49, 63, 65
Camino de Santiago, the Way of St James,
    50, 75
Canaan/Canaanite, 217, 221, 226
Canada Park, *see* Latrun Valley
Canterbury, x, xviii, 15, 34, 39, 40
'Carlos the Jackal', 79
Carmel settlement, 249-52
'Cast Lead' attack on Gaza, 5, 181
Castel San Pietro di Terme, 112-13, 117, 120,
    126
Castro, Fidel, 50
Cattolica, 118, 126
Cave/Tomb of the Patriarchs, Hebron, 238,
    243, 244, 246
Cenotaph, 4, 6
Cesena, 118
Champagne region, 72, 73-89;
    Henry I, Count of Champagne, 78, 124;
    Henry II, Count of Champagne, 74;
    Hugh, Count of Champagne, 77
'Change the Record', slogan for Just Walk to
    Jerusalem, 3, 9, 161, 214, 228, 284-5
Charlemagne, 94

Charles V, Holy Roman Emperor (1519–56), 58
Châteauvillain, 72, 84
Châtillon, 106, 108, 109
Christian Peacemaker Teams, 245
Churchill, Winston Leonard Spencer, MP for Dundee, Secretary of State for the Colonies, later Prime Minister, 7
Circuit des Lavoirs, 88
Cistercian Order, 77, 79, 80, 81
Clairvaux, 72
Clairvaux Abbey, 77–83
Clairvaux Forest, 76–7
Claudius, Roman Emperor (AD 41–54), 91
Cohen, Robert, writer and Amos trustee, 12–15, 242–3, 255, 272–3, 283–4
Collage of God, The (by Mark Oakley), 97
Colombey-les-Deux-Églises, 76
Combatants for Peace, 254
Combe des Morts, 101–2
Conservative Friends of Israel, 10
Constantine I, 'Constantine the Great', Roman emperor (AD 306–337), 73, 123, 141, 151–2, 186
Constantine II, Roman emperor, 188
Constantinople (originally Byzantium, later Istanbul), 87, 112, 173, 190, 191
Convent of Hortus Conclusus, 234
Convent of St Mary Coronata, 117
Corbyn, Jeremy, 1, 8, 61, 235, 276
Corfu, 127
Corinth, 127
Crusade, First, 78
Crusade, Second, 78, 79, 124
Crusade, Third, 40, 74
Curzon, George Nathaniel, 1st Marquess Curzon of Kedleston, former Viceroy of India, Foreign Secretary (1919–25), 6
Cyprus, 10, 11, 85, 199

Damascus, 40, 78, 147, 202, 207
Dampierre, 88–9, 99
Dardanelles, Strait of the, 179
Darwish, Mahmoud, 248
Dead Sea, 201, 202, 211–12, 213, 214, 215, 216
Deir Sneid, 4
Democratic Unionist Party (DUP), 1, 7–8
Department for International Development (DfID), 214, 273
Divion, 60
Dover, x, xviii, 11, 38–41, 42
Dranse, River, 91, 92, 97, 98
Durrës, xi, 125–32, 146, 150

EAPPI (Ecumenical Accompaniment Programme in Palestine and Israel), 94, 215, 245

East Jerusalem, *see* Jerusalem
Easter Rising, 7
edelweiss, 99
Edirne, 167, 170, 172, 180
Edward III, 42
Egypt, 4, 40, 71, 94, 107, 145, 188–9, 224, 241, 265
Al-Eizariya, 62, 235
Elbasan, 137, 140, 141, 143
Elizabeth I, 47
Erdogan, Recep Tayyip, President of Turkey since 2014, previously Prime Minister (2003–2014), 179, 180–1, 187
EU (European Union), 7
Eurotunnel, 43, 46
Evros, River and border crossing, 179
Excelsior, poem (Longfellow), 102–3

Faenza, 117, 126
Fano, 118–19
Fateh, 17, 192, 265, 273, 274–5
Feres, 172
Field of the Cloth of Gold, The, 46
Finsbury Park mosque terrorist attack, 55, 58
Floringhem, 59–60
Focara headland, 118, 119
Foreign and Commonwealth Office (FCO), 6, 8, 272
Forêt de l'Orient, 73
Franco, Francisco, 50
Frashëri, Neem, Albanian poet, 136–7
Frederick I, 'Barbarossa', Holy Roman Emperor (1155–90), 78
'Free Speech on Israel' (FSOI) campaign group, 10, 14
Friends of Al-Aqsa, 9

Galerius, Roman Emperor (AD 305–311), 151, 153
Galilee, 20, 215, 238
Gallipoli, 179
Gambia, The, 48, 62
Gandhi, 30, 276
Gaulle, Charles, President of France, 42, 76
Gaza, 6, 30, 85, 100, 231, 294;
    2010 aid convoy to Gaza, 181–2;
    2010 flotilla to Gaza, *see* Mavi Marmara;
    Gaza Beach, 188;
    blockade of, 3, 4, 5, 11, 14, 94, 236, 259–260, 262, 265, 266, 273, 275, 284;
    border of, 267;
    'Cast Lead' attack on Gaza, *see* 'Cast Lead';
    DfID programmes in, *see* DfID;
    Erez crossing, 255;
    Escape From Gaza (BBC radio drama), 4–5;
    Great March of Return, 285;

(Gaza *cont.*)
 Jewish Boat to Gaza, 10-11;
 Leane Mohamad 'Birds not Bombs'
  speech on Gaza, 10;
 living conditions, 3, 5, 33, 94-5, 257;
 map, 224;
 massacres, 285;
 Oh rascal children of Gaza (poem by
  Khaled Juma), 259;
 Palestinians from Gaza denied freedom of
  movement, 12;
 Rafah crossing, 4, 175, 265;
 restriction of exports from Gaza,
  25;
 settlers from Gaza, 250;
 Third Battle of Gaza, 207, 209;
 tunnels from Egypt into Gaza, 145, 188;
 wall enclosing Gaza, 255-6, 257-8, 285;
 wars and attacks against, 3, 5, 32, 181,
  257, 266-7, 269;
 zookeepers in Gaza, 239;
Gaza City, 32;
Gethsemane, Garden of, *see* Jerusalem
Golan Heights, 3, 260
Golem, 132
Golgotha, 73
Great March of Return, 285
Great St Bernard Pass, 91
Greek Orthodox Church, 21, 125, 162, 163,
 177, 190-1, 270
Greenbelt Festival, 11, 20, 27, 28
Grenfell Tower Fire, 48
Guardian, The, newspaper, 32, 42, 138, 176,
 192, 264
Gueux, Claude, 82
Guines, 36, 47, 49, 62
Gülen, Fethnullah, 180-1
Gush Etzion settlement, 28
Guzul, 183

Haaretz newspaper, 28, 244, 264, 276,
 285
Hadow, Pen, 34
Hadrian, Roman Emperor (117-38), 123
Haganah, Jewish paramilitary organisation in
 Palestine during Mandate, 217, 245
Hagia Sophia (Istanbul), 112, 129, 151, 185,
 186, 188-92
Hagia Sophia (Thessaloniki), 153
Haifa, 199
Hainault, Philippa of, 43
Hall, Nive, 20, 219
Hall, Philip, OBE, British Consul-General in
 Jerusalem, 255, 271-4
Halper, Jeff, 24
Hamas, 17, 29, 192, 256, 258, 265, 273
Hannibal, 92, 94, 105, 120
Al-Haq (Palestinian human rights
 organisation), 213

hawiya (ID card compulsorily issued to
 Palestinians), 5
Heaney, Seamus, 52, 62, 75
Hebron, 17, 28, 29, 119, 212, 224, 226, 227,
 229, 232, 233, 238, 239-45, 247, 248,
 254, 261, 264, 266, 268, 274, 278;
 Hebron massacre, 1929, 244-5;
 Hebron massacre, 1994, 243-4;
Henry II, 39-40
Henry VIII, 46
Herzl, Theodor, founder of the Zionist
 Organisation, playwright, journalist
 and author of *Der Judenstaat*, 193,
 195
Heschel, Rabbi Abraham Joshua, 14, 100
Hewitt, Garth, 9, 10, 15, 270, 281
Hijaz Railway, 202
Hildegard von Bingen, 51
Hippodrome of Constantine, 186, 188
Holocaust, 10, 11, 14, 26, 31, 269
Holy Land, 3, 13, 15, 20, 22, 25, 27, 32, 33,
 37, 74, 78, 85, 123, 207, 208, 215, 236,
 238, 254, 260, 262, 270, 272, 277,
 280, 281, 284, 285
Holy Land Trust, 24-7, 29, 31-2, 203, 220-1,
 237, 239-40, 262, 264, 285
Hopkins, Ben, 67, 185
Horse Guards Parade, 6
Hoxha, Enver, Albanian head of state (1944-
 85), 137
Hugo, Victor, 60, 82
Hussein ibn Ali, Sharif of Mecca, 71

Iasmos, 167
Imola, 117
Incarnation (of Christ), 161-5
Indiana Jones, 20, 122, 204, 205
Indiana Jones and the Last Crusade (1989 film,
 starring Harrison Ford, directed by
 Steven Spielberg), 204
Innocent, Pope (1130-43), 77-8
Intercontinental Hotel, Bethlehem, 264, 266
International Holocaust Remembrance
 Alliance, 10
Intifada, First, 30, 232, 233, 278-9
Intifada, Second, 25, 230
Ipsala, 180
Iran, 25, 26
Iraq, 41, 105, 167, 168, 185
Iraqis, 155, 167-168, 202
Irene, see Gaza
Irish War of Independence, 7
'Iron Harvest', 75
Isidore of Miletus, 189-90
ISIS/Daesh, 48, 94, 167
Israel, 3, 4, 95, 99, 113, 238, 239, 242, 249,
 259, 265, 279, 284;
 2014 war on Gaza, 32;
 Albania's attitude to, 136;

Association of Civil Rights in Israel, *see* ACRI;
attacks on Gaza, 266;
attitude to Iran, 26;
barred to Palestinians, 12, 199;
barring Palestinian access to Dead Sea, 212;
biblical kingdom of, 194;
'Blue Line' (war front with Lebanon), 199;
border with Jordan, 211;
'Cast Lead' attack on Gaza, *see* 'Cast Lead';
collective punishment of Palestinians, 17;
Conservative Friends of, 12;
control of Palestinian Authority, 267;
creation of, 4, 235, 236, 260, 273-4, 280, 285;
criticism of, 10, 14, 193, 274;
dispute with passengers of *Mavi Marmara*, 188;
Dissident Israeli voices, 10-11;
Ecumenical Accompaniment Programme in Palestine and, *see* EAPPI
government of, 19;
house demolitions carried out by, 7, 18-20, 23, 24, 28, 250-1;
human rights violations, 232, 266-8;
Israeli army, *see* Israeli Defence Force;
Israeli blockade of Gaza, *see* Gaza;
Israeli military detention and deportation of activists, 11;
Israeli naval attacks on Free Gaza vessels, 11;
Israeli occupation of Palestinian Territories, *see* Occupation
Israel/Palestine, 20, 21, 262, 272-3;
Israeli Separation Wall, *see* Wall;
Knesset, 285;
Law of Return, 5;
maps, 16, 224;
Palestinian attitude to, 250, 267-8, 277;
Palestinians imprisoned for working without a permit in, 19;
perception in Palestinian media, 269;
responsibility for Sabra and Shatila massacre, 114;
theft of Palestinian resources, 212-213, 236;
Theresa May's view of, *see* May, Theresa;
The Times of Israel (newspaper), 28;
tourist industry, 283;
trauma of collective psyche of, 26, 31, 32;
UK government support for, 274;
Israeli Committee Against House Demolitions (ICAHD), 24
Israeli Defence Force (IDF), 12, 23, 27, 31,
51, 113, 212, 230, 235, 250, 256, 258, 264, 266, 268;
destruction of Palestinian crops by, 23;
house demolitions, 2, 24;
intimidation and violence in Dheisheh Refugee Camp, 231, 233-4;
origins, 245;
presence and role in Hebron, 243-8, 261;
role in Sabra & Shatila massacre, 113-14;
Issogne, 108, 109-111
Istanbul, xi, 129, 130, 146, 151, 180, 182-97, 198, 214, 275
Ivrea, 106, 110, 111

Jabaliya Refugee Camp, Gaza, 4
Al-Jabari, Nidal, 247-8
Jaeger, Ben, 254
Jaffa/Yaffa Riots, 7
James I, 7
Jeanne d'Arc, 75
Al-Jehali, Suleiman, 249-54
Al-Jehali, Tariq, 248-53
Jericho, 20, 201, 215, 219-22, 235,
Jerusalem, 20, 29, 51, 62, 63, 159, 240, 264, 266, 271, 282;
access barred to Palestinians from Gaza, 12;
Al-Aqsa Mosque/Compound, 238, 254, 270, 279;
American embassy, 285;
Anglican mission/St George's Cathedral, 15, 194, 271;
British capture and rule of, 7, 71;
British Consulate-General, Jerusalem, 255, 271-4;
capital of future Palestinian state/Al-Quds, 33;
Church of the Holy Sepulchre, 20, 73, 123;
Confraternity of Pilgrims to Jerusalem, 34;
Crusader kingdom, 40, 74, 78, 85;
destination for Just Walk, 2, 3, 9, 14, 33, 34, 37, 61, 89, 95, 124, 132, 142, 192, 259, 261, 262, 285;
destroyed villages, 232;
Dome of the Rock, 230;
Dominus Flevit, Church of, 279;
East Jerusalem, 3, 24, 30, 33, 260, 271;
East Jerusalem YMCA, *see* YMCA;
Gethsemane, Garden of, 20, 271;
Heavenly Jerusalem, 152;
Hebron-Jerusalem Road, 119, 240, 264;
home of San Ciriaco, *see* San Ciriaco;
Jerusalem Syndrome, 225, 276;
Jewish Cemetery, 279;

Kidron Valley, 279;
Knights of the Hospital of St John of
    Jerusalem/Knights Hospitaller, 84-7;
Lions' Gate, 129, 280;
maps, 16, 224;
mountains of, 222;
Mount of Olives, 20, 254, 270, 279-80;
new Jerusalem, 285;
Old City, 254;
pilgrimage destination, 15, 104, 118, 215;
prophecy of Micah, 281;
Sabeel Ecumenical Liberation Center,
    280;
shared city, 14, 33, 280;
Silwan Necropolis, 279;
Temple Mount, 238, 245, 279;
Via Dolorosa, 23, 280;
wilderness of, 226
'Jesus trail', 20, 32, 74, 215
Jewish Nation-State Law, 285
Jews, 9, 212, 241, 243;
Albanian sanctuary for Jews in WWII,
    135-6;
attacks on Jews during Second Crusade,
    78;
attitudes in British Cabinet to Jews
    during WWI, 193-5;
civil, political and religious rights
    affirmed in New Balfour Declaration,
    272-3;
coexistence with other Abrahamic faiths,
    51, 61-2, 121-2, 238;
forced conversion of Jews in Ancona,
    124;
Jewish Boat to Gaza, see Gaza;
Jewish critiques of Israel's actions, 14;
Jews for Justice for Palestinians, see JJP
massacres of Jews in Buruq Uprising,
    244-5;
Orthodox Jews, 29, 238, 243, 246;
patients at Hospital of St John, 85;
rights and political status affirmed in
    Balfour Declaration, 5-6;
Russian persecution of Jews, 194-5;
'self-hating Jews', 10;
threat from American Zionist Christians,
    26-7;
tradition of dissent, 13;
violence against Jews perpetrated by
    Christians, 284;
'Wrong Kind of Jews', 13-14;
JJP (Jews for Justice for Palestinians), 9, 10,
    14
Johnson, Boris, MP, Foreign Secretary, 6, 43,
    254, 267, 272
Jones, Max, 105
Jordan, 12, 25, 119, 186, 187, 199-217, 224,
    231, 241, 259, 261, 270, 280
Jordan Valley, 63, 226, 274

Jubran, Husam, 231-2, 233-4, 278
Julian, 'the Apostate', Roman Emperor
    (361-3), 123-4
Justinian I, 'the Great', Eastern Roman
    Emperor (AD 527-565), 186, 189-190

kanun (traditional Albanian laws or ethical
    code), 136
Kavajë, 137-8
Kavala (refugee camp), 167
Kensett, Mark, 221, 245
Keşan, 177, 179-181, 182
Kfar Etzion settlement, 240
Al-Khader, 2, 17-19, 28, 32, 182, 282,
    284
Al-Khazneh, 'The Treasury' of King Aretas
    IV, 206-9
Khreitoun Valley, 232
King's Highway, 201-2, 211
King Hussein/Allenby Bridge crossing, 12,
    200, 215-19
King Jr, Rev Dr Martin Luther, 14, 30
Kipi/Peplos border crossing (from Greece to
    Turkey), 171, 175-7
Knights Templar, 85
Koestler, Arthur, see Balfour Declaration

Labour Party, 1, 10, 232
Lac du Der, 73
Lagos, 167-8
Lake Geneva, 91
Latrun Valley, 283
Law of Return, 5
Lawrence of Arabia (1962 film, starring Peter
    O'Toole, directed by David Lean),
    201, 210
Lawrence, Colonel Thomas Edward, archae-
    ologist, soldier, diplomat and writer,
    202, 207-9
Lear, Edward, 130-1, 137, 143
Lentilles, 72, 73, 74-5
Le Pen, Marine, 48
Liberal Democrat Party (Lib Dems), 1
Librazhd, 143, 146-7
Livy (Roman historian), 92
Lloyd George, David, MP for Carnarvon
    Boroughs, Prime Minister (1916-22),
    later 1st Earl Lloyd-George of
    Dwyfor, 71, 193-4
London, 1-15, 33, 42-3, 48, 71, 91, 94-5,
    100, 119, 180, 192, 235, 258, 259, 271;
Balfour Centenary celebrations, 235,
    237;
building replica Wall, 21-2, 28;
destination for future pilgrimage from
    Palestine, 221;
Down and Out in Paris and London
    (George Orwell memoir), 146;
East End, 195;

Regent's Park, 191;
starting point for Just Walk, 76, 89, 120,
186, 241, 248, 253, 269, 272, 275,
276, 282
London Regiment, 64-6

Macron, Emmanuel, President of France, 48
Madagascar, 56
Magi, Journey of, 25, 34
Malkala, 181
Malta, 85, 260
Manchester, 2, 13;
Manchester University, 105, 243
Mandolini, Laura, 119
Manger Square, Bethlehem, 268-71
Marmara, Sea of, 182, 183
Martigny, 91-2, 97, 108
Mary I, 'Bloody Mary', 47
Masoud, Ahmed, writer, academic and Amos
trustee, 4, 5, 9, 12, 13, 32, 33, 94-6,
145, 218, 258
Matterhorn, 91
Mavi Marmara, 181-2, 187, 188
Mawtini ('My Homeland'), old Palestinian
national anthem, 240, 270, 278
May, Theresa -
celebration of Balfour Centenary, 235,
236, 237, 252-3;
loses majority in general election, 1;
open letter to, 254, 259-62, 273;
pact with DUP, 1, 7 8;
presentation of New Balfour Declaration
to, 272-3;
speech at Conservative Friends of Israel
meeting, 10;
McCabe Pilgrimages, 48, 62, 63
Medina, 202, 207
Mehmet II, 'the Conqueror', Sultan of the
Ottoman Empire (1444-6 and 1451-
81), 85, 87
Merkel, Angela, Chancellor of Germany, 76
Micah, prophet, 281
Michelangelo, 115-6
Monastery of St George, Jordan Valley, 63
Mont Blanc, 91
Monte Rosa, 91
Moreb, Mahdi, 245-6
Mormant, 72, 84-7;
Maison-Dieu de Mormant, 84-7
Moses, 194, 201, 204
Mount Hermon, 52, 216
Mount of Olives, *see* Jerusalem
Mousa, Ali Salim, 2, 17-20, 32, 282, 284
Musleh, Hanna, 283

Nabataean civilisation, 201, 204-10
Nakba (catastrophe), 4, 29, 200, 231, 283
Napoleon (Napoleon Bonaparte), Emperor of
the French (1804-14), 79, 81, 91, 94

Nassar, Daoud, 23, 32
Nativity Church, Bethlehem, 20, 215
NATO (North Atlantic Treaty Organisation),
61, 179
Nazareth, 20, 238, 275
Near East Council of Churches, 275
Negev Desert, 255, 274
Netanyahu, Binyamin, Prime Minister of
Israel, 235, 237, 260, 265
Netiv Ha'Ashara, 255-6
New York Times, The, newspaper, 24, 48
Next Big Think, The, 56
Noli, Fan, Albanian priest, politician and
writer, 137
Normandy, 40, 46, 63
Northern Ireland, 7
Nunc Dimittis, 104

Obelisk of Theodosius, 188
Occupation of Palestinian Territories by
Israel, 3, 9, 14, 18, 19, 20-30, 32, 34,
48, 62, 96, 110, 131, 164, 203, 227-9,
231, 232, 236, 238, 239, 243, 247-50,
252, 260, 262, 268, 273, 275, 278,
280, 283, 284
Occupied Palestinian Territories (OPT), 5,
28, 85, 94, 259, 271
Olham, 36, 61, 63
One-State Solution, 143
Open Bethlehem (film by Leila Sansour),
32
Orsières, 91, 97-8, 108
Orwell, George, *Down and Out in Paris and
London*, 91
Oslo Accords, 213, 217
Oslo Peace Process, 25
Ospedale della Pietà, 114
Ottoman Empire, 23, 51, 71, 85, 128, 130-1,
137, 145, 152, 173, 183, 184, 188,
194, 207-8, 217, 240, 244, 268,
280
Outines, 73

Paisley, Ian, 1
Pajova, 141-2
Pale of Settlement, 194-5
Palestine, 2, 15, 18, 79, 94, 117, 119, 164, 187,
192, 195, 197, 230, 232, 235, 245, 248,
260, 264, 265, 268, 269, 271, 282,
284;
advocacy initiatives for, 21-2, 28, 32-5,
237;
arrival in, 219-22, 261;
Artists for Palestine UK, 9, 12;
British conquest of, 4, 71, 207-9, 263;
British High Commissioner for, *see*
Samuel, Sir Herbert;
British promise to establish 'a national
home for the Jewish people' in, 4;

(Palestine *cont.*)
British strategic interest in, 194;
British withdrawal from, 4;
communities of hope, 22-4;
compared to Plantation of Ulster, 7;
disregard for the wishes of the 'present inhabitants', 6;
dog ownership in, 238-9;
Ecumenical Accompaniment Programme in Palestine and Israel, *see* EAPPI;
ethnic cleansing of, 29, 241, 258;
Jewish return to, 194;
Kairos Palestine, 27;
landscape, flora and fauna of, 139, 225-8;
maps, 16;
McCabe Pilgrimages to, 48, 62, 63;
'non-Jewish communities' in, 4;
non-violence movement, 25-7, 29-31, 247, 252, 275;
oasis of Palestine, 222;
Palestine/Israel, 272-3;
Palestine National Initiative, 33;
Palestine Solidarity Campaign, *see* PSC;
Palestine sunbird, 227;
Roman remains in, 234, 240, 283;
setting for the Incarnation, 20-1, 74, 123, 165, 215, 216, 238, 277;
solidarity movement in UK, 236;
statehood not recognised by UK, 12, 262, 276;
walking in Palestine, 225-8, 234, 240-1, 274, 275
Palestine Broadcasting Corporation (PBC), 235-237, 254, 268-269
Palestine Marathon, 225-228
Palestinian Authority, 25, 185-6, 212, 235, 239, 267
Palestinian Medical Relief Society, 33
Palestinians, 3, 6, 9, 18, 23, 79, 85, 188, 193, 216, 219, 262, 265, 266, 269, 270, 272, 273, 274, 275, 277, 280, 283, 284, 285;
advocacy projects on behalf of, 32-3, 237, 275;
American attitudes to, 26;
attitude to Balfour Declaration, *see* Balfour Declaration;
barred from travelling through Israel, 12, 199;
black Palestinians, 220;
blamed for conflict, 267-8;
British-Palestinians, 10, 200;
Palestinian Centre for the Study of Non-Violence (PCSN), 30;
century of suffering precipitated by Balfour Declaration, 3, 18, 22, 32, 220, 236, 241, 248, 251, 252, 260, 261, 269, 273, 275, 278, 284;

children, 3, 10, 17, 19, 23, 114, 212, 221-2, 230, 241, 247, 248, 257, 258, 259, 261, 263, 266, 275, 276; *see also* Alrowwad;
Christian Palestinians, 22-32, 51, 228, 229, 238;
coexistence with Israelis, 51, 61-62, 107-8, 121, 232;
collective punishment by Israel, 17, 28, 31, 232;
compulsory ID cards, *see* Hawiya;
cuisine, 9, 11, 12, 22, 277;
Palestinian Delegate to the UK, Dr Manuel Hassassian, 12;
demolition of Palestinian houses, 2, 17-20, 23, 24, 28, 87, 182, 251, 274, 275, 284;
denied access to Dead Sea, 211-13;
disappointment with Oslo Peace Accords, 25;
driven into exile in *Nakba*, 4;
economy, 30, 62-3, 212, 238, 278-9;
Palestinian flag, 9, 172, 183, 185, 214, 227, 264;
'Palestinian Gandhi', 24;
hunger strike prisoners, 17;
Jewish support for, 14, 24;
Jews for Justice for Palestinians, *see* JJP;
keys of houses, 4, 229-31;
landscape, flora and fauna, *see* Palestine;
living conditions in Gaza, 3;
living as refugees, 5, 22, 29, 113, 114, 202, 231-3, 236, 240, 241, 242, 261, 283;
loss of land maps, 1948-2010, 16;
Palestinian Mission to the UK, 9;
music, 9, 11-12, 15, 240, 242, 270, 276, 278, 280, 281;
olive oil, *see* Zaytoun;
Palestinian parliament, 33;
restriction of movement, 25, 33, 94, 95, 199, 215, 216, 220;
right of return denied, 3, 4, 5, 33, 35, 94-6, 230;
Right to Movement (activist group), *see* Palestine Marathon;
statehood, 7, 33, 233, 236, 241, 254, 262, 267, 276, 278;
victims of British *realpolitik*, 193;
Palfest (Palestinian Festival of Literature), 12
Palmach, *see* Haganah
Panagia Kosmosoteira, Monastery of, 172-3
Papua New Guinea, 56-7
Paraguay, 117
Paris, 2, 64, 79, 190
Parliament Square, 2, 8, 42
Paths to Peace Centre, *see* Netiv Ha'Ashara
Paul the Silentiary, 190
Peqin, 137, 144
Peristera, 158-9

Persod, 111
Petra, 201, 204-10
Phalangists (Lebanese Maronite Christian militias), 113-4
HRH Prince Philip, the Duke of Edinburgh, 6
Philip I, King of France, 46
Philip II, King of Spain, 47
Philip II, King of France, 74
Philippines, The, 48, 117
Piacenza, 113, 117
Picardy, 63
Pierini, Don Valter, 121-5
PLO (Palestine Liberation Organisation), 276
Pont Saint Martin, 106, 111
Procopius, 190
PSC (Palestine Solidarity Campaign), 9, 232

Al-Quds (Jerusalem), 33, 118, 275

Rachel's Tomb, 231
Raft of the Medusa, The, 115
Ramadan, Jihad, 232-3
Ramallah, 12, 33, 235, 238, 247, 254, 268, 274, 276, 278
Ranchicourt, 60-1
Really Good (sculpture by David Shrigley), 1
Rhodes, 85-7
Rhodope Mountains and region, 167-70
Rhone, River, 91, 93
Richard the Lionheart, 40, 50, 74
Rift Valley/Jordan Rift/Dead Sea Rift, 201, 216, 226
Rimini, 117, 118
Rodolivos, 161
Roma (Romani), 98, 165
'Roots' forum, 237-8
Rose, Chris, director of Amos Trust, 11, 34, 40, 93, 103, 106, 107, 109, 140, 142, 144, 186, 197, 200, 214, 215, 218, 219, 237, 240, 242, 253, 254, 255, 258, 262, 264, 265, 270, 273, 274, 275, 276, 278
Rothschild, Lionel Walter, 2nd Baron Rothschild, banker, politician, zoologist and leading Zionist, recipient of Balfour Declaration, later President of the Board of Deputies of British Jews, 195
Rothschild, Nathaniel Charles Jacob (current Lord Rothschild), 235
Rotonda of Hagios Giorgios, Thessaloniki, 151-3
Route de Podemainge, 98

Sabra and Shatila massacres, 99, 113-114
Sa'ir, 240-2, 261
Saladin, Sultan of Egypt, 40, 74
Samaria, 26
Samothrace, 170-1

Samuel, Sir Herbert Louis, Liberal MP, Home Secretary during Easter Rising of 1916, 1st British High Commissioner for Palestine, later 1st Viscount Samuel, 7
San Ciriaco (Judas Cyriacus), Bishop of Ancona, 123-4
Sansour, Leila, Palestinian film-maker and CEO of Open Bethlehem campaign, 22, 32
Santa Maria della Pietà, 114-16
Sarajevo, 115
Sarkozy, Nicolas, President of France (2007-12), 76
Savoy/Savoie, County and Kingdom of, 101, 106
Sderot, 255-9
Secker, Glyn, 10, 11, 14
Sembrancher, 91, 92, 93, 96-7
Senigallia, 119-20, 126
Settlers, Israeli, 7, 17-19, 28, 203, 213, 233, 235, 237-9, 244-6, 249-51, 261, 278
Sharon, Ariel, Israeli Defence Minister, later Prime Minister, 114
Sharp, Professor Gene, 30
Shawamreh, Salim, 24
Shkumbin, River, 143-7
Shlaim, Avi, 10
Shrigley, David (creator of *Really Good* sculpture), 1
Shroud Maker, The, 32
Six-Day War of 1967, 217, 283
Skanderbeg Mountains, 138-9
SNP (Scottish National Party), 1
Somme, Battle of the, 63-5, 69
South Africa, 27, 68, 278
Southwark Cathedral, the Cathedral and Collegiate Church of St Saviour and St Mary Overie, 15, 242, 283
St Benoît-Joseph Labre, 58-9
St Bernard of Clairvaux, 77-9; Fountain of St Bernard, 77; Rule of St Bernard, 81; Saint-Bernard Stream, 80
St Bernard of Menthon, 91, 1-2; Hospice du St Bernard, 99, 1-4; St Bernard dogs, 102-3
St George, 17, 151, 157, 282
St George's Cathedral, *see* Jerusalem
St Helena, 73, 123
St Jacques, 75
St James's Piccadilly, 21-2, 28
St Luke's Church, West Holloway, London, 89, 112, 125, 163, 271
St Martin-in-the-Fields, 2
St Paul, 152, 160
St Simeon Stylites, 57
St Théodule, 92-3

Storrs, Colonel Sir Ronald, Military Governor of Jerusalem, then Civil Governor of Jerusalem and Judaea, 7
Suleiman I, 'the Magnificent', Sultan of the Ottoman Empire (1520–66), 85, 183, 279
Sumud Freedom Camp, 254
Syria, 25, 35, 94, 105, 160, 187, 197, 202, 211, 216, 224, 231, 241, 261
Syrians, 105, 154-156, 196-197, 207

Taybeh beer, 229, 270
Tel Aviv, 20, 136, 219, 224
Tel Rumeida settlement, 244, 246-7
Tent of Nations, 23
Therma Loutri Traianopolis, 172
Therouanne, 36, 55-8
Thessaloniki, 130, 147, 151-7, 171, 275
Thomas, Mark, 15
Thrace, 166, 173, 175, 176, 179
Tirana, 130, 133, 138, 145, 146, 147, 148
Tour de France, 76
Trafalgar Square, 1-3
Trans-Aegean pipeline, 166, 169
True Cross, 73, 123
Trump, Donald, President of USA, 38, 192, 263, 285
Tuqu, 234-5, 236, 260
Tuqu'ur, 225
Two-State Solution, 137, 278

Ulster, 1, 7
UN (United Nations), 5, 16, 169, 230
UN Declaration of Human Rights, 5
UNRWA (United Nations Relief and Works Agency for Palestine Refugees in the Near East), 17, 230-2

Valley of the Siq, 204
Vasilika, 159
Venice, 114-16, 128
Via Egnatia, 130, 131, 132, 133, 139, 141, 142, 143, 144, 146, 153, 166, 168, 180
Via Emilia, 112, 117
Via Flaminia, 117, 118, 121
Via Francigena, 34, 55, 76, 84, 86, 92, 99, 106, 108, 117
Victor Emmanuel II, 'Le Roi du Savoie', King of Italy (1861-78), 106
Vladimir, Prince of Kiev, 190

Wadi Jihar, 225-6
Wadi Musa, 204, 208
Wall/Separation Wall, 10, 18, 21-3, 28, 32, 33, 110, 221, 230, 231, 234, 236, 237, 262-4, 266, 275, 281, 284
Walled Off Hotel, 262-4

Weizmann, Chaim, President of the Zionist Organisation, academic biochemist and first President of Israel, 13, 193, 242-3
Welsh, Nick, 219, 221, 255
West Bank, 3, 14, 17, 30, 33, 46, 153, 203, 215, 235, 238, 239, 259, 260, 270, 272;
    access barred to Dead Sea shoreline, 211-13;
    Amos Trust partners, 34;
    border region with Jordan, 200, 201;
    Christian population, 229;
    haven for refugees fleeing the Nakba, 29;
    Israelis forbidden from entering, 28;
    map, 224;
    Masar Ibrahim-al-Khalil (the Abraham Trail), 225-8;
    occupation by Israel, see Occupation;
    ophthalmic care, 85;
    refugee camps, 117, 231-4;
    restriction of imports, 25;
    walking in, 224, 225ff. 274
Western Front, 4, 69, 71, 75
Westminster Bridge terrorist attack, 8
Whitehall, 4, 6, 8
Wi'am Palestinian Conflict Transformation Centre, Bethlehem, 23, 34, 264
Williams, Rowan, Baron Williams of Oystermouth, previously Archbishop of Canterbury, Master of Magdalene College, Cambridge, 164
Wimborne-Idrissi, Naomi, 10
Wink, Walter, ix, 31, 285

Xanthi, 165

Yatta, 249, 251
YMCA, East Jerusalem, 22
Youth Against Settlements, 242, 245-7

Zamir, Tsameret, 256-8
Zaytoun (Fairtrade importer of Palestinian olive oil and produce), 9, 12, 146
Zec, Safet, 114-16
Zedong, Chairman Mao, Chinese head of state (1949-76), 137
Zennor, 65, 69, 96
Zinn, Howard, 34
Zionism, 6, 7, 10, 13-14, 19, 26-7, 29, 61, 71, 193-5, 242-3
Zochrot, Israeli NGO, 283
Zog, King of Albania (1928-39), 130, 135-6
Al-Zoughbi, Dr Zoughbi, ix, 23, 32, 281